Burnin' Down
the House

VALERIE SWEENEY PRINCE

Burnin' Down the House

the House

Home in African American Literature

COLUMBIA UNIVERSITY PRESS / NEW YORK

Columbia University Press wishes to express its appreciation for a donation toward the cost of publishing this book, given to Hampton University in memory of Frank Carmines.

Grateful acknowledgment is given to Steve A. Prince for use of the following:

"When I Think of Home" (linoleum print, 9" x 12", 1998) from the
  Home Series [frontispiece]
"Urban Dirge" (linoleum print, 9.5" x 14", 2003) from the *Home Series*
"Ghetto Squares" (linoleum print, 8" x 15", 2003) from the *Home Series*
"Migratory Tracks" (linoleum print, 8" x 10", 2003) from the *Home Series*
"Pot to Piss In" (linoleum print, 5.5" x 10", 2003) from the *Home Series*
"I'll Lay My Head on Some Lonesome Track" (linoleum print, 7.5" x 14",
  2003) from the *Home Series*
"Sugarman Blues" (linoleum print, 7" x 10" 2003) from the *Home Series*

Columbia University Press
Publishers Since 1893
New York   Chichester, West Sussex
Copyright © 2005 Columbia University Press

Library of Congress Cataloging-in-Publication Data
Prince, Valerie Sweeney.
Burnin' down the house : home in African American literature / Valerie
  Sweeney Prince.
    p. cm.
ISBN 0–231–13440–1 (alk. paper) — ISBN 0–31–13441–1–X (pbk. : alk. paper)
PS374.N4P75   2004
813.009'3552—dc22   2004049444

Columbia University Press books are printed
  on permanent and durable acid-free paper.

Printed in the United States of America
Designed by Lisa Hamm
c 10 9 8 7 6 5 4 3 2 1
p 10 9 8 7 6 5 4 3 2 1

To Amee, who said, "Go!"

Contents

Acknowledgments

How does any work get done except by the labor of many hands? This particular project has been in the making for more years than I generally acknowledge, but it initially crystallized in a single word during graduate school. The word was, of course, "home." I returned "home by the sea" to finish this book and was received into the welcoming arms of so many people—Margaret Simmons, Barbara Whitehead, Lois Benjamin, William R. Harvey, Joann Haysbert, John Alewynse, Joyce Jarrett, Mamie Locke, April Burris, Bradford Grant, Regina Blair, Jacqueline Regina Blackwell, and Amee F. Carmines—who stood tirelessly urging me forward. Amee, in particular, has been my friend and ally, reading and critiquing when no one else was around. My cousin Lois read an early draft and helped me find my own voice. I write of home because I have a family, not untroubled, not without conflict, not romanticized; I come from somewhere.

Over the years of work on this project, many students have inspired me and helped me to better articulate exactly what I mean.

They have endured my obsession with the themes of "space" and "place" and "home." But those at home have endured the worst of it. My parents, Robert and Lurlene Sweeney, are battle-worn soldiers who stood at the ready for me, always doing whatever was required. My children, Imani and Elijah, have learned patience, independence, and strength, having been born to a mother who simply must write. And my beloved husband, Steve, who can make art out of anything, makes it possible for me to do this work day to day. I thank him for the designs that grace the cover and head each chapter. He continues to be my inspiration.

My sister, Maria, her husband, Neil Osborne, and their daughter, Drexel, opened their home to me and endured my endless chatter without complaint on my trips to Cambridge during the last phase of this project. Their generosity and hospitality were invaluable to its timely completion. The editors at Columbia University Press, Jennifer Crewe and Leslie Kriesel, provided invaluable assistance in refining the finished product.

Carlo Rotella also motivated me. As I watched him speak at the MLA convention in San Francisco in 1998, he was a stranger, but during a time when I needed encouragement, his professionalism and intelligence made me hold to my convictions. His words about working until he finds just the right way to express what he means were not lost on me. One can be a hero without even trying sometimes.

Without the inspiration given by the Holy Spirit to lay everything down and to pick up only those things that Christ allows, I would never have been able to bear all the costs of seeing this project through. Most of all, I thank God for being my home in this world.

I would not change a moment of this walk. Although the work is secular, the journey has been sacred.

Burnin' Down the House

Introduction: A House Is Not a Home

The search for justice, opportunity, and liberty that characterized the twentieth century for African Americans can be described as a quest for home. During the early part of the century, America witnessed the largest mass migration in history. African Americans left the South looking for opportunity promised by the industrial North. The North did offer relief from the despotism of Jim Crow, which was ruthlessly enforced by mob violence, but poverty and

When I think of home, I think of a place
Where there's love overflowing.
I wish I was home, I wish I was back there
With the things I been knowing. . . .

—Charlie Smalls, "Home"

BONO: . . . Searching out the New Land. That's
what the old folks used to call it. See a fellow
moving around from place to place . . . woman
to woman . . . called it searching out the New
Land. . . . Ain't you never heard of nobody
having the walking blues?

—August Wilson, *Fences*

Not a house in the country ain't packed to its
rafters with some dead Negro's grief.

—Toni Morrison, *Beloved*

racism also awaited the migrants in northern cities. Overcrowded
ghettos began to fester with the stench of unfulfilled promises and
the rotting corpses of failed dreams lying unburied and unmourned
upon hard ground. By the mid-twentieth century, Claude Brown
had joined a chorus of talented black writers including Arna Bontemps, Countee Cullen, Claude McKay, Sterling Brown, Lorraine
Hansberry, Richard Wright, Ralph Ellison, Ann Petry, and James
Baldwin, who were already voicing their frustrations. The dream
that Harlem Renaissance author Langston Hughes wrote about
had indeed been deferred. Anger arose as a wall built in defense of

this sacred place of home. Black writers had invested too much to let the ideal die so unceremoniously. Passion for home ran like lifeblood through the African American psyche.

A look back upon the century of African American literature shows that home is ubiquitous and nowhere at the same time. Perhaps that is why authors express the longing for home utilizing the language and the sentiment of the blues. The blues form arose near the turn of the twentieth century out of the privation experienced by African Americans. It gives voice to the frustrations suffered by the masses of black people living in a culture of white supremacy and presents a unique worldview. The blues introduces a logic drawn from African American sensibility that makes the notion of home seem possible in a chaotic world.

Like home, blues expressiveness grows out of paradoxical associations. Its themes are born from the duality inherent in African American culture. In his renowned *The Souls of Black Folk* (1903), W. E. B. Du Bois coined the term "double consciousness" to describe the psyche as it had developed for African Americans by the opening of the twentieth century, a description that can be aptly applied to the formation of the blues as well. As a distinctly African American genre, it reflects the double-mindedness of the culture out of which it grows. In his theorization of the blues, however, Houston A. Baker Jr. is clear in emphasizing its complexity:

> As driving force, the blues matrix . . . avoids simple dualities. It perpetually achieves its effects as a fluid and multivalent network. It is only when "understanding"—the analytical work of a translator who translates the infinite changes of the blues—converges with such blues "force," however, that adequate explanatory perception (and half-creation) occurs. The matrix effectively functions toward cultural understanding, that is, only when an investigator brings an inventive attention to bear. (9)

African American authors like those studied in these pages, and others such as novelists Albert Murray, Ntozake Shange, Alice Walker, Bebe Moore Campbell, and Walter Mosley, have attempted to be such "investigator[s] bring[ing] an inventive attention to bear" through the end of the twentieth century.

Blues expressiveness appears, in the works studied here, as a form that helps individuals as well as the African American collectivity to negotiate contradictory positions. When the material site fails to nurture and to protect, blues expressiveness is given to function as home in its stead. Farah Griffin writes that blues performance "serves as a transitional space, making the transformation from migrant to urban dweller a little less harsh. It does this by providing the stability of 'home,' as well as offering a means to negotiate the 'here'" (54). It becomes a "safe space," in Patricia Hill Collins's language, wherein migrants can seek shelter. Seemingly, the musical and ideological structure of the blues give it the potential to bring order to the chaos of life by finding meaning in otherwise meaningless and dehumanizing circumstances.

Over the course of the next five chapters, I chart the journey toward home through five novels: *Native Son, Invisible Man, The Bluest Eye, Corregidora*, and *Song of Solomon*. By 1940, a lexicon emerged in African American literature that formed the basis of a vocabulary about home. The city, the kitchen, and the womb recur as sites that specifically inform our understanding of an African American sense of home. Each author draws upon these terms. Each novel repeats and revises the sites and each revision inflects them with new meaning. The pattern of home represented in these novels is configured similarly to the blues matrix described in Baker's *Blues, Ideology, and Afro-American Literature: A Vernacular Theory*. While Baker argues that the "black (w)hole," his blues matrix, seems to offer the potential for retreat and regeneration, the "black holes" in the novels are increasingly destructive. Baker's androcentric metaphor of the black hole invokes the notion of home even as it relies heavily upon a metaphor drawn from the female body. However, Baker is content to imagine a matrix with generative power that does not make room for woman.

The black hole, Baker argues, offers a way of reading literature in the context of vernacular culture. He suggests that the language of the folk is the blues, and the blues is conceived within a cultural matrix that subsumes literary experiences and ultimately "gives birth to light":[1]

> A matrix is a *womb* [emphasis added], a network, a fossil-bearing rock, a rocky trace of a gemstone's removal. . . . The matrix is a point of ceaseless input and output, a web of intersecting, crisscrossing impulses always in productive transit. Afro-American blues constitute such a vibrant network. . . . They are the multiplex, enabling *script* in which Afro-American cultural discourse is inscribed. (3–4)

Having defined the blues as a "matrix" that he describes elsewhere as "always already"—an eternal womb existing apart from the female body—Baker evades the responsibility of dealing with the "whole" individual. As a result, he deals with only part of the community he seeks to champion—the whole male and the female "hole." Such oversights have prompted sometimes acrimonious exchanges between Baker and African American feminist scholars. Yet his study can be productively mined for its underlying assumption: a connection between the blues and the womb.

In order to unpack the conflation that reduces the blues, which Baker reads as a sign of material conditions, to the matrix, which is a womb of sorts, we must keep both the material environment and the female body in sight. Baker removes the body in an effort to divert attention from the individual to the general black populace. He looks to the sign of a railway junction, the X, as a mark that indicates the generic "you" (or "me") and serves as a free-floating signifier of black subjectivity. He writes, "Its mark is an invitation to energizing intersubjectivity. Its implied (in)junction reads: Here is my body meant for (a phylogenetically conceived) you" (5). Baker elides the productive space of the womb (within a woman's body) in order to privilege the "vibrant network" that becomes an asexual, creative junction engineered by male hands and encoded as the blues. The railway crossing X stands as a sign of the mother's erasure, which, in Baker's logic, allows a black nation to be brought forth from the void left in place of her *whole* body.

In contrast to Baker's work, which substitutes symbols for the black female body, Hortense Spillers, in her often anthologized

"Mama's Baby, Papa's Maybe: An American Grammar Book," seeks to resurrect the black woman's flesh. On a symbolic level, she suggests that African American identity is developed around the black (she uses the word "captive") womb. Spillers discusses in "Mama's Baby" how slavery shifted the ground upon which black identity was founded away from the notion of the Father, as found in Lacanian theory. Instead, African American identity is built upon the construct of the Mother: because the newborn black child followed the "condition of the mother," the mother reads as the primary symbolic field. Unfortunately, such an identification serves to perpetuate the institution of slavery rather than to give African American women any real power. Yet they have been used as the scapegoat for the black community's numerous ailments since the time of slavery because they are the sole bearers of the black womb. African American female authors Toni Morrison and Gayl Jones explicitly take issue with the logic that reduces the African American woman to her womb and demand—even to the point of dismemberment and murder—that black female subjectivity be understood as distinct from the black womb.

While Baker looks at the slave narratives of the male authors Olaudah Equiano and Frederick Douglass in order to locate the economics of the blues, he cites Harriet Jacobs's *Incidents in the Life of a Slave Girl* to enable a shift from particular individuals (here Equiano and Douglass) to a generic human community. Baker writes, "A community of women, as represented by Linda Brent, controls its own sexuality, successfully negotiates (in explicitly commercial terms) its liberation from a crude patriarchy, and achieves expressive fullness through the literate voice of the black, female author" (55). Not coincidentally, this community consists of women. Baker thus effectively reinscribes the patriarchal domination that Spillers describes as "patriarchal-matriarchy."

Baker shows neither much regard for psychic consequences nor a great sensitivity to the considerably reduced territory in which Brent is allowed to negotiate her liberation, compared to her male counterparts. She is forced to choose her womb—seducing Mr. Sands in order to resist Dr. Flint's advances—and as a result, she gives birth to two children. The consequence of producing offspring is that Brent is further bound to the institution of slavery because she feels responsible for liberating them as well as herself. In order to do so, she is forced to choose a womb again. Rather than setting forth on the adventure that Baker notes characterizes the male narratives, Brent must be "buried" in what Baker calls a "tomb"—which might be read as "womb"—space inside her grandmother's home (53). Her material environment mirrors and reifies her bodily condition.

While Baker suggests in his introduction that he would like to look at the *gestalt,* loosely translated as "whole to the part," he actually makes one part so large that it takes on mythic proportions. Then he goes on to read the part as the whole. The womb becomes the black hole, which, for Baker, functions as a home wherein a man can safely hibernate until such time as he is ready to (inevitably) emerge. Baker's project validates the blues as a viable means of framing literary analysis. Unfortunately, he imagines the blues matrix as an all-consuming black hole at the expense of women. Baker posits the blues as a "womb" able to "give birth" without the complicating presence of the female body.[2]

In the twenty years since the publication of *Blues Ideology,* many scholars have attacked Baker's work as sexist while others have been content to apply his ideas blindly to their own reading of other texts. My effort in this study is not to dismiss Baker's work as antifeminist; however, I am not willing to apply his framework without offering critique. Instead, I attempt to reclaim the matrix as a black female place and suggest ways to explore representations of home in order to expand upon the lexicon used to read African American literature.

This study charts a dual trend. First, it explores the intratextual movement away from material structures toward metaphorical blues expressions, creative responses complementing the built environment that help characters survive. But it is equally concerned with a larger pattern of movement as authors represent the African American quest for home. This intertextual quest reveals a hitherto covert yearning for a primordial home. "Home" begins as a broad term—a universal ideal to which we aspire. Its locus, repeated in *Native Son*, *Invisible Man*, *The Bluest Eye*, and *Corregidora*, has been getting increasingly smaller—from city to kitchen to womb. Home is configured as a vortex, like Houston Baker's black hole, drawing all things into itself. Finally, the whirlwind can bear no more: this vortex is disrupted by an explosive demolition in *Corregidora*. With the house demolished, readers are left to gather the scattered pieces and rebuild, using the blues sensibilities acquired in the journey through the storm.

Unfortunately, it is not easy to recover what has been lost. In *Native Son*, we meet Bigger Thomas in Chicago after his family has migrated from Mississippi. Clearly, their dreams have been deferred. What Bigger knows as home he confronts in the austere façade of the city that restricts his access and constrains his mobility. It is an understatement to say that the kitchenette apartment where he lives with his family is inadequate. But the kitchenette (a kitchen place) is representative of the Southside (a city place), the black assigned section of Chicago, and the restrictions it places upon his life. *Native Son* chronicles Bigger's rebellion against the station and the designation imposed by the spatial politics that declare, "You can't win." In fact, Bigger cannot win. He can't even sing. Bigger has no use for music. Because it seems he has little regard for blues expressiveness, he must use other means—ultimately, destructive means—to reconfigure a home for himself. He reconfigures the Dalton household by murdering Mary and placing her body in the basement furnace. Thus he transforms his assigned place, the Daltons' basement (a womblike place), into the center of the household as the community searches for the missing girl.

In contrast, the character Mary Rambo in *Invisible Man* tempers her poverty and flavors her home with the sound of her blues. Mary runs a rooming house where the narrator stays for a time. Situated by the blues she sings in the kitchen, she becomes a sign of home for the narrator. Unfortunately, the dynamics that govern Mary's house are presaged in the Southern past at Jim Trueblood's cabin. His sordid history as a sharecropper comes forth as a blues tale centering around poverty, rape, and incest. The Trueblood tale is a blueprint that prefigures Mary's house and begins to clarify the connection suggested in *Native Son* between the built environment (kitchen and city places) and the womb. Ellison emphasizes the black woman's womb by linking it to the Trueblood cabin, through the double pregnant figures of Jim's wife and daughter; then he revises Bigger's basement by sheltering his protagonist in his own dark hole (a womblike place).

In each of the novels, home is correlated with the womb; however, the connection and, more importantly, its implications are not made explicit until Toni Morrison's *The Bluest Eye*. The Northern city that marks the encounter for the male protagonists of Wright's and Ellison's novels is not available to a little black girl like Pecola Breedlove. Her encounters with home are dominated not by city streets but by the geographically smaller sites of kitchens. In representing these sites, Morrison demystifies Mary Rambo's blues kitchen. And because Pecola decides that her problems originate in a failure of sight rather than in a failure of sound, she tries to mitigate them with the blues of her eyes rather than the blues of her mouth. The end of the novel reveals the failure of Trueblood's blues as Pecola brings forth her father's dead seed.

In the fourth chapter, I examine the contrast Gayl Jones represents between Catherine Lawson's kitchen experiences in *Corregidora* and Ursa's experiences as a blues singer. Home takes Ursa even further inside than the kitchen, into the place of the female body. However, it does not prove a suitable home, and what was internalized in the site of the womb becomes painfully externalized. Rather than the black (female) place of the kitchen, as it has been designated by the racialized terms of domestic servitude, Jones offers a graphic blues site that "makes room" for home through a traumatic dismemberment. Ursa is left to find the voices, the others with whom she might sing herself a blues home. In so doing, she reconfigures her relationship with both the past and present. Ultimately, it is unclear whether Ursa finds a viable home place. What is clear, however, is that it is not constructed in an isolated act of individual will. If she is to invent a home, it must be constructed in concert with others.

Finally, *Song of Solomon* presents the city as "ghetto"—but not in the sense of Bigger Thomas's segregated and impoverished Southside, nor in the sense of *Invisible Man*'s ever-changing Harlem. Morrison signifies on the leitmotif of the earlier novels and reconfigures the places of the city, the kitchen, and the womb in terms that are more viable. The African American quest for home, irresistibly attracted toward increasingly smaller sites, breaks free from the vortex and explodes in *Corregidora*. Morrison gathers the scattered pieces, inverts the pattern, and leads the way out of the womb. It is dead; the kitchen opens outward; and the city becomes ghetto. Rather than being a black place because it is so interior that there is no light, as is the case with Baker's black hole, home becomes a black place because of the presence of all color. To be at home, then, Morrison suggests in *Song of Solomon*, the African American community must embody the blues paradox of holding its opposite within itself. The novel declares that home is untenable—yet it must be defended, even at the cost of our lives.

Notes

1. Baker characterizes the black hole as "The symbolic content of Afro-American expressive culture [which] can thus be formulated in terms of the *black hole* conceived as a subcultural (underground, marginal, or liminal) region in which a dominant, white culture's representations are squeezed to zero volume, producing a new expressive order" (152). Without lodging any specific critique about the model of the "black hole" itself, feminist scholars like Deborah McDowell, Barbara Christian, and Joyce Ann Joyce are not particularly persuaded by his case. Their arguments against Baker largely surfaced as critiques of the value and effectiveness of poststructuralist criticism in the reading of African American womanist texts. Barbara Christian, "The Race for Theory," *Cultural Critique* 6 (Spring 1987): 51–63; Joyce A. Joyce, "'Who the Cap Fit': Unconsciousness and Unconscionableness in the Criticism of Houston A. Baker, Jr., and Henry Louis Gates, Jr.," *New Literary History* 18 (Winter 1987): 371–83. Michael Awkward and Ann du Cille, however, do offer specific critiques. See Michael Awkward, *Inspiriting Influences: Tradition, Revision, and Afro-American Women's Novels* (New York:

Columbia University Press, 1989); Ann du Cille, "'Who Reads Here?': Back Talking with Houston Baker," *Novel: A Forum on Fiction* 26.1 (1992): 97–106.

2. In *Race Men,* Hazel Carby lodges a similar critique in her reading of W. E. B. Du Bois's *The Souls of Black Folk*: "The map of intellectual mentors he [Du Bois] draws for us is a map of male production and reproduction that traces in its form, but displaces through its content, biological and sexual reproduction. It is reproduction without women, and is a final closure to Du Bois's claim to be 'flesh of the flesh and bone of the bone,' for in the usurpation of the birth of woman from Adam's rib, the figure of the intellectual and race leader is born of and engendered by other males" (25–26). See Hazel Carby, *Race Men* (Cambridge: Harvard University Press, 1988).

Works Cited

Baker, Houston A., Jr. *Blues, Ideology, and Afro-American Literature: A Vernacular Theory.* Chicago: University of Chicago Press, 1984.

Griffin, Farah Jasmine. *"Who Set You Flowin'?": The African-American Migration Narrative.* New York: Oxford University Press, 1995.

Ghetto Squares

I had discovered the crowning error of
the city. . . . The city was not the endless
succession of canyons. . . . The city had limits.

—F. Scott Fitzgerald, "My Lost City"

Ain't you heard
The boogie-woogie rumble
Of a dream deferred?

—Langston Hughes, "Dream Boogie"

1

Living (Just Enough) for the City: *Native Son*

The novels in this study span nearly forty years, beginning in 1940 with Richard Wright's *Native Son* and concluding in 1977 with Toni Morrison's *Song of Solomon*. In this chapter I look at *Native Son* because it speaks of home in broad terms that are characteristic of this period of great transition. At the outset of the century the Northern city was presented as the African American's best chance for locating a viable home. And after the advent of the mechanical cotton harvester, World War II, and other mitigating circumstances, many put their hope of finding a home in the North. At the time Wright published *Native Son*, 77 percent of African Americans lived in the South. Over the next 30 years, 5 million of them would move to Northern cities. This is the backdrop of the novel (and of this book). Although his protagonist, Bigger Thomas, is part of this great wave of sojourners, Wright declares that he has natural rights of inheritance. Bigger is a *native* son. He inherits the city, but it refuses him. Many scholars have considered the ways the city fails to be home for Bigger, but I read this topic from a new perspective. *Native Son* introduces a blueprint for home that will be revised by Ralph Ellison in *Invisible Man*, Toni Morrison in *The Bluest Eye* and *Song of Solomon*, and Gayl Jones in *Corregidora*.

Read chronologically, the novels show the African American longing for home as a pattern of movement, first to the outdoor place of the city, then to the indoor place of the kitchen, and finally, to the quintessentially interiorized place of the womb. Southerly winds blew African Americans away from Southern ground. Even if they had not been persuaded by the façade of the "Promised Land," many migrants believed life in the North could not be worse than the conditions they experienced in the South. In fact, if half of what they heard—from fast-talking Northern industrialists about wages and from recent migrants bragging of new conquests—was true, the North was a free train ride to a land of opportunity. For a time, the Northern city stood as the symbol of home's potential. So migrants went north in search of their dreams.

By 1940, when Wright published *Native Son*,[1] a generation of African Americans had been raised in Northern cities. Wright had migrated as a child, and his work reflects the disillusionment characterstic of novels like *The Street* by Ann Petry, *Home to Harlem* by Claude McKay, and *God Sent Sunday* by Arna Bontemps. African Americans had discovered that the potential embodied by the city was bounded.

In *Native Son*, Bigger's experiences with the city are in the foreground. Nevertheless, the kitchen, configured as both the kitchenette apartment and a place within the Dalton household, plays a vital role. The kitchenette provides a sharp contrast to Bigger's experience in the city streets. The womb in the novel is less obvious. The Dalton basement, Bigger's assigned place, is a womblike place from which Bigger hopes to emerge into a new life. However, the city refuses to accept Bigger's claim of belonging and forces him to occupy increasingly confined places.

Kitchen: The Kitchenette Apartment

The opening "Brrrrrrriiiiiiiiiiiiiiiiiiiiiinng!" awakens the Thomas family. The harshness of the tone sets the mood for what will follow. The kitchenette apartment at the beginning of *Native Son* is restrictive for Bigger as well as the other members of his family living there. This place introduces the tensions at work in the built environment that will frustrate Bigger's aspirations. Our attention is drawn to Bigger and his natural (male) desire to escape the stultifying (female) place of the apartment. Segregationist housing practices forced African Americans in Chicago to live in such ghetto kitchenette apartments. Wright describes the social dynamics this fostered in *12 Million Black Voices*: "the kitchenette throws desperate and unhappy people into an unbearable closeness of association, thereby increasing latent friction, giving birth to never-ending quarrels of recrimination, accusation, and vindictiveness, producing warped personalities" (108). The kitchenette places tangible and intangible boundaries around the lives of its inhabitants. These barriers constrain their growth and restrict their movements.

A narrow space of one room is the Thomases' living area. The living space is so contained by the kitchenette that it leaves the natural connections between mother and son, brothers and sister distorted, if not completely compromised. As Dan McCall states, "Wright's point [in representing the kitchenette] is not to deny the Negro's 'folk culture.' He was trying to show that for those slum dwellers the folk culture was swallowed in unbearable closeness" (7). The architectural design maximized (white) profit and almost completely neglected (black) human needs. Bigger's effort to draw invisible, defensive curtains around himself for protection and privacy cannot help but violate others' personal boundaries. People living in this household are simply pressed too close.

Bigger has difficulty identifying with those around him. His mother nags him in lieu of his deceased father to take a relief job in order to help make ends meet. Bigger sees her as another obstacle to control over his own life. Poverty and anger constrain him and limit his ability to interpret his experiences more productively. The problem that arises out of these circumstances, as Keith Gilyard points out, is that Bigger "cannot give voice to either his rage or his vision" (158–59). His frustrations have few expressive outlets. Once Bigger loses respect for his family and their cultural practices, he loses sight of a vital resource. Although limited, Mrs. Thomas is rooted by her participation in expressive practices. Constricted as he is, Bigger does not recognize folk culture as such and thus can only mock folk practices that might otherwise serve as emancipatory gestures. This mockery is evident in the exchange Bigger has with his mother over breakfast:

> "Bigger's setting here like he ain't glad to get a job," [Mrs. Thomas] said.
> "What you want me to do? Shout?" Bigger asked. (15)

Mrs. Thomas is contemptuous of Bigger because, unlike his sister, Vera, he does not share her limited aspirations and is not satisfied by the offer he has received for a relief job. The sarcasm Bigger expresses here is eclipsed by irony later as the significance of this exchange is highlighted by his unexpected "shout"— manifested as Mary's homicide. For Bigger, his mother—like Bessie, the girlfriend he later murders in cold blood—embodies folk culture.

While to the uninitiated, Bigger may appear to be asking his mother if she wants him to yell (speak in a loud voice), Bigger is really asking if she expects him to perform a shout. A shout is a particularly African American expression of joy, gratitude, and praise to God, wherein one dances with religious abandon. Anthropologist Zora Neale Hurston reads the practice of shouting in *The Sanctified Church*:

There can be little doubt that shouting is a survival of the African "possession" by the gods. In Africa it is sacred to the priesthood or acolytes, in America it has become generalized. The implication is the same, however, it is a sign of special favor from the spirit that it chooses to drive out the individual consciousness temporarily and use the body for its expression. (91)[2]

Practiced widely in Holiness and Pentecostal churches popular among Southern migrants,[3] such charismatic expression is far more active than a mere outburst. Instead, as Hurston notes, "Shouting is a community thing" (91) that engages an individual as part of a congregation in fellowship with God. Bigger has no intention of expressing joy, particularly not in the form of a shout, over the offer of a relief job. He views shouting as frivolous. Thus he cuts himself off from a potentially meaningful engagement with this community within the household.

An effective exploration of home in *Native Son* begins with an understanding of the social dynamics at work in the kitchenette. The material constraints the kitchenette imposes upon Bigger mold his sense of home, and not simply by instigating his alienation from expressive gestures; there is also a clear division between genders. The kitchenette is designated as female by the dominance of Mrs. Thomas's myopic worldview. Mrs. Thomas and the home she represents cannot accommodate the lifestyle that Bigger wants. In the opening scene when a black rat invades the apartment, fear of exposure, embarrassment, or shame are all put aside for the immediate concern. The women huddle together as Mrs. Thomas locates the rat: "Frantically, Vera climbed upon the bed and the woman caught hold of her with their arms entwined about each other, the black mother and the brown daughter gazed open-mouthed at the trunk in the corner" (8). From the bed, she directs her son toward the threat. Bigger's role as "man" thrusts him into the position of defender of his home place; conversely, Vera and Mrs. Thomas's role as "women" suggests that they are defenseless. These roles are rigidly imposed and further demonstrate the impermeability of the space. It is Bigger who must kill the rat, and so he does. Wright utilizes this fierce imagery to foreshadow what is to become of Bigger himself. The dynamics inside the apartment are but a reflection of larger social forces.

The sense of triumph produced by Bigger's defeat of the rat is short lived, as his attempt to be "the man of the house" ends with this primal act of aggression. The "house," from Bigger's perspective, is hardly worth defending. Yet Bigger acts, as opposed to the inaction of his sister. He operates from the perspective that he will make a difference in this situation. On the other hand, Vera is so afraid of the rat that she cannot even think to jump onto the bed. Instead she shrinks into a corner until her mother orders her to move. Clearly, this is not the first encounter this family has had with a rat, nor, the novel also implies, will it be the last; yet Vera has not found an active way to manage the situation. Trudier Harris explains the gender dichotomy as part of a larger schema of oppositions:

> Wright sets up an opposition in the novel between the native and the foreign, between the American Dream and American ideals in the abstract and Afro-Americans trying to find their place among the ideals, between Bigger as a representative of something larger and freer, indeed more American, than the limitations of the black community and the black women as representatives of a culture and a way of life that would stifle such aspirations. (63)

Vera is paralyzed to the point of utter vulnerability and is, therefore, completely subject to the forces of her environment. The rat is an imminent threat to the family and they know it must be killed.

The rat race begins here for Bigger in the kitchenette, the lived reality of black life within the ghetto. Bigger is not really invested in protecting his family. In fact, he considers this place a threat to his own emotional well-being:

> He hated his family because he knew that they were suffering and that he was powerless to help them. He knew that the moment he allowed himself to feel to its fullness how they lived, the shame and misery of their lives, he would be swept out of himself with fear and despair. So he

held toward them an attitude of iron reserve; he lived with them, but behind a wall, a curtain. And toward himself he was even more exacting. He knew that the moment he allowed what his life meant to enter fully into his consciousness, he would either kill himself or someone else. So he denied himself and acted tough. (14)

Vera and Mrs. Thomas are living behind a "curtain" that obscures their ability to see the mechanisms operating in their world to control them. But in this passage, we find that Bigger also lives behind a curtain of sorts—a wall of "iron reserve." In the absence of physical walls set in place to make a space livable—for example, to separate male and female sleeping areas—Bigger's barrier of "iron reserve" is a defensive boundary he erects in an attempt to protect himself from the debilitating realities of his life. These barriers reconfigure the space of the apartment and serve to direct Bigger's movement through it.

But there are moments when Bigger's barrier fails him. His mother's voice transgresses this ephemeral border and reaches Bigger from behind her curtain as she sings:

Life is like a mountain railroad
With an engineer that's brave
We must make the run successful
From the cradle to the grave. . . . (14)

This song evokes the image of the junction—a crossroads of movement through territory that evokes the image of the South. Significantly, the song she sings is a gospel, but the hope of Christ as Savior is absent from the segment represented here.[4] Instead, her song charts the challenges and potential triumphs of life in terms of geographical markers. Success is measured by one's ability to negotiate the spatial obstacles and to move from one site to another. To change locale, then, is to change one's relationship to the world. Rather than appearing as a form of praise or worship centered around the figure of Christ (since Christianity is the implied context) that would mark her text as sacred, Mrs. Thomas's music functions like blues. The train, a common symbol of the blues, suggests both the hope embodied by arrivals and the sorrow found in departures. Her song helps her negotiate the here and now that is circumscribed by the historical context of migration.

The song irks Bigger, and he is glad when she stops singing and returns to him with a pot of coffee and a plate of crinkled bacon (14). Bigger is not consoled by the superficial comfort offered by his mother's song. He focuses instead on the immediacy of his physical hunger. His unfulfilled desires within the stultifying environment of his home are assuaged momentarily by food.

In an effort to escape the constrictions of the kitchenette, Bigger expands his sense of home to incorporate the masculine space of street culture. "Domestic space is stifling and provincial," according to Farah Griffin's reading of male migrant characters. She continues, "The male migrant characters of . . . [particular migration literature] attempt to develop a street culture and/or attempt to acquire a critical consciousness as a means of resisting the negative impact of the city" (123). In many ways, the street culture these characters develop is antithetical to the maintenance of home and family. But as Wright demonstrates, the kitchenette does not adequately sustain that family either. It fails to be home, a shelter from the inhospitable city, so the culture of the streets is established to fill that role. Ironically, Bigger's soulish longings are a more complicated manifestation of the expressions of hope about which Mrs. Thomas sings. In their own ways, both of them have invested place with so much yearning that they believe it might yield the route to their liberty. So Bigger goes outside to try to catch a glimpse of what it means to be at home.

City: The Street

Just after the novel's opening scene, Bigger exits his apartment and goes downstairs before going out into the morning. He stops to smoke a cigarette and watches two white men putting up a billboard across the street and talking of politics. Their discussion reveals the presence of an invisible class structure that separates blue-collar workers like themselves from politicians like Buckley, who is pictured on the billboard: "I bet that sonofabitch rakes off a million bucks in graft a year. Boy, if I was in his shoes for just one day I'd *never* have to worry again" (16). At the same instant that their work reveals the distance between themselves and men with power and money like Buckley, it also suggests Bigger's societal position in relationship to them all.

Bigger's sense of home has been predetermined by a system that predates him and relies upon his subjugation for its existence. In "Richard Wright and the Dynamics of Place in Afro-American Literature," Houston Baker posits a reading of place that coheres with this reading of home for Bigger. As a subset of place, home is subject to the dynamics and politics associated with it. Reading the significance of location, Baker writes:

> For place to be recognized as actually PLACE, as a personally valued locale, one must set and maintain the boundaries. If one is constituted and maintained, however, by and within boundaries set by another, then one is not a setter of place but a prisoner of another's desire. Under such conditions what one calls and perhaps, feels is one's own place would be, from the perspective of human agency, *placeless*. Bereft of determinative control of boundaries, the inhabitant would not be secure in his or her own space but maximally secured by another. Such confinement is always a function of interlocking institutional arrangements. ("Richard Wright" 87)

Baker's assertion is that the notion of place originates within the primary displacement of the slave trade wherein African peoples were dispersed as property throughout the white, western world. Without the fundamental acknowledgment of human agency, African Americans were left to circulate under the control of economic institutions in the same manner as any other resource. Baker argues that place for them "begins in a European DIS-PLACEMENT of bodies for commercial purposes" ("Richard Wright" 91). While I am less interested in the economics than in issues concerning race and gender, Baker's Marxist reading works well with Wright's communist slant.

The hands of these two white men literally bring Buckley's visage into Bigger's daily life as a sign of the "true" policing power (unlike the critical watch of someone like his mother). Operating on various levels, white society has the authority to post signs of that power throughout culture. The accusatory glare follows passersby who fall beneath the point of the finger as the billboard revises the standard World War II motto of "Uncle Sam wants you" with its own variation: "IF YOU BREAK THE LAW, YOU CAN'T WIN!" (16–17). Although the billboard will randomly accuse *every* viewer with the same glare, the politics associated with location guarantee that some groups of individuals will be addressed more often than others.

Still, the street culture Bigger participates in with his male friends seems to offer a less restrictive alternative to life inside the kitchenette. On the street or in the pool hall that is an extension of the male street culture, Bigger is able to conjure up defiant visions of robbing a white man's store or of becoming an airplane pilot. In these spaces he can think bigger thoughts than those his mother could ever imagine. His dreams are understood and even shared by Gus and the others. This masculine culture is set in contrast to the purportedly female dominated space of the apartment. Men and boys can gather and scheme without the policing eye of frightened women like his mother and Vera.

In the street spaces, Bigger and his friends plan a bold robbery of a white man's store, but like the women, these boys are scared. Bigger foils the planned robbery before it can begin by attacking his friend, Gus—masking his fear under the guise of anger. Although he is able to maintain his masculinist front with his friends and, by extension, male street culture in general, in this act he succumbs to another thinly veiled level of white oppression.

Like the kitchenette apartment, which only offers Mrs. Thomas imaginary power in exchange for effective control, the street is yet another realm of white domination. It seems to expand the constrictive boundaries of the kitchenette and give Bigger the chance to lust after the freedom suggested by flight. While standing in the street, Bigger spies a plane and recognizes that a lack of opportunity rather than a lack of ability keeps him from flying, too. But Gus reminds him of the other barriers that Bigger neglects to consider: "If you wasn't black and if you had some money and if they'd let you go to that aviation school, you *could* fly a plane" (20). The cinema, airplanes, and billboards serve as constant reminders of his allotted station in life. Bigger is not freer on the streets. The black street culture pictured here by Wright is as limited and limiting for men as the kitchenette apartment is for women.

All around Bigger as he stands talking with Gus on the street, people are moving. The seemingly purposeful action of vehicles, birds, and people captivates him: "Automatically, his eyes followed each car as it whirred over the smooth black asphalt. A woman came by and he watched the gentle sway of her body until she disappeared into a doorway" (19). As Bigger and Gus stand on the street "playing white," they are set apart by the seemingly goal-directed movement around them.

Invoking the rich history of the dozens, a mean contest of wit and words, played on porches and in outdoor, street places, this game of "playing white" holds the potential to serve as a blues moment. Such a moment occurs when one is able to translate painful experiences through a filter of African American expressive culture in order to impose meaning upon potentially devastating contradictions. For instance, Mrs. Thomas's singing serves as a blues moment because she is able to glean some meaning and a measure of comfort from it in the midst of a difficult situation. Bigger's efforts to use folk expression are thwarted, however. The men's play finally gives way to frustration, resentment, anger, and fear. Bigger's effort to reencode his position within the world through this game with his friend is ultimately no more consoling for him than his mother's (blues) singing. Finally he tells Gus: "It's just like living in jail. Half the time I feel like I'm on the outside of the world peeping in through a knot hole in the fence" (23). Bigger has no expressive vehicles through which to either effectively articulate his feelings to those outside his small circle of friends or reinterpret and affirm the value of his life and his experience.

He dismisses the value of his common black experiences—as evidenced by the movement of the community passing by him—in favor of things outside his grasp: flight, material wealth, and the power signified by "whiteness." The meaning of the movement in the streets is lost on him. Instead he is a bystander as others move about. He cannot help noticing this movement, but his gestures toward expression in the play with Gus fail to engage him in the surrounding action, reinforcing Bigger's disengagement from the community. Community, an expressed connection between human beings, is vital to the institution of home. Without such ties, an individual like Bigger is unlikely to build such a place on his own.

While the street may feel more like home in that it is less provincial than the apartment, for Bigger, it is also a place that stifles his creative expression and restricts his ability to engage others in meaningful ways. After sabotaging the planned robbery of Blum's store, Bigger must take the relief job his mother wanted for him as chauffeur for the Dalton family. In this way Bigger moves from the kitchenette apartment and the streets to the Daltons' house, a kitchen place that begins to introduce a connection to the womb.

Between the Kitchen and the Womb: The Dalton House

After the kitchenette and the streets of the Southside fail to provide adequate shelter, it is doubtful that the Dalton house will meet Bigger's needs. In some ways, his sense of place expands as he takes the trek across the city to the Dalton household to accept the chauffeur position. The job gives him justification for going into a prohibited part of town. But his place within the Dalton household as servant mitigates any perceived expansion. Instead, Bigger's sense of place becomes smaller. Although he will venture back into the Southside after his murder of the socialite Mary Dalton is uncovered, his encounter with this household seals his fate. The city closes in and his sole expressions of power are forged out of his experiences there.

Despite the liberal sentiment that is the subtext of the relief job offer, apart from his naïve hope that the Daltons might be like the whites in the movies, Bigger finds no reason to share his mother's optimism about his new employment. As James Giles astutely notes, "Mr. and Mrs. Dalton primarily represent a devastating satire of misguided, white liberalism. They attempt to atone through meaningless philanthropic gestures for their guilt as exploitative capitalistic landlords. By doing so, they succeed only in temporarily confusing black rage and, thus, delaying essential social reform" (80). Over the course of the novel, it becomes evident that hiring Bigger is one of those "philanthropic gestures." The shallowness of their actions implicates the Daltons in a system of oppression that victimizes Bigger. John M. Reilly connects the Daltons' social position to their race politics. In their apparent naïveté, they partner with more blatant forms of racist oppression:

[The Daltons'] responsibility for institutionalizing racism through the exploitation of their tenants and the enforcement of segregated housing patterns cannot be attributed directly to their characters, in the way that Britten and Buckley may seem to be motivated by race hatred. Yet, as the logic of the novel shows, the Daltons' complicity in exploitation is a greater evil than the Klan-like behavior of Britten or Buckley, for their controlling role in the economic and social system of Chicago creates the conditions that frustrate and oppress not only the Thomases but all blacks in the city, conditions that in turn require the active reinforcement of the overt racism that the Daltons are too respectable to indulge, too self-deluded to acknowledge as necessary to the maintenance of their social position. (43)

The Daltons' sense of home (and place) grows out of their economic authority, which requires policing by spatial directives such as the billboard outside the Thomases' kitchenette apartment.

As landlord, Mr. Dalton knows neither the people nor the circumstances of his property. He does not even seem to know the addresses of his holdings. Thus the sincerity of his liberal concern demonstrated through his gifts of Ping-Pong tables and offers of menial jobs to black people is undermined by his detachment as landlord. This dynamic is evident in his brief exchange with Bigger.

Shortly after meeting him, Mr. Dalton inquires about Bigger's living conditions:

> "How much rent do you pay?"
> "Eight dollars a week."
> "For how many rooms?"
> "We just got one, suh." (50)

Mr. Dalton's line of inquiry places Bigger's family under a microscope that mirrors his daughter's later, more obviously offensive assertions. Mary Dalton more directly expresses:

> "You know, Bigger, I've long wanted to go into those houses," she said, pointing to the tall, dark apartment buildings looming to either side of them, "and just *see* how your people live. . . . They're *human*. . . . There are twelve million of them. . . . They live in our country. . . . In the same city with us. . . ." Her voice trailed off wistfully. (70)

Mary speaks of the black belt, the African American's assigned portion of the city, as if she is rendering a dream world created not through interrelating systems of power, access, and control but through her own naïvely dehumanizing imaginings.

While attempting to orient Bigger to his new job, the Daltons' housekeeper, Peggy, tells him, "It's really more than a job you've got here. . . . It's just like home" (58). It *is* just like home, inasmuch as home overtly and covertly restricts access and constricts movement. Bigger's place there is, after all, a room in the back, above the kitchen, entered through the basement. This place can be home for him as long as he remains confined within these parameters. (Of course, it is the transgression of those boundaries and Bigger's fear of being discovered in a white lady's room that compel the action of the novel and literally frighten Bigger to the point of murder.) Yet, for a brief moment, there is potential for Bigger to ally himself with this household.

As in the earlier scene that day when his mother brings him breakfast, food helps satiate Bigger's feeling of longing. The temporary satisfaction of eating fosters a sense of connectedness that is necessary in the establishment of home. After Bigger eats the food Peggy prepares for him, he succumbs to the pleasure of the moment: "He had quite forgotten that Peggy was in the kitchen and when his plate was empty he took a soft piece of bread and began to sop it clean, carrying the bread to his mouth in huge chunks. . . . He stopped chewing and laid the bread aside. He had not wanted to let her see him do that; he did that only at home" (56). The problem that Bigger experiences here, as in the earlier scene, is that the comfort only lasts for a short while; the sense of alienation returns to him after the food is gone.

In a similar scene in *Invisible Man* the narrator is reminded of the South while eating hot, buttery yams from a street vendor in Harlem. But the kind of connectedness that the invisible man feels is not sustained here because Bigger does not acknowledge or accept the importance of such affiliations. Unlike the invisible man, who desires to return to his roots in the South, Bigger is clearly detached from his Southern past. He is able to emotionlessly recount the fact of his father's murder to Jan and Mary in the same detached way that he steels himself to his family's conditions in the kitchenette. And only rarely, in moments involving food or song, does Bigger seem to have even a glimmer of recognition of his heritage.

Bigger returns to the Southside with Mary and her boyfriend, Jan. However, his experiences there are permanently altered by the events that occur after his initial encounter with the Daltons. The Southside, the kitchenette, and the Daltons' basement are enclosed by monolithic walls that Bigger's rage alone is unable to surmount. The friction between him and Mary ignites anger in Bigger that must find expression. Otherwise, Bigger cannot start the creative task of building useful shelters. Instead of creativity, his anger finds the wrecking ball of violence. Alienated as he is, Bigger is not able to effect enough of a change to dramatically alter the African American experience of home. The walls erected to contain him remain unmoved even as Bigger's fate is sealed.

City: The Black Belt

Bigger's efforts are generally to disassociate himself rather than look for ties that might bind him to other people. Perhaps this inclination fuels his contempt for Mary, who makes foolhardy attempts to pronounce her solidarity with him upon their initial meeting. Instead of provoking kinship, her unmerited trust elicits his confusion. Consequently, whatever impulse might be motivating her demonstrations of concern for black people is undermined by her lack of insight into Bigger's individual character. Without sincere acknowledgment of his humanity, her behavior toward him is both asinine and offensive. For example, while in the car with Bigger, a drunken Mary begins to sing:

> Swing low, sweet chariot,
> Coming fer to carry me home. . . .

Bigger refuses to sing along:

> Jan joined in and Bigger smiled derisively. Hell, that ain't the tune, he
> thought.
> "Come on, Bigger, and help us sing it," Jan said.
> "I can't sing," he said again. (77)

Bigger listens to Mary and Jan's effort to sing the Negro spiritual and realizes the words are right, but something in the rendition is wrong. Yet he cannot sing the song either.

Bigger's refusal to sing might be read as a means of resisting the liberal advances Jan and Mary offer. However, his ability to actually sing the spiritual would connect him with the cultural productions of black people—who, from Bigger's perspective, have no valuable commodities. This song, like Mrs. Thomas's earlier, alludes to the African American history of movement through space and transcendence of place, of which each has but a limited understanding. Thus, the potential power of the music is subverted. (Later, Ellison will exploit the tension suggested by the cultural disparity between black people and white liberals, captured by this scene in *Invisible Man*. Mary and Jan's request for Bigger to sing is echoed by a "broad" white man in the brotherhood who asks the protagonist to sing. Brother Jack tells him that the invisible man does not sing, but, of course, he does. He answers the request without music, but by performing a blues riff nevertheless: he exclaims, "He hit me in the face with a yard of chitterlings!" [304]. His performance evokes laughter born of both pleasure and pain.)

It is Mary who provokes the musical exchange in the car. She is heir to the liberal guilt embodied by the combination of her philanthropic parents—a blind mother and an entrepreneurial father. She urges Bigger to express himself in ways he is incapable of, particularly in her presence. Continually, Mary calls for Bigger to express his voice. And even after he has un-selfconsciously complied with her wishes, she calls attention to his behavior in a manner that arouses his resentment:

> "You know, for *three* hours you haven't said *yes* or *no*."
> She doubled up with laughter. He tightened with hate. Again she was looking inside of him and he did not like it. (80)

This observation bothers Bigger. As in the earlier conversations, Mary wants to compel him to speak. Here she sees through his "iron reserve," and Bigger is caught off guard. Essentially she is trying to affirm the significance of his unarticulated voice by urging him toward expression. The problem is that she thinks she knows what he has to express. Her rendition of the spiritual is characteristic of her presumptuousness. While Mary may know the words, she does not know the tune, familiarity with which comes from reconciling the words and melody with intimate knowledge of a cultural past not her own. On the other hand, Bigger might recognize both the tune and the lyrics, but he cannot sing.

Earlier that day, he had asked his mother across the breakfast table, "What you want me to do? Shout?" (15). In an ironic twist on shouting, an expression of religious (emotional) abandon, Bigger does shout, responding to Mary's call for voice. What he learns, however, is neither a dance nor a yell. It is murder masked as voice: "He had learned to shout and had shouted and no ear had heard him" (123). In part, Mary's ignorance of the "tune" she wants to sing and even the fact that her perspective on things might be wrong conspire in her death. Her good intentions cannot overcome centuries of racial history. Getting so drunk that she needs to be carried to her room places both Mary and Bigger in a compromising position that leads to her suffocation. It is only afterward, however, that Bigger realizes he has answered the question he posed to his mother. He shouts and finds a creative expression. While creative expressiveness is fundamental to establishing an African American sense of home, it is illogical to suggest that Bigger could use murder to locate a stable place. Instead, the dynamics enacted by this kind of expression intrude upon the making of a home.

The exhilaration of murder supplants the momentary satisfaction provided by distractions like the game of "playing white" with Gus. Now tools such as this game, which are only minimally cathartic for Bigger, lose their effectiveness altogether. His desire to do *something* has been fulfilled through his very significant act of murder, which makes all his other practices seem trivial. Not long afterward, Bigger goes out with his girlfriend, Bessie, to a bar. While they sit listening to the music playing, Bigger realizes:

> He knew that he should have asked her to dance, but the excitement that had hold of him would not let him. He was feeling different tonight from every other night; he did not need to dance and sing and clown over the floor in order to blot out a day and night of doing nothing. (133)

Bigger's altered perspective on dance mirrors his position on religion and alcohol; in his mind they are simply passive means of coping.

Despite his estrangement from the black community and its cultural practices, after the murder, Bigger retreats into the relative safety of the Southside. The black belt provides a cover of normalcy that at least temporarily masks his guilt. Beyond the superficial camouflage, however, the food, music, and lifestyle that so fascinated Mary and Jan offer little solace for Bigger. In fact, he is disdainful of both his mother and Bessie, who are so immersed in their own cultural practices. Clearly, he views them as the same kind of individual. Bigger consistently compares the crutches they utilize to sustain themselves: "The same deep realization he had had that morning at home at the breakfast table, while watching Vera and Buddy and his mother came back to him; only it was Bessie he was looking at now and seeing how blind she was" (131). They are weak in the same way; therefore, they are dangerous to Bigger in the same way. Bessie uses alcohol as an opiate; Mrs. Thomas practices her religion. Bigger feels these women threaten his ability to survive in the world as he makes it and as it makes him. In the end, he believes he *must* kill Bessie.

After coercing her into participating in his murder/kidnapping scheme, he is prepared to murder her in cold blood, too. When Bessie realizes that Bigger has actually murdered a white woman, she tells him, "If you killed *her* you'll kill *me*" (168). Her growing awareness appears as a blues idiom:

"Lord, don't let this happen to me! I ain't done nothing for this to come to me! I just work! I ain't had no happiness, no nothing. I just work. I'm black and I work and don't bother nobody. . . ."

"Go on," Bigger said, nodding his head affirmatively; he knew the truth of all she spoke without telling it. "Go on and see what that gets you." (170)

Bigger rejects the vernacular sentiment of Bessie's common, urban experience. She speaks of the blues, but he refuses to accept her expression as valuable.

Here again, Bessie and Mrs. Thomas's religion are conflated. Bessie's pleading could read as a prayer, but not one born of faith— the fundamental element of Christianity. Consequently, like Mrs. Thomas's songs, Bessie's expression is fundamentally not Christian. So while her pleas take the form of a prayer, they have the cadence and the sentiment of the blues. They become an urban blues performance for which Bigger is her audience. As John McCluskey explains, "Surprisingly, the lament of Bessie Mears, Bigger Thomas' girlfriend, is the statement which most closely parallels the blues tradition. Bessie's plea is the plea of a woman who has known only heartache and poverty. Though she remains thinly characterized, we can hear faint strains of Bessie Smith and Ma Rainey in her voice" (336). However, Bessie's blues pleadings only confirm Bigger's alienation: "Her words had made leap to consciousness in him a thousand details of her life which he had long known and they made him see that she was in no condition to be taken along and at the same time in no condition to be left behind" (216). So even while acknowledging the truth of Bessie's blues, he dismisses them as ineffectual: "Go on and see what that gets you" (170). It's not truth that Bigger seeks—it is change in the conditions that shape his life.

Because Bigger refuses to acknowledge the intrinsic value of Bessie's blues, he denies the kinship implicit among common folk. But his sense of place is intrinsically connected with his sense of race: "How easy it would be for him to hide if he had the whole city in which to move about! They keep us bottled up here like wild animals, he thought" (233). Bigger is afraid of what Bessie knows about him and the murder, and he is afraid of how that information could be used by the authorities who are hunting him. But when he dismisses Bessie's words as worthless, he rejects the potential shelter of the black belt—the place is bound with the people and the narratives that influence the way it operates. For a short while he is able to hide in abandoned buildings and travel unmolested: "He climbed through the window and walked to the street, turned northward, joining the people passing. No one recognized him" (232). But this relative freedom does not last. His confinement can be diagrammed on two levels: the discursive realm, which seemingly offers no liberatory modes of expression apart from murder; and geographical place, which offers only limited access to material resources. The reality of his confinement is revealed as he plots his escape within the constricted boundaries of the black city, held captive by a symbolic, white blizzard: "There were many empty buildings with black windows, like blind eyes, buildings like skeletons standing with snow on their bones in the winter winds" (163).

Until he kills Mary, Bigger feels he has no means to adequately vent his frustration because the expressive vehicles of his community do not satisfy him. Yet this feeling of estrangement motivates him to deny the murder, despite the fact that Bessie has already figured it out. The expressive modes already established within the community are not expedient and leave Bigger's sociopolitical dilemma unchanged. The other influence upon Bigger's worldview is the lack of genuine cohesiveness within the black community. He, a black man, has killed a white woman, and that reality alone prohibits Bigger from speaking openly. The myth of a unified black community is unraveled after his crime is discovered. Two residents of the Southside exchange:

> "Ef Ah knowed where tha' nigger wuz Ah'd turn im up 'n' git these white folks off me."
>
> "But, Jack, *ever'* nigger looks guilty t' white folks when somebody's done a crime." (73)

While white authorities hold the entire black belt under siege for the actions of one man, the black community is polarized by their ideals and fears. Bigger's act sets events in motion that distort everything but the fundamental fact of Mary's murder.

By the end of the novel, Bigger cannot help but view himself as connected with black people and ultimately satisfies himself by situating his actions outside a moral dichotomy of right and wrong. Finally, the morbid creativity of his first expressive gesture gives way to a blues ethos. Through this mediating lens, Bigger recognizes what on some level his attorney, Max, refuses to see: that his actions might be considered somehow "appropriate" and "natural" if agency is attributed to the individual parts of the system that limits black people. While Max labels that racist system co-conspirator in Bigger's crimes, he is unwilling to take that next step that would allow Bigger to justify his actions as somehow proper within that larger schema, housed within the entire framework of his crime. Max stops short of becoming a participant in the urban blues performance—a means of translating murder into creative expression—that helps Bigger, as black migrant, impose meaning upon his environment and gives significance to his tragic experiences. Max's response of shock and horror foreshadows Mr. Norton's response in *Invisible Man* to Trueblood's tale of rape and incest. The liberal sensibilities that allow them to enter into a discussion about race mask the true horror of racism and, further, their place within racist practices.

The media representation of Bigger's trial demonstrates the degree to which the state apparatus has been able to bring the Frankenstein's monster of the threatening black man to life. "It is this Bigger of the media," Griffin says—the black, oversexed animal—"who is pursued, captured, tried, and executed. The overwhelming state apparatus leaps to violence when it can no longer contain him through housing and discourse" (129). Yet it is this Bigger who has managed to become a creator in and of himself. By daring to step outside the parameters defined by his socioeconomic circumstances into a realm not just of fear but also of flight, Bigger has managed to transform energy and bring his own monster to life.[5] This creative energy leads ultimately to Bigger's own violent end, but he does achieve a moment of flight via that rebellion. Although Bigger is never able to remove himself from the constraints of race imposed by the larger society and his flight takes shape inside a collapsing circle, for a short time, he has been able to sustain a sense of liberty that grows out of a self-awareness that complicity would never permit him to know.

As with any carnivalesque inversion, however, the original balance of power remains intact. However frightening Bigger's defiance may have been, he, like the black rat in the opening scene, is perceived as the intruder; no matter how valid his position, no matter how powerful his cause, he will be hunted, caught, and slain. Bigger is moving within a dynamic system that has many ways of maintaining itself.[6] The space[7] he carves out cannot be read as a frontier, the unexplored expanse suggested by the seemingly empty space that allows him to look up at the airplane in the sky; it is instead a small part of the Daltons' basement where he plots his cover-up. Doreen Massey reads place as "a subset of the interactions which construe space, a local articulation within the wider whole"

(115). While "space" is generally conceived in larger terms than "place," Bigger creates a space for himself that is a subset of someone else's place—the Dalton household. For this reason, he is doubly confined. Bigger is homeless in the sense in which Baker uses the term "placeless," and his space is liberating insofar as the terms defined by his blues performance are still functional.

On the subject of music and dance in *Native Son*, John Mc-Cluskey states:

> As a Marxist, *however*, Wright could not unqualifiedly extol the power and vitality of folk culture, as Harold Cruse has pointed out. Thus, for Wright in his early analysis, though folk expression might help define a group, its insights could not suffice to guide Black people to power (and, presumably, guide Black artists to a searching social critique) within a broader political context. (334)

The character that Wright created in Bigger reflected the author's perspective. To Bigger, people like his mother, who want to sing and shout, and Bessie, who wants to drink and dance, are foolish because they do not see the uselessness of their own actions. Moreover, it is difficult for him to separate the family from the place they inhabit.

Bigger's reading of his mother and siblings signifies upon his reading of the apartment and vice versa. He himself reads as part of and in contrast to the interior landscape of the kitchenette. In setting Bigger beside Vera and his mother and then moving him outward into the increasingly larger geographical planes of the streets, the Daltons' house, and the black belt, Wright charts a schematic of urban territory upon which these power dynamics are enacted. The interplay of insider versus outsider is initiated by Bigger's name, which overtly states his claim to a space outside his family and this cramped apartment. It is not simply that Bigger is literally that, bigger than his family and this stultifying space they are forced to occupy. Rather, in the dialectical language of blues expressiveness that characterizes so much of Wright's ultimate worldview, Wright asserts that the nation is BIGGER—bigger than the man, bigger than the black belt, but, importantly, bigger than the Daltons and Buckley, too. Thus the largeness of the city is merely an illusion. In this dialectical framework, then, the black rat remains a threat and explodes the notion of home. Home is not reconciled with Bigger. And we find that Bigger is biggest—too big for the city, the kitchenette, or the Daltons' basement.

Notes

1. Richard Wright's *Native Son* (1940) is the literary forebear of Ralph Ellison's *Invisible Man* (1947). Perhaps no other African American authors have been more accepted into the traditional canon of American literature than these two men. Their masterpieces of fiction have become a standard part of a liberal arts curriculum. While we might find varied representations of both the city and home in the work of other male authors like Langston Hughes, Jean Toomer, and Alain Locke from the Harlem Renaissance era or more contemporary authors like James Baldwin, Ernest Gaines, and LeRoi Jones (Amiri Baraka), it seems prudent to spend some effort examining home as it is represented in these two works, which are so accepted. Not only do they speak directly to the issues of home within the context of African America, but they also inform the writings of those who follow. No major African American author since the publication of *Native Son* and *Invisible Man* is unaware of or unaffected by the novels' legacies.

2. Hurston's reading of shouting is distinctly secular. It serves well in this discussion of secular expressions like the blues, which is very often set in opposition to sacred practices of worship.

3. Until recent decades these churches, which are now the fastest growing Christian denominations in the world, had been classified as cults by sociologists like E. Franklin Frazier. They were looked upon with disdain by the black middle class. See *The Negro Church in America* (New York: Schocken Books, 1974).

4. The verse continues: *Watch the curves, the hills, the tunnels; never falter, never quail. Keep you hand upon the throttle and you eye upon the rail.*

5. Craig Werner notes the ways in which Wright utilizes a line from T. S. Eliot's "The Love Song of J. Alfred Prufrock"—"There will be time to murder and create"—which is based upon "the momentary exhilaration associated with Bigger's discovery of his own significance." *New Essays on Native Son* (New York: Cambridge University Press, 1970), 132.

6. In the manner described by Ross Chambers's *Room for Maneuver: Reading (the) Oppositional (in) Literature* (Chicago: University of Chicago Press, 1991), power structures are designed to permit a level of opposition: "Oppositional behavior consists of individual or group survival tactics that do not challenge power in place, but make use of circumstances set up by that power for purposes the power may ignore or deny. It contrasts, then, with revolution, which is a mode of *resistance* to forms of power it regards as illegitimate, that is, as a force that needs to be opposed by a counter force" (1). Toni Morrison's *Playing in the Dark: Whiteness and the Literary Imagination* (Cambridge: Harvard University Press, 1992) also describes such a systematic approach to resistance. As she writes about slave narratives, "Whatever popularity the slave narratives had—and they influenced abolitionists and converted anti-abolitionists—the slave's own narrative, while freeing the author in many ways, did not destroy the master narrative. The master narrative could make any number of adjustments to keep itself intact" (50–51).

7. Space and place work cooperatively. Generally, space is read as undefined or expansive while place is perceived as defined and therefore limited. Understanding one requires knowledge of the other because as spatial terms function, their oppositions gain their meaning when set one beside the other. See Michel de Certeau, *The Practice of Everyday Life* (Berkeley: University of California Press, 1984), 117–18. Here I use the term "space" rather than "place" because it connotes the freedom of movement Bigger has been denied by the tyranny of place.

.

Works Cited

Baker, Houston A., Jr. *Blues, Ideology, and Afro-American Literature: A Vernacular Theory*. Chicago: University of Chicago Press, 1984.

——. "Richard Wright and the Dynamics of Place in Afro-American Literature." In Keneth Kinnamon, ed., *New Essays on* Native Son. New York: Cambridge University Press, 1970.

Ellison, Ralph. *Invisible Man*. New York: Vintage, 1947.

Giles, James. *The Naturalistic Inner-City Novel in America: Encounters with the Fat Man*. Columbia: University of South Carolina Press, 1995.

Gilyard, Keith. *Modern Critical Interpretations:* Native Son. Ed. Harold Bloom. Philadelphia: Chelsea House, 1988.

——. "The Sociolinguistics of Underground Blues." *Black American Literature Forum* 19 (4) (1985): 158–59.

Griffin, Farah Jasmine. *"Who Set You Flowin'?": The African-American Migration Narrative*. New York: Oxford University Press, 1995.

Harris, Trudier. "Native Sons and Foreign Daughters." In Keneth Kinnamon, ed., *New Essays on* Native Son. New York: Cambridge University Press, 1970.

Hurston, Zora Neale. *The Sanctified Church*. New York: Marlowe and Company, 1981.

Kinnamon, Keneth, ed. Introduction to *New Essays on* Native Son. New York: Cambridge University Press, 1970.

Massey, Doreen. "Double Articulation: A Place in the World." In Angelika Bammer, ed., *Displacements: Cultural Identities in Question*. Bloomington: Indiana University Press, 1994.

McCall, Dan. *The Example of Richard Wright*. New York: Harcourt, Brace and World, 1969.

McCluskey, John, Jr. "Two Steppin': Richard Wright's Encounter with Blues-Jazz." *American Literature* 55 (3) 1983: 332–44.

Reilly, John M. "Giving Bigger a Voice: The Politics of Narrative in *Native Son*." In Keneth Kinamon, ed., *New Essays on* Native Son. New York: Cambridge University Press, 1970.

Wright, Richard. *Native Son*. New York: Bantam, 1940.

———. *12 Million Black Voices*. New York: Thunder's Mouth Press, 1941.

2

Keep on Moving Don't Stop: *Invisible Man*

The title *Native Son* is clearly ironic; Bigger Thomas has no home or paternity. Yet the novel lays out three terms that sketch a blueprint for the place of home within African American literature traceable through works produced over the following three decades: the city,

the kitchen, and the womb. The city dominates Bigger's landscape
even as he is pressed into geographically more restrictive spaces.
The kitchen is represented as the kitchenette, an abbreviated version
of a more complete place; and Bigger's retreat into the basement of
the Dalton house is but the initial stage of a literary retreat into the
womb.

In Ralph Ellison's masterpiece published twelve years later, *Invisible Man* (1952), the nameless protagonist goes on a journey that begins at the end, when he seems to have found "a home of sorts"— a basement apartment in an "all white" building outside Harlem. I will examine the ways that Ellison picks up and revises the theme of home that appears in *Native Son* specifically as the three geographical markers. I am interested in the changes Ellison makes in representing these sites so that they seem to yield the possibility of community fundamental to establishing home. The womb is defined more clearly in this novel, and the kitchen also plays a more significant role in *Invisible Man* than in *Native Son*. However, the city still dominates the landscape and serves as the chief concern in the narrator's quest for home.

Invisible Man augments the scenes of home found in *Native Son* as Ellison explores other possibilities of the Northern city. Numerous scenes, most within the city, provide the backdrop for the plot. Of all the settings featured in *Invisible Man*, Mary Rambo's house most reads as "home" because it contains her blues kitchen. In addition to Mary's house, only the basement apartment and the South are overtly characterized as home for the invisible man. The narrator looks over his shoulder to the South, a place to which he will never return. For a time, it guides his movements as Kansas does Dorothy's on her journey through Oz. The basement is a more overt representation of the womb than Bigger's basement in *Native Son*. In contrast to the city, which resists being configured as home, Mary's house, with its blues kitchen, and the basement apartment, a womblike place, lend themselves to being read as home. Yet something remains in place to trouble such a reading. We imagine home to be stable and therefore stabilizing, but Ellison builds upon Wright's problematization of stability as a quality of home. The impermeability of Wright's city does not prove stabilizing, despite the fact that it remains static. In contrast, Ellison focuses on the changing face of the city that refuses to be known or knowable, and thus refuses to engender the familiarity fundamental to the construct of home.

As in *Native Son*, in this novel the blues seems to be part and parcel of the black (home) place. Unlike Wright, Ellison believed music was a vital aspect of his literary aesthetic. Instead of social protest, Ellison sought to create art; and his art would be infused with the movement and cadence of the blues. Berndt Ostendorf says:

> Vernacular dance, vernacular language, and vernacular music represent for this high cultural modernist a total body of culture. And Ellison wants to translate that energy into the organized discipline of his art. . . . Jazz, dance, and language all partake of a total world view and a total way of life. Hence, one of the harshest estimates that Ellison ever made of Richard Wright was that "he knew very little about jazz and didn't even know how to dance." (97)

Wright's inability to dance is tantamount to Bigger's inability to sing. Stereotypically, "Black folk got rhythm," if they do not have anything else. Ellison, believing that music and dance are fundamental to African American culture, suggests that for a black man, not knowing how to dance means lacking a crucial foundation. It is through understanding of these cultural practices that black people become connected with one another. Although the blues cannot mitigate all of the debilitating effects experienced at home, it provides a cadence through which some of the occupants make a culture of privation more bearable.

Womb: The Truebloods' Cabin

By the second chapter of the novel, two of the three terms have been introduced. The narrator, in the prologue, is already underground in New York City. But the novel goes back to the time when his journey began in the South. The Trueblood episode appears in the second chapter of *Invisible Man*. Jim Trueblood is a sharecropper who lives with his family near the campus of the college the narrator attends briefly. The narrator inadvertently escorts Mr. Norton, a wealthy white trustee, to the Truebloods' cabin. Initially Mr. Norton is struck by the age and style of the structure: "It was an old cabin with its chinks filled with chalk-white clay, with bright new shingles patching its roof" (46). He notices the cabins first, then, "looking across the bare, hard stretch of yard . . . two women dressed in new blue-and-white checked ginghams," both of whom "moved with the weary, full-fronted motions of far-gone pregnancy" (47). Filled with wonder that the buildings have lasted since slavery, Mr. Norton exclaims, "The human stock goes on, even though it degenerates. But these cabins!" (47). Mr. Norton expects the "human stock" to continue despite its degeneration but he is full of wide-eyed amazement that the man-made cabins endure so well. From his perspective, the pregnant black woman is part of an old scene of the black South. These structures and the women working in the yard, he intimates, are enduring evidence of a more wholesome past.

The narrator is mortified by his own impropriety, having stumbled upon the Truebloods without forethought. Jim Trueblood is a disgrace to the local black community, particularly the petit bourgeoisie at the college. He has brought shame to everyone by impregnating both his wife, Kate, and his eldest daughter, Matty Lou. These are the two women dressed alike and bearing the weight of pregnancy, like twins, working together in the yard. In introducing Mr. Norton to Jim Trueblood, the narrator discloses the dark underbelly of the poverty of black domestic life. The pregnant womb is necessarily part of this construction because, as even Mr. Norton recognizes in his pejorative understanding of African Americans, home is built around family. Patriarchy relies upon the woman as the kin source, and men operating under this philosophy look to women to bring forth the next generation. While no home place can be constructed around gender without some inherent conflict, the terrain of the black (home) place of the sharecropper pictured here is made even more treacherous by poverty, racism, and the imbalance of power between the genders.

Mr. Norton is attracted to the Truebloods' tale as if by a force beyond his control. He demands that the narrator stop and let him speak to Trueblood himself. Trueblood willingly narrates his woeful tale to the Northern, white, liberal philanthropist. Unable to afford coal, the family conserves body heat by sleeping together in two pallets on the floor. The younger children are in one and Matty Lou between her parents in the other. Trueblood recounts his thoughts, which include reminiscing about a past love and fending off a current suitor interested in Matty Lou, but he places responsibility for his behavior on a "dream-sin": he awakened from a dream to discover he was having intercourse with his daughter.

Initially, Ellison describes the setting as "dark, plum black. Black as the middle of a bucket of tar" (54). In this black place, he lays out the dynamics of home at work in this novel. The Truebloods' log cabin is a remnant of slavery. This part of the material landscape has hardly been altered since prior to the Civil War. This black (home) place that began in racist Southern oppression and poverty ends in the same shack with a mother and daughter impregnated by the same man. Although Mr. Norton hardly can be credited with recognizing the nuances of these sophisticated racial dynamics, he is correct in that, indeed, one incestuous seed "degenerates." Kate and Matty Lou bear the tragedy of home literally in their bodies. The two pregnant women, mother and daughter, signify the privation out of which Trueblood's blues are created.

At first, the narrator is baffled by his confrontation with Trueblood, but the sharecropper contributes one of the most profound lessons the unnamed protagonist receives in his long journey. Trueblood's blues are characterized by John S. Wright as the "creative will to transcendence" (176). Upon awakening from his nightmarish dream and recognizing his quagmire (that he is having intercourse with his daughter while his wife is lying next to them in bed), Trueblood explains, "Once a man gits hisself into a tight spot like that there ain't much he can do. It ain't up to him no longer. There I was, tryin' to git away with all my might, yet having to move without movin'. I flew in but I had to walk out. I had to move without movin'" (59). Trueblood is caught within a situation that inflicts terrible pain upon himself as well as his family; at the same moment he experiences pleasure great enough to create an unresolvable predicament. Movement is both the problem and the solution. The narrator himself will come to accept Trueblood's quintessential blues paradox: having to arrive at the result without ever performing the action. As John S. Wright explains, "In his full awareness, then, of the irredeemable cost of freedom from sin and the attendant consequences of freely sinning, Trueblood gives eloquent testimony to his own tragic sense of life and to that need for transcendence he finally satisfies only in the resolving poetry of the blues" (176).

Incest is not the shocking new ground Mr. Norton discovers that hot afternoon as he listens to the tale. Instead, he ventures into "new territory" when he stumbles upon Trueblood's yard and encounters the black (home) place and the blues. What confounds him even more than the fact of incest is the fact that Jim Trueblood seems to have escaped judgment: "You did and are unharmed!" (51). It seems Trueblood has found a resolution to his personal dilemma. He *can* move without moving, as Norton demonstrates by rewarding his performance. Along with so many other guilt-ridden, wealthy white men, Norton is moved by Trueblood's tale while Trueblood, as blues performer, does not have to *move* at all.

The sharecropper's home, which had been threatened by poverty, the mock charity of Northern liberals, and the racial pragmatism of the black college, is now maintained by Jim Trueblood's retellings of his story. He transforms his own painful experience into a blues performance. Already known for his singing and storytelling, Trueblood has polished his tale, reconfiguring tragic circumstances to make his life more livable. His family is clad in new clothing, his roof patched with new shingles bought with money garnered from patrons of his art. Trueblood is an agent of the blues. In contrast, the women are not heard. The mark left on Jim's face from Kate's swing of an ax is the sole evidence of her resistance. Matty Lou is just silenced; she "won't speak a word to nobody" (67).

Rape is a high price for Matty Lou to pay in order for her father to be rewarded as an agent of the blues. And as Ann du Cille, Hortense Spillers, and other African American feminist critics have emphasized, care must be taken not to reduce her to an object of patriarchy.[1] She does not get to narrate her own tale; that authority is given (quite naturally) to her father, who, even after violating the (natural) rights of his daughter, retains his domestic dominance (as evidenced by the failure of his wife's attempt to kill him). To deny the horror of the scene and only acknowledge the blues expression that emerges from it risks, as Ann du Cille suggests in a critique of Houston Baker's reading of the episode, reducing race to rape. Rape is the means through which Trueblood gains his power, at the expense of Kate and, most notably, Matty Lou. His role as father is doubly confirmed by the two pregnant women. In this household, as opposed to that of Bigger Thomas, paternity is clear—all too clear.

Kitchen: Mary Rambo's Blues Kitchen

While Bigger is unable to discover a safe place to roost in the course of his desperate flight, that is precisely what the invisible man unwittingly finds in Mary Rambo's house. The novel actually begins "underground," in the basement of an apartment in New York City, as the invisible man recites the story of how his journey to that point began. He has been propelled from place to place by a series of events that makes it impossible for him to have the comfort of a stable home. After arriving in New York, he must come to understand the naïveté of the hope that he will be allowed to return to the deep South (somehow improved by his experiences). Still reeling from yet another sudden shift in place, the narrator emerges from a subway and finds himself ushered into Mary Rambo's house.

Mary meets the visibly ailing narrator on the street, and with some assistance from another passerby, helps him into her home. This house, more than any other in the novel, manifests the mythic possibilities of home that must be constructed, at least partially, around the familiarity fostered by the past. Yet it too is part of urban blues culture and reflects the tension of blues vernacular. The blues speak of a dialectic created in the opposition of privation, poverty, and racism with privilege, wealth, and liberty. Mary's position as caregiver is well known within the community, and she expects the residents to be familiar with her reputation. She reassures the ailing protagonist, *"You take it easy, I'll take care of you like I done a heap of others, my name's Mary Rambo, everybody knows me round this part of Harlem"* (252). Mary ushers the protagonist into his next venue as she compels him to take refuge in her home.

Mary allows him to reside in her house without fear of eviction or of the social elitism that is so pervasive at the Men's House—from which he has just been banished for pouring a spittoon over the head of a reverend, whom he has mistaken for Dr. Bledsoe. Bledsoe is the Southern administrator who betrayed him by sending him to work in New York in the futile hope of returning to school. At Mary's house, he finds the comfort of good company, rest, and food. He explains his relationship with her in this way, "Other than Mary I had no friends and desired none. Nor did I think of Mary as a 'friend': she was something more—a force, a stable, familiar force like something out of my past which kept me from whirling off into some unknown which I dared not face" (258).

Friends have become obsolete in the narrator's world after Bledsoe's betrayal. Mary does not serve as "friend"; rather, she is an anchor of sorts that rescues him from an unfamiliar, and therefore terrifying, abyss of urban Northern life. The greater the "unknown," the more familiar and stabilizing is Mary. The "unknown" that the narrator so fears is not an identifiable place. Instead, it is an expanse of unencoded space that would consume him, were it not for the grounding Mary provides. The expanse feels threatening when set within the context of Harlem, the city that refuses to be constant for the invisible man. Mary's house offers the consolation of a definite site sheltered from the city, which only exacerbates the perceived chaos.

The expanse of the Northern city had seduced the protagonist and left him sick and stumbling up from the subway. Mary's "familiarity" contrasts with this large strangeness. But the narrator has difficulty articulating Mary's relationship to him. Like music, she is beyond words. Her house becomes "the South right in the middle of Manhattan" that Farah Griffin describes in *"Who Set you Flowin'?" The African American Migration Narrative*. Like the atmosphere created by the blues performance Griffin describes, Mary embodies not the South so much as "home." She becomes a meta-place that exists as a locale in the abstract. As such, Mary suggests the familiarity of Southern ritual culture without actually materializing the South. In her house, the narrator is able to find the solace of Southern practices without leaving town. She opens her doors selflessly to this man who could be categorized as a "stranger." The dichotomies inherent in the construct of home, which operate to make Mary recognizable inside the strangeness of the city, conversely function to make the protagonist known, or at least not a stranger, to her. In this way Mary and her guest develop a relationship that is not contingent upon knowing the personal details of each other's life. Mary is familiar to him because of the cultural values she represents; consequently, her house reads as "home." The blues performance that makes "the South right in the middle of Manhattan" is a musical configuration. Hence, Mary is reconfigured in this way as well.

The musical value system she embodies is made up of blue notes that begin with a man sick and stumbling into the arms of a care-taker. The narrator explains, "When I came out of the subway, Lenox Avenue seemed to career away from me at a drunken angle, and I focused upon the teetering scene with wild, infant's eyes, my head throbbing" (251). Here again the underground is a womblike place. Coming out of the subway station is like being reborn and given to a new mother. Mary shelters the narrator without concern for how his presence might impact her own well-being. When she is low on food and money, she serves cabbage instead of complaining or refusing to feed someone. What she demands in return appears as a benign pressure to perform "some act of leadership, some noteworthy achievement" (258).

The underlying tension in Mary's house is reflected by this pressure and the cabbage—suggesting the permeability of home and its potential to be infiltrated by larger forces like economics associated with maintaining such places. In another sense, the circumstances at Mary's house demonstrate the flexibility of the blues. Within the context of the blues, strangers can be allied unproblematically with each other, as are Mary and the protagonist. Further, the blues creates a space where circumstances like poverty can be integrated into the structure of home, Mary's house, without complete ruin.[2] While contemplating the meaning of the cabbage and the pressure in his room, the narrator hears Mary in the kitchen: "Then from down the hall I could hear Mary singing, her voice clear and untroubled, though she sang a troubled song. It was the 'Back Water Blues.' I lay listening as the sound flowed to and around me, bringing me a calm sense of my indebtedness" (297).

The blues serves Mary as a repository into which she can pour her pain and negative emotion. Mary's blues kitchen emerges as part of a larger cultural practice of establishing "home ground." The blues becomes a metaphorical bottle tree that is constructed to guard the home and protect its occupants by containing the evil.[3] Mary's blues, in effect, seeks to capture the evil "spirit" that troubles her home. The blues kitchen helps her negotiate the conflict between her home as a safe space and poverty as a threat to that perceived serenity—and the song brings order and meaning to her guest's experience.

The narrator's sense of indebtedness to Mary motivates the invisible man to accept a job with a political organization known as the Brotherhood so that he can repay her. Ironically, this job requires him to move. On his last day at Mary's home, the invisible man is awakened by a jarring sound. The cacophony has a very different effect on him than the blues tones of Mary's kitchen. The disembodied sound of metal striking against the metal of the radiator pipes reverberates throughout the building and infuriates the protagonist. He expresses hostility toward the people behind this commotion by looking for a weapon with which to contribute his own noisy blows to the pipe:

Then near the door I saw something which I'd never noticed there before: the cast-iron figure of a very black, red-lipped and wide-mouthed Negro, whose white eyes stared up at me before his chest. It was a bank, a piece of early Americana, the kind of bank which, if a coin is placed in the hand a lever pressed upon the back, will raise its arm and flip the coin into the grinning mouth. For a second I stopped, grabbed it, suddenly as enraged by the tolerance or lack of discrimination, or whatever, that allowed Mary to keep such a self-mocking image around, as by the knocking. (319)

Mary wonders at the racket caused by the numerous tenants throughout the building, and her bewilderment is expressed in her characteristic blues idiom, "They know when the heat don't come up that the super's drunk or done walked off the job looking for his woman, or something. Why don't folks act according to what they know?" (320). This kind of expressiveness is what allows the potential for pleasure to coexist with the likelihood of pain, and contrasts with the narrator's cacophony. Her vernacular gives voice to the rage that he so vehemently desires to articulate through his attack upon the pipe. It seems appropriate to him to use the bank that he finds so offensive. But Mary is puzzled by the self-centeredness of a response that focuses on one's own feelings of discomfort rather than recognizing the interconnectedness of human beings in the struggle to endure.

Mary identifies with the super's position as another expression of need, akin to her own. She has the unusual ability to recognize and, further, to validate another person's pain. This is significant precisely because it is a difficult thing to do, as Elaine Scarry describes:

> For the person in pain, so incontestably and unnegotiably present is it that "having pain" may come to be thought of as the most vibrant example of what it is to "have certainty," while for the other person it is so elusive that "hearing about pain" may exist as the primary model of what it is "to have doubt." Thus pain comes unsharably into our midst as at once that which cannot be denied and that which cannot be confirmed. (4)

Mary bridges the chasm between the certainty embodied by her own experience of pain and the doubt about another's. Through her blues vernacular, she correlates her own experiences with the actions of those around her (even as their actions further inconvenience her), incorporating new circumstances into her blues vocabulary as they arise. In contrast, the narrator cannot handle the disruption and has trouble identifying with the figure that he finds so offensive. Yet he is able to note the pain in the bank's expression, which "seemed more of a strangulation than a grin" (312). The bank's visage shows the classic paradox of blues expressiveness that balances between pain and pleasure. This face both "grins and lies" in the way that Paul Laurence Dunbar describes in his poem "We Wear the Mask":

> We wear the mask that grins and lies,
> It hides our cheeks and shades our eyes,—
> This debt we pay to human guile;
> With torn and bleeding hearts we smile,
> And mouth with myriad subtleties.

The "subtleties" of the expression are key to understanding a complex history.

Mask wearing is inseparable from the African American historical experience; no amount of shame or anger can erase the past. African Americans have been forced to contort their sorrow into laughter, anger into a grin. As Wright states in *12 Million Black Voices*, "The ridiculousness and sublimity of love are captured in our blues, those sad-happy songs that laugh and weep in one breath, those mocking tender utterances of a folk imprisoned in steel and stone" (128). The "steel and stone" framework of the city promotes the contradictory impulses that began centuries earlier, in the Middle Passage, the smiling through tears. The bank is a blues artifact that could anchor the invisible man's profound history of pain, resistance, fortitude, and pride. Yet the narrator is so angry about the stereotype it represents that he refuses to identify with the pain inherent in its expression.

He quickly dismisses the observations that might help him identify with the hidden pain (and Scarry suggests that pain is always concealed if it is not experienced personally); hence, he misses the lessons that might be learned by empathizing with others and sharing their grief. As Griffin notes, his judgment is impaired by his inability to comprehend the multifaceted layers of his experiences:

This question, "What does it mean?" is Invisible Man's constant refrain. He is ambitious and somewhat pretentious. He feels that in order to reach his goal of leadership, he must shun those elements that bind him to a racial past. While he seeks to lead black people, it is an empty aspiration that fails to recognize the value of racial wisdom. Nowhere is this contradiction more evident than in his relationship with Mary. (131)

For the narrator to empathize with and share the grief expressed by the bank, he would have to be willing to ally himself with the collectivity the figure represents. The blues ethos that permits this kind of identification is, after all, a vernacular expression. But he is not yet ready to make the conscious choice to identify with this segment of his racial community. He dismisses his observation of the "strangulation" and the awareness it might bring. Instead, he uses the bank as a weapon to unleash his anger upon the unseen forces. Not surprisingly, in the process he smashes the head apart; and that which he hoped to destroy, he will not be permitted to discard.

City: Dispossession

Ellison assigns value to Mary's house by juxtaposing it with a scene of an eviction (one potential effect of that "unknown" space that the narrator fears) involving an old black couple. The narrator uses Mary as the point of contrast by which he assigns meaning to the city. The metropolis is large; Mary is small. While her house is not large enough to accommodate the invisible man's needs, she is an invaluable resource for him as he comes to understand his place within the urban territory.

Like the sense of homelessness found in *Native Son*, dispossession illustrates the relationship certain people have with the places they occupy. At the first eviction the narrator has ever witnessed, he makes an impassioned speech in an attempt to subdue an angry crowd, trying to explain the meaning of "dispossession." He expounds:

"'Dispossess,' eighty-seven years and dispossessed of what? They ain't *got* nothing, they can't *get* nothing, they never *had* nothing. So who was dispossessed?" I growled. "We're law abiding. So who's being dispossessed? Can it be us? These old ones are out in the snow, but we're here with them. Look at their stuff, not a pit to hiss in, nor a window to shout the news and us right with them. Look at them, not a shack to pray in or an alley to sing the blues! (279)

After eighty-seven years, the elderly couple has little of material value, and their condition presages the state of the entire community. Ellison draws upon William Faulkner's use of the dispossession theme in *Go Down, Moses,* where Ike struggles with the idea when he inherits land because the rightful heir, Lucas Beauchamp, is black. Ike dispossesses his cousin, Lucas, of the land (only to repudiate it later). Ike laments, "Dispossessed of Eden. Dispossessed of Canaan, and those who dispossessed him dispossessed him dispossessed" (247). Ellison recasts this literary theme from Faulkner's Mississippi within the setting of the Northern city. Dispossession is an active condition enforced upon the community by officials with orders such as those who block the old couple's door. The narrator captures in his speech the sense of transience and indeterminacy that residents, recast as travelers, experience in city life.

When we meet the invisible man in the prologue, he has taken up residence in the basement of an apartment building. He has lit it with 1,369 light bulbs illuminated by unregulated electricity. The protagonist uses the lights to establish this territory as his home. Marking territory in this way can be situated within the African American practice of establishing "home ground." Anthropologist Grey Gundaker claims that such practices exist within the context of African America from coast to coast in both urban and rural settings: "Scale varies, but the claim, I am here, stays the same" (1). In this gesture, the narrator declares, "I am here," but with much less emphasis on the "here" than on the "I am." One reason is that place, within the context of the novel, continues to be unstable, as tenuous a construct as any seemingly fixed identity.

In fact, Monopolated Light & Power, the electric company responsible for distribution of current for the area, believes that "a lot of free current is disappearing somewhere into the jungle of Harlem" (5). The power company is, of course, a faceless white corporation whose primary goal is to serve its own interests (which may overlap with the interests of the larger white community), presumably without considering the interests of the black community. The company is quick to place blame for the loss of current on the African American community. Harlem is a black place. It is indisputably the section of New York City reserved for African Americans, so the reference to it as a "jungle" carries racist connotations. Harlem is read here as a barbaric wilderness, an untamed expanse that is far too frightening and free to be conquered. From the white perspective represented by ML&P, at best such a place can only be contained.

The invisible man exploits the image of Harlem as jungle to avoid the possibility of being discovered. Harlem during the 1920s was the scene of a great rebirth of African American culture; the contemporary Harlem pictured here contrasts with the image of that era.[4] The protagonist explains, "The joke, of course, is that I don't live in Harlem" (5). This is part of the irony. ML&P's expectation that a power drainage must come from inside the "jungle" is so restrictive that no one with this perspective could imagine that the drainage is coming from elsewhere—let alone an "all white" building *outside* of Harlem. Yet the lines delineating Harlem from the rest of Manhattan are more permeable than ML&P wishes to admit. As Gloria Anzaldúa writes, "Borders are set up to define the places that are safe and unsafe, to distinguish *us* from *them*. A border is a dividing line, a narrow strip along a steep edge. A borderland is a vague and undetermined place created by the emotional residue of an unnatural boundary. It is in a constant state of transition" (3). Borders, as Anzaldúa defines them, are a type of threshold that is constantly in flux. In the prologue, the invisible man has made this basement into a borderland home of sorts. If he embraces the border as his home, we might expect that he is also embracing the idea of change and mixtures. The despotism of one culture over another, of the power company's monopoly over Harlem, is challenged by the metaphor of in-betweenness. So the invisible man finds comfort in this retreat: "The point now is that I found a home—or a hole in the ground, as you will" (5).

The basement hideaway may be read as a transitional space between what is characterized as the "jungle"—representing the African American ghetto—and civilization, the white city. According to the logic employed by ML&P, a black man should not reside outside the "jungle" of Harlem and no white person in this apartment building would be siphoning electricity. But having recently come to the awareness that his identity is more precisely fixed as an *invisible* man than a *black* man, the narrator is able to orchestrate this ruse and manipulate the power structure into deceiving itself. He manages this scam because of society's insistence upon classifying places as well as people in the ways that Anzaldúa illuminates—according to race, gender, nationality, etc. It is important to ML&P and the culture associated with the corporation to be able to delineate its boundaries of power in order to maneuver the opposition (either real or imagined) onto a plane that operates under its authority. As Doreen Massey articulates:

> Two points seem clear. First, and very obviously, the way in which we characterize places is fundamentally political. But second, and far less obviously perhaps, the politics lie not just in the particular characteristics assigned to places (whether they include racist or sexist features, to which social class they are assigned) but in the very way in which the image of place is constructed. (114)

The division that demarcates the jungle and separates it from the rest of the city draws a line of safety with which the white community is able to assuage their fears of an African American threat. Identifying the territory of the jungle and African Americans as its occupants allows the whites to blindly insist upon the truth of its boundaries.

Perhaps the narrator turns on 1,369 bulbs in order to shed light on the intangibility of the barriers between the races. He then contradicts the authority of these boundaries through his tale. The reader, aware from the prologue of the narrator's true location, is not deceived by the apartment building's claim of being "all white." Hegemony's borders are not hard and fast. Instead it is the very permeability of those delineations that allows the structure to endure.

By the time the invisible man has gone through the Brotherhood and encountered Todd Clifton and Ras the Destroyer, he has come to accept the movement that compels him from place to place as a part of the African American collective condition. As he is moved, he is forced to receive both material and psychological signs that connect him to the collective experience. His briefcase is now full of indicators of his travels, and he has the potential to identify himself as part of a larger community of racialized people and sites. But that community still refuses to yield itself to the invisible man's needs. The Harlem riot is one of the last venues depicted in the novel. During the riot the illusion of stability ordinarily associated with place gives way to chaos. In the midst of this extreme disorder, the narrator again longs for home.

The portrait of Mary surfaces as a maternal, stable, and ordering figure that comes to be read overtly as home: "It was not a decision of thought but something I realized suddenly while running over puddles of milk in the black street, stopping to swing the heavy brief case and the leg chain, slipping and sliding out of their hands" (551). Those signs of his journey—the case heavy with the weight of the coins, the bank he broke at Mary's house, and the leg chain given to him earlier by Tarp—become the physical manifestations of the vernacular blues expressiveness inherent in black experiences, which have the potential to defend him against hostile enemies. Although the physical weight of the metal blues artifacts protects him during the upheaval of the riot, like Bigger in his doomed flight, the narrator is searching for a safe place to roost. He is trying to reach Mary's house, but he is running the wrong way. He cannot go back to Mary's—the maternal imagery is rendered useless as the milk already wasted upon the ground.

The past is not available to the protagonist because of the laws of physics, regardless of social, cultural, or personal history. Further, as Doreen Massey suggests, "There is no one essential past about which to get nostalgic. This is true in the sense that there has never been a historical movement untouched by the world beyond" (116). Time is the inevitably corrupting presence that complicates the ability to construct home as an ideal in the present. The knowledge required to construct home as a perfected shelter is predicated upon experience that comes through living over time. The invisible man cannot go home to Mary's because of the impossibility of returning through time and space with the knowledge he has acquired through the act of moving away. He is, indeed, moving in the wrong direction if he is trying to go home, because Mary's house becomes home for him only after he leaves. The challenge facing the invisible man is to use the tools available to him to create a home in the present. In the midst of this confusion, he suddenly finds himself falling to safety underground.

Womb: "A Home of Sorts" in the City

The narrator finds himself below ground after falling through an open manhole: "I was never to reach Mary's, and I was overoptimistic about removing the steel cap in the morning. . . . I tried to find the usual ladder that leads out of such holes, but there was none" (567). Falling underground, into a womblike place, in effect represents an impossible return. The serendipitous event parallels the desire to deliberately return to an originary moment while drawing upon the knowledge accumulated in his journey away from that very place. The narrator is able to use the things he has carried with him from his past as fuel. He burns the combustible objects in his briefcase in order to light his way out of the hole. Just as the leg chain and bank became pragmatic tools for his survival, these other things literally are able to help him survive.[5] This moment represents the culmination of past events as he tries to create a livable future out of the tools he has acquired.

The characterization of a place is, as Massey argues, "fundamentally political" because it is how societal institutions are able to sustain control over areas that otherwise would not belong to them. Although the characterizations may be presented as "natural," or unchanging essences already determined by the very existence of particular locations, they are dynamic rather than fixed. Consequently, Harlem is read as "jungle," not to determine accurately who is illegally pilfering power from ML&P, but to maintain the illusion of definitive boundaries and therefore the semblance of absolute control through the metaphor of containment. "Very often," Massey writes, "moreover, that intrinsic nature [of place] is seen as eternal, unchanging. And even where change is acknowledged, this approach often views the 'essence of place' as having evolved through a history which is read as a sense, an internal history" (11). If the narrator is African American and he lives outside the "jungle," then he challenges the logic embodied in the establishment of boundaries. However, it is the narrator's claim to invisibility that sets the ruse into action.

Motion is, of course, the primary directive of the novel: "Keep that nigger boy running." This directive sets the narrator in motion. Jerry Gafio Watts quotes Albert Murray saying, "'Improvisation,' Murray tells us 'is the ultimate human (i.e. heroic) endowment.' The blues-oriented hero is a matter of improvisation" (58). The narrator is such a blues hero, although the characterization is conflicted. By the end of the novel, he is claiming, "I would have to move them [Harlem] without myself being moved" (507). This sentiment echoes one he heard earlier from Jim Trueblood—"I had to move without movin'" (59). The narrator returns to that sentiment, derived from Trueblood's immoral rape and impregnation of his daughter alongside the legitimate impregnation of his wife. He tries to employ the sharecropper's blues logic in the environment of the ever-changing city. But the narrator cannot perform his way out of the blues paradox of the Harlem riot. His world has become one of sight, not invisibility, which illuminates rather than obscures the mechanisms that operate to maintain place. So Trueblood's solution to his perverse situation is thwarted in the narrator's relationship to Harlem. He cannot employ the blues strategy, so he is both physically and emotionally moved.

Another aspect of the home life captured in this revision of Trueblood's blues must not be overlooked. Jim Trueblood's blues reappear in the language of the protagonist, sanitized of the female body, that reminds us of the high stakes involved in blues production. Kate and Matty Lou are not accommodated by the narrator's blues sentiment, or more precisely, they are used and discarded. The black (home) place is subsumed within the more attractive figure of the pregnant black woman even as the woman is effaced by her womb. The slave cabin does not endure in the narrator's revision of Trueblood's blues—it has fallen away during the migration to the Northern city—and the "human stock . . . degenerates." From the outset, the narrator has been trying to get home—first back to the South, then to Mary's—and finally he finds himself underground. "I was in strange territory now and someone, for some reason, had removed the manhole cover and I felt myself plunge down, down . . . and I lay in the black dark . . . no longer running, hiding or concerned" (565). The womb reappears as a *man*hole, in Baker's terminology, "an irresistible attractive force" drawing all things into itself. This is indeed a black hole: "I tried to reach above me but found only space, unbroken and impenetrable" (567).

It would be nearly twenty years before Toni Morrison offered another vantage from which to view this impoverished black (home) place and its impact upon family life by introducing Pecola Breedlove in *The Bluest Eye*. In *Inspiriting Influences*, Michael Awkward reads Pecola, who suffers rape by her father, as a feminist revision of Matty Lou. I will discuss Pecola and the relationship incest has to the place of home further in the next chapter. The external specter of the city that haunts the migrants' early encounters in Wright's and Ellison's works is not the focus for Morrison in *The Bluest Eye*. While the male authors choose to focus on the confrontation between races that implicates the city, paying little deliberate attention to gender, home for this female author tends to read more specifically as the built physical structure. Yet, even as Morrison looks to the dynamics of a more intimate sphere, she records evidence of a devastating conflict that has the potential to destroy the quality of her characters' lives. The protagonist is threatened by directives issued from home that characterize human action and behavior as either legitimate or illegitimate. The city seems to fall away as we move further inside the built structure of home. Kitchens become the focal point in *The Bluest Eye*, before we again are pulled tragically into the womb.

Notes

1. Baker's reading of this scene in *Blues Ideology* ignited a firestorm among African American feminist critics because he suggests:

> Only the Trueblood encounter reveals the phallus as producing Afro-American generations rather than wasting its seed upon the water. The cosmic force of the phallus thus becomes, in the ritual action of the Trueblood episode, symbolic of a type of royal paternity, an aristocratic procreativity turned inward to ensure the royalty (the "truth," "legitimacy," or "authenticity") of an enduring black line of descent (183).

Baker arges that Trueblood's union with his daughter produces a royal lineage, and thus Matty Lou becomes the source who ensures a black line through the act of rape by her own father. The phallus is supreme and compassion for the daughter is sublimated by the dominance of patrimony.

2. John Bardi of Pennsylvania State University, Mont Alto, performed a witty, philosophical interpretation of three musical forms at the "Blues Traditions: Memory, Criticism, and Pedagogy" conference at Pennsylvania State University in June 2000. His performance on electric guitar read music as a metaphor for political systems. He presented a baroque piece as "exclusive"—any notes from outside the classical scale are banished from the "kingdom" by the resolution of the piece. An avant-garde piece represented a chaotic and unstable government, while the blues successfully presented a system that afforded both order and inclusiveness.

3. Such practices can be seen throughout the American landscape as African Americans lay claim to the territory and structures they inhabit. Containers like gourds, jugs, and bottles are often hung from trees or set on porches near doorways to both guard and mark the home. The blues is another such container. Like the bottle trees that appear as a distinctly African American aesthetic practice, the blues plays a significant role in maintaining Mary's home ground. Robert Farris Thompson explains such cultural practices in "Bighearted Power: Kongo Presence in the Landscape and Art of Black America" (in Grey Gundarker, ed., *Keep Your Head to the*

Sky: Interpreting African American Home Ground [Charlottesville: University Press of Virginia, 1998]):

> The *nkisi* tradition, brought to the United States from Kongo and Angola by Gullah Jack and other legendary healers, was a matter of embedding spirits in earths, keeping the spirit in a container to concentrate its power, and including with these earths material signs which told the spirit what to do. The gist of those expressions are seemingly regained in a creole art wherein the house guards the spirit of the owner and the icons in the yard guard or enhance that spirit with gestures of protection and enrichment.

A collection of *minkinsi* figures were featured in an exhibition at the Smithsonian as an introduction to a show featuring art by sculptor Renee Stout. At the entrance to the exhibition were these figures and a prominent sign explaining their presence and significance. The sign explained that the English language has no direct parallel for the word "*minkinsi*." "*Minkinsi* are fabricated things, yet they can be invoked to produce desired effects, they have a will of their own, and they may willfully command the behavior of human beings . . . people depend on *minkinsi* to do things for them, even to make life itself possible" (quoted in Wyatt Macaffey and Michael D. Harris, *Astonishment and Power: The Eyes of Understanding and the Art of Renee Stout* [Washington, D.C.: The Smithsonian Institution Press, 1993], 13).

4. For a comprehensive examination of the image of Harlem in literature see James De Jongh, *Vicious Modernism: Black Harlem and the Literary Imagination* (Cambridge: Cambridge University Press, 1990).

5. Ellison romanticizes this site by imagining a disembodied womb wherein his protagonist can hibernate only to emerge, some time later, renewed. In chapter 4, "She's a Brick House," about *Corregidora*, I deal with the futility of the gesture as well as some of its gendered implications.

Works Cited

Anzaldúa, Gloria. *Borderlands*/La Frontera: *The New Mestiza*. San Francisco: Spinters-Aunt Lute, 1987.

Faulkner, William. *Go Down, Moses*. New York: Vintage, 1940.

Gudaker, Grey, ed. *Keep Your Head to the Sky: Interpreting African American Home Ground*. Charlottesville: University Press of Virginia, 1999.

Griffin, Farah. *"Who Set You Flowin'?": The African-American Migration Narrative.* New York: Oxford University Press, 1995.

Massey, Doreen. "Double Articulation: A Place in the World." In Angelika Bammer, ed., *Displacements: Cultural Identities in Question.* Bloomington: Indiana University Press, 1994, 110–21.

Ostendorf, Berndt. "Ralph Waldo Ellison: Anthropology, Modernism, and Jazz." In Robert O'Meally, ed., *New Essays on* Invisible Man. New York: Cambridge University Press, 1988, 95–121.

Scarry, Elaine. *The Body in Pain: The Making and the Unmaking of the World.* New York: Oxford University Press, 1985.

Watts, Jerry Gafio. *Heroism and the Black Intellectual: Ralph Ellison, Politics, and Afro-American Intellectual Life.* Chapel Hill: University of North Carolina Press, 1994.

Wright, John S. "The Conscious Hero and the Rites of Man: Ellison's War." In Robert O'Meally, ed., *New Essays on* Invisible Man. New York: Cambridge University Press, 1988, 157–86.

Wright, Richard. *12 Million Black Voices.* New York: Thunder's Mouth Press, 1941.

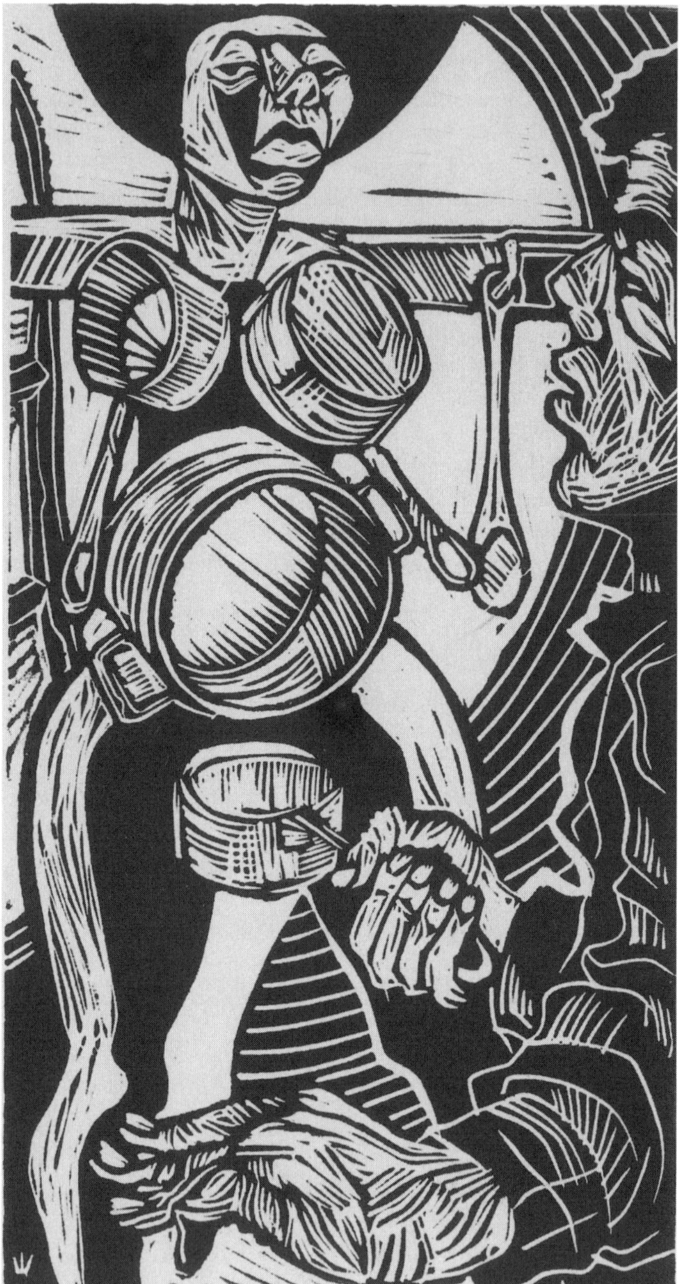

Pot to Piss In

3

Get in the Kitchen and Rattle Them Pots and Pans: *The Bluest Eye*

Harriet Beecher Stowe and her sister, Catherine Beecher, coauthored a work entitled *The American Woman's Home* for middle-class Victorian women, to help them use the site of home, and specifically the kitchen, as a means of ordering their lives. Home as the domestic sphere, as opposed to the broad geographical landscape of the city, had been deemed, and remains, the woman's realm. Such readings of place are "fundamentally political," to borrow Doreen

Massey's language.[1] In other words, persistent readings of home as the feminine place serve a political end. Yet as Lori Askeland writes, "The vulnerability of this domain, however, must not be overlooked; the house remains a sheltered 'feminine' space, that is, a *hus* for true spiritual growth, which by virtue of its enclosure in the 'masculine' domain of materialism and commercialism, always remains in danger of being invaded and corrupted by it" (782). While the values promoted by Stowe and Beecher's reading of the Victorian "model home" were deconstructed by later writers like Toni Morrison, many of their notions about the site of home persist due to the influence of larger patriarchal paradigms. "The woman's place is in the home"—even if that home abuses, confines, perverts. The home as shelter is an enduring myth that both men and women found reason to support. So even when the built environment did not support the mythology through architectural design, women found ways to imagine a new place. As Askeland explains:

> Implicitly, then, the "model home" represented both shelter from and dominance over the chaos of the world. As several scholars have noted, the kitchen was one place where Stowe and Beecher in particular believed that order and control could be brought to bear on society's problems. . . . [But Victorian homes were not built according to the innovations suggested by these two women.] Thus because their domain was always undermined by their need for shelter in the larger masculine domain, Victorian women were often forced to enact the reverse of Rapoport's dictum: to "think" their domain, create a mental ideal of it, after it had already been built, and thereby remodel as best they could. (787)

Women began "remodeling" within the space of their own imaginations, and the degree to which they were able to act on their thoughts determined the success of their "renovation."

This chapter turns to the material constraints out of which women's experiences are forged. Toni Morrison's representation of home moves away from the concern with the city in Wright's and Ellison's works. Morrison's focal point shifts to the kitchens in *The Bluest Eye*. Thus I shift from the city in the previous chapter that surrounds Bigger's kitchenette apartment and the Daltons' basement in *Native Son* and the ever-changing face of Harlem that contrasts with Mary Rambo's blues kitchen and his well-lit underground hideaway in *Invisible Man*. Presumably, had the narrator of *Invisible Man* been able to go back over the puddles of milk to the home he was running toward during the Harlem riot, he would have found Mary where he left her. While the narrator's identity is so vital that he *cannot* go home again, Mary's presence is so fundamental that she cannot *leave* home. In contrast, in *The Bluest Eye*, Morrison demystifies Mary's blues kitchen by offering first Big Mama's imaginary kitchen, then Mrs. MacTeer's greens and blues kitchen, Polly's black and blue kitchen, and finally the Breedloves' kitchen that seems to have no music, no food, no comfort at all. The dynamic imposed by these kitchen places, so limiting to the vital male protagonists of Wright's and Ellison's novels, is ultimately subverted by the perverse behavior of Cholly Breedlove in his own kitchen.

Central to the construct of home because of its function as hearth that both heats and feeds the household, the kitchen is crucial to the survival of the inhabitants. Even the Thomas family of *Native Son* has an oven, the presence of which justifies the naming of the whole apartment a "kitchenette." Of course, the oven is woefully inadequate in sustaining the family and consequently, the oven/hearth fractures into the consuming furnace in Bigger's alternate place within the Dalton home. Thus the centrality of the kitchen/oven is usurped by the basement/furnace, which, in serving as crematorium for Mary Dalton, holds something even more imperative for Bigger (as well as for Mary's parents) than heat in the middle of a Chicago blizzard.

In Morrison's *Paradise* (1998), the oven is quite literally the center of the town of Haven until the residents feel compelled to move. The town established by former slaves has been threatened by an undefinable "outside":

Ten generations had known what lay Out There: space, once beckoning and free, became unmonitored and seething; became a void where random and organized evil erupted when and where it chose—behind any standing tree, behind the door of any house, humble or grand. . . . But lessons had been learned and relearned in the last three generations about how to protect a town. So, like the ex-slaves who knew what came first, the ex-soldiers broke up the oven and loaded it into two trucks even before they took apart their own beds. (16)

The oven is taken apart brick by brick and moved to the center of the new town, where it is reassembled. The hearth is home for the residents of Haven and later, the newly established Ruby. And, significantly, it is not located inside a kitchen place. Instead it is outside, in the center of the town. Once the oven is removed from the kitchen, just as in *Native Son*, the illusion of (black) female authority is shattered. In *Paradise*, Morrison literally removes the kitchen walls that might otherwise reinforce the pretense of (black) female power, concealing the true male authority that maintains identity, passes along traditions, conducts business, and polices the community.

The material site plays a direct role in authorizing behavior. Moreover, place to some degree can dictate behavior. As both a material and psychological construct, home is given to impose structure and purpose on an otherwise meaningless space. However, if it fails to produce order, then its occupants must create order by some other means. The ultimate tragedy of home as place is that when it fails to be precisely that which it is promoted to be (fixed, inherently locatable, stabilizing), it asserts itself despotically upon the lives of its inhabitants by dictating what they can and cannot do. Yet, rather than being abandoned as a failed, even impossible, construct, it becomes the focus of a power struggle instigated by the politics of place to maintain the elusive/illusionary site of home.

On the most fundamental level, of course, homes are built. Carving physical space into definitive places is an aggressive act. For once space is cut into units of meaning such as room, house, city, state, school, and store, which gain their significance as particular locales in relationship to one another, we who are invested in those distinctions must first acknowledge their existence in these specific terms. Yet it is not enough simply to acknowledge the labels; we must stand ready to defend them. The act of place making, like all other constructions of identity, is necessarily communal. It operates in terms of inclusion and exclusion, and consequently precipitates the construction of binary oppositions like inside versus outside or "us" versus "them"—and these are debatable constructs. Kathleen M. Kirby explains that place operates on the presumption of definitive borders that can be used to determine key aspects of individual identities:

> Place seems to assume set boundaries that one fills to achieve a solid identity. Place settles space into objects, working to reinscribe the Cartesian monad and the autonomous ego. It perpetuates the fixed perimeters of ontological categories, making them coherent containers of essences, in relation to which one must be "inside" or "out," "native" or "foreign," in the same way that one can, in the Euclidean universe, at least, be in only one place at one time. (176)

Once these boundaries demarcating the perimeters of place have been established, place begins to dictate which human activities should occur there and elsewhere, and moreover, is endowed with the ability to construct signposts of identities in order to determine who should participate in which activities. The inhabitants necessarily enter into a struggle. Henri Lefebvre explains that space is not simply a void waiting to be filled by a fertile presence; instead, it functions as a mechanism of power: "That space signifies is incontestable. But what it signifies is dos and don'ts—and this brings us back to power. Power's message is invariably confused—deliberately so; dissemination is necessarily part of any message from power" (142).[2] Place is conflicted, and the intensity of the struggle surrounding spatial delineations is dictated by the level of commitment and power occupants have to apply to defending them. Thus, for example, in Morrison's *The Bluest Eye*, Pecola Breedlove is the most completely victimized because she is the weakest person in the struggle.

The tragedy of place is demonstrated with dramatic clarity by Pecola's rape at the hands of her father. Preceding this devastating climax, however, are indications that more than simply address *how* these events come to pass, as the narrator, Claudia, modestly asserts in the early pages of the novel, but *why* as well. For Pecola, home never succumbs to the order of place because place has no structure in the Breedlove home, which therefore does not function as place. Instead the claim of groundedness, articulated by "home as place," that circumscribes knowledge of and experiences with home, is contradicted by the lack of order. And the disorder that might otherwise be accepted as space or unencoded expanse is contradicted by the material structure built as house (home). This home, then, is left dysfunctional. Without structure, Pecola finds only the chaos that leads to her dementia within the amorphous abyss of blue eyes. While she experiences the complete loss of meaning and value for her own subject position, some of those around her are able to maintain a semblance of order in their lives. Sites of meaning often appear for other (female) characters in the oasis offered by the blues kitchen, like the one Mary Rambo has in *Invisible Man*, that serves to translate the pain of experiences and deprivation of present conditions into the cathartic form of blues expressiveness.

Our examination of home for the male characters Bigger and the narrator of *Invisible Man* goes outside of the structure to grapple with the geographically larger sites of the city and thus alludes to the imagery of state and nation. Bigger encounters the city and kills two women who threaten his survival there, and the invisible man must leave women behind. In contrast, our study of home for the female character, Pecola, leads further inside, to a room within the structure (to grapple with the physically smaller site of the kitchen that evokes the imagery of family and nourishment). It is no mere coincidence that for the narrator in *Invisible Man*, Mary is figured as a mother *in* her kitchen—located safely under patriarchal control. Despite the potentiality signified by Mary Rambo's blues kitchen, the male protagonist there has more options available when he begins engineering the site of home than does a little girl like Pecola. Home for her centers around her family, and her mother in particular.

Kitchen: Mrs. MacTeer's Greens and Blues Kitchen

The closest Morrison comes to Mary Rambo's blues kitchen in *Invisible Man* is Mrs. MacTeer's kitchen. Mustard greens are cooking there instead of cabbage. Greens, like cabbage, are African American soul food. As in *Native Son,* when Bigger's hunger helps him forget he is not at home (sopping his plate clean with bread),[3] and in *Invisible Man,* when the narrator enjoys the hot, buttery yams that remind him of his cultural heritage in the South, the greens play a key role in making Mrs. MacTeer's home. Morrison uses the word "greens" as a pun, introducing a play that deliberately conflates the taste and the smell of the greens with the sound of the singing and the experience of place.

While Mrs. MacTeer is not singing in her kitchen when we meet her, even as a young child, Claudia MacTeer notices the effect her mother's kitchen blues have on the mood of the house. Lonesome Saturdays are transformed by song:

> If my mother was in a singing mood, it wasn't so bad. She would sing about hard times, bad times, and somebody-done-gone-and-left-me times. But her voice was so sweet and her singing-eyes so melty I found myself longing for these hard times, yearning to be grown without "a thin di-i-ime to my name." I looked forward to the delicious time when "my man" would leave me, when I would "hate to see that evening sun go down . . ." 'cause then I would know "my man has left this town." Misery colored by the greens and blues in my mother's voice took all the grief out of the words, and left me with a conviction that pain was not only endurable, it was sweet.
>
> But without song, those Saturdays sat on my head like a coal scuttle, and if Mama was fussing, as she was now, it was like somebody throwing stones at it. (24)

The blues, of course, thrive within a culture of contestation. Mrs. MacTeer is fluent enough in a blues vernacular to rid many "lonesome Saturdays" of their bitterness, but Claudia states clearly that there are moments when her mother's blues idiom fails. One such occasion is in autumn, soon after the novel opens, when Pecola Breedlove comes to stay with the MacTeer family.

Mrs. MacTeer makes no secret of the fact that Pecola will not be staying long since she is irritated with the girl at the moment. The curt manner with which Mrs. MacTeer deals with Pecola mirrors her expressions of love to her own daughters, Frieda and Claudia. Her concern for Pecola's well-being is tempered by her poverty. Once she discovers that the visitor has drunk three quarts of milk over the course of a single day, she begins a harangue implicating Pecola and everyone else by whom she feels she has been wronged. The milk becomes a symbol that incriminates Pecola's family and her mother, in particular, for their failure to nurture or even properly nourish her. Pecola can drink three quarts of milk, but she remains thirsty for the love that Mrs. Breedlove refuses to give her.

Mrs. MacTeer assumes Pecola's motivation for drinking the milk is greed, but Claudia understands it to have another source—her desire to engage the picture of Shirley Temple on the cup. Both Frieda and Pecola talk of how they adore her. Pecola imbibes the milk because it gives her the opportunity to worship the image of Shirley Temple; it is a simple conduit legitimating her relationship with the girl on the cup. She drinks the milk like an insatiable infant who believes that by drinking she will somehow become closer to that cute and adored image. What she discovers, unfortunately, is that her efforts only cause her further alienation.

Pecola is thrown away by her family and left to sink or swim at the mercy of God or the world around her. Neither of her parents bothers to check on her well-being. Unlike Shirley Temple, who seems to have nearly the whole world's love, Pecola has few who care whether she lives or dies, and they are not empowered to do much to alleviate her suffering. Pecola's presence is like the presence of the cup in the MacTeer home. The cup suggests a value system decreeing who is or who is not lovable in society. The image that gives complex meaning to an otherwise insignificant cup, bolster the mainstream's claim of ownership over the ideal American home. Even if icons such as Shirley Temple serve to anger or dismiss, as for Claudia and Pecola respectively, they have managed to infiltrate the MacTeer household, creating confusion and keeping it a site of contestation.

While Mrs. MacTeer overlooks the negative significance of both the cup and blue-eyed dolls, Claudia is acutely aware of their devastating potential. Instead of offering a character like Mary Rambo, who consistently expresses herself in a blues idiom, Morrison juxtaposes Mrs. MacTeer's moments of failed blues expressiveness with Claudia's naïve insight. Claudia destroys the doll she is given for Christmas in an effort to expose its value. In scenes like the following, Claudia's latent blues expressiveness incubates, only to erupt in gestures such as the dismantling of the doll:

> I fingered the face, wondering at the single-stroke eyebrows; picked at the pearly teeth stuck like piano keys between red bowline lips. Traced the turned-up nose, poked the glassy blue eyeballs, twisted yellow hair. I could not love it. But I could examine it to see what it was that all the world said was lovable. (20)

Claudia speaks as the uncorrupted voice of a threatened black subjectivity. As Gurleen Grewal asserts, "Morrison's invocation of black music is significant, for it related to a nonbourgeois consciousness not co-opted by the dominant culture" (16). Rather than literal music, the black "music" here is the sentiment of the blues. Claudia employs this blues logic even as a child. She is as perplexed by the adults' response to the doll as they are by hers. Her mother assumes that she desires the unyielding plastic white doll for Christmas; no one asks her what she wants. If they had, she would have been ready with an answer:

> "I want to sit on the low stool in Big Mama's kitchen with my lap full of lilacs and listen to Big Papa play his violin for me alone." The lowness of the stool made for my body, the security and warmth of Big Mama's kitchen, the smell of the lilacs, the sound of the music. . . . (21)

Importantly, what Claudia wants for Christmas is to experience a kitchen scene wherein she is central. The scale of an adult area is

brought into proportion by her "low stool." The kitchen is both secure and warm due to her relationship with and proximity to her
grandparents. This experience is characteristically vernacular and
resists the force imposed by the dominant structure as represented
by the Shirley Temple cup and the doll.

It's no wonder that the adults do not ask Claudia what she wants
for Christmas, since they could not have given her what she desires.
Barbara Johnson's observations made in reference to *Sula* are ap-
plicable here:

> Morrsion's novel conveys so strong a sense of what she calls "rootedness"
> precisely by writing under the sign of uprootedness. Yet it is not simply
> that there was once a *there* there and now it is gone, but that there is
> from the beginning something profoundly uncanny about "that place."
> Home is familiar precisely to the extent that, as Renita Weems puts it, it
> is somehow a place one has never been. (4)

Claudia has never been figured in Big Mama's kitchen in the ways
she imagines. The "experience" there is the sole item on Claudia's
Christmas wish list. Claudia imagines the interior space of Big
Mama's kitchen to be without contradictions. There are no appara-
tuses like the cup and the doll to disrupt the fantasy in which she
is central. However, we know that "real" space is fraught with contradictions. Building upon Steve Pile's work in *The Body and the
City: Psychoanalysis, Space, and Subjectivity*, Katherine McKittrick
asserts that multiple narratives simultaneously compete for space:

> Homes and the nation become hybrid intercultural spaces that encour-
> age different kinds of ambivalence in the mind. . . . Pile explains that
> spaces—emotional, bodily and environmental—produce "many spaces
> in the same space: space projected from the inside onto the surface of
> the body. . . . Objects forever preserved within the body-mind; outsides
> inside; insides outside. . . . Lines of demarcation, ideals; and so on. . . ."
> There is a messiness, then, to occupying space, and in *The Bluest Eye* the
> relationship between place and identity is about mental and corporeal
> movement, is cursive inscriptions, naturalisation, and contestation. The
> inside is out, and vice versa. (13)

As is evidenced by the environment outside of Claudia's imagination, identity for a black girl in 1941 Lorain, Ohio is contested. But for Claudia, contradictions are mediated by eruptions of blues expressiveness. As Grewal explains, "What makes it possible for . . . [Claudia] to resist the dominant culture is the strong presence of an alternative culture at home passed on to her by her mother, whose blues songs . . . and kitchen conversation with the neighborhood black women . . . emit the resilience of a cultural identity of resistance" (37). Pecola, on the other hand, cannot even imagine an experience like that of which Claudia dreams. The intimacy of Big Mama's kitchen site is the polar extreme of the detachment fostered by the "outdoors." So while one girl has a fantasy in which she is solidly placed (at home), the other girl is operating out of another fantasy in which she is maximally displaced (homeless).

Pecola comes to be in the MacTeer home as a "case" who needs a place to live for a few days because she and her family are "outdoors." Claudia explains what that means: "There is a difference between being put out and being put outdoors. If you are put *out*, you go somewhere else; if you are out*doors*, there is no place to go. The distinction was subtle but final. Outdoors was the end of something, an irrevocable, physical fact; defining and complementing our metaphysical condition" (18). Being outdoors suggests a literal homelessness that means more to the community than the abstractions of race and class because of its tangibility. Nothing elicited more sympathy or fear in Lorain, Ohio than the thought of being put outdoors. The experience is no more "real" than the scene Claudia imagines of Big Mama's kitchen because, likewise, it is a place imagined without contradictions. The community agrees to overlook discrepancies that might suggest that "outdoors" is anything other than what it needs that space to be.

Claudia informs the readers that Pecola is "outdoors," then explains what it means in order to dissipate any confusion that might arise from the fact that Pecola actually first appears inside. In fact, Claudia and Frieda have graciously agreed to set aside petty arguments so that they can focus their attention on "trying hard to keep her from feeling outdoors" (19). The reality is, of course, that the Breedloves are not literally outside. Each of them has some-place to stay until they can be reunited. Pecola's father, Cholly, is in jail for setting their residence on fire; her brother is with another family; and Mrs. Breedlove is staying with the Fishers, where she works as a maid. They are not forced to lounge in the gutters like those mired in the contemporary, urban sense of homelessness. Yet the exercise of these two little girls is futile within a community that needs to have the Breedloves "outdoors." A more mature Claudia later admits:

> All of us—all who knew her—felt so wholesome after we cleaned our-selves on her. We were so beautiful when we stood astride her ugliness. Her simplicity decorated us, her guilt sanctified us, her pain made us glow with health, her awkwardness made us believe we were eloquent. Her poverty kept us generous. Even her waking dreams we used—to silence our own nightmares. And she let us, and thereby deserved our contempt. We honed our egos on her, padded our characters with her frailty; and yawned in the fantasy of our strength. (159)

The community balances its own insecurities against Pecola as if their positive characteristics could only exist when directly con-fronted by the opposite extreme. She embodies the negative traits those around her never wanted to be—black, ugly, poor, etc.—and they use her as a scapegoat to free themselves of being identified as those things. So even as Pecola has a place to rest her head in the MacTeer home, she is still "outdoors" because she cannot—is not allowed to—stay in the place where she is. Marc C. Conner ob-serves that "the house serves as the antidote to the evil of being out-doors, offering shelter and safety. . . . But the home as the haven is soon translated into the home as prison. . . . The house is simulta-neously respite and jail; like the community, for which it stands as synecdoche, the house seems to promise rest and comfort, but it provides neither, especially for Pecola" (53). While the house con-figured simultaneously as respite and prison might be more clearly illustrated by a text like Harriet Jacobs's *Incidents in the Life of a Slave Girl*, the dynamic, as Conner suggests, is played out here also.

Jacobs's protagonist, Linda Brent, experiences both rest and imprisonment as a fugitive in the confines of her grandmother's home; here, Morrison creates a triumvirate.[4] The polar, imaginary experiences of Claudia in Big Mama's kitchen (at home) and Pecola's experience of being "outdoors" (homeless) diverge from the more "real" and, at least within this context, more central locale marked by Mrs. MacTeer's kitchen.

Kitchen: Polly's Black and Blue Kitchen

Mrs. Breedlove escapes the fate of homelessness after Cholly puts their family outdoors because she can stay at the Fishers' home. Polly's kitchen is a "black" place in the ways that Dilsey's kitchen is in *The Sound and the Fury*—a place where Pauline Breedlove serves her surrogate white daughter and her white family. Mrs. Breedlove is resentful of intrusions into this realm, which might remind her of the ugliness of her life at the storefront. While she is leery of defending that place, she is fierce in defense of Fisher family affairs. In this other place, her employers' kitchen, Mrs. Breedlove seems to escape the repercussions associated with her own family. Here she can lord over canned goods, shiny floors, and other things that seem to give her life value: "Power, praise, and luxury were hers in this household. They even gave her what she had never had—a nickname—Polly" (101).

Even the little pink-and-yellow girl at the Fishers' home calls Mrs. Breedlove "Polly." Hearing the name from the lips of a child younger than she incites Claudia to anger: "Her calling Mrs. Breedlove Polly, when even Pecola called her mother Mrs. Breedlove, seemed reason enough to scratch her" (86). The designation, which seems arrogant and disrespectful to Claudia, contributes to Mrs. Breedlove's possessiveness over the space of this home. She is able to function within a relatively viable construction of "ideal servant," which, although constrictive, is nonetheless a seductive contrast to the ugliness of her life at home. Rather than deconstructing such designations, as Claudia does in her dismemberment of the doll or as Bigger Thomas does by decapitating the murdered corpse of Mary Dalton in *Native Son*, Mrs. Breedlove accepts her role within the Shirley Temple world signified by the cup. So while Pecola hungrily laps at the white milk to no avail, as mammy, her mother is received into this alternative household. Claudia describes the effect the kitchen has on Mrs. Breedlove: "Mrs. Breedlove's skin glowed like taffeta in the reflection of white porcelain, white woodwork, polished cabinets, and brilliant copperware" (86)—and it is Polly, of course, who keeps the kitchen glowing. Her presence in the pink-and-yellow girl's kitchen is as vital to maintaining the whiteness of the cabinetry, the counters, and the family who lives there as the black drops are in the optic white paint of *Invisible Man*'s Liberty Paint Factory.

Conversely, Pecola is the one black drop too many. Pecola's presence in the Fisher household disrupts the precarious balance and threatens to destroy the whole system. She is only there to handle a chore for her mother, and she is not even invited in until Claudia and Frieda arrive. With a stern admonition to stay still, Mrs. Breedlove leaves the three girls in the kitchen. When she returns with a bag of wet laundry and to answer the small child's call, Mrs. Breedlove discovers that Pecola has accidentally knocked over a freshly baked pie and is hopping around the floor in its hot insides: "In one gallop she was on Pecola, and with the back of her hand knocked her on the floor. Pecola slid in the pie juice, one leg folding under her. Mrs. Breedlove yanked her up by the arm, slapped her again, and in a voice thin with anger, abused Pecola directly and Frieda and me by implication" (86).

Polly's maternal feelings seem to be directed at the pink-and-yellow child rather than her own daughter's obvious humiliation and pain. It is the black child who is hurt and sliding across the floor in the dark juice, yet Mrs. Breedlove is invested in whiteness and defends her place in it without realizing that she has internalized the terms of her own oppression. Just as the narrator of *Invisible Man* must be expelled from the Liberty Paint Factory, so too must Pecola be expelled from the Fisher household. This kitchen, like the other kitchen site in the storefront, serves as a place of torment for Pecola. So the dimension of physical violence is added to her experience of this material "black" site. Instead of a blues kitchen like the one that mediates on behalf of Claudia, with greens flavoring the sound of her mother's singing, the "black" place of Polly's kitchen, a place of domestic servitude, becomes for Pecola a "black and blue" place.

Because of its proximity to the white household, Polly's kitchen is a "black" site, and unlike the characters seen in their "own" kitchens, Polly does not have a blues vocabulary with which to temper the despotism of that site. Unlike Bigger Thomas, who is frustrated by his "relief" job at the Dalton home, Polly laps up her job as domestic for the Fisher family as readily as Pecola drinks the three quarts of milk. The household that keeps Pauline from being outside when her husband, Cholly, sets their house on fire cannot accommodate her children. This house, then, serves as both Pauline's refuge and her prison in the way that Conner suggests. To stay there, she must reject her family, and in so doing she sacrifices crucial parts of herself. Barbara Johnson notes in her psychoanalytical reading of *Sula* that "Freud exclaims over the fact that the German word for 'homey' extends itself to turn into its opposite—that the meaning of 'heimlich' moves with a kind of inevitability from cozy, comfortable, and familiar to hidden, secret, and strange, so that one meaning of 'heimlich' is identitcal to its opposite, 'unheimlich'" (4). In the German sense of the word, home is at once home and not home. Consequently, Pauline is fragmented into multiple selves who mirror Morrison's earlier triumvirate: Mrs. Breedlove's experiences at the storefront (homelessness) and Polly's at the Fishers' (at home) are mediated by Pauline's memories of her teenaged years.

Long before Pauline became Polly or even Mrs. Breedlove, she had stepped on a rusty nail and was left with a mild deformity in one of her feet:

> Slight as it was this deformity explained for her many things that would have been otherwise incomprehensible: why she alone of all the children had no nickname; why there were no funny jokes and anecdotes about funny things she had done; why no one ever remarked on her food preferences. . . . Why she never felt at home anywhere, or that she belonged

anyplace. Her general feeling of separateness and unworthiness she blamed on her foot. Restricted, as a child, to this cocoon of her family's spinning, she cultivated quiet and private pleasures. She liked, most of all, to arrange things. To line things up in rows—jars on shelves at canning, peach pits on the step, sticks, stones, leaves—and the members of her family let these arrangements be. (88)

The significance of common occurrences such as teasing and nicknaming is easily overlooked. These communal practices bind individuals around a shared past and give them a sense of cohesiveness that helps unite them into a family unit.[5] Being excluded from these practices leaves Pauline feeling isolated. She acknowledges her sense of alienation and identifies her misshapen foot as the source of her world's failings. Her foot is the foundation upon which she builds a vocabulary for interpreting an "incomprehensible" situation. Without this key element, the young Pauline has no means of systematically confronting the chaos of her life. Her family has excluded her from the cultural practices that structure their existence and left her alone to develop a framework for rendering her experiences intelligible.

For brief periods during her early adulthood, Pauline does experience moments of blues expressiveness. Cholly comes with music—"a kind of city-street music where laughter belies anxiety, and joy is as short and straight as the blade of a pocket knife. She listened carefully to the music and let it pull her lips into a smile" (91). So when she narrates her experience of meeting him for the first time, she expresses herself in a rare blues idiom: "When I first seed Cholly, I want you to know it was like all the bits of color from that time down home when all us chil'ren went berry picking after a funeral and I put some in the pocket of my Sunday dress, and they masked up and stained my hips. My whole dress was messed with purple, and it never did wash out. Not the dress nor me" (91–92). Cat Moses suggests that Pauline articulates a blues narrative of her own, "in lyrically expressing a longing for the rural Southern community that revolved around church ("Sunday dress") and ritual ("berry picking," "funeral"), Pauline accomplishes what the blues singer accomplishes: she recreates that which is lost and for which she longs, transforming lack into poetry. Unfortunately, the transformation is temporary and exists only in her memory" (6). Pauline divests herself of the value of such expressive gestures that paint her experiences with color in favor of more calculated, less intuitive systems. The exclusion she feels manifests itself as restriction, so she founds her teleology on "quiet and private pleasures" rather than social practices like those of her family:

> She liked, most of all, to arrange things. To line things up in rooms—jars on shelves at canning, peach pits on the step, sticks, stones, leaves—and the members of her family let these arrangements be. . . . During all of her four years of going to school, she was enchanted by numbers and depressed by words. She missed—without knowing what she missed—paints and crayons. (88–89)

This teleology operates like blues expressiveness to fulfill the psychological need for order in Pauline's life. However, the smallness of her spatial terrain dictates the smallness of the system she employs. She is relegated to the porch step and the kitchen, left alone to give order to trivialities that neither impose upon nor impede the welfare of others.

While the omnipresence and deprivation of her foot motivate Pauline to find a way to maintain her mental faculties, they also serve, later in life, to draw her effectively into complicity with her own victimization and, subsequently, that of her daughter. The space of the Fishers' kitchen (the site where she becomes "ideal servant") and the porch step are so constricted that the system Pauline has erected to order her life is not able to accommodate anyone other than herself. Because it does not interfere, her childhood family allows her the privilege of that order, but later as a mother she is not able to derive creative expressiveness from the system that might protect her children also. So just as if someone had doomed her to act out a tragic script written at the time her foot was permanently marked by that nail, Mrs. Breedlove refuses to read any signs as warnings and instead accepts them almost fondly, as fate.[6] This is how she comes to have ugly children and to live in an abusive home.

The children Sammy and Pecola are ugly because she and Cholly are ugly. Their ugliness is a simple confirmation of what her foot, missing front tooth, and newfound education at the movies[7] had already told her—that she and her family are not worthy of either attention or love. As the rotten seed planted by this derision festers, Mrs. Breedlove comes to despise those things and people who are most closely allied with her: "More and more she neglected her house, her children, her man—they were like the afterthoughts one has just before sleep, the early-morning and late evening edges of her day, the dark edges that made the daily life with the Fishers lighter, more delicate, more lovely" (101). In the Fisher home, Mrs. Breedlove finds affirmation that she does not get elsewhere: "Really, she is the ideal servant" (101). She hungrily accepts her position as maid because it offers her a place to escape the ugliness she believes characterizes the rest of her life.

Kitchen: The Breedloves' Kitchen

The Breedloves' storefront has very few interior walls. The kitchen is a separate room, but the bedroom and living area are distinguished primarily by furnishings. In this regard, the storefront is similar to the kitchenette apartments of Chicago and the Truebloods' cabin in *Invisible Man*. For reasons discussed in the previous chapters, such living conditions affect people's lives in sometimes rather disturbing ways. As Richard Wright laments in *12 Million Black Voices*, "The kitchenette blights the personalities of our growing children, disorganizes them, blinds them to hope, creates problems whose effects can be traced in the characters of its child victims for years afterward. . . . The kitchenette fills our black boys with longing and restlessness, urging them to run off from home" (110–11). The same effects are evident in the lives of Pecola and Sammy Breedlove. "[Sammy] was known, by the time he was fourteen, to have run away from home no less than twenty-seven times. . . . Pecola, on the other

hand, restricted by youth and sex, experimented with methods of en-
durance. Though the methods varied, the pain was as consistent as
it was deep" (38). The storefront is not a hospitable place to live. As
Shelley Wong asserts, "Nowhere in this novel is this legacy of slavery—the disfigurement of human relationships by the marketplace—more ironically stated than in Morrison's decision to locate a
family by the name of 'Breedlove' in a converted (and poorly converted at that) storefront" (462).

Drinking, having sex, fighting, sleeping, and even waking up are
all spectacles available for "public" display, in the Breedlove home.
It seems that nothing can happen in this storefront without everyone present at the time knowing about it. The physical barriers that
would serve as signposts, issuing prohibitions ("Do not enter"; "Do
not exit"; "Watch this, not that") are simply not present. In their
place is space with very few socializing directives. Thus few barriers exist to separate girlhood experiences, like Claudia's Christmas
wish, from adult episodes, like the times when Mrs. Breedlove will
not allow herself to have an orgasm until she knows that "my flesh
is all that be on . . . [Cholly's] mind" (103). Her parents do not shelter Pecola. Instead, she is forced to confront situations that they
might have veiled for her. Furthermore, she has never had access to
childhood experiences like the one that Claudia imagines in Big
Mama's kitchen, that function as signs of love, so she is left to interpret her parents' sexual intercourse through her own limited
knowledge:

> Into her eyes came the picture of Cholly and Mrs. Breedlove in bed. He
> making sounds as though he were in pain, as though something had him
> by the throat and wouldn't let go. Terrible as his noises were, they were
> not nearly as bad as no noise at all from her mother. It was as though
> she was not even there. Maybe that was love. Choking sounds and
> silence. (48–49)

Because Pecola is forced to confront her parents' sexuality, she
imagines that this is love.[8] Certainly, walls create an illusion of safety that can, and indeed must, be challenged. But walls also serve to

foster the sense of security a young girl needs until such time as she develops into a mature adult.

The fact that the walls are around the kitchen and not a bedroom, for example, is a measure of Mrs. Breedlove's inadequacy. In this statement I do not mean to absolve Cholly of his charge within the household; however, we must carefully examine the power at work here. While Mrs. Breedlove cannot be held responsible as an architect, literally designing walls, it is she, in particular, who superintends many of the spatial dynamics. The walls around the kitchen serve as a normalizing gesture that helps to distinguish the storefront as a home. Mrs. Breedlove is able to identify with this particular site and the norms the kitchen seeks to represent (that of the hearth). By acting out the role of wife and mother in her gestures of caretaking, she demonstrates her investment in maintaining the illusion of normality. "Mrs. Breedlove considered herself an upright and Christian woman, burdened with a no-count man, whom God wanted her to punish" (37). The kitchen, then, becomes a mere tool she uses, along with its accoutrements, to maintain her perceived authority.

On a Saturday morning near the beginning of the novel, these dynamics are played out in a ceremonial conclusion to one of Cholly's drunken episodes. Mrs. Breedlove's actions, as the narrator recounts, are well choreographed: "in the kitchen . . . [Mrs. Breedlove] made noises with doors, faucets, and pans. The noises were hollow, but the threats they implied were not. . . . There was direction and purpose in Mrs. Breedlove's movements that had nothing to do with the preparation of breakfast" (35). The eruptions of violence in the Breedlove household can be gauged on Saturday mornings like this one by the clamor in the kitchen. These sounds function similarly to those Mrs. MacTeer makes in her (blues) kitchen to influence her daughter's perceptions and to shape the order and events of the day. But the regularity with which these menacing sounds emanate from this kitchen is not balanced by the comfort offered by the smell of mustard greens cooking on the stove and songs, "about hard times, bad times, and somebody-done-gone-and-left-me times" (24) that make life tolerable for Claudia and her mother in the MacTeer house. Mrs. Breedlove uses frying pans and pokers as weapons rather than for cooking and tending the stove.

This kitchen serves Mrs. Breedlove's needs as much as the Fisher kitchen does. Her role in relationship to the family, however, is inverted. Where she embraces the Fisher family, she rejects her own. Here again we are reminded of Barbara Johnson's use of Freud's notion of *heimlich*; clearly, Mrs. Breedlove's storefront home is also, simultaneously, not home. The Breedloves' kitchen is not a place of soul food and singing, like the kitchen in the MacTeer household and Mary Rambo's blues kitchen from *Invisible Man*. Instead, Mrs. Breedlove's kitchen is the ceremonial backdrop for repercussions of routine episodes of drunkenness.

Womb: Collapsing Inward

If *The Bluest Eye* is a study of spatial politics, then the struggle comes down to a battle between Cholly and Pecola: he is a sign of boundless passion and operates without restraint; she is passion without an outlet. The former bursts outward and the latter collapses inward. Energy seeks the most expedient route to the ground; thus given their proximity, Cholly finds Pecola the most expedient conduit for his expression. She has no order or meaning apart from the perception of her ugliness to use as a framework for interpretation, so space collapses inward.

The Breedloves' kitchen is dysfunctional because they have placed no restrictions on the activities authorized to happen there. Each character attempts to flee the stultifying power of the constructs imposed by this storefront home in his or her own way. Mrs. Breedlove rejects all but the most superficial connections to her family for her identity as Polly in the Fisher home. Sammy runs away for however long he can manage. Cholly drinks as an escape. Pecola has the least effective means of escape, with her earnest desire to become beautiful by turning her eyes blue.[9]

So the perception of ever-extending, empty expanse, which has already been condensed for Pecola by the impermeability of the kitchen walls, is further condensed by the lack of interpersonal directives that might order or restrict any activity. Consequently, all that remains to define the perimeters of the kitchen are the unpredictable impulses of Cholly Breedlove. Cholly invades Pecola's body as territory and establishes borders, thereby constructing an extended realm for his expression of pleasure and domination. The deprivation created by this unstructured chaos leads to Pecola's dementia.

Perhaps more than any other character depicted in the novel, Pecola lives the contradictions expressed by the blues. Yet she has no understanding of blues culture or its significance. The "hollow" sounds Mrs. Breedlove makes in the kitchen do not contain the substance of the blues that makes grief seem "sweet." In fact, at the one moment in the novel when Pecola articulates a blues refrain, she is *outside* of her home and lying in bed with the other girls at the MacTeer home. Earlier the neighbor child, Rosemary, presumed when she saw Pecola with her panties down that the girls were "playing nasty." Actually, they had been assisting Pecola because she had just "become a woman." The shared feelings of confusion, fear, frustration, and finally revelation among female characters after this encounter dealing with Pecola's first menstrual cycle lead the young girls to try to express themselves through the language of the blues.

The pain of experience itself, not deliberate effort, compels Pecola to inquire about her new procreative abilities using the syntax of the blues. After Frieda explains that before you can make a baby "somebody has to love you," Pecola asks, "'How do you do that? I mean, how do you get somebody to love you?' But Frieda was asleep. And [Claudia] didn't know" (29). Unfortunately, Pecola does not sustain the potentially transcendent expressiveness of this moment; she locates the failure of her home and family to nurture her in sight rather than in sound—the blues of her eyes rather than the blues of her mouth.

Characters like Mrs. MacTeer and Claudia use blues expressiveness to temper the harsh experiences of their lives. The blues serves to codify place with signposts that offer Claudia direction as she navigates her surroundings. So Claudia first appears with her sister, Frieda, in a naïve blues moment, trying to utter the "right words" over seeds they plant in the ground. Of the few in the community who care enough to pay Pecola attention, it is only the young girls, Claudia and Frieda, who think her baby is worth saving: "So deeply concerned were we with the health and safe delivery of Pecola's baby we could think of nothing but our own magic: if we planted the seeds, and said the right words over them, they would blossom, and everything would be all right" (9). However, as Michael Awkward argues, language fails in *The Bluest Eye* to express the "right words":

> For in the face of Pecola's intense self-hatred and the disdain of an entire community where Pecola and her pregnancy are concerned, discursive acts such as the MacTeer girls' incantations of putative (but, curiously unspoken in the novel) "right words" cannot avoid being anything but insufficient. What is required . . . is the bonding of women, or what Ntozake Shange calls in *For Colored Girls'* final scene of an achieved female community which, not coincidentally, is directly preceded by a male's murder of children—"a laying on of [female] hands." This communal laying on of hands results in the liberation of the female self and "the holiness of myself released." (119)

Pecola does not have access to this communal female healing. Her mother does not bring the milk that she desires and the milk she drinks from the Shirley Temple cup cannot satiate her thirst; instead, it results in a backlash from Mrs. MacTeer about why she cannot satisfy Pecola either. Rather than a female laying on of hands that might offer spiritual renewal and healing, home leaves Pecola bereft of maternal sensitivities and alone to deal with perverse fatherhood: Cholly's destructive masculine laying on of hands. The earth itself refuses to yield for Pecola, and there are no "right words" to say over a child impregnated by her father that will make it otherwise.

Both the words and the ground are crucial here. Even as children, these girls know that they might speak something that can be vital to their ability to negotiate the dynamics of place. Ultimately, the earth proves to be more powerful than their "right words," which cannot intercede to save Pecola or her child. But in choosing to tell Pecola's story, an older Claudia gains authority that the younger Claudia has yet to acquire. *The Bluest Eye* becomes, as Cat Moses describes it in "The Blues Aesthetic in Toni Morrison's *The Bluest Eye*," Claudia's blues narrative.

On the other hand, to survive the kind of assaults directed at her, Pecola needs to reinterpret painful experiences in order to render them intelligible. But the conflict she confronts is too powerful for her meager defense—the hope of becoming pretty. In a dysfunctional household without order, it is even more important that Pecola have a viable means of offense, or at least of coping. Without either, however, Pecola is unable to lessen the tragic impact of the inevitable confrontation. Place is even more constricted for her than the sites of the porch and the Fishers' kitchen are for her mother. Without codifiers to organize her surroundings around a set of established norms, like the walls of a more traditional house[10] or the blues idiom of the MacTeer household,[11] the Breedloves' kitchen randomly signifies contradictory, odd, and even perverse demands that function as expressions of power. If barriers are not established to maintain the order that might protect and defend inhabitants, then the power naturally levels any restrictions. Rather like electricity, power seeks the conductor offering the least resistance as it makes its way to the ground. Pecola is that medium.

Pecola's story is, of course, framed by the narrative of the Dick and Jane primer and its depiction of the green-and-white house. Yet as Wong suggests, its message conceals a problematic interrelationship between residents and the places they occupy:

> The lesson of this passage in fact goes well beyond acknowledging or presenting white bourgeois values—it goes as far as enacting the very conditions of alienated self-containment which underlie those values. We might note, for instance, that the "house" precedes the "family" in order of both appearance and discussion. In this scheme of things, human relations are preempted by property and commodity relations. (472)

Just as Mr. Norton notices the log cabins before he sees the women in *Invisible Man*, the built structure appears first. The primer hearkens back to the Victorian "model home" that Stowe and Beecher extol in *The American Woman's Home*; however, in both Morrison's obvious manipulation of conventions and this more subtle dynamic highlighted by Wong, the primer reveals the essential need for imaginative "remodeling." Without such renovations, place remains despotic.

Pecola's rape attests to the devastating potential of ideological constructs permitted to cohabit freely in the Breedlove storefront. As Wayne Franklin and Michael Steiner explain, "We experience issues such as consumerism, colonialism and patriarchy in concrete locales, whether those locales be the high-toned architecture of a department store, the partitions imposed on a countryside by a foreign power, or the domestic sphere as a material—not just ideological construct. It is the rare human issue that is truly placeless" (4). As a site of culture, this storefront—which is neither house nor home in any mythical sense—implicates larger issues of consumerism, colonialism, and patriarchy, among others. Morrison suggests that incest is *placed* in this storefront at the perverse intersection of racism, poverty, the failure of community, and unfulfilled desire.

That fateful Saturday afternoon when Cholly staggers in drunk, he sees his daughter in the kitchen, washing dishes. Pecola is fulfilling the role she has inherited from her mother. And Cholly barely distinguishes between mother and daughter. She reminds him of Pauline when he met her in Kentucky. "[Pecola's] hands were going around and around a frying pan, scraping flecks of black into cold, greasy dishwater. The timid, tucked-in look of the scratching toe—that was what Pauline was doing the first time he saw her in Kentucky. Leaning over a fence staring at nothing in particular" (128). Pecola makes a similar gesture to the one her mother made years earlier, her foot scratching a place on the back of her leg. Cholly wants to scratch the itch with his teeth. "The confused mixture of memories of Pauline and the doing of a wild and forbidden thing excited him, and a bolt of desire ran down his genitals, giving it length" (128). As always, Cholly acts upon his impulse.

Cholly is contrasted with Mr. MacTeer, who defends his daughter, Frieda, from the illicit, predatory advances of Mr. Henry. Cholly becomes the predator. He does not gauge his actions against a scale of right or wrong, so it never occurs to him that he should not touch his daughter like this: "The creamy toe of her bare foot scratching a velvet leg. It was such a small and simple gesture, but it filled him then with a wondering softness. Not the usual lust to part tight legs with his own, but a tenderness, a protectiveness. A desire to cover her foot with his hand and gently nibble away the itch from the calf with his teeth" (128). He rapes Pecola on the floor in front of the sink. The tragedy of home for Pecola is described best in this scene. The space of home has become so compressed that she is left to maneuver psychologically within the confined space of the kitchen floor.

In 1941 the unyielding black ground signified the terrible cost at which home might be established for the black community of Lorain, Ohio. The barriers that delineate the place of home are erected upon this foundation: the unyielding black ground and the Breedloves' kitchen floor. The storefront is what remains for cultural outcasts like the Breedlove family. Their internalization of white normative values and their inability to find any productive coping mechanisms ultimately pin Pecola tragically to the ground under the weight of her father's "embrace."

Her escape into madness only leaves her more completely bound. The expanse of space that had been segmented into home/kitchen is further condensed into the stultifying and incestuous site of Pecola's own body, raped and impregnated by her father. Claudia and Frieda attempt to change the dynamics of the dichotomy of Pecola versus the community or outdoors versus a sense of spatial security. They try to impose order through their own blues expressiveness by speaking their magical "right words" over seeds planted in the black earth, in order to ensure that Pecola brings forth the life that would "bear witness" to an otherwise forgotten tragedy. Their magic fails, and remembrance of Pecola is left to Claudia's narrative recollection as text.

At the end of *The Bluest Eye* Claudia describes a pathetic picture of Pecola as a peculiar bird attempting to deliver herself from the bondage of walking upon the ground. Now completely insane, she is a hopeless spectacle. Claudia narrates:

> The damage done was total. She spent her days, her tendril, sap-green days walking up and down, her head jerking to the beat of a drummer so distant only she could hear. Elbows bent, hands on shoulders, she flailed her arms like a bird, in an eternal, grotesquely futile effort to fly. Beating the air, a winged but grounded bird, intent on the blue void it could not reach—could not even see—but which filled the valleys of the mind. (158)

The fragility of the gesture of flying without speed, wind, or anything more than arms for wings bespeaks the severity of her dementia. Yet there is something eerily lucid about her act. Pecola recognizes that she is constrained by the tyranny of place and of home (her family and her community) and unable to draw upon its resources. In contrast to the unforgiving apathy with which the ground confronts her, flight might possibly release her from the tyranny of place into an alternative reality. Despite the fact that Pecola understands that her groundedness is affiliated with her victimization, she does not comprehend any of the physical or metaphorical mechanics involved in achieving flight.

In *Corregidora* by Gayl Jones, this study of home will continue further inside than Morrison goes in *The Bluest Eye*. The body becomes the place of contention and the womb the crucial "black place." My concern, then, will shift from the physical site of kitchen places to the womb, or more precisely, the absence thereof. The novel suggests that the African American home ground must move away from the body to find room within the context of blues culture.

Notes

1. Doreen Massey, "Double Articulation: A Place in the World," in Angelika Bammer, ed., *Displacements: Cultural Identities in Question* (Bloomington: Indiana University Press, 1994), 110–21.

2. I share Lefebvre's emphasis on social space rather than a Lockean notion of "preexisting" space. I am concerned about the ways that people move in and through space/places.

3. Richard Wright, *Native Son* (New York: Bantam, 1940), 56.

4. Actually, the entire novel is an exploration of these experiences and nearly every character might be discussed in these terms. However, I am concerned here with the prominent kitchen sites that will offer a solid framework, if not all the gradations, for a discussion of home, blues, gender, race, and migration. For more comprehensive readings of *The Bluest Eye* see Madonne M. Minor, "Lady No Longer Sings the Blues: Rape, Madness, and Silence in *The Bluest Eye*" in Harold Bloom, ed., *Toni Morrison* (New York: Chelsea House, 1986), 85–99. Also Philip Page, *Dangerous Freedom: Fusion and Fragmentation in Toni Morrison's Novels* (Jackson: University Press of Mississippi, 1995); Ruth Rosenberg, "Seeds in Hard Ground: Black Girlhood in *The Bluest Eye*," *Black American Literature Forum* 21.4 (1987): 435–45; and Jane Somerville, "Idealized Beauty and the Denial of Love in Toni Morrison's *The Bluest Eye*," *Bulletin of the West Virginia Association of College English Teachers* 9.1 (1986): 18–23.

5. Unity and family are fundamental elements in the construction of home. In spatial terms, we can explore the significance of collectivities in the establishment of borders. Kathleen Kirby asserts that the establishment of place is directly related to how we are identified and what we are labeled (native or foreign, friend or foe, us or them). The act of delineating the boundary that distinguishes home from everything else necessarily includes the creation of a collectivity as well (this aspect of home and place making is explored more thoroughly in the next two chapters).

6. Mrs. Breedlove is given at least one warning when her tooth falls out. The narrator describes in some detail how the tooth could have been read as a sign and used to mount a resistance against a force like the tyranny of place. But Mrs. Breedlove does not act on this warning.

7. As in *Native Son*, the movies appear as a way for the larger society to promulgate its messages and to legitimize its authority. By refusing to depict anything other than black stereotypes, if it depicted African Americans in the movies at all, Hollywood helped distribute a racist discourse and value system.

8. This same point of confusion prompts one of Pecola's rare moments of blues expression while she is staying at the MacTeer household. "How do you get somebody to love you?" she asks Claudia and Frieda, as if she is repeating a classic blues refrain. The line is not so much a question to be answered, let alone by three little girls, as it is a line to be sung.

9. This novel is set in a period prior to the invention of colored contact lenses that could literally make brown eyes appear to have transformed to blue. The transformation, of course, would be affect rather than effect, so the underlying point of contestation would remain unresolved.

10. The green-and-white house depicted in the Dick and Jane reading primer is such a house. Morrison's point in offering this representation is to contrast the experiences of her various black characters with this image of a supposedly ideal, and harmless, home. See Chikwenye Okonjo Ogunyemi, "Order and Disorder in Toni Morrison's *The Bluest Eye*," *Critique: Studies in Modern Fiction* 19 (1977): 112–20.

11. We might even see how the blues idiom mediates on behalf of the prostitutes who live above the storefront. These women are not indicted by the self-righteousness of their neighbors; instead, their neighbors, in refusing to accept and to love Pecola, are indicted by them. See Denise Heinze, *The Dilemma of "Double Consciousness": Toni Morrison's Novels* (Athens: The University of Georgia Press, 1993).

Works Cited

Askeland, Lori. "Remodeling the Model Home in *Uncle Tom's Cabin* and *Beloved*." *American Literature* 64.4 (Dec. 1992): 795–805.

Awkward, Michael. *Inspiriting Influences: Tradition, Revision, and Afro-American Women's Novels*. New York: Columbia University Press, 1989.

Conner, Marc C. "From the Sublime to the Beautiful: The Aesthetic Progression of Toni Morrison." In Marc C. Conner, ed., *The Aesthetics of Toni Morrison: Speaking the Unspeakable*. Jackson: University Press of Mississippi, 2000, 49–76.

Franklin, Wayne and Michael Steiner, eds. "Taking Places: Toward the Regrounding of American Studies." In *Mapping American Culture*. Iowa City: University of Iowa Press, 1992, 3–23.

Grewal, Gurleen. *Circles of Sorrow, Lines of Struggle: The Novels of Toni Morrison*. Baton Rouge: Louisiana State University Press, 1998.

Hurston, Zora Neale. *Their Eyes Were Watching God*. New York: Harper and Row, 1937.

Johnson, Barbara. "'Aesthetic' and 'Rapport' in Toni Morrison's *Sula*." In Marc C. Conner, ed., *The Aesthetic of Toni Morrison: Speaking the Unspeakable*. Jackson: University Press of Mississippi, 2000, 3–11.

Kirby, Kathleen M. "Thinking Through the Body: The Politics of Location, Subjects, and Space." *Boundary* 2 20.2 (1993): 176.

Lefebvre, Henri. *The Production of Space*. Trans. Donald Nicholson-Smith. Cambridge: Blackwell Publishers Ltd., 1991.

McKittrick, Katherine. "'Black and 'Cause I'm Black I'm Blue': Transverse Racial Geographies in Toni Morrison's *The Bluest Eye*." *Gender Place and Culture: A Journal of Feminist Geography* 7.2 (June 2000): 125–43.

Morrison, Toni. *The Bluest Eye*. New York: Holt, Rinehart and Winston, 1970.

———. *Paradise*. New York: Knopf, 1998.

Moses, Cat. "The Blues Aesthetic in Toni Morrison's *The Bluest Eye*." *African American Review* 33 (Winter 99): 623–38.

Toomer, Jean. *Cane*. New York: Liveright, 1975.

Wong, Shelley. "Transgression as Poesis in *The Bluest Eye*." *Callaloo* 13.3 (Summer 1990): 471–81.

Wright, Richard. *12 Million Black Voices*. New York: Thunder's Mouth Press, 1941.

4

She's a Brick House: *Corregidora*

Although much has been written in the nearly twenty years since Houston A. Baker Jr. published *Blues, Ideology, and Afro-American Literature: A Vernacular Theory* (1984), his book offers a cogent place to begin discussion about home focused on *Corregidora*, by way of Toni Morrison's *Sula*. African American feminist scholars like Ann du Cille, Barbara Christian, Michael Awkward, and Deborah Mc-Dowell have critiqued Baker's work, in general, because of its sig-

She
rises from impulses of
hurt/to sing fine
print on the pain

—Sterling Plumpp, "Billie Holiday"

"Where did you get those songs?" . . .
"I made them up."

—Gayl Jones, *Corregidora*

A word is a bridge thrown between myself
and another.

—V. N. Volosinor, *Marxism and the Philosophy of Language*

nificant oversights and phallocentricism.[1] Even when Baker discusses purportedly symbolic aspects of literature, Ann du Cille argues, he tends to collapse the symbolic into the material at the expense of women. Writing about Baker's use of the Lacanian term "phallus" as a "signifier of the Father, or, better, of the Father's LAW," in his reading of *Invisible Man*'s Trueblood episode, du Cille suggests that Baker and Ellison both have "oversimplified" the fact that the "signifier and signified are not so easily separable." She continues, "For while the phallus may not be a material object, its action, its 'phallic energy,' its 'Father LAW' are not immaterial—certainly not to Matty Lou Trueblood, Pecola Breedlove, and other objects of its power" (448). Nevertheless, I return to *Blues Ideology*, in particular, because Baker's formulation of a blues matrix depends so heavily upon a metaphor drawn from the black female body. I do not mean to dismiss Baker's *Blues Ideology* as antifeminist, but neither am I willing to blindly apply his framework without offering a critique. Instead I am hoping to reclaim the matrix and to suggest ways to use the construct of home to expand upon the lexicon used for reading African American literature.

In chapter 1, "Living (Just Enough) for the City," and chapter 2, "Keep on Moving Don't Stop," the city is shown to circumscribe the experiences of "home" for the male protagonists, Bigger Thomas of *Native Son* and the narrator of *Invisible Man*. Ultimately, Bigger "can't win" against the austere façade of Chicago's Southside, and the invisible man cannot rest for running through the ever-changing face of Harlem. Neither can be "at home" in the Northern city—at least not for long. As limiting as home is for these characters, it is more so for Pecola Breedlove in *The Bluest Eye*. Home decreases from the (male) outdoor place of the city to the stultifying site of the black (female) indoor place of the kitchen. Nowhere is this reality more clearly demonstrated than in the tragic climax of the novel when Pecola is pinned bodily to the kitchen floor by the incestuous "embrace" of her father. Similarly, in Gayl Jones's *Corregidora*, the geographically limited space of kitchens, which shape Pecola's experiences of home, collapses into the even smaller site of the womb.

As illustrated in the previous chapter, "Get in the Kitchen and Rattle Them Pots and Pans," the spatial politics associated with the site of home in the novel shift from the indoor site of the kitchen to the quintessentially interior site represented by the pregnant figure of Pecola, who carries her father's dead seed. In its mapping of home, *Corregidora* follows a similar pattern, conflating kitchen and bedroom places that seem to lead inevitably to the womb.

In this chapter, I analyze Eva Peace from Toni Morrison's *Sula* and Catherine Lawson and Ursa from Gayl Jones's *Corregidora*. These characters, when read in succession, demonstrate the failure of the construct of Baker's "black hole," which is built upon the notion of a return to the womb, and show what is at stake for African American women at home. First, Eva becomes homicidal and kills her son when she perceives him as attempting to return to her as a "black hole." Then Catherine connects the physical place of home, specifically black, female-assigned places like the kitchen, with the black woman's body. Finally, Ursa's experiences as a producer of the blues culture Baker foregrounds reveal the dire price exacted from African American women in their attempt to overthrow the power dynamics imposed by the site of home.

Womb: A Black Hole

While Baker's *Blues Ideology* makes a significant contribution to the field of African American studies by utilizing the blues in literary analysis, his "matrix" reconfigures the blues as a womb, embodied in the metaphor of the "black (w)hole." But the body is the crucial aspect that the metaphor lacks. In Freudian terms, as Jane Gallop describes in *The Daughter's Seduction: Feminism and Psychoanalysis*, "Woman is then the figuration of phallic 'lack'; she is a hole" (22). Hazel Carby's critique of Du Bois's *The Souls of Black Folk* applies to Baker, who likewise "traces in its form, but displaces through its content, biological and sexual reproduction" (25). In his project, the woman has been discarded in favor of an asexual reproductive order that allows men to give birth to themselves. The man-made hole in *Blues Ideology* is given to do the work of the woman's body.

Nevertheless, a character like Ralph Ellison's nameless narrator of *Invisible Man* cannot simply fall underground, "into a home of sorts," and then, at the appropriate time, deliver himself fully actualized back into the world. Perhaps this is why we finally see him not reborn but trapped underground in a snapshot; he only appears to be in motion. The unsexed hole is neither a viable home place nor a place for rebirth. Instead, it can be described by Eva Peace's violent response to her son, Plum, in Morrison's *Sula*: "No!" she proclaims, "You can't be 'hole' and 'whole' at the same time." Eva kills Plum because, having come home from war addicted to drugs, he tries "to crawl back up into [her] womb." She discovers his need. He is not "whole" in any of its connotations.

In the following scene, Eva explains to her daughter, Hannah, why she killed Plum:

> It was such a carryin' on to get him born and to keep him alive. Just to keep his little heart beating and his little old lungs cleared and look like when he came back from that war he wanted to git back in. After all that carryin' on, just getting' him out and keepin' him alive, he wanted to crawl back in my womb and well. . . . I ain't got the room no more even if he could do it. . . . I couldn't do it again. . . . I would have let him if I'd've had the room but a big man can't be a baby all wrapped up inside his mamma no more; he suffocate. (71–72)

Eva adds rooms onto the house that took her years to build, so she is able to accommodate Plum *in her house*; but she has no room for him *in her home*, which she represents as womb. Here Morrison offers a more accurate representation of the power dynamics at work in Baker's black hole than any that Baker himself chooses in *Blues Ideology*. Like the protagonists in "Big Boy Leaves Home" and "The Man who Lived Underground" cited by Baker, Plum seeks a hole wherein he can escape the damaging effect of his experiences outside the black community. Having found that regenerative place, Baker suggests that these characters may reemerge whole at some time in the future. He envisions a model that would allow the male to utilize the reproductive power of a type of womb, but it does so by usurping the agency of the mother.

As Eva's son, perhaps Plum has a natural right to believe that if a place of healing and recovery exists for him, he will find it with his mother. From Eva's perspective, Plum imagines an idyllic return to wholeness, without seeming to be aware of its costs. Her response to Plum's effort to return home suggests that Eva is aware; in addition to the economic, emotional, and social costs, Eva would have to bear Plum's return bodily. Though he returns carelessly, in coming home Plum asserts the privilege of a man-child in a patriarchal society. But instead of seeing this gesture as natural, his mother reads his behavior symbolically. He has not simply come home; he is seeking to return to her womb. In this way, Eva is not just his biological mother. She becomes his ideological matrix. Plum seeks to disembody her to serve his own needs.

As Laura Doyle explains in *Bordering on the Body: The Racial Matrix in Modern Fiction and Culture*, kinship patriarchy is created by a dominant group of males who "control marriage in order to define and mythologize kin boundaries in a way that serves their needs as rulers" (25), and it is maintained at the expense of the woman who, as "mother," serves as the means through which men sustain their wealth, health, and control. "Not just psychologically but politically and aesthetically, then, the logic of kinship patriarchy turns a man against his kin source and leaves a woman to her own resources. The underlying problem, of course, begins when kinship patriarchy defines the mother as kin source" (27).

No matter how compelling Plum's needs may be, despite his desperate circumstances, Eva acts as if she can only give him what he desires at the expense of herself. Marianne Hirsch suggests, "In trying to explain to Hannah an act that is so obviously beyond comprehension, Eva dwells on an intense need for self-protection, a clear drawing of her own boundaries, a definitive expression of the limits of what she has to give, and she insists as well on Plum's boundaries, which, as a mother, she was forced to violate" (421). This seems contradictory since Eva repeatedly demonstrates her willingness to sacrifice herself on behalf of her children. After Boy Boy leaves she makes very difficult choices, the most legendary being the loss of her leg, which is rumored to have something to do with acquiring money for her starving family. Hirsch looks to this moment as the source of what she calls a "maternal discourse": "Eva's missing leg is the mark of maternal discourse in the novel and the key to its (thematized) ambivalence toward it" (419). Hirsch continues:

> There is an ellipsis in the text, a silence surrounding Eva's eighteen-months' absence from Medallion. This gap gives rise to numerous tales,

some told by Eva herself to amuse the children . . . others invented by the townspeople in their effort to explain her return without one leg, but with a new black pocketbook full of money. The tales are clearly apocryphal: The mother's (self-)mutilation in the service of her own and her children's survival remains, to the end of the novel, unnarrated, and perhaps unnarratable, but the source of endless narration. (419)

If we import Hirsch's argument into Baker's, the "maternal discourse" symbolized by the missing leg functions like a black hole within the text. The unspoken narrative becomes both the known origin and the mystery into which narrative attention is drawn. Not coincidentally, the moment that Hirsch points to in order to locate her "maternal discourse" is represented as an irresistible void, "the long fall of space below . . . [Eva's] left thigh" (31). Morrison builds her image of the maternal around the significant *something* that is missing. In its absence the leg becomes central; I agree with Hirsch's assessment that this absent something is central to the way that Eva functions as mother.

Of course, killing Plum comes with some emotional if not physical costs. What makes this different than any previous situation is the pressure exerted on Eva by Plum's desire to return home—since she is identified as that original home. Eva chooses to see herself as "whole" rather than to allow herself to be made into a "hole" into which he can climb. She makes the choice to be woman rather than womb. Unfortunately, Eva has a narrow perspective. Having thus limited her options, she is forced to make a *non*choice—to kill rather than be killed. Her "death" would come in the form of a transformation from woman to womb and would be symbolic; on the other hand, Plum's death is literally murder by his mother.

Eva refuses to distinguish between metaphor and reality. She is unwilling to bear the son, the child she fought so hard to keep alive, again. In her attempt to step outside the damaging gender dynamics of the black hole, she becomes alternately life-giver and destroyer. Hirsch argues that in *Sula* there is no escape from the "irresistible attraction" (to borrow Baker's language) of the construct of the maternal:

Holding on to a pervasive belief in the danger of the maternal, and reiterating that danger not only in the deaths of Chicken Little and of Plum, but also in the death of a large part of the town in the half-built, womblike tunnel at the end of the novel, the text demonstrates the trap that lies within the attempt to escape from the maternal. (426)

The problem lies in the metaphor. Once something goes into a black hole, it never comes out; not even light ever comes out again. In witnessing Eva's murder of her son, we learn in *Sula* what it takes four generations of women to discover in Gayl Jones's *Corregidora*: the dynamics of the black hole that privilege the womb over the woman must be dismantled, or the blues matrix will consume itself and threaten everything around it.

Kitchen: Mr. and Mrs. Hirshorn's Kitchen

The home Baker imagines is a womb without a woman; in *Corregidora* Gayl Jones tells the story of a woman struggling to be at home without a womb. The protagonist, Ursa Corregidora, has been given a directive passed down from her mother, grandmother, and great-grandmother—"make generations" in order to "bear witness" of past atrocities. The womb is the site her mothers insist she use as the means of bearing her (and their) experiences. Consequently, home becomes very local for Ursa. The women in this novel are sacrificed in favor of the womb and the men vilified in the name of the father.

The father in Ursa's home is Corregidora. Ursa represents the fourth generation of women to bear the name of the Portuguese Brazilian slave owner who prostituted his slaves. Her great-grandmother bore a daughter by him and this daughter, Ursa's grandmother, did too. The women keep the name Corregidora as a testament to this legacy of sexual domination and abuse. The boundaries of home for Ursa are constructed and maintained by a small (dying) community of women and still ruled by an absent father/lover. After her first husband, Mutt, causes her to fall down a flight of stairs, she is forced to have a hysterectomy. Ursa suddenly must confront a black hole, but a different one than Baker imagines. Rather than a womb, this black hole is the void left in place of her womb.

Ursa's uterus is rendered useless, and its premature fruit, a month-old fetus, is discarded. The womb, a most private and intensely personal place, becomes completely public when it is literally thrown away. This new black (female) public place supersedes the black hole and in so doing, makes room for Ursa to imagine an alternative home. She fills this new black (female) place with the blues. Unlike the previous discourse associated with home—"make generations"—the blues are necessarily social. Home shifts markedly from the perverse incestuous place that Ursa bears bodily to a site that is externalized and created in concert with others.

I begin my reading of this novel, however, not with Ursa but with Catherine Lawson. Although she is a minor character in the novel, Catherine's experiences are peculiarly black and female, and furthermore, they are characterized in terms of home. Catherine explicitly connects the built home with the black woman's body and moves us from Eva's resistance to the force exerted by the "black hole" (read as home) to Ursa's blues. Catherine provides the crucial insight that helps illuminate the dynamics at work in the material place of home, which seem to demand that any radical reconfiguration occur first in the material rather than the metaphorical realm—even if that material is a woman's body.

Catherine, called Cat, is not *at* home insofar as she has no assigned station that will afford her both liberty and humanity; instead, she struggles with being *not* home in the places where she lives and works. Cat struggles to explain to Ursa the relationship between her experiences at work, in Mr. and Mrs. Thomas Hirshorn's house, and her experiences at home. The recounting of those experiences allows us to import meaning into Ursa's similar confrontations with the place of home.

Catherine appears soon after the novel opens, bringing soup to Ursa during her recovery from the hysterectomy. She leaves town abruptly, soon after Ursa uncovers her lesbian relationship with Jeffy, the teenaged daughter of a friend. Cat is absent throughout the rest of the novel and only mentioned in Ursa's dreams and a passing conversation Ursa has on the street with an older Jeffy. Jeffy tells about a terrible accident involving Cat:

> She work over at the Wax Works, you know. One that makes Dixie Cups or something like that. She was reaching down to get something and got her hair caught in one of these machines and it pull all her hair out. Well, it pulled all the top part out. Might as well say all of it. She was in the hospital about six months. (176)

The relevance of this passage is obscured by its physical distance from a house, yet the forces at work in this scene are directly related to the power dynamics of home. As the older Jeffy states plainly in reference to the accident, "Bad thing to happen to a woman, ain't it?" (176). Long hair is a hallmark of womanhood and beauty. In this accident Jones quite deliberately represents "a bad thing" that happens "to a *woman*" [emphasis added] as opposed to a man. This *woman's* injury serves as blatant indication of those deeper scars that are more effectively concealed within Cat's past. At the beginning of the novel, she makes her living doing hair out of her kitchen. This affords her both economic means and the freedom "to keep [her] own hours" (29). For the time being, working out of her own home liberates Cat from the oppressive demands of the factory and the domestic work she used to perform. Unfortunately, she does not emerge from this past unscathed. In fact, by the end of the novel, she wears a bad wig in an effort to hide her disfigurement. Rather than functioning as a mask, the wig serves as a sign of the injury and reinforces the reality of Cat's debilitation.

The irony is that Cat knows employment in the factory is not very different from domestic work, in that black women's labor is exploited in order to serve the needs of white men and women.[2] Despite the fact that Cat's experiences, like Ursa's, are bound up with the blues, she seems to have no received cultural framework within which to express the value of her life. So instead, she replicates (and in so doing, falls victim to) the very systems of her oppression. Unable to utilize blues expressiveness, Cat tries in vain to explain her motivations to Ursa:

She was telling me about Mr. and Mrs. Thomas Hirshorn and something
that happened in the kitchen . . . one morning he [Mr. Hirshorn] was sitting at the table while she was fixing coffee. "You pretty, Catherine, you
know that? You pretty, Catherine. A lot of you nigger women is pretty." . . .
He kept sitting, thumping on the table watching her . . . and then when
she'd got the can of coffee grounds down and was opening it to pour it in
the pot, he was behind her, touching her arm, and she dropped the can,
and it banged and rolled across the kitchen floor spilling grains. (65)

In this scene, Jones lays out the black place of the kitchen as it has
been constructed by the racialized, Southern past. Emancipation
and the subsequent conditions leading to the Great Migration
began dismantling the quarters and signaled the fall of Southern
aristocracy. The kitchen is a "black" place in the ways that Jean
Toomer describes in *Cane* in "Blood Burning Moon":

Bob Stone sauntered from his veranda out into the gloom of fir trees and
magnolias. The clear white of his skin paled, and the flush of his cheeks
turned purple. As if to balance this outer change, his mind became con-
sciously a white man's. He passed the house with its huge open hearth
which, in the days of slavery, was the plantation cookery. He saw Louisa
bent over that hearth. He went in as a master should and took her.
Direct, honest, bold. (31)

Bob Stone's prescribed place allows him free access to any and all
sites within the plantation system. There are no limitations upon
where and when he may enter any place—including Louisa's vagina. His actions are justified by the authority that deems Stone (as
would-be master) *naturally* "direct," "honest," and "bold" in regard
to Louisa (as would-be slave).

This passage makes explicit the fact that both terms, "hearth"
and "home," are not only gendered but also racialized and as such,
set within a matrix of power relationships. As Spillers explains:

"Gendering" takes place within the confines of the domestic, an essential metaphor that then spreads its tentacles for male and female sub-

ject over a wider ground of human and social purposes. Domesticity appears to gain its power by way of a common origin of cultural fictions that are grounded in the specificity of proper names, more exactly, a patronymic, which, in turn, situates those persons it "covers" in a particular place. (266)

Precisely because Cat is both black and female, she is assigned the role of domestic servant in a white family's kitchen. Consequently, her body as the signifier of that black female identity becomes the focal point. White male attention is directed toward her, and thus, her assigned place (the kitchen) and her experience of that place are expressed bodily.

Cat satisfies her need for control over her own home places by assuming a position of power over a young girl. She exercises that control according to the same despotic norms that have been used against her. Ursa overhears an exchange between Cat and Jeffy that demonstrates the dynamics:

> "If you bother [Ursa] again I'll give you a fist to fuck." . . .
> There was a loud slap, and then low crying.
> "Laugh now."
> "Please, Miss Catherine."
> "I said, 'Laugh now.'"
> Low crying. (47)

White patriarchy forced the black woman into the kitchen as domestic labor, then went further to dominate her body sexually. In response, Cat tries to move from the assigned black (female) "kitchen" place to invade and dominate Jeffy's womb. Cat justifies her lesbian relationship with this teenaged daughter of a friend who has been entrusted to her care by saying, "I wanted to come back home to my own bed and not be made a fool of. You know what I mean?" (66).

Early in the novel, Cat struggles to articulate her understanding in a way that might function as a mapping of her own as well as Ursa's experiences (at home). Cat clearly understands if she is ever to be *at* home, she must not be forced to stay in the kitchen. Referring to Ursa's employment as a blues singer, she tells her:

> You got talent. A talent or a craft, that's what I say, and don't have those sons of bitches hanging on your neck all the time. And daughters of bitches. When I was young I worked in white women's kitchens, so I know how it is. Leastwise the factory ain't a kitchen, but ain't much different. (29–30)

Ultimately, Cat is unable to successfully explain herself. In this way she operates as the foil who highlights the value of Ursa's contrasting experiences. Ursa's singing signifies off of Cat's experiences as a domestic worker and displaces her own would-be domestic experiences with the blues. However, Cat's experiences as a domestic should not be dismissed because they are intrinsically bound with Ursa's blues.[3]

The distance between the kitchen and the bedroom is compromised by the relatively unrestricted sexual appetite of Thomas Hirshorn, who sees Cat as simply an apparatus for feeding his hunger. She becomes, for him, an extension of the kitchen. As owner, Hirshorn can occupy Cat as territory almost as readily as he might eat the meal she prepares. In effect, the white man's response to her presence in *his* kitchen transforms the kitchen into a "bedroom" place.

The discursive walls that might be established by place to prohibit particular activities are absent within the racist aftermath of the slave economy. The owner of the house asserts his position of power over Cat through sexual harassment. She is forced to negotiate the slippery terrain that separates her livelihood from her "private" life while confronting a treacherous adversary. As her boss, Hirshorn has both the access and the power to make Cat "feel foolish all day in a white woman's kitchen" (64). Moreover, the experience is so destructive that it compromises the walls that might otherwise restrict "public" access to the "private" place of Cat's sexual body. The barriers that might distinguish the site of the kitchen from the site of the bedroom are obscured, and Cat's response is equally confused.

Through her relationship with Jeffy, Cat challenges the value she is assigned by the place of the kitchen and of the bedroom. Rather than acquiesce, she struggles to escape her designated place. Cat is seeking to reconfigure the nature of her own experience. In the effort, she becomes a "clumsy nigger" who is ultimately left a shadow of her former self, poorly masking her obvious disfigurement. Ursa, on the other hand, maps her journey home in the language of the blues.

Womb: Making Room

Jones uses Cat to demonstrate the material significance of kitchen places in the lives of African American women, but she underscores the quintessential blues paradigm at the heart of the novel. Ursa retains the paradoxical impulse to "make generations" even while she is left wombless by her fall. The patriarch Corregidora rejects even the façade of the kitchen in favor of the bedroom and capitalizes on black women's bodies as sexual commodities. The mothers dispute this relationship first by trying to assert their humanity, then by refusing to allow the testament to Corregidora's inhumanity to die.

Unfortunately, they co-opt the womb as a site for domination and, instead of liberating themselves, thus risk reifying the terms of their oppression. Amy Gottfried considers the ironic implications of their response: "The Corregidora women respond to their early enslavement by defining themselves and their daughters as wombs intended for the literal bearing of witnesses. Sexual violence doubly limits desire and pleasure for these women. First defined as 'pussy,' they are now self-defined as womb" (560). Trying to liberate herself from Corregidora, Great Gram sought to make a home for herself and her daughters. She moves from her distinctly black (female) would-be kitchen/bedroom place as "little gold piece" in Brazil to her womb in Kentucky as an attempt to control the productivity of her own body.

By Ursa's time, however, Great Gram's desire to control her own body serves as a mandate for Ursa and her mother, Correy. The question they grapple with over the course of the novel is whether or not the position depicted by Corregidora is any better than the one Great Gram and Gram actually held.[4] Ursa's journey home must move her away from the kitchen as well as from the womb. In "Mama's Baby," Spillers evokes the image of the Mother within the context of African America. In contrast to the symbolic realm overshadowed, in the Lacanian view, by the specter of the Father, here the Father is absent by design. While Lacan suggests that the Father is always in doubt, from Spillers's perspective, he is both doubted and denied, and the offspring are given over to the "condition of the mother." Such a shift requires more than a simple reading of race and gender and evokes a complicated lexicon upon which we might build a vocabulary for literary analysis.

The Corregidora women attempt to invert the pastoral image of home by insisting that the father is the source of their kin, and their black female bodies testify to the sins of his house. The quest is not to achieve regeneration, as for Plum in *Sula*, but to pass on the legacy of Corregidora. As H. A. Ashraf notes:

> In Ursa's memories of Great Gram's slave heritage, there's no ambivalence (since Great Gram had ensured that there would be no questioning her version of the past), no paradoxes since the tale is of pure victimage and equally pure evil, and little feeling that Ursa was supposed to be searching for her own identity at all. The ghosts are not being exorcised; they're being embalmed. (276)

Ashraf borrows an image from Salman Rushdie of a haunting, but it is the women themselves who are haunted.[5] Ursa is charged to "make generations" in order to pass down the legacy as it was told to her: Corregidora is the incontestable paternal figure who shamelessly harbored Great Gram and Gram as property—his "little gold piece"—and sexual chattel.[6]

Ursa understands enough about this legacy to reject kitchen places and to seek a more viable home place. She chooses the stage as the place to begin the arduous journey away from Corregidora's memory toward her own home, created through the blues. On the blues performer's stage, female bodies are both liberated through the reduction of incomprehensibly painful experiences into manageable terms and policed by the intervening presence of mothers and men. Yet the stage is not the site of Ursa's tragedy. She is knocked down a flight of stairs by her drunken husband on her way home after an evening performance. Ursa's fall marks the violent flashpoint when all the dynamics of place making come together within the text.

On the surface, Mutt is angry about Ursa's occupation because her performances arouse other men. He threatens her: "'That's what I'm gon do,' he said. He was standing with his arms all up in the air. I was on my way to work. 'One a y'all wont to bid for her? Piece a ass for sale. . . . That's what y'all wont, ain't it? Piece a ass'" (159). In isolation, Mutt's actions might read as a domineering man trying to control his wife's interactions. However, when read in the context of history as well as the Corregidora women's quest to "make generations," they reveal a more complicated dynamic at work.

While the kitchen collapsed into the bedroom for many black women, Corregidora was only invested in the latter. Great Gram's assigned place within the Brazilian household was as a concubine—his "little gold piece." In the tradition established by Great Gram, Ursa tries to walk away from her black (female) home place. But she is not completely liberated from the kitchen/bedroom dynamic simply because she resists it. The Corregidora women are subject to the force exerted by the larger construct of home. So when Ursa is ultimately scarred by place, it is as the result of a fall down a flight of stairs, a liminal place between the stage—the home of Ursa's choosing—and the assigned black (female) kitchen and bedroom.

The Corregidora women use their bodies to establish a place for themselves secure enough to withstand Corregidora's dominion. Unfortunately, as Gottfried asserts, "Sexual commodification is supplanted by a deliberate, political self-definition. But as Ursa . . . discovers, this political move has a double-edged drawback: The Corregidoras' agenda severely limits their sexual identities, a limitation which in turn provokes domestic violence" (559). Like Ursa, Mutt is trying to secure a home for himself, and he responds violently to the perceived threat to it by transforming the site of Ursa's body. In the process, Ursa loses her womb[7]—the place that had been configured as the enduring site of the Corregidora legacy. The absence of her uterus becomes a *"well that never bleeds"* (99). This black hole contains neither water nor blood with which to sustain life. In Ursa's imagination she hears Mutt say to her, *"Let me get up in your hole, I said. I wont to get up in your goddamn hole"* (100). Mutt transforms the quintessential *something* embodied by Ursa's womb into a void. In so doing, he physically expresses his desire to enter the place that was occupied by Ursa's womb; once again, as with Eva and Plum, home is imagined in these terms.[8]

Although she resists mystifying the material site of home, at the end of the story when Mutt finally reenters her life, Ursa is drawn back to the specific place where they lived, presumably in the hope of rectifying past mistakes. The last pages of the novel offer a hope not present anywhere else, because at this moment language intersects with body, place, and memory as both Mutt and Ursa articulate what they want and need on their own terms:

> A moment of pleasure and excruciating pain at the same time, a moment of broken skin but not sexlessness. . . . I held his ankles. It was like I didn't know how much was me and Mutt and how much was Great Gram and Corregidora. . . .
> "I could kill you."
> He came and I swallowed. He leaned back, pulling me up by the shoulders.
> "I don't want a kind of woman that hurt you," he said.
> "Then you don't want me."
> "I don't want a kind of woman that hurt you."
> "Then you don't want me."
> "I don't want a kind of woman that hurt you."
> "Then you don't want me."
> He shook me till I fell against him crying. "I don't want a kind of man that'll hurt me neither," I said. He held me tight. (184–85)

Ursa's epiphany comes at the end of the novel, when she finally understands that in order to construct a viable home place, she must shift the emphasis, bodily, from "the well which never bleeds"—its life-giving, and more important, life-sustaining powers all inarguably gone—to her mouth, the site that permits the expression of her blues. The difficulty as well as the deliberateness of this shift is emphasized by her concluding posture. Certainly, the novel ends ambiguously. But in its last pages, Ursa successfully integrates the past into what Deborah McDowell calls a "continuous present"[9] that allows her finally to imagine a home built out of her experiences as well as those of her foremothers, Corregidora, and Mutt.

Much has been said about the concluding lines of *Corregidora* as a blues exchange.[10] The blues, of course, have been associated with both movement and the translation of experiences into alternative terms. They permit disparate experiences to converge at a single moment in time and so facilitate Ursa's epiphany. The suffocating site of the womb needs to be discarded, the novel suggests, in favor of a less "totalizing" narrative, to borrow language from Michel de Certeau.[11] The concluding blues song Ursa sings with Mutt is "jerry-built" from fragments of the past. The blues narrative produced in place of the womb opens up room for maneuvering outside the stultifying interior site configured by Great Gram and Corregidora.

The integrity of the structural blueprint introduced in *Native Son* and revised by Ellison in *Invisible Man* and Morrison in *The Bluest Eye* is threatened by complete collapse in *Corregidora*. Jones begins her demolition with the womb, but by the end of the novel, even the blues Ursa sings is compromised. In *Song of Solomon*, Morrison will recover the patronym and collect the remnants of the city, the kitchen, and the womb to reconstruct the African American place of home. Finally, in this novel, we find a representation of home, not without contradictions or completely unproblematic, but with enough conflict resolved that we can imagine laying down our bones to rest for a while.

Notes

1. The 1980s and '90s were the backdrop for much infighting between women seeking to validate literary representations of their experiences at home and men seeking control over the master's tongue and house. Alice

Walker's search for Zora Neale Hurston's grave took her to her "mother's house." As a result of her efforts and those of many others before her, African American female authors like Margaret Walker, Gwendolyn Brooks, Toni Morrison, Octavia Butler, Gloria Naylor, Ntozake Shange, Toni Cade Bambara, and Gayl Jones rose to dominate the field of fiction writing. However, men sought a home of a different sort within the house of the academy. Into the twenty-first century, the most renowned criticism and theory continue to be produced by men like Henry Louis Gates Jr. and Houston A. Baker Jr. Such a reality does not suggest an inherently divided house that opposes "writers" and "readers"; nonetheless, it seems a disparity between "writing" and "reading" arose along gender lines.

2. White Americans read the presence of African American domestic workers as a sign of their own domestic security. Nearly a hundred years after the collapse of the slave economy, home for white people continued to be stabilized at the expense of black laborers (even if much of the "stabilizing" was more symbolic than actual labor). For this reason, African American women had few employment opportunities besides domestic work. Home is invented in a contest for power from which someone will emerge victorious and someone will invariably lose. Domestic service is but a by-product of this struggle.

3. Lindon Barrett makes this connection between domestic service and the blues explicit in his reading of a scene from Billie Holiday's autobiography. Despite the questions of authenticity that have been raised in relationship to this work, his discussion is relevant not only because Holiday (as character if not historical person) writes about her experiences of black (female) places as a domestic worker who employs relevant cartographical strategies, but also because, like the fictional Ursa, "the lady sings the blues." Barrett's discussion is in reference to the following scene he cites from Holiday's autobiography, *Lady Sings the Blues*:

> All these bitches were lazy. I knew it and that's where I had them. They didn't care how filthy their damn houses were inside, as long as those white steps were clean. Sometimes I'd bring home as much as ninety cents a day. I even made high as $2.10—that's fourteen kitchen or bathroom floors and as many sets of steps.

It is [Holiday's] "originary" labor that affirms the site (sight) of the valued and the not-valued, the inside and the outside; it is her antinominan presence on the boundary and, finally, within the house—primarily kitchens and bathrooms, architectural sites of inside meeting outside—

that maintains the value of the valued. Insofar as Holiday is outside, the low, down, dirty, maid, the commanded, the not-valued, she is a source of value. . . . (874)

Holiday is housed insofar as she stays put, in those built places that require the services of black females—steps, kitchens, bathrooms. Yet, as Barrett suggests, designations such as "high" versus "low," "rich" versus "poor," "dirty" versus "clean" are relative rather than essential. Holiday gains a level of control over these home places by reformulating the terms of her oppression. She literally rewrites them through the language of autobiography and the blues. In the passage from *Lady Sings the Blues*, Holiday curses the women and calls them "nasty." The white women whose homes she works in become "dirty" while she, by implication, is clean. See "'In the Dark': Billie Holiday and Some Sights and Sounds of American Value," *Callaloo* 13.4 (1990): 872–85.

Leon Forrest also connects a discussion about Billie Holiday with *Corregidora* in his article "A Solo Long-Song: For Lady Day" in *Callaloo* 16.2 (Spring 1993): 332–67. Forrest writes, "The mythical power of Billie Holiday's life, charged by the immediate abuse from men throughout her life, and the mythical-sexual victimization by the slave master of her great grandmother becomes an obvious scale-model for a most troubling and memorable novel *Corregidora*, by Gayl Jones" (364).

4. Nancy Jesser makes the following observation in her insightful reading of Toni Morrison's *Beloved*: "The specificity of historical moments allows for and demands certain and, at times, mixed-up choices. None are choices for all time, and none are apocalyptic enough to end the history in which we find ourselves. But, Morrison suggests [in *Beloved*], we bear a kind of haunting from these choices that in turn haunts the future" (341). The house in Bracktown is haunted with ghosts of her mother's past, and Ursa must leave in order to begin her *own* journey toward "home." See Nancy Jesser, "Violence, Home and Community in Toni Morrison's *Beloved*," *African American Review* 33.2 (Summer 1999): 325–45.

5. From the start of the novel, Ursa's sense of place grows primarily from two directions: from the demand that she "make generations" in order to record past atrocities, as she literally has been born to do; and out of her desire to sing the blues. I do not mean to suggest that the command to "make generations" and the blues are divergent. In fact, at times they are nearly synonymous. Once we also consider the conditions that lead to Ursa's hysterectomy, we have the necessary tensions established to nurture the

blues. A black woman's encounter with her assigned place, either in the kitchen (ultimately pinned to the floor by her father, as Pecola is in *The Bluest Eye*) or on the steps (like Pauline Breedlove ordering meaningless things or Billie Holiday polishing white marble) or in the factory (as Cat comes to be), ends with her wearing the scars of her experiences bodily.

6. In her reading of *Beloved*, Doyle makes an observation that is relevant to this discussion:

> Like the white men who steal Sethe's milk in Toni Morrison's *Beloved*, dominant-group men drink the milk that would nourish the cultural expressions of subordinate-group men. As Halle dramatizes, this theft renders the men emotionally numb and strikes them symbolically deaf and dumb. Meanwhile the theft of literal and metaphorical milk leaves the women to create a "told story" out of nothing but their own scarred and sequestered bodies. In fact, all women who would be artists, whether they belong to dominant or subordinate kin groups, must struggle to de-symbolize themselves, which they often begin to do by withdrawing, either voluntarily or involuntarily, from the marriage circuit. (26–27)

Certainly we see this pattern reflected in *Corregidora* where, in her struggle to forge a place for herself, Ursa is forced from both marriage and reproduction.

7. Mutt's perverse response to Ursa, in knocking her down a flight of steps, is similar to Paul D's encounter with the ghost in *Beloved*. As Nancy Jesser observes in her reading of the novel, "[Paul D's] coming [to 124 Bluestone Road] disrupts the physical spaces of the house. He 'broke up the place, making room, shifting [the ghost], moving it over to someplace else, then standing in the place that he had made'" (338). See Nancy Jesser, "Violence, Home, and Community in Toni Morrison's *Beloved*," *African American Review* 33.2 (Summer 1999): 325–45.

8. Deborah McDowell, "Negotiating Between the Tenses: Witnessing Slavery After Freedom—*Dessa Rose*," in Deborah E. McDowell and Arnold Rampersad, eds., *Slavery and the Literary Imagination* (Baltimore: Johns Hopkins University Press, 1989), 144–63.

9. See Katherine Boutry, "Black and Blue: The Female Body of Blues Writing in Jean Toomer, Toni Morrison, and Gayl Jones," in Saadi A. Simawe, ed., *Black Orpheus: Music in African American Fiction From the Harlem Renaissance to Toni Morrison* (New York: Garland, 2000), 91–118; Melvin Dixon, *Singing a Deep Song: Language as Evidence in the Novels of Gayl Jones* (Garden City, NY: Anchor-Doubleday, 1984), 236–48; Gunilla T.

Kester, "The Blues, Healing, and Cultural Representation in Contemporary African American Women's Literature," in Lilian Furst, ed., *Women Healers and Physicians: Climbing a Long Hill* (Lexington: University Press of Kentucky, 1997), 114–27; and Claudia Tate, "*Corregidora*: Ursa's Blues Medley," *Black American Literature Forum* 13 (1979): 139–41.

10. In *The Practice of Everyday Life,* trans. Steven Rendall (Berkeley: University of California Press, 1984), Michel de Certeau theorizes that: "For the technological system [embodied by the city] of a coherent and totalizing space that is 'linked' and simultaneous, the figures of pedestrian rhetoric substitute trajectories that have a mythical structure . . . [for] a story jerry-built out of elements taken from common sayings, an allusive and fragmentary story whose gaps mesh with the social practices it symbolizes" (102).

Works Cited

Ashraf, H. A. "'Relate Sexual to Historical': Race, Resistance, and Desire in Gayl Jones's *Corregidora.*" *African American Review* 34 (2) (2000): 273–297.

Baker, Houston A. *Blues, Ideology, and Afro-American Literature: A Vernacular Theory.* Chicago: University of Chicago Press, 1984.

Carby, Hazel. *Race Men.* Cambridge: Harvard University Press, 1998.

Doyle, Laura. *Bordering on the Body: The Racial Matrix of Modern Fiction and Culture.* New York: Oxford University Press, 1994.

du Cille, Ann. "Phallus(ies) of Interpretation." In Winston Napier, ed., *African American Literary Theory.* New York: New York University Press, 2000, 443–59.

Gallop, Jane. *The Daughter's Seduction: Feminism and Psychoanalysis.* Ithaca: Cornell University Press, 1982.

Gottfried, Amy S. "Angry Arts: Silence, Speech, and Song in Gayl Jones's *Corregidora.*" *African American Review* 28 (4) (1994): 559–70.

Hirsch, Marianne. "Maternal Narratives: 'Cruel Enough to Stop the Blood.'" In Henry Louis Gates Jr., ed., *Reading Black, Reading Feminist: A Critical Anthology.* New York: Meridian, 1990.

Jones, Gayl. *Corregidora.* Boston: Beacon, 1975.

Morrison, Toni. *Sula.* New York: Knopf, 1973.

Spillers, Hortense J. "Mama's Baby, Papa's Maybe: An American Grammar Book." In Winston Napier, ed., *African American Literary Theory: A Reader.* New York: New York University Press, 1990, 257–79.

Toomer, Jean. *Cane.* New York: Liveright, 1975.

[Home is] *this* world, the world of which we
are normally aware . . . the social setting in
which man may expect to find his secure
place. [The unhomely, t]hat which is 'secret',
and that which usually remains hidden but
is brought to light, is the unconscious mind
of the individual, and through and beyond this
is a wider region of the unconscious that we
find embodied in myths, legends and fairy
tales throughout the world; it is the realm of
primitive fears, of what has been forgotten and
left behind, yet returns on occasions to plague
us; it is the sense of alienation, of things we
have made turning against us, of historical
and social forces that we are helping to shape
and that yet escape our control and even our
knowledge; and it may also be a sense of the
'wholly other' invading our lives.

          —Siegbert S. Prawer, "The 'Uncanny' in Literature"

Europeans living in America have undergone
a transformation. [Carl] Jung calls this process
"going Black."

          —Ishmael Reed, *Mumbo Jumbo*

5

God Bless the Child That's Got His Own: *Song of Solomon*

In *Mumbo Jumbo* (1972), Ishmael Reed muses about the possibility
of "blackness" sweeping the country like a contagion of pandemic
proportions. Reed suggests that during the 1920s, inspired by the
rhythms of black cultural productions, the United States suc-
cumbed to its urge to jelly roll, betraying its white façade by exposing its dark underbelly. In this satire, Reed paints a picture of a
nightmarish plague that the establishment is unable to quell.

The infestation is not, however, a foreign agent introduced to a virgin population. Instead, the phenomenon arises from inside the nation. It is a repressed part of our national identity manifested as blues, ragtime, jazz, returning to seize control of the dominant consciousness. The "alien" black presence so vital to building and maintaining the nation, in Reed's vision, spreads beyond white supremacist stopgaps and Jes Grew out of control. Funk infests the country and alters its pulse to match the rhythm of the soft-shoe that reveals more than a trace of resemblance to the African foot stomp upon bare ground. Without regard for accepted norms and practices, people began to show their color; otherwise "good" people began to "act black" in their style of dress, music, speech, and performance.

For a time, Jes Grew emerged from the recesses of our consciousness and proved itself a crucial part of our national identity. In this parody, Reed shows what is at stake for a country and a people still struggling to define itself as home for African Americans only a few generations removed from slavery. Even the suggestion that Jes Grew's elusive Text ever existed challenges ontological beliefs about racial divisions within society. Such categories are not hermetic. The distinctions between communities were becoming increasingly difficult to identify by the tracks that had previously separated them. Reed's notion of Jes Grew is important because knowing *where* we are cartographically relies upon knowing *who* we are as a people. These, of course, are not new questions, and they continue to permeate the writings of successive generations at least in part because they are so difficult to answer.

Reed's critique and his reference to Jung's observation about the European American "going Black" provide a convenient metaphor upon which to anchor the concept of home. American national identity is founded upon formulations of race. Consequently, we utilize the language of race to help us articulate the ways in which we inhabit the land. As a result, home is built upon metaphors of racial identity. But what might appear at a great distance to be simply black and white becomes infinitely complicated the more closely it is examined.

While not overtly concerned with addressing the needs of a white audience in the ways reflected in Reed's *Mumbo Jumbo*, Toni Morrison creates an unapologetically black home place that nevertheless manages to demonstrate a sophisticated understanding of race. The natural world of borders—walls, fences, streets, streams, and mountains—that define home in *Song of Solomon* is accompanied by the ghettoized world of breast milk, bones, peaches, blues, and ghosts. Unfortunately, the credence lent to the world of borders by the authority of maps, government agencies, and other institutions usually occludes the significance of the ghetto.

The ghetto is, of course, a portion of the city assigned to disenfranchised members of society who generally share a common racial identity. But in the African American vernacular, "ghetto" is also a characterization for something or someone, or an act or behavior that is identified with the place of the ghetto. It is both a particular material site identified in terms of spatial markers like street signs and housing projects and the more arbitrary label assigned to nearly anything "black" that might be associated with that locale. To be "ghetto" is to act flagrantly out of one's impulses in spite of the presence of strangers. For example, in *Song of Solomon,* Porter's public display of drunkenness, shouting and urinating out of an attic window, might be called "ghetto."

In *Song of Solomon*, the city itself becomes "ghetto"—not in the sense of Bigger Thomas's segregated and impoverished Southside, which he knows intimately but which refuses to know him, nor in the sense that *Invisible Man*'s Harlem is a black jungle that keeps slipping out of view. I do not want to dismiss the standard usage of the term; obviously, the word "ghetto" denotes slums African Americans were forced by economic pressures to occupy. What I am suggesting, however, is that in its standard usage the term is pejorative; the derivative from the vernacular includes this connotation but is inflected with a broader meaning. These black cities can barely house the protagonists and are not home to them. To be "ghetto" in the vernacular sense is to have a home even if it is an illegitimate nonplace that emerges alongside that which appears to be more natural. *Song of Solomon*'s Southside, for example, is ghetto because it is the dark underbelly that is home to the characters' blacker selves.

In this chapter I will examine the ways in which Morrison signifies on the leitmotif of the earlier novels and reconfigures the places of the city, the kitchen, and the womb in terms that are more livable. The representation of home, drawn as an irresistible attraction toward increasingly smaller sites—the city, the kitchen, the womb—in the previous works, breaks free and explodes in *Corregidora*. Morrison gathers the pieces Jones scatters and in *Song of Solomon* inverts the pattern, leading us out of the womb rather than into it. The womb is dead; the kitchen opens outward; and the city becomes ghetto. Rather than being a black place because it is so interior that there is an absence of light, as is the case with Baker's black hole, home becomes a black place because of the presence of all color. To be at home, then, Morrison suggests in *Song of Solomon*, the African American community must embody the blues paradox of holding its opposite within itself. The novel declares that home is untenable, yet it must be defended even at the cost of life itself. The protagonist, Milkman, having gained the knowledge of how to integrate the material world embodied by his father with the ghetto symbolized by his aunt, can finally fly home.

Womb: A Dead Place

While Baker's theoretical framework in *Blues Ideology* erases the mother by subjugating the productive space of the biological womb to the male-engineered matrix, *Song of Solomon* resists such a reading by privileging the woman's body. Although the womb is clearly a hostile place that can be invaded by potentially lethal forces, Morrison refuses to let the reader forget that the womb is located within a woman's body. She creates dynamic characters with individual personalities not easily ignored, even when the novel moves from the literal womb into metaphor. In *Song of Solomon*, representations of the womb are repeated and revised in a range that spans the mythical, the literal, and the metaphorical. The most obvious example of a mythical womb is, of course, Pilate's emergence from Sing's dead womb. Milkman's life is literally threatened when he is still in Ruth's womb, and as an adult he helps to destroy Hagar's barren womb. Finally, the novel offers the Butlers' house as a metaphor for a decaying womb through which Milkman reconnects with his ancestral past.

Although much has been written about Pilate's mythic origins, I return to this point because her birth is a clear demonstration of Morrison's concern for the womb as it relates to the quest for home. Even Pilate's brother, Macon Dead II, who, in his pursuit of material gain, has become estranged from his sister and detached from his ancestry, recognizes Pilate's link to the past. He tells his son, Milkman, "If you ever have a doubt we from Africa, look at Pilate" (54). She represents the African who was wrested from her homeland only to be denied the liberty of establishing a home in the new land. The struggle in the novel to acquire an estate to pass on to future generations is similar to the contest depicted in *Corregidora* to "make generations" that "bear witness" of the past. In an attempt to liberate Ursa from the perverse dogma instituted by her great-grandmother, Jones literally cuts the womb out of the woman's body. However problematically, the hysterectomy and its precipitating violence free Ursa from the cycle of maternity and allow her to withdraw from the marriage circuit in an effort to redefine her relationship to home. The womb and fetus lost in *Corregidora* are reclaimed in *Song of Solomon*. While Ursa's fetus is premature and discarded along with the womb, Sing's baby matures to full term.

Morrison understands the need to reconfigure the role the female body plays in the African American construction of home. The novels discussed in the previous chapters become increasingly critical of the effort to retreat into the womb. Morrison revises Jones's violent dismemberment, which radically alters the place of Ursa's body, by keeping the womb intact even while insisting that it not be considered a viable home. Morrison accomplishes this by allowing the woman to choose death over the responsibilities of motherhood. Pilate declares, "People die when they want to and if they want to" (141). Unfortunately, in choosing to die *before* Pilate is born, Sing literally holds the future captive in her womb. Pilate's sheer determination to live overcomes death. She delivers herself from the cavern of dead flesh that might have been her tomb.

In this birth, Morrison posits a paradox that is characteristic of the blues expression that will come to shape Pilate's life. Pilate embodies the blues sentiment expressed by lyrics like "Sometimes I feel like a motherless child," growing out of the slave past. Slave families were torn apart and children routinely denied a relationship with their mothers. This terrible reality is supported, perhaps ironically, by an equally heinous law supporting the institution of slavery, which mandated that children "follow the condition of the mother." This law in conjunction with governing practices functioned to erode the natural right of a black individual to control access to her own body and her offspring. In "Mama's Baby," Spillers maintains that "Under these arrangements, the customary lexis of sexuality, including 'reproduction,' 'motherhood,' 'pleasure,' and 'desire' are thrown into unrelieved crisis" (272). I have already discussed at some length how the blues emerges from this troubled past and works to impose meaning upon the chaos of black experiences. In fact, the blues is one of the few narrative traditions that can accommodate the hyperbole and truth, hope and angst, of a mother who dies *before* the child is even born. Sing's womb, then, is a blues crossing, that black (female) place Baker might call a "black hole." Pilate must overcome the condition of her mother— and her own quintessential blues condition of being a motherless child—before she can claim the right to be alive.

The black hole that Baker describes is indicated by the X, the sign of the railway juncture. The X, however, evokes the image of America's mechanization and thus diverts attention from the female body. However, Pilate emerges from her mother's dead womb bearing no mark of this crossing at all. The narrative describes the scene of Pilate's birth from Macon's perspective:

> After their mother died, she had come struggling out of the womb without help from throbbing muscles or the pressure of swift womb water. As a result, for all the years he knew her, her stomach was smooth and stur-

dy as her back, at no point interrupted by a navel. It was the absence of a navel that convinced people she had not arrived through normal channels. . . . Once the new baby's lifeline was cut, the cord stump shriveled, fell off, and left no trace of having ever existed. (27–28)

The absence of a navel suggests the polar opposite of Baker's junction. Pilate's smooth belly brings to mind anything but the manmade. The absence of a navel bears witness to her mother's death, but it also indicates an unnatural break with the past. Morrison moves toward resolving the dilemma of the absent mother by reinscribing her in Pilate's flesh as the absence of a navel. Pilate is *unmarked* by her mother's death. Like Adam, who as the first man has no need for a navel, Pilate with her smooth belly signifies originality. Further, she is given dominion over the tools that will reconnect the next generation with its past. This heritage transcends the black hole of her mother's womb and reaches beyond the vortex of the Middle Passage to an African past. Consequently, that "captive flesh," which had been "seared, divided, ripped-apart . . . riveted to the ship's hole, fallen, or escaped overboard" (Spillers 260) in the ancestral past, is permitted to begin again. In this way, Pilate's belly becomes a blues paradigm simultaneously signifying the problem and the solution.

Morrison reinforces the idea that the womb is a hostile place through the figures of Macon's wife, Ruth, and Pilate's granddaughter, Hagar. These women desperately long for a viable home that will nurture their embattled psyches. The devaluation of the womb corresponds with the dynamics established by their respective homes: Ruth's is too big and Hagar's is too detached. As a result, the womb again emerges as a sign of home and its dysfunction.

Ruth is the lonely daughter of the first African American doctor in town. She never discovers any meaningful ways of expressing herself in the overwhelmingly masculinist space of Not Doctor Street and her father's house. Southside residents integrate the doctor's home into their cultural landscape but they do not accommodate Ruth; and the house that justifies the expanded reading of African American space for the community at large collapses in upon his daughter. Without a sense of ownership, Ruth *belongs* to the house. Consequently, the social space that might read as an expanded site of power for the African American community in general, Ruth finds nearly impossible to negotiate. As Lefebvre explains, "The subject experiences space as an obstacle, as a resistant objectality: at times as implacably hard as a concrete wall, being not only extremely difficult to modify in any way but also hedged about by Draconian rules prohibiting any attempt at such modification" (57). Because the house is expansive, it seems available to be encoded at will, but instead of yielding itself as a void, it refuses to be fitted to Ruth's female sensibilities. Her efforts to resist the sense of smallness her home imposes upon her are ineffectual and usually result in negligible changes in her mundane routine. The birth of her son, Milkman, is her only significant victory over the conditions that shape her life.

Nevertheless, Ruth would not have been able to conceive Milkman without Pilate's assistance. Pilate arrives in town after discovering that her granddaughter, Hagar, is not like her daughter, Reba, or herself. Hagar's appetites cannot be satiated by wandering. She needs a home, so Pilate seeks to reconnect with her more conventional brother. The reunion is brief, just longer than the time it takes Milkman to grow from conception to birth. When Macon discovers that Ruth is pregnant, he initiates a regimen designed to induce an abortion. While Milkman has not yet become "real" to her, Ruth is terrified by the possibility of aborting the fetus. Nevertheless, she is unable to resist her husband and submits to castor oil, scalding pots, soapy enemas, and knitting needles. When he punches her in the stomach, she finally looks to Pilate for help.

For Ruth, the womb is not a haven; nor is it perverted into a record through which she can "bear witness" of the past. With Pilate's assistance, Ruth asserts the sovereign right to control access to her body. Her womb, under siege by Macon, characterizes the struggle of African American women to liberate themselves from oppressive domestic dogma that seems to extend the reach of male governance to the female body. When paired with Pilate, Ruth no longer serves as the malleable conduit for expanding and maintaining male territory. Rather than functioning as a mere kin source, Ruth begins to exercise dominion over her life and affect the lives of others. She manipulates Macon into impregnating her and she manages to resist his threats long enough for her son to be born.

Within a larger context, *Song of Solomon* contains none of the nostalgia associated with Ruth, as mother, found in some of the earlier literature. For example, we cannot imagine Milkman running and jumping over puddles of milk to get to Ruth in the way the narrator does in his attempt to get to Mary Rambo in *Invisible Man*. The dark hole into which the invisible man falls during the Harlem riots is a surrogate for Mary Rambo's body. The basement apartment is simply an extension of this same association. The apartment reads as Baker's matrix, a womblike blues home wherein the narrator can withdraw from his experiences in the world. Morrison reconfigures Ellison's vocabulary—man, milk, mother, home, and womb—and inflects the terms with new meaning. Milkman's experiences quell the optimism associated with a retreat into the womb. The womb, in *Song of Solomon*, does not bear even the trace of romance. For Milkman, home must be a broader place, located elsewhere. The womb is not safe for Milkman as it was not safe for Pilate.

Pilate says that Milkman "come into the world tryin to keep from getting killed" (140); but this reality seems to have made him selfish. He treats Pilate's hungry granddaughter, Hagar, with the same callous disregard his father gives his mother. Ultimately, Hagar drowns in a pool of her own longings, manifested as a mad desire for Milkman. Though he falls in love with Hagar the moment he sees her, over the course of time his lust wanes; meanwhile, her passion for him becomes more concentrated. Although the bodily consequences are just as severe for Hagar as they are for Sing or Ruth, she begins to move the conceptualization of home out of the womb. She does not produce a child (in fact, the novel infantilizes her). And unlike Great Gram in *Corregidora,* who looks to the womb to produce hope for the next generation, Pilate rests the future of the Dead family upon Milkman's shoulders.

Hagar begins a ritual rampage, ostensibly to kill Milkman, after their breakup. News of this threat to her son's life once again sends

Ruth to Southside, seeking to defend him, where she confronts Hagar. Hagar is hurt and disappointed by Ruth's hostility. She tries to explain her motivation for stalking Milkman: "He is my home in this world"; Ruth retorts, "And I am his" (138). They are both wrong. Hagar cannot curl up inside Milkman any more than he can crawl back inside of Ruth. Ruth's womb was inhospitable even when his presence there was appropriate. Yet, in employing this imagery, Morrison signifies on Eva Peace in *Sula*—in this case, the mother would have the son come "home" to her womb, but he refuses to accept her on those terms. It is Pilate who states the wrenching truth neither woman wants to acknowledge: Milkman "wouldn't give a pile of swan shit for either one of you" (138).

This exchange encapsulates the inconsistencies that make it impossible for Ruth and Hagar to be at home and rooted. The scale they use to measure home is too restrictive because it begins and ends with the body—Hagar uses Milkman's and Ruth uses her own. Beyond the obvious futility of an attempt to do what is biologically impossible, both women fail to recognize that the nature of the womb is to thrust outward rather than to draw in. Despite the resonance of Baker's argument, the womb is not a vortex, "charged with extraordinary attractive force" (154–55), and any home conceived in these terms will not long endure. Home must be configured as a broader model that can accommodate progress and growth. The shortcomings of these women are not individual and personal; rather, they indict the African American literary tradition for its insistence upon the preeminence of patrimony over a woman's life and for its failure to appreciate the needs of the whole community in search of home.

Milkman's apathy toward Hagar is typical of his attitude toward women and reflects a social pattern that offers males privilege without responsibility. He no longer feels a connection to Hagar, so he responds to the threat she poses to his life by imposing his will upon her. His will invades her embattled psyche, displacing her desires with his. Milkman finally decides upon an ultimatum, "Either I am to live in this world on my terms or I will die out of it. If I am to live in it, then I want her dead" (129). It is a simple binary: she goes or

I go. This dichotomy, however, demonstrates his failure to integrate the blues sensibilities embodied by his aunt, which disrupt simple dualities. Neither is Hagar equipped with a language adequate to express her overwhelming emotions. Instead, paralyzed by her desire, Hagar is unable even to release her arms holding the knife above her head.

Hagar proves incompetent at killing Milkman. Rather than attempting to understand her motivations or to show compassion, Milkman is relentless: "'If you keep your hands just that way,' he said, 'and then bring them down straight, straight and fast, you can drive that knife right smack in your cunt. Why don't you do that? Then all your problems will be over'" (130). The knife becomes a surrogate for Milkman's penis, invading and violating Hagar's vagina. He wills her death by directing her to mutilate the passage that leads to her womb. Milkman is so completely self-absorbed that he is blind to his responsibility for Hagar's behavior and unaware of the power he wields over her life. His behavior mirrors Macon's toward Ruth, although Hagar's womb, which might hold the promise of the future, is apparently barren. Even her vagina has been emptied of pleasure. The journey to and from the uterus is a dangerous passage, threatened by male agents who show little regard for women or the fruit of the womb. Sing's womb is the cavern of dead flesh from which Pilate must escape and Ruth's womb is the site where Milkman's life is threatened by his father. Milkman's last encounter with Hagar signifies the continuing threat to the womb. But by not actually involving the uterus, choosing instead to operate on the plane of wit and will, this encounter also provides the segue that leads out of the body.

Finally, Morrison reinforces the image of the dead womb first represented in Pilate's birth and repeated and revised in the figures of Ruth and Hagar by moving into metaphor. The Butler mansion is a womb site that speaks of death and the Dead family past. "If metaphor," as Susan Willis maintains, "and much of Morrison's writing in general, represents a return to origins, it is not rooted in a nostalgia for the past. Rather, it represents a process for coming to grips with historical transition" (264). The collapsing ruins of the

Butler house suggest a gangrenous womb, but the house also serves to shift spatial orientation away from the female body toward the materiality of the built environment. Retracing Pilate's steps in his search for a secret cache of gold, Milkman soon finds his way to the Butler's mansion, out of reach by car. Milkman must go the distance from the road on foot. He makes his way down a dark tunnel into an interior site deep in the woods. "He looked back down the path and saw the green maw out of which he had come, a greenish-black tunnel, the end of which was nowhere in sight" (240–41). It is a primordial place that is literally and figuratively larger than his mother's womb. He steps into the past, a time before his birth, into a place large enough to hold clues to his father's past and his grandfather's past too.

His unwitting quest for home begins with an allusion to the German folktale, *Hansel and Gretel*. While the familiar childhood characters salivate over a witch's gingerbread house, Milkman vomits from the stench of a different witch's house before Circe comforts him (as the two fictional forebears were similarly comforted) with the smell of ginger root. Now the only human occupant, Circe literally steps out of the past in a moment of what Susan Willis calls "funk." Willis defines "funk" as "nothing more than the intrusion of the past in the present" (280), but such moments play a vital function in helping Milkman to overcome major failings of his past. This "funk" also reads as the uncanny, which indicate for Siegbert Prawer "that we are nearing that dark, transpersonal realm of . . . [Jung's] collective unconscious, that realm of mythological forms where things and persons become magical, taboo, dangerous and yet full of the promise of enrichment and salvation" (14). Circe is far too old to be alive, yet she remains to watch the Butlers' house decay and to feed the dogs so that they can help assure the demise of this property. She wills herself to live in order to see this process through.

While Mary Rambo is an archetypal maternal figure serving to expand the male sense of home by staying in her place, Circe transcends that archetype. At the end of the novel the narrator of *Invisible Man* intends to run home, where presumably Mary remains available to receive him. Like Mary's, Circe's obligation is also in the home, but she transcends the limitations of her assigned black (female) place simply by staying there too long. The invisible man cannot return to Mary (in the body) although he retreats into her surrogate womb. Macon II, on the other hand, can literally return to Circe through the eyes, feet, and mouth of his son. This crucial distinction helps Milkman make the transition from egocentrism to social responsibility. Carl Jung asserts that our efforts should be to "connect the life of the past that still exists in us with the life of the present, which threatens to slip away from it" (157). The consequence of missing this sort of connection is "a kind of rootless consciousness" (157)—the kind that characterizes Milkman's life. As a signifier of the maternal, Circe *recalls* the past and provides Milkman with tangible evidence of his place within it. She is the cord that reaches through time and keeps the past from slipping away. That is why this midwife who never lost a baby (and only one mother) smells like "ginger root—pleasant, clean, seductive" (241).

More than magic, the smell of ginger suggests deep, strong roots, like those found in Southside. The luxury of air conditioners deprives the upwardly mobile middle-class African Americans of the smell that rides into open windows of Southside on the air: "there the ginger smell was sharp, sharp enough to distort dreams and make the sleeper believe the things he hungered for were right at hand" (185). The scent of ginger suggests the hope that the women of *Corregidora* believe is offered only in the womb. This root, like the herbs Ruth uses to bewitch Macon, works like black magic, enticing Milkman into the dark hull of the Butler house.

Milkman has an erection when he enters and climbs the stairs to meet Circe's embrace (242). He is aroused and succumbs to her seduction. In this seminal moment, Milkman enters and becomes present in his ancestral past. It is similar to the scene at the end of *Corregidora* when the distinctions between identity and time collapse for Ursa—"I didn't know how much was me and Mutt and how much was Great Gram and Corregidora" (184). Ursa's epiphany is the recognition that the ability to gain control over our past "had to be sexual." It has to be because rootedness is sexual; it is the present act we perform with our bodies to invoke the past and reach into the future through the process of reproduction. The womb, in this final configuration as the rotting shell of the Butler mansion, emerges as a place of thinly veiled yearning—the desire to be remembered, the longing to be productive, the need to live on one's own terms—placed in constant jeopardy by the corruption of material culture. Time threatens to destroy both the material environment produced as a monument to this yearning and the human life the womb promises to bear. The womb, first metonymic of the African American woman, becomes synecdochic for home and ultimately reads as a sign of decay brought on by the supreme investment in material culture. By demystifying the womb, the novel frees Milkman to go elsewhere in his journey home.

Kitchens: Open Outward

In *Song of Solomon,* the black hole is not the nostalgic, restful haven into which men fall to recuperate; instead, it is more directly identified with the black woman's body as a womb. Likewise, kitchen places are complicated by the presence of men who conspire, laugh, and talk through late evening hours. While there are numerous scenes that occur in the kitchen, I will discuss two brief passages: Circe's confrontation with Milkman about her commitment to the Butler household and Pilate's description of a man falling off a cliff in his kitchen. Together, these two scenes help us understand how Morrison continues to redefine the terms given to represent home by making the kitchen into a site of resistance. While Morrison demystifies the womb by reading it more literally, she mystifies the place of the kitchen by asking to suspend our disbelief. Analysis of these scenes will not provide a complete picture of home; however, it is a concise reading of the dynamics at work within the place of the kitchen and how those dynamics differ from kitchen scenes represented in the previous novels.

The kitchen is, of course, that place of domestic servitude within the white household assigned to the African American in the racist past. It is also an interior site crucial to developing kinship within the place of home. The kitchen fosters connections that help alienated people like Bigger Thomas or the narrator of *Invisible Man* to feel at home. For a moment, even Bigger lets down his guard when he sops his plate with his bread in the Daltons' kitchen. But Mary Rambo's and Mrs. MacTeer's blues kitchens offer only meager resistance to a huge white supremacist apparatus that distorts notions of home to its own ends. This apparatus continues to demand that an individual stay in her place (even when removed from an occupation as a domestic servant), which sexism and the legacy of slavery insist, for African American women at least, remains the kitchen. The blues kitchen that gives a measure of comfort to the invisible man proves unable to penetrate the madness that ensues in *The Bluest Eye*, a short time after Pecola's father rapes her on the kitchen floor. Cat Lawson, in *Corregidora*, is more aware than any of the other characters of how the kitchen works to victimize her. Unfortunately, awareness alone is not enough to compete with that despotism. Awareness must be accompanied by an effective means of resistance that might function, like the blues, to comfort individuals who are able to identify with this mode of expression; or that, like Circe (and her deep ginger roots), works to dismantle the authority given to the material environment of the kitchen altogether.

The image of the kitchen plays a significant role in America's historical development and expansion. It is not hyperbolic to assert that Circe's presence within the Butler household has global implications. While I am certainly not suggesting that a line leads from Circe to World War II, Amy Kaplan argues, after examining the writings of Harriet Beecher Stowe and others, that domestic rhetoric is a vital counterpoint to nationalist rhetoric. During the mid-nineteenth century, in particular, the language of domesticity suffused debates about national expansion. Kaplan says, "Women's work at home . . . performs two interdependent forms of national labor; it forges the bonds of internal unity while impelling the nation outward to encompass the globe" (587). Domestic discourse both redresses and reenacts the contradictions of the empire through its own double movement—to expand female influence beyond the home and the nation, while simultaneously contracting the woman's sphere to police domestic boundaries against threats from within and without. The movement inward, which in African American literature is a movement into the body, like the trend represented in nineteenth-century discourse, is really a subset of a larger, masculinist expansion. This outward thrust is fueled, in part, by African American domestic labor. Circe, then, arises out of this discourse as the localized black female figure who serves as the mechanism of American expansion. She must somehow become larger than her assigned station, root herself deeper than the nationalist movement, or simply outlive it in order to challenge the meaning of her place within the kitchen.

Although Circe does not actually appear there, the kitchen is a station that dictates how she is permitted to act within a given environment. Circe's assigned place in the Butler household is the black (female) kitchen, traditionally designated for African American women. Just as William Faulkner laments in his grotesqueries the emaciated landscapes in the fallen South and wrestles with the implications of race and servitude, Morrison depicts a sophisticated dynamic at work in the now defunct Butler household. Like Clytie in *Absalom, Absalom!*, Circe's presence within the household complicates our reading of the power relationships set in place to perpetuate and to disrupt racial hierarchies. As Homi Bhabha describes, "In a feverish stillness, the intimate recesses of the domestic space become sites for history's most intricate invasions. In that displacement, the border between home and world become confused; and, uncannily, the private and the public become part of each other, forcing upon us a vision that is as divided as it is disorienting" (445). The subjugated, eternal black presence within the household invites the question: Whose side is she on?

Circe disrupts the myth of the "loyal servant" who holds no personal ambitions by, among other things, harboring the children of the man the Butlers killed. She is a defiant figure who clearly understands her social responsibilities. Yet she endures like Dilsey in *The Sound and the Fury* to see "de first en de last" (375). Milkman misinterprets this dedication as her love of the Butler family and their home. When he confronts her with this perspective, Circe responds curtly, "They loved it. Stole for it, lied for it, killed for it. But I'm the one left. Me and the dogs. And I will never clean it again. . . . Everything in this world they lived for will crumble and rot" (249). Circe's dedication is not to the Butler family, but to overseeing the demise of their estate. When faced with financial ruin, the remaining Butler killed herself. Circe has witnessed the end of the family line, but she wants to see the material legacy destroyed, too. She and Milkman sit together in the last room in the house that has not yet been demolished. Her dedication is a triumph of the human spirit over the unconscionable pursuit of wealth.

Circe's survival symbolizes the African American collective will to endure nearly insurmountable conditions. The rotting hull of the Butler mansion, then, represents the inevitable demise of an unjust system that dehumanizes its agents and contorts a testament of their strength into a sign of their weaknesses. Yet, in this mixed-up world of kitchens and home, Circe's fate remains tied to that site. The kitchen is a cauldron built upon the myth of white supremacy, maintained by male dominance, and threatened by the potential for treachery. If the kitchen no longer can be trusted to serve the home, then the integrity of the home is compromised. By expanding Circe's presence from background in the national landscape to foreground within the domestic portrait and by pushing the limits of mortality, Morrison creates a figure that is simultaneously real and mythical. When Milkman leaves Circe, the authority of the black (female) kitchen place is all but dismantled.

Pilate is another character who refuses to behave according to the demands of the kitchen. Having discovered that she is virtually alone in the world, she throws "away every assumption she ha[s] learned and beg[ins] at zero" (149). At an age when most people have already stopped imagining, Pilate discards her beliefs. She does not allow preconceived notions about people or places to dictate her experiences. This unburdening is the crucial step in "opening up" the kitchen for Pilate. Philosopher Martin Heidegger suggests that "spaces open up by the fact that they are let into the dwelling of man" (157). The kitchen maintains its authority over the lives of its subjects by obscuring obvious conflicts and functioning within a set of given expectations. Because Pilate has rejected those expectations, she is able to accept the improbable story her employer offers:

> He said he couldn't figure it out, but he felt like he was about to fall off a cliff. Standing right there on that yellow and white and red linoleum, as level as a flatiron. He was holding on to the door first, then the chair, trying his best not to fall down. I opened my mouth to tell him wasn't no cliff in that kitchen. Then I remembered how it was being in those woods. I felt it all over again. So I told the man did he want me to hold on to him so he couldn't fall. He looked at me with the most grateful look in the world. (41)

Pilate does not concern herself with the impossibility of falling off a cliff inside the kitchen of his home. Instead she opens up her mind to receive his version of events and enters into the scene just enough to attempt a rescue. Pilate is receptive to his belief that he is falling but resistant enough to remain standing safe in his kitchen.

This kitchen, like any other social space, is fraught with inconsistencies. Heidegger offers the following example to explain the quality that space has of becoming quite malleable given the right set of circumstances: "If all of us now think, from where we are right here, of . . . [a particular outdoor place], this thinking toward that location is not a mere experience inside the persons present here; rather, it belongs to the nature of our thinking *of* that . . . [specific site] that *in itself* thinking gets through, persists through, the distance to that location" (156). Personal experience with a particular site formulates an understanding that coalesces in the *making* of that space. The space becomes "real" in the present environment even when the physical site is at some distance.

As liberal as Heidegger's reading of dwelling places is, Morrison manages to imagine something larger through the medium of fiction. In the kitchen scene Pilate describes, Morrison challenges Heidegger's notion that building produces locations that "allow spaces" by moving further into the immaterial. Pilate asks, "What difference do it make if the thing you scared of is real or not?"

(40–41). Regardless of what the built environment of walls and floors *allows*, belief is more powerful. The man's belief in the cliff and Pilate's investment in that belief defy the laws of physics operating inside the kitchen. The wife of the man Pilate is working for is not as receptive to her husband's perspective. She makes Pilate release him before he feels safe on his own. Once Pilate lets go, it takes him "three whole minutes to go from a standing upright position to when he mashed his face on the floor" (41). Space, according to Henri Lefebvre, signifies "dos and don'ts;" but the logic of place that dictates that a man cannot fall off a cliff while standing in his kitchen is disproved by the incontrovertible evidence of the amount of time it takes him to fall.

The place of the kitchen is opened up for the man because it contains a dangerous cliff from which he is falling. It is also opened up for Pilate because she accepts this alternative viewpoint as viable. Once walls (or in this case, floors) are undermined as effective barriers that restrict what logically can happen in a place, they lose their authority. Lefebvre asserts that "rather than signs, what one encounters here [in a social space like a kitchen] are directions—multifarious and overlapping instructions" (142). Lefebvre's "dos and don'ts" signify an infinite range of possibility; the viability of what is *not* real, in Pilate's experience in this kitchen, undermines the legitimacy of what seems to be more tangible. The monolithic walls that seek to confine those assigned to a particular station, such as the kitchen, become permeable and wholly unreliable. The price of his wife's disbelief in the possibilities is her husband's death. What the location allows is challenged by the reality of that event. And truth moves beyond what has been built as a kitchen into what is experienced as belief.

City: The Ghetto

Finally, the city returns to the notion that home is accompanied by a dark copy of itself. This copy usually remains a mere shadow, but at moments, the ghetto Jes Grew out of control. Then we see the blackening of the great white city in Wright's *Native Son*—white made more palpable by its thick covering of blizzard snow. Funk erupts and uncannily forces us to confront the reality that the distance between the bourgeois aspiration of owning the "Erie Lackawanna" and giving up nearly everything there is to own is as thin as the flip side of a dime. The blues is one means ghetto inhabitants like Pilate use to reverse the field of play—submerging the city and recalling the ghetto.

In *Song of Solomon*, the city is neither an adversary, as it appears to be in *Native Son*, nor an obstacle course, as it is in Ellison's *Invisible Man*. Nor does the city simply serve as the backdrop against which Morrison in *The Bluest Eye* and Jones in *Corregidora* can foreground the increasingly interior space of home. The first part of *Song of Solomon* is set in a modest-sized city in Michigan. The city is small enough for people to know who lives there but Northern enough to accommodate a burgeoning black middle class. It is here that the siblings Macon and Pilate Dead first appear. I have already discussed Pilate's mythical birth and how she liberates herself from the tyranny of the kitchen. What remains is to situate Pilate within the framework of home.

In the introduction of *Blues Ideology*, Baker records an epiphany he experienced during his study of African American culture, "I found myself confronted with a figure to ground reversal. A fitting image for the effect of my reorientation is the gestalt illustration of the Greek hydria (a water vase with curved handles) that transforms itself into two faces in profile" (2). This metaphor describes for Baker the relationship vernacular productions have to dominant culture. While I have already offered an involved critique of Baker's blues matrix in the previous chapters, I consider this image appropriately applied to the characters Macon and Pilate. If the novel, according to Morrison, is about "a journey from stupidity to epiphany, of a man, a complete man" (quoted in Grewal 62), then it bears upon Baker's theoretical black whole.

A man becomes "whole," in Baker's terms, or "complete," in Morrison's, when he is immersed within a culture that knows its *whole* self. The play between the figure and the ground captured in the image of the Greek hydria is represented by Morrison in the interchange between Macon and Pilate. As Denise Heinze observes, "Pilate, as manufacturer of a pleasurable product and an adversary to squeezing money out of neighbors—though not necessarily of making it—is the aesthetic antithesis of her utilitarian brother who makes people pay dearly for a basic necessity so that he may live in comfort" (85). Pilate's rejection of material concerns diametrically opposes Macon's total investment in "owning things." Yet neither character can be understood fully except in contrast to the other. Without becoming involved in the intricacies of rhetorical composition and design, I suggest that Macon is presented as the figure and Pilate as the ground (or vice versa); each is created through the play between positive and negative space. Together they represent the *complete* picture.

In other words, as a product of the ghetto—by which I mean a site encouraging the return of that repressed African identity—Pilate is *unheimlich,* while as an inhabitant of the city—by which I mean that normative metropolitan lifestyle involving work and play within a fairly densely populated built environment—her brother, Macon is *heimlich*. These German terms, *unheimlich* and its apparent opposite, have no ready equivalents in standard English. In a discussion about the uncanny in literature, Siegbert Prawer offers these definitions for the word *unheimlich*:

> (a) The 'un-homely', that which makes you feel uneasy in the world of your normal experiences, not quite safe to trust to, mysterious, weird, uncomfortably strange or unfamiliar. In this sense, *unheimlich* has frequently been used as the equivalent of a word that would seem to be its opposite, the word *heimlich* meaning 'secret' or 'hidden.' And from here, from this dialectical tension between *heimlich* and *unheimlich*, we arrive at a second meaning which has interested several writers from Schelling to Freud: (b) The 'un-secret', that which should have remained hidden but has somehow failed to do so. (6–7)

If Macon is the figure who has safely concealed that private, black part of his experience since his father's violent murder, Pilate is the figure who exposes the same Africanist past. The siblings split after their father is killed defending his land from the jealous and greedy Butlers. Macon resorts to the city in order to build a place of his own that cannot be stolen, and Pilate retreats into a ghetto experience that keeps "her just barely within the boundaries of the elaborately socialized world of black people" (150).

Macon's pursuit of things results in the acquisition of numerous properties that he manages from his desk in Sonny's Shop. However, Macon lives on Not Doctor Street, which town legislators and town maps only acknowledge as Mains Avenue. The street was renamed by Southside residents, patients of the only African American physician in town, in part because none of them lived there. The African American community is largely housed within Southside until the doctor's distinct social position situates him economically and geographically outside the predefined parameters of the general black populace. With his entrance the community has grown more complex than that which can be effectively contained within the Southside; so it must accommodate the doctor's social and physical proximity, integrating him into the communal landscape. The doctor's house expands the African American sense of place and Macon envisions himself, as a property owner, a suitable heir to his estate; "entertain[ing] thoughts of marrying the doctor's daughter was possible because each key [in his pocket] represented a house which he owned at the time" (22). Macon's success at integrating himself into the existing landscape suggests that he has found a place for himself in this growing city.

Macon's labor to establish a place of his own culminates in considerable wealth, but it also alienates him from the other black people in the community. A man's labor, according to Karl Marx, can take "on its own existence . . . it exists outside him, independently, and alien to him . . . it stands opposed to him as an autonomous power. The life which he has given to the object sets itself against him as an alien and hostile force" (quoted in Prawer 18). Macon works to "own things" so that those things will "own other things" and he can own himself and "other people too" (55). Unfortunately, material gain alone is not enough to satisfy the human longing for rootedness projected onto the place of home. The physical distance of his house on Not Doctor Street from the properties in Southside is mirrored by his emotional and psychological distance from Southside residents. Ironically, his labor turns against him, holding him outside of the community that reaps the fruit of his harvest.

Macon hordes dwelling structures in an attempt to fix his established place within the city and makes routine public displays in order to maintain it. His behavior proclaims to those around him that he *has* a home; conversely, his behavior accuses them of being without. But this is not the perspective from the Southside. According to Homi Bhabha, "To be unhomed is not to be homeless, nor can the unhomely be easily accommodated in that familiar division of the social life into private and the public spheres" (445). Bhabha is referring, of course, to the *unheimlich,* which I identify with the ghetto. Although Macon now lives in the house that expanded the horizons of the local African American sense of home, he feels challenged by Southside. Even the buildings themselves seem defensive at times: "Scattered here and there, his houses stretched up beyond him like squat ghosts with hooded eyes. He didn't like to look at them in this light. During the day they were reassuring to see; now they did not seem to belong to him at all—in fact he felt like the outsider, the propertyless, landless wanderer" (27). Under the shadow of night, the black, ghetto place comes to the foreground. Macon, in his refusal to identify with it, becomes more clearly the disinherited city dweller, wandering aimlessly about someone else's land.

Originally, ghettoes were ethnic enclaves carved out by Jews who settled in Italy, segregated communities where they could preserve their religious practices and culture. By the time of the Crusades, the increasingly militant medieval Christian church began to formalize the ghetto by imposing legal restrictions on Jews. However, as Louis Wirth observes, "The historians of the ghetto are usually inclined to overemphasize the confining effect of the barriers that were set up around the Jew, and the provincial and stagnant character of ghetto existence. They forget that there was nevertheless a teeming life within the ghetto which was probably more active than life outside" (19). In twentieth-century America, the ghetto has come to be associated with the disenfranchisement of African Americans. Yet, like the original Jewish settlements, the black ghetto is teeming with life. Like Bhabha's description of the "unhomely," the ghetto cannot be fixed within simple dichotomies. In fact, in this scene Macon is ghettoized by his status as outsider. The figure who is secured, both literally and figuratively, by the keys in his pocket slips into the background. In the evening shadows, Macon becomes dispossessed of his land.

Macon's attempts to own property so that he can own himself and other people prove finally as impotent as Bigger's carnivalesque inversion of the Daltons' home. Bigger is thwarted most immediately by his ignorance of the furnace mechanics but more significantly by the larger institutional structures that predetermine his failure. The billboard's policing eye, which insists that "you can't win," may be absent from Macon's setting, but his wholehearted internalization of Eurocentric systems of power leaves him nearly as vulnerable as Bigger. While Macon's response to his father's murder may not be physical violence, it is far from self-affirming.

More remarkable in this context is his sister Pilate's practice of respecting the people and things she encounters as she meets them within their own environment. Heidegger might define this quality as "sparing" and "preserving": "Sparing . . . takes place when we leave something beforehand in its own nature, when we return it specifically to its being. . . . *The fundamental character of dwelling is this sparing and preserving*" (Heidegger 149). Pilate spares by meeting an individual where he is (as she does, for instance, with the man in his kitchen) and preserves by respecting the contributions others bring to encounters. Thus Pilate, according to the terms laid out by Heidegger, *dwells* in the land.

This sense of dwelling is manifested in Pilate's incessant wandering after her father's murder and her subsequent estrangement from Macon. Her lack of attachment to any particular place is contrasted with her ability to locate and retain significant communal signposts. Pilate keeps the inheritance of her home literally in the form of her father's bones and figuratively in the partial narrative of the blues text. She is an agent of the blues like the classic blues artists Angela Davis considers in *Blues Legacies and Black Feminism*. Davis explains, "The women who sang the blues did not typically affirm female resignation and powerlessness, nor did they accept the relegation of women to private and interior spaces" (20). Pilate's journey continues to affirm the new pattern of expansion rather than retreat, supported by the expressive mode of the blues. "And Pilate embodies the image of the black blues woman, for her song of the lost man, flown away, departed, leaving the beloved behind in suffering and pain" (Skerrett 195).

That she continually interprets her world through the lens of the blues song (as she does on the day of Milkman's birth at the opening of the novel) keeps her perspective from being forgotten. Gurleen Grewal, borrowing her vocabulary from Baker, suggests, "Pilate's blues song and its referent, the historic/mythic flying African, depicts the despairing Robert Smith with blue wings; it succeeds in unifying, in 'an Afro-American expressive field' (Houston Baker's phrase), people as far removed from each other as the genteel Ruth Foster Dead and the poor Mrs. Bains, Guitar's mother" (70). The blues does indeed have the potential to unify disparate individuals into a community.

By using material wealth as a signifier of his superiority over those who do not have access to the same capital resources, Macon cuts himself off from the support of this community, leaving himself vulnerable in its presence. In his effort to hasten his trip from Southside, where he feels like an outsider, Macon passes in front of Pilate's house, where her song meets him in the street: "He was rapidly approaching a part of the road where the music could not follow, when he saw, like a scene on the back of a postcard, a picture of where he was headed—his own home. . . . There was no music there, and tonight he wanted just a bit of music—from the person who had been his first caring for" (28–29). The sound of the voices lures Macon, under the cloak of darkness, to Pilate's window, where he can secretly watch his extended family. Susan Willis suggests that Pilate's house gains its value within the novel because of its contrast to Macon's. "The utopian aspect of Pilate's household is not contained within it, but generated out of its abrupt juxtaposition to the bourgeois mode of her brother's household" (Willis 273). The music forces Macon to confront the image of his own home. Macon considers his own sense of isolation in contrast to Southside generally but to these women specifically. Yet, "as soon as man *gives thought* to his homelessness," Heidegger maintains, "it is a misery no longer" (161). Macon recognizes his own homelessness and allows Pilate's blues song to bridge the chasm between the siblings, at least for as long as the singing lasts. Scenes such as this one illustrate how borders become confused.

As children, Macon and Pilate face the world together, knowing that they are at odds with everyone else after their father's murder (including Circe, who had harbored them for a short while); they make a coherent unit for the time being. Before long, however, the murderous disruption that initially set them together against the world destabilizes even that last remaining certainty. Their father's farm having been stolen, their parents both dead, and their safety tenuous, when Macon and Pilate disagree on whether or not to take the mortally wounded hunter's gold, the final thread of unity that bound them is nearly completely severed. Yet years later, as Macon is pushed into the background by the ghetto of Southside at dark, he seeks solace in the shadows beneath his sister's window. While he may be standing outside the home, it is his identification with the people inside as family that resituates Macon in relationship to Southside. By allying himself with this household of women, he is able to use proximity and his ties to Pilate to identify with the ghetto and to assuage his feeling of loneliness.

As he stands outside Pilate's window in the darkness, Macon's sense of alienation melts away. For this instant, he becomes part of the ghetto. Meaning is created in the interchange between the siblings. This scene depicts a black whole—a fleeting moment of recognition that Macon and Pilate come from the same source. Unfortunately, this moment is tragically brief and leaves the distinct revelation that the city alone does not satisfy the yearning to be a "complete man," and neither does Pilate's ghetto lifestyle. But we see the potential for the same blues that draws Macon to the shadows outside Pilate's window to bring him home.

So much of African American literature has been represented as a quest for home. I could have chosen any number of texts. For the sake of cogency, I have focused on a few works, drawn from a period in American history during the latter part of the largest mass migration the nation has ever known. African Americans were seeking a place of their own, and this postmigration literature depicts the struggle to deal with the knowledge gained in its aftermath. Hortense Spillers maintains that "Domesticity appears to gain its power by way of a common origin of cultural fictions that are grounded in the specificity of proper names, more exactly, a patronymic, which, in turn, situates those persons it 'covers' in a particular place" (266). Her reading of the domestic can be readily applied to *Song of Solomon*, with its central quest for the name of the father that has been lost over time through the carelessness of racism and the drive toward upward mobility. But in reaching for those material comforts that seem to be available to all who labor for them, we must be aware of what might be lost.

The nearly forty-year span of African American literature represented here culminating in *Song of Solomon* reveals that home is somehow beyond place, beyond life, and even beyond death. It is an un-selfconsciously black place where men and women live alongside the ghosts of their past. We cannot walk away without carrying the bones inherited from our years of struggle. Even so, we must be able to encode those experiences honestly, in order to pass the *complete* story to the next generation. Home is a *whole* place captured sometimes in song, sometimes in fleeting moments of recognition.

The blues, these authors seem to suggest, is the expression that best represents the African American's peculiar position within the mid-twentieth-century American landscape. The city that looms so large in the literature produced during the Great Migration is not home. The kitchen is far too stultifying and the womb is little more than a romantic notion. Yet these sites form the basis of an African American vocabulary about home. We are left with the ghetto—the poor, black enclave nevertheless teeming with life—and the blues. Morrison seems to be saying finally that we must be willing to accept the possibility that we may be damned to walk beside home in a nether region of shadows and ghosts—lurking near but apart from the place we call home. This realm belongs to the ghetto.

Works Cited

Baker, Houston A., Jr. *Blues, Ideology, and Afro-American Literature: A Vernacular Theory*. Chicago: University of Chicago Press, 1984.

Bhabha, Homi K. "The World and the Home." In *Dangerous Liaisons: Gender, Nation, and Post-Colonial Perspectives* (Minneapolis: University of Minnesota Press, 1997), 445–55.

Davis, Angela. *Blues Legacies and Black Feminism: Gertrude "Ma" Rainey, Bessie Smith, and Billie Holiday*. New York: Pantheon, 1998.

Faulkner, William. *The Sound and the Fury*. New York: Vintage, 1929.

Grewal, Gurleen. *Circles of Sorrow, Lines of Struggle: The Novels of Toni Morrison*. Baton Rouge: Louisiana State University Press, 1998.

Heidegger, Martin. *Poetry, Language, Thought*. New York: Harper and Row, 1971.

Heinze, Denise. *The Dilemma of "Double Consciousness": Toni Morrison's Novels*. Athens: The University of Georgia Press, 1993.

Jones, Gayl. *Corregidora*. Boston: Beacon, 1975.

Jung, Carl Gustav. *The Archetypes and the Collective Unconscious*. 2nd ed. Princeton: Princeton University Press, 1969.

Kaplan, Amy. "Manifest Domesticity: No More Separate Spheres!" *American Literature* 70.3 (Sept. 1998): 581–606.

Lefebvre, Henri. *The Production of Space*. Trans. Donald Nicholson-Smith. Cambridge: Blackwell, 1991.

Morrison, Toni. *Song of Solomon*. New York: Signet, 1977.

Prawer, Siegbert S. *The 'Uncanny' in Literature: An Apology for its Investigation*. London: Westfield College, 1965.

Spillers, Hortense J. "Mama's Baby, Papa's Maybe: An American Grammar Book." In Winston Napier, ed., *African American Literary Theory: A Reader*. New York: New York University Press, 1990, 257–79.

Willis, Susan. "Eruptions of Funk: Historicizing Toni Morrison." In Henry Louis Gates Jr., ed., *Black Literature and Literary Theory*. New York: Routledge, 1984, 263–84.

Wirth, Louis. "The Ghetto." In Joe T. Darden, ed., *The Ghetto: Readings with Interpretations*. Port Washington, NY: National University Publications, 1981, 15–26.

Index

WEIGHTY ISSUES

SOCIAL PROBLEMS AND SOCIAL ISSUES

An Aldine de Gruyter Series of Texts and Monographs

SERIES EDITOR

Joel Best, Southern Illinois University at Carbondale

Joel Best (*editor*), **Images of Issues: Typifying Contemporary Social Problems** (Second Edition)

Joel Best (*editor*), **Troubling Children: Studies of Children and Social Problems**

James J. Chriss (*editor*), **Counseling and the Therapeutic State**

della Porta, Donatella and Alberto Vannucci, **Corrupt Exchanges: Actors, Resourses, and Mechanisms of Political Corruption**

Jeff Ferrell and Neil Websdale (*editors*), **Making Trouble: Cultural Constructions of Crime, Deviance, and Control**

Anne E. Figert, **Women and the Ownership of PMS: The Structuring a Psychiatric Disorder**

Mark Fishman and Gray Cavender (*editors*), **Entertaining Crime: Television Reality Programs**

James A. Holstein, **Court-Ordered Insanity: Interpretive Practice and Involuntary Commitment**

James A. Holstein and Gale Miller (*editors*), **Reconsidering Social Constructionism: Debates in Social Problems Theory**

Gale Miller and James A. Holstein (*editors*), **Constructionist Controversies: Issues in Social Problems Theory**

Philip Jenkins, **Intimate Enemies: Moral Panics in Contemporary Great Britain**

Philip Jenkins, **Using Murder: The Social Construction of Serial Homicide**

Valerie Jenness, **Making It Work: The Prostitutes' Rights Movement in Perspective**

Valerie Jenness and Kendal Broad, **Hate Crimes: New Social Movements and the Politics of Violence**

Stuart A. Kirk and Herb Kutchins, **The Selling of *DSM*: The Rhetoric of Science in Psychiatry**

John Lofland, **Social Movement Organizations: Guide to Research on Insurgent Realities**

Donileen R. Loseke, **Thinking About Social Problems: An Introduction to Constructionist Perspectives**

Leslie Margolin, **Goodness Personified: The Emergence of Gifted Children**

Donna Maurer and Jeffery Sobal (*editors*), **Eating Agendas: Food and Nutrition as Social Problems**

Gale Miller, **Becoming Miracle Workers: Language and Meaning in Brief Therapy**

Bernard Paillard, **Notes on the Plague Years: AIDS in Marseilles**

Dorothy Pawluch, **The New Pediatrics: A Profession in Transition**

Erdwin H. Pfuhl and Stuart Henry, **The Deviance Process** (Third Edition)

William B. Sanders, **Gangbangs and Drivebys: Grounded Culture and Juvenile Gang Violence**

Theodore Sasson, **Crime Talk: How Citizens Construct a Social Problem**

Wilbur J. Scott, **The Politics of Readjustment: Vietnam Veterans since the War**

Wilbur J. Scott and Sandra Carson Stanley (*editors*), **Gays and Lesbians in the Military: Issues, Concerns, and Contrasts**

Jeffrey Sobal and Donna Maurer (*editors*), **Weighty Issues: Fatness and Thinnness as Social Problems**

Jeffrey Sobal and Donna Maurer (*editors*), **Interpreting Weight: The Social Management of Fatness and Thinness**

Robert A. Stallings, **Promoting Risk: Constructing the Earthquake Threat**

Frank J. Weed, **Certainty of Justice: Reform in the Crime Victim Movement**

Rhys Williams (*editor*), **Cultural Wars in American Politics: Critical Reviews of a Popular Myth**

WEIGHTY ISSUES

Fatness and Thinness as Social Problems

Jeffery Sobal and Donna Maurer
Editors

ALDINE DE GRUYTER

New York

About the Editors

Jeffery Sobal is Associate Professor in the Division of Nutritional Sciences at Cornell University, where he teaches about social science analysis of food, eating, and nutrition. His research interests focus on social patterns of obesity, body weight and marriage, and the role of weight in society, particularly stigmatization of obese individuals and medicalization of obesity as a social problem. He co-edited, with Donna Maurer, *Eating Agendas: Food and Nutrition as Social Problems* (Aldine, 1995).

Donna Maurer is a John S. Knight Postdoctoral Fellow in the Writing Program at Cornell University. In 1997, she received her doctorate in sociology from Southern Illinois University-Carbondale, where she won the Outstanding Dissertation Award. She co-edited, with Jeffery Sobal, *Eating Agendas: Food and Nutrition as Social Problems* and is currently completing a book on the North American vegetarian movement.

ALDINE DE GRUYTER
A division of Walter de Gruyter, Inc.
200 Saw Mill River Road
Hawthorne, New York 10532

This publication is printed on acid free paper ∞

Library of Congress Cataloging-in-Publication Data

Weighty issues : constructing fatness and thinness as social problems
/ Jeffery Sobal and Donna Maurer, editors.
    p. cm.—(Social problems and social issues)
   Includes bibliographical references and index.
   ISBN 0-202-30579-1 (alk. paper).—ISBN 0-202-30580-5 (pbk. :
alk. paper)
    1. Obesity—Social aspects. 2. Food—Social aspects.
3. Nutrition—Social aspects. I. Sobal, Jeffery, 1950–   .
II. Maurer, Donna, 1961–   .   III. Series.
RA645.023W45   1999
306.4'61-dc21   99-13616
                                      CIP

Manufactured in the United States of America

10 9 8 7 6 5 4 3 2 1

Contents

PART IV   GENDERED DIMENSIONS

PART V   INSTITUTIONAL COMPONENTS

PART VI   COLLECTIVE PROCESSES

Preface

While many people consider their weight to be a personal problem, when does body weight become a social problem? Until recently, the major public concern was whether sufficient food was available. As food systems developed the capability to provide increasingly stable and abundant food supplies, people focused more on limiting their individual food intake. Questions about food insufficiency were replaced with concerns about food excess that led to a focus on "ideal weight" and appearance. These interests have aggregated into public concerns about people who are defined as "too fat" or "too thin."

Historically, food, nutrition, and body weight have been marginal sociological concerns. Notable early exceptions include Thorstein Veblen's (1899) consideration of the significance of food as a status marker and George Simmel's examination of the sociology of a meal (Symons 1994). More recently, sociologists have paid more attention to food, eating, and nutrition in research, teaching, and practice (Beardsworth and Keil 1997; Germov and Williams 1999; McIntosh 1996; Mennell, Murcott, and Van Otterloo 1992; Sobal 1992; Sobal, McIntosh, and Whit 1993; Whit 1994). In particular, sociologists have begun to address the gendered nature of food preparation and dieting (Charles and Kerr 1988; DeVault 1991; Lupton 1996) and weight-related social problems such as obesity and eating disorders (Hesse-Biber 1996; Millman 1980).

Understanding body weight problems requires insight into how social problems rise and fall. To explain the emergence, development, and attenuation of social problems, the chapters in this volume borrow from and contribute to a social constructionist perspective.

THEORETICAL APPROACHES TO EXAMINING BODY WEIGHT AND SOCIAL PROBLEMS

Social problems analyses generally take one of two major orientations: objectivist or constructionist (Miller and Hostein 1993). Most analyses of body weight as a problem use an objectivist perspective that fits within positivist social facts paradigms (Ritzer 1975). Constructionist analyses of body weight are increasing, however, in line with the growing application of social definition paradigms in many disciplines (Ritzer 1975).

OBJECTIVIST ORIENTATIONS

Objectivist approaches to social problems take a positivistic stance, seeking to document and describe the reality of particular social problems (Spector and Kitsuse 1977). Such analyses usually focus on the prevalence, patterns, and severity of a particular problem. Objectivists assume that when a negative condition reaches an intolerable point, it self-evidently becomes recognized as a social problem. Objectivists view overweight, for example, as a condition in which individuals develop excess fat stores. They define obesity as a social problem to the degree that people's weights are above medically accepted standards or ideals (Dalton 1997b).

Objectivists' analyses of weight may document epidemiological patterns, seek to determine their causes, and propose solutions that may include engineering social institutions. Sociological objectivist analyses of body weight have examined the relationship between weight and such factors as depression (Ross 1994), socioeconomic status (Sobal and Stunkard 1989), marital status (Sobal, Rauschenbach, and Frongillo 1992). Nutritional scientists characteristically take an objectivist approach, describing weight problems and developing interventions to minimize or eliminate them (Dalton 1997a; Stunkard and Wadden 1993).

CONSTRUCTIONIST ORIENTATIONS

Many people see the condition of massive obesity as a social problem. A difficulty is evaluating the point at which obesity should be addressed as problematic. There are always people fatter or thinner than others, but how does this become a local, national, or international problem? Endless potentially problematic conditions exist, but only a limited number can come to the forefront of public attention at a given time (Hilgartner and Bosk 1988). The question is how weight becomes a social problem and where it is ranked with respect to other issues.

While an objectivist designates particular conditions as problems, a constructionist examines the processes by which people come to identify certain phenomena as problematic (Schneider 1985; Spector and Kitsuse 1977). Constructionists focus on processes rather than "facts," viewing social problems as the products of collective definitions. Consequently, constructionists set aside rigid social problems categories, and instead consider the claims that people make regarding these conditions. From a constructionist standpoint, a social problem has no independent ontological status; it depends on public definition. As social constructions, problems have life cycles that may or may not correspond with the objective prevalence or severity of the conditions (Best 1989:139–140; Downs 1972).

Why is it useful to study social problems as processes rather than as objective "facts"? Objectivist analyses of social conditions tend to reify empirical data and position the sociologist as the moral arbiter of "good" and "bad." The study of social problems as processes, on the other hand, enables the development of a sociological theory of how issues become recognized as problematic and how definitional processes depend on other structural and cultural conditions.

VARIETIES OF SOCIAL CONSTRUCTIONISM

While all constructionists recognize the negotiated, intersubjective nature of knowledge (including scientific knowledge) (Aronson 1982; Kitsuse and Cicourel 1963), they disagree on constructionism's direction and applications (Miller and Holstein 1993). In one camp, strict constructionists maintain that only the process of construction itself should be described (Ibarra and Kitsuse 1993; Spector and Kitsuse 1977). Any recourse to "facts" results in "ontological gerrymandering," which grants privileged status to certain information that the analyst regards as "true" (Woolgar and Pawluch 1985). Strict constructionists view the use of such facts as a return to objectivism—which they see as detracting from a "pure" social constructionist theory (Troyer 1992).

Although strict constructionists call for research that makes no recourse to "facts" and therefore makes no claims of its own, such a pure approach remains elusive. Some theorists argue that strict constructionism is empty because it can only explain the broadest generalities of social processes (Best 1993; Rafter 1992). In their recent prologue to a collection of constructionist research, strict constructionist advocates Sarbin and Kitsuse (1994:14) admit that "None of the chapters in this volume is an exemplar of strict constructionism. . . . It is questionable whether researchers can sustain any method that would be consistent with (its) requirements. . . ." Since any form of analysis requires leaving the claimsmakers' narratives, even attempts at strict constructionism create claims that others can analyze sociologically.

A more moderate stance, contextual constructionism, maintains that claims need to be addressed in their cultural and structural contexts, even though this may require the use of some objectified "facts" (Best 1993). This view is reinforced by recent efforts to integrate constructionist and objectivist perspectives (Jones, McFalls, and Gallgher, 1997). Contextual constructionists do not necessarily "debunk" popularly assumed objectivist explanations—claiming that some seemingly objective facts are more "true" than others (a practice which incurs the strongest accusations of ontological gerrymandering). Instead, they suggest that a constructionist perspective enables the explanation of the rise and fall of a variety of social problems with reference to interest groups, government, science, the media, historical conditions, and cultural values. Contextual construction-ism also permits the differentiation between sets of claims—as some sets may be more worthy of study than others. Strict constructionists have dif-ficulty with this approach, as they view all claims as equally valid and soci-ologically interesting.

CONCLUSION

Social constructionist perspectives can contribute to our understanding of weight problems because they focus our attention on how these prob-lems are created, maintained, and promoted within various social envi-ronments. While there is much objectivist research concerning weight problems, few studies address the socially constructed aspects of fatness and thinness. The chapters in this volume both draw from and contribute to social constructionist perspectives.

Donna Maurer
Jeffery Sobal

REFERENCES

Aronson, N. 1982. "Nutrition as a Social Problem: A Case Study of the Entrepre-neurial Strategy in Science." *Social Problems* 29: 474–487.

Beardsworth, A., and Keil, T. 1997. *Sociology on the Menu: An Invitation to the Study of Food and Society*. New York: Routledge.

Best, J. (ed.). 1989. *Images of Issues: Typifying Contemporary Social Problems*. Haw-thorne, NY: Aldine de Gruyter.

———. 1993. "But Seriously Folks: The Limitations of a Strict Constructionist Interpretation of Social Problems." Pp. 109–127 in *Constructionist Controversies: Issues in Social Problems Theory*, edited by G. Miller and J. A. Holstein. Hawthorne, NY: Aldine de Gruyter.

Charles, N., and M. Kerr. 1988. *Women, Food, and Families*. Manchester: University Press.

Dalton, S. 1997a. *Overweight and Weight Management*. Gaithersburg, MD: ASPEN.

Dalton, S. 1997b. "Body Weight Terminology, Definitions, and Measurement." Pp. 1–38 in *Overweight and Weight Management*, edited by S. Dalton. Gaithersburg, MD: ASPEN.

DeVault, M. 1991. *Feeding the Family: The Social Organization of Caring as Gendered Work*. Chicago: University of Chicago Press.

Downs, A. 1972. "Up and Down with Ecology: The Issue-Attention Cycle." *The Public Interest* 28:38–50.

Germov, J., and L. Williams (eds.). 1999. *A Sociology of Food and Nutrition: Introducing the Social Appetite*. Melbourne: Oxford University Press.

Hesse-Biber, S. 1996. *Am I Thin Enough Yet? The Cult of Thinness and the Commercialization of Identity*. New York: Oxford University Press.

Hilgartner, S., and C. L. Bosk. 1988. "The Rise and Fall of Social Problems. *American Journal of Sociology* 94:53–78.

Ibarra, P. R., and J. I. Kitsuse. 1993. "Vernacular Constituents of Moral Discourse: An Interactionist Proposal for the Study of Social Problems." Pp. 21–54 in *Constructionist Controversies: Issues in Social Problems Theory*, edited by G. Miller and J. Holstein. Hawthorne, NY: Aldine de Gruyter.

Jones, B. J., J. A. McFalls, and B. F. Gallgher. 1996. "Toward a Unified Model for Social Problems Theory." *Journal for the Theory of Social Behavior* 19(3):337–356.

Kitsuse, J. I., and A. V. Cicourel. 1963. "A Note on the Uses of Official Statistics." *Social Problems* 11(2):131–139.

Lupton, D. 1996. *Food, the Body, and the Self*. London: Sage.

Mennell, S., A. Murcott, and A. H. Van Otterloo. 1992. *The Sociology of Food and Eating*. Newbury Park, CA: Sage.

McIntosh, Wm. Alex. 1996. *Sociologies of Food and Nutrition*. New York: Plenum.

Millman, M. 1980. *Such a Pretty Face: Being Fat in America*. New York: W. W. Norton.

Miller, G., and J. Holstein. 1993. "Constructing Social Problems: Context and Legacy." Pp. 3–18 in *Constructionist Controversies: Issues in Social Problems Theory*, edited by G. Miller and J. Holstein. Hawthorne, NY: Aldine de Gruyter.

Rafter, N. 1992. "Some Consequences of Strict Constructionism," *Social Problems* 39(1):38–39.

Ritzer, G. 1975. *Sociology: A Multiple Paradigm Science*. Boston: Allyn and Bacon.

Ross, C. E. 1994. "Overweight and Depression." *Journal of Health and Social Behavior* 35:63–78.

Sarbin, T. R., and J. I. Kitsuse. 1994. "A Prologue to Constructing the Social." Pp. 1–18 in *Constructing the Social*, edited by T. R. Sarbin and J. I. Kitsuse. London: Sage.

Schneider, J. W. 1985. "Social Problems Theory: The Constructionist View." *Annual Review of Sociology* 11:209–229.

Sobal, J. 1992. "The Practice of Nutritional Sociology." *Sociological Practice Review* 3(1):23–31.

Sobal, J., W. A. McIntosh, and W. Whit. 1993. "Teaching the Sociology of Food and Nutrition." *Teaching Sociology* 21(1):50–59.

Sobal, J., Rauschenbach, B., Frongillo, E. 1992. "Marital Status, Fatness, and Obesity." *Social Science and Medicine* 35(7):915–923.

Sobal, J., and A. J. Stunkard. 1989. "Socioeconomic Status and Obesity: A Review of the Literature." *Psychological Bulletin* 105(2):260–75.

Spector, M., and J. I. Kitsuse. 1977. *Constructing Social Problems*. Menlo Park, CA: Cummings.

Stunkard, A. J., and T. A. Wadden. (eds.). 1993. *Obesity: Theory and Therapy.* 2nd ed. New York: Raven Press.

Symons, M. 1994. "Simmel's Gastronomic Sociology: An Overlooked Essay." *Food and Foodways* 5(4):333–351.

Troyer, R. 1992. "Some Consequences of Contextual Constructionism." *Social Problems* 39(1):35–37.

Veblen, T. 1899, 1953. *Theory of the Leisure Class.* New York: Mentor.

Whit, W. 1994. *Food and Society: A Sociological Approach.* Flint, MI: General Hall.

Woolgar, S., and D. Pawluch. 1985. "Ontological Gerrymandering: The Anatomy of Social Problems Explanations." *Social Problems* 32(3):214–237.

I

INTRODUCTION

1

Body Weight as a Social Problem

JEFFERY SOBAL and DONNA MAURER

While body weight is a salient personal issue to many individuals, weight is also increasingly seen as a broader social problem. Numerous analyses of weight as a public health problem claim that there are "epidemics" of obesity and eating disorders (van't Hof and Nicolson 1996; Jeffery and French 1998; Rippe 1998). In contrast, body weight as a social problem has received less attention (Maurer and Sobal 1995), and many questions remain. What are the historical foundations of current conceptions of body weight? How have medical models dealt with weight issues? How do the gendered dimensions of weight relate to it as a social problem? Do the institutional components of society determine how fatness and thinness are constructed? How are collective processes involved in defining and negotiating weight issues?

The chapters in this volume address these questions by examining socially problematic aspects of weight. All of the contributions use a constructionist perspective to examine weight as a social problem, but in different forms. Authors from multiple disciplines provide different orientations about how weight interpretations occur in society. History, sociology, nutrition, communications, psychology, and public health all elicit different constructionist orientations. The chapters in this book are grouped into sections that reflect fundamental perspectives that can be employed to examine social aspects of body weight: historical, medical, gendered, institutional, and collective.

HISTORICAL FOUNDATIONS

Historical analyses examine prior periods of time and search for patterns of changes, considering precursors and precedents that shape contemporary phenomena (Breisach 1994). Current concerns about body weight are located in a stream of time, and historical analyses provide insights about how weight was cast and recast into its current patterns and interpretations. A growing number of social history analyses have examined weight and eating disorders, primarily as narrative histories (e.g., Bell 1985; Brumberg 1988; Levenstein 1993; Schwartz 1986; Seid 1989; Stearns 1997). The chapters in this volume provide more specific analyses of how weight has been constructed differently over time.

Comparative historical analyses consider how societies deal with issues differently, contrasting them to reveal alternative social trajectories. The chapter by Peter N. Stearns examines the different ways American and French societies dealt with body weight among children, revealing strikingly different national paths. The French focus on eating discipline produced few obese children, while American laissez-faire eating patterns contributed to weight problems. Cultural contrasts provide evidence that interpretations of weight are constructed and not inherent, as exemplified by the earlier and stricter reactions of the French to overweight children.

The social construction of children's eating patterns and body weight over time can also be examined through a biographical lens, as seen in Paula Saukko's chapter, which provides historical contextualization for the work of Hilde Bruch. Bruch was a pioneering figure influential in the construction of contemporary thinking about obesity and eating disorders among both health professionals and the general public. Saukko explains how the interweaving of Bruch's personal history, psychiatric history, and such events in world history as the depression and the cold war produced complex portraits of weight as historically and socially located within specific times and contexts.

MEDICAL MODELS

Medical history examines general and specific examples of the ways that health professionals and the health system deal with medical phenomena (Breiger 1984). Medical historians examine historical precedents, precursors, and patterns that can provide insights into contemporary events and practices. The study of the medical history of body weight is no exception to the usefulness of examining past medical events and processes.

The chapter by Mark T. Hamin cuts a broad path in describing the scope of "historical legacies" and their effects on approaches to obesity, tracing the early development of several scientific communities during the twentieth century. Hamin analytically differentiates five major biomedical traditions that were held in different scientific and clinical communities, each with its own diagnostic views about weight, which led to different therapeutic interventions. His case studies of each tradition reveal important links with current conceptual schools and their practices.

Assessment techniques play a crucial role in the success of medical practice, and the development and adoption of a new assessment method can be an important development in the state of a field. However, if a technique later proves to be inadequate, or even worse, inappropriate, then considerable time and trust have been lost. David Smith and Sally Horrocks's chapter provides a case study of the rise and fall of the assessment of physical well-being developed by Georges Dreyer. Their analysis of this historical case reveals that the adoption and rejection of a method is not simply an objective and technical matter, but rather it is a social product constructed through a web of dynamic organizational relationships. Their account gives sobering pause to the unconsidered acceptance of contemporary scientific body weight procedures.

GENDERED DIMENSIONS

Weight and gender are so tightly intertwined that they often seem inseparable (Bordo 1993). The gendered nature of bodies, and the weight of these bodies, cannot be ignored. Differences and inequalities between women and men permeate all aspects of body weight, with the higher salience of weight among women a central consideration in thinking about fatness and thinness. Obesity is feared by most women, and eating disorders are largely gender bound. The social construction of weighty issues among women can be examined from many perspectives, and several are illustrated by chapters in this volume.

The construction, change, and enactment of cultural ideals have a powerful influence on the way women have dealt with weight. Nita Mary McKinley's chapter considers the gendered nature of weight ideals in a society where women are evaluated on their appearance and adherence to notions of femininity. The many dimensions of womanly ideals also carry weight ideals, revealing a complex (and contradictory) amalgam between being a woman and being a particular weight. McKinley shows that the case of fat women is an exception that demonstrates the current cultural rules, with their resistance to weight norms making it difficult to break free of entanglement with gender norms.

The extent of penetration of concern about weight into the social construction of women's bodies is perhaps most clearly apparent in the practice of dieting. The chapter by John Germov and Lauren Williams describes how women engage in continuous surveillance of other women's bodies as well as their own, which leads to perpetual dieting often becoming a taken-for-granted component of women's roles. Their examination of the dieting discourse, however, moves beyond a simple description of women's social oppression to a presentation of alternative discourses of resistance to pressures to be thin.

Role contrasts are frequently invoked to seek insights about gender and weight, as in the juxtaposition of professional football players and ballerinas as examples of heros and heroines of different weight identities. Martha McCaughey's chapter pursues parallels between female anorexia and male compulsive bodybuilding in the similar underlying processes involved in seeking opposite body types. She explains how the pursuit of control by both anorexics and bodybuilders leads down a pathway of addiction to body projects that consume the individual in the process of constructing his or her body.

INSTITUTIONAL COMPONENTS

Social institutions are important forces that shape the ways society deals with issues such as body weight. The role of industries, professions, governments, organizations, and other institutions in shaping perceptions and actions related to fatness and thinness is often not widely recognized, and should not be underestimated. Chapters in this volume begin to lay out some of the institutional landscape within which body weight is interpreted, negotiated, and performed.

S. Bryn Austin's chapter focuses on the processes involved in the making of the diet industry, which has emerged only in the last several decades to become a major force in food and health arenas. Austin traces the development of mass consumerism and how it incorporated a focus on healthy eating, focusing on how the evolution of dietary fat reduction serves diet food markets at least as much as the public's health. The intertwining of industrial and public health interests raises important questions about the institutional underpinnings of the pursuit of diet foods and dieting.

Professions also play an important role in the landscape of fatness and thinness. Ellen S. Parham's chapter discusses the multiple meanings of weight among dietitians and nutritionists. Parham provides important insights about the ways that dietitians are caught up in and cope with what she identifies as a weight dilemma, in which they are trained to feel responsible for helping clients lose weight, but do not have effective therapeutic options that can successfully help patients lose weight and maintain the weight loss. This weight dilemma has important consequences for perceptions of dietitians as professionals in the weight arena.

COLLECTIVE PROCESSES

Collective behavior involves social movements that change the way society frames and deals with particular issues, such as fatness and thinness (Bash 1995; Lofland 1996). Social movements may attempt to change how the food and nutrition system operates, using a toolbox of strategies to present their points of view and to modify others' perspectives and actions. Collective processes have been examined with respect to some aspects of food, eating, and nutrition, but relatively little attention has focused on how movements deal with body weight.

Social movements attempt to present themselves to the public in the best possible light to advance their causes and avoid criticisms or problems. Donna Maurer describes how the vegetarian movement deals with issues of fatness and thinness. Maurer shows how public images of vegetarians as "skinny" are considered, negotiated, and managed in the vegetarian movement's presentation to the broader public by de-emphasizing weight loss aspects of vegetarianism and neutralizing the "skinny vegetarian" image.

Some social movements deal directly with body weight, attempting to change the way society constructs fatness and thinness. The chapter by Jeffery Sobal examines the size acceptance movement, which acts as an advocate for fat people. Sobal examines the structure and processes of the size acceptance movement, considering origins, allies, strategies, and other aspects of the movement as it establishes a niche among the diversity of players in the broader body weight arena.

CONCLUSION

Society deals with weight not just as an objective physiological condition, but also as a set of social meanings. These chapters examine some important aspects of the social construction of weight as a social problem. However, there is much more work to be done to more fully elaborate the social discourses, interpretations, claims, negotiations, management, and presentation of body weight in society. Constructionist insights offer additional tools for those who practice in areas that deal with body weight as both a personal problem and a social issue.

REFERENCES

Bash, H. H. 1995. *Social Problems and Social Movements: An Exploration into the Sociological Construction of Alternative Realities.* Highlands, NJ: Humanities.

Bell, R. M. 1985. *Holy Anorexia*. Chicago: University of Chicago Press.

Bordo, S. 1993. *Unbearable Weight: Feminism, Western Culture, and the Body*. Berkeley: University of California Press.

Breiger, G. H. 1984. "History of Medicine." Pp. 121–94 in *A Guide to the Culture of Science, Technology, and Medicine*, edited by P. Durbin. New York: Free Press.

Breisach, E. 1994. *Historiography*, 2nd edition. Chicago: University of Chicago Press.

Brumberg, J. J. 1988. *Fasting Girls: The Emergence of Anorexia Nervosa as a Modern Disease*. Cambridge, MA: Harvard University Press.

Jeffery, R. A., and S. A. French. 1998. "Epidemic Obesity in the United States: Are Fast Food and Television Viewing Contributing?" *American Journal of Public Health* 88:277–80.

Levenstein, H. 1993. *Paradox of Plenty: A Social History of Eating in Modern America*. New York: Oxford University Press.

Lofland, J. 1996. *Social Movement Organizations: A Guide to Research on Insurgent Realities*. Hawthorne, NY: Aldine de Gruyter.

Maurer, D., and J. Sobal (eds.). 1995. *Eating Agendas: Food and Nutrition as Social Problems*. Hawthorne, NY: Aldine de Gruyter.

Rippe, J. M. 1998. "The Obesity Epidemic: A Mandate for a Multidisciplinary Approach." *Journal of the American Dietetic Association* 98(10, Supplement 2):S5–54.

Schwartz, H. 1986. *Never Satisfied: A Cultural History of Diets, Fantasies, and Fat*. New York: Free Press.

Seid, R. P. 1989. *Never Too Thin: Why Women Are at War with Their Bodies*. New York: Prentice Hall.

Stearns, P. 1997. *Fat History: Bodies and Beauty in the Modern West*. New York: New York University Press.

van't Hof, Sonja, and Malcolm Nicolson. 1996. "The Rise and Fall of a Fact: The Increase in Anorexia Nervosa." *Sociology of Health and Illness* 18(5):581–608.

II

HISTORICAL FOUNDATIONS

2

Children and Weight Control
Priorities in the United States and France

PETER N. STEARNS

France and the United States began to evince new concerns about fat and weight, and a new penchant for dieting, in the late nineteenth century. In both societies, increasingly sedentary jobs plus middle-class affluence and the abundance of available food set off new alarms after several decades in which plumpness had been valued esthetically and as an assurance against consumptive illness. Growing realization of the problems of degenerative diseases, as the classic communicable killers began to be brought under control, added to the modern concern. Nutritional studies, promoted by doctors (with the French initially more active than their American cousins) and (but here particularly in the United States) by actuarial tables, added to the mix. Fashion changes increasingly emphasized slenderness. A battle against corsets, launched in France but quickly taken up in the United States, led to a new valuation of natural thinness among women, but there were pressures for less weight and more musculature on men as well. The modern campaign against fat, complete with the first generation of commercial gimmicks, was well launched. Again in both countries, this campaign persisted, with recurrent intensification of standards, through the twentieth century (Banner 1984; Delbourg-Delphis 1982; Fields 1995; Stearns 1997).

Basic similarities in standards and approaches in the two countries, enhanced by mutual imitation, did not eliminate important distinctions. Attitudes toward children's weight differed significantly, and the differences were reflected not only in popularized advice to parents, but in injunctions by physicians dealing with heavy children and carried through in parental practice. Nutritionists have long pointed to poor eating habits in childhood as a key source of the unusually extensive weight problems among American adults. Not surprisingly the greater average slenderness of French adults (who weigh in about seven pounds lighter than their American counterparts in the late 1990s, height held constant) (Laurier, Guiguet, Chau, Wells, and Valleron 1992), owes much to stricter eating controls imposed in childhood. The differences can be both traced and explained historically, and while this analysis does not indicate easy remedies for the American anomaly—simply intoning, Do as the French do, would solve little—it does point to several factors that must be addressed. For while American approaches toward weight control in childhood lagged well behind the strictures aimed at adults during the first half of the twentieth century, the gap began to narrow at the level of official medical standards from the 1940s onward. Yet popular practice did not follow suit—which is where the comparative historical analysis really pays off, in showing why parents and children alike had trouble adjusting their expectations about eating, in such marked contrast to their French analogs (Kuczmarski, Flegal, Campbell, and Johnson 1994; Statistical Bulletin of the Metropolitan Life Insurance Company 1970; Stearns 1997).

"THE SAFE POLICY IS: EVERY CHILD ABOVE HIS NORMAL WEIGHT LINE" (EMERSON 1921)

Once launched in the 1890s, the American rhetorical commitment to weight control developed quickly. The *Ladies Home Journal* began to carry regular diet advice by 1901: "Every pound of fat that is not needed for some purpose is a burden and should be disposed of as soon as possible." Esthetic and health factors conjoined in the pleas. On the men's side, Bernarr Macfadden introduced his body-building shows in the 1890s; his magazine *Physical Culture* had a subscriber list of 150,000 by 1906, touting such slogans as "Early old age shows at the waistline." Special weight-reducing products and diet books were being advertised in the daily press, while faddists like Horace Fletcher, the chewing enthusiast, won such eminent converts as William James, who sponsored a lecture at Harvard. Doctors gradually added weight control to their standard health recommendations. Most striking was the moral stigma quickly attached to overweight. As a magazine noted in 1914, "Fat is now regarded as an indiscretion, and almost as a crime" (Summerville 1916:28–29). A novel in 1900, describing the perfect figure of its heroine—"sensuous, graceful, slender"—also cited the reactions toward more corpulent women: "It was sheer horror that held Susan's gaze, upon Violet's incredible hips and thighs, violently obtruded by the close-reefed corset" (Ashmore 1906; Bray 1995; Patten 1897; Phillips 1900; Rorer 1906; Summerville 1916; Walker 1904–5; Way 1995).

Amid this multifaceted, steadily mounting pressure, however, children were notably absent. To be sure, *Ladies Home Journal* articles offered advice in columns for "girls," but the target was not in fact age-specific in a period in which mature women were urged to delight in girlishness. Both in formal pediatric publications and in popularized materials for parents, concerns about underweight surpassed attention to excessive eating several-fold, into the 1940s. Presentations such as Addington's *Your Growing Child* (1927) were typical. A full chapter lamented the problems of the finicky eater, with strategies to build up underfed children; there was no comment whatsoever on the opposite problem. Special recipes to build up under-weight children, particularly boys, dotted the pages of the new *Parents' Magazine,* including praise for snacks between meals and the consumption of fatty foods. Food was also recommended as motivation: "Children will eat when they won't do anything else, especially if they're tempted by something sweet" (Faegre, Anderson, and Harris 1958:38). Even superficial chubbiness, parents were warned, might not suffice: "The face of a child may look plump, owing to the particular cast of his features, but when he is stripped, noticeable depressions may appear between the ribs" (Kemp 1930:108). "He may be round and fat and still be poorly nourished" (Taylor 1949:65).

To be sure, there were a few qualifications to this general separation of children from the reigning adult weight standards. A number of doctors dealt with parents who pressed for help for children only slightly under-weight. Doctors tried to downplay the concern, realizing that moderate underweight might not be a bad thing, but they might not be able to pre-vail against the dominant lay culture. Certainly, there were nutritionists by the 1930s, and doctors even earlier, aware that children's overeating could pose health problems, at the time and in adulthood. Girls were particularly likely to be noted for problems of overweight, in a period when the pressures for slenderness bore strongly on women. Doctors and parents alike might combine to deplore girlish fat, primarily on esthetic grounds. Boys were unquestionably more likely to be exempt. "The situation is more serious for girls, than for boys," a *Woman's Home Companion* article intoned in 1920: "The latter usually have better opportunities to be normally active, and also they are not so much disturbed about their appearance as the members of the other sex" (Emerson 1921). Fat girls, it was sometimes noted, were often teased by peers. Only girls were pictured in the rare interwar articles that dealt with problems of overweight before adulthood (Anderson 1931; Child Study Association of America 1947; Crossley 1931; Emerson 1921; Richardson 1930).

But the exceptions should not becloud the basic patterns. When parents and most physicians worried about children's eating habits, they over-whelmingly stressed undernutrition. Doctors could easily dismiss concerns about children even twenty pounds over normal weight, using words like "stocky" and "husky," particularly about boys. "But a little padding on the frame doesn't hurt the child" (Wishnik 1935:185). Parents might be even more cavalier, insisting that plumpness signaled children's health and fulfillment of parental responsibilities. Pride in children's appetites redounded favorably on the mother as cook and caretaker. The simple process of growing up, both parents and most experts assumed, would take care of any problems on the part of younger children. In contrast, what to do when the child was "too thin" generated massive worry, intensified during the depression, when stories of hunger so readily seized center stage (Gay 1936; Granger 1930; Wishnik 1935).

Thus the main parental fare through the first half of the twentieth century concentrated on inadequate eating. Monthly columns in women's magazines like *Good Housekeeping* emphasized tips on how to get thin children to consume more. Elaborate strategies might be needed for "reluctant eaters": "Please, lovey, take one more spoonful for Mummy (or Daddy or Santa Claus)" (Holt 1956:132); "I won't love you anymore if you don't eat" (Kenyon 1933:98). "One child would never eat unless his father crawled around the room on all fours braying like a donkey" (Farren 1934:256).

Medical opinion began to correct this imbalance from the 1940s onward. Pediatric articles on problems of overweight children increased in number, gradually surpassing those on inadequate nutrition. But there were strong indications, unsurprising given the previous focus, that parental opinion remained slow to catch up. Indeed, popularized materials were fully echoing the pediatric standards only by the 1960s, as attention to excessive thinness persisted. Even Dr. Spock, while warning against sugary snacks in the 1950s mainly on grounds of tooth decay, devoted most of his attention to adequate intake, noting how a mother showed her love by making foods the child liked (Spock and Lowenberg 1955). Doctors commented frequently on parents who insisted that fat babies reflected health and familial love: "Your Fat Baby Is Not Necessarily a Prize Baby," one attempt at redress proclaimed. "To boast that a fifteen-months old baby 'eats everything' is not a tribute to its precocity but to the ignorance or willful negligence of its mother" (Dunbar 1949:386). In this context, many parents not only overlooked children's obesity but positively resented doctors who ventured to call it to their attention. New slogans, indeed, supplemented older notions in prompting children to clean up their plates. References to starving children in Europe, in the years after World War II, or then to their counterparts in India or elsewhere, offered additional goads for parents who defined satisfactory mealtimes in terms of everyone finishing whatever was on the plate (Rose 1955; Dunbar 1949; Holt, McIntosh, and Barnett 1953).

Of course, by the late 1940s if not before, teenagers frequently changed their tune after childish indulgence, and literature directed at them, such as the new magazine *Seventeen*, were filled with diet advice and dire warnings, particularly to girls. Not health alone but, even more, beauty and boy-catching depended on slenderness. For many girls, this meant the necessity of losing weight, not maintaining restrained eating patterns, precisely because childhood standards had been so lenient (Benjamin 1945).

For children themselves, American culture seemed strangely to lag, in two related respects beyond the ongoing struggles with the revision of medical views. First, as indicated, a gap widened steadily, for at least a half-century, between what adults read, and in many instances at least apparently accepted, about their own weight goals, and what they urged on their children. It was possible indeed that weight-conscious adults gained some indirect relief by letting their children eat away. Second, more broadly still, the impact of growing abundance and affluence on the young, translated into fairly steadily diminishing problems of sheer food supply, was only slowly and incompletely translated into popular beliefs. Dominant middle-class opinion, of the sort that clearly defined most widely read magazines and prescriptive literature, did not adjust to actual eating patterns, as the prevailing tone implied a massive incidence of malnutrition and excessive thinness where children were concerned.

This huge anomaly, obviously productive of adult weight concerns, obviously providing a historical explanation for the prevalence of much childhood overweight even today, must and can be explained. But before turning to this essential analysis, a counterexample will further define the causation involved. France, on the whole no more advanced than the United States in weight control advice for adults, differed early on in the approach to children—and the difference persists to the present day. The comparison highlights the need to probe American beliefs and precedents for a childhood anomaly that, clearly, was by no means inevitable.

FRANCE: DISCIPLINED EATING

Despite many differences in specific settings, the French seemed to agree that childhood eating required serious discipline. A group of devoted experts certainly stressed this theme explicitly across class lines, as they tried to improve the child-rearing habits of workers and peasants. Here was a major divergence from American patterns, and from this a crucial explanation of why other aspects of French weight culture, and of success in restraint, diverged as well.

For a striking feature of the French movement to control overweight was its smooth mesh with dominant attitudes about children and children's eating. Traditional child rearing, to a degree across class lines, insisted on childhood as a period of regulation. Long centuries of limited food supplies conditioned peasants, at least, to insist that their children neither waste food nor use it excessively. None of this was new, but it was given new attention as doctors turned their sights on obesity—and notes on childhood obesity occurred far earlier in French medical literature than in American, scattered references aside. Specific research on childhood obesity was underway by the 1930s, again in advance of developments in the United States. More important still, the idea of regulating children's eating gained both legitimation and wide publicity by its incorporation into the endless pamphlets and courses on child care that spread throughout France from the late nineteenth century through the 1930s as part of the *puériculture* campaign (Comité National de l'enfance 1936; Devraigne 1928).

Discussions of child rearing might have generated more indulgence in the French context than the American. The dominant concern was the nation's population problem, correctly defined as a lagging birth rate in comparison with competitors such as Germany. The remedies, widely publicized and granted government support in the decades between the 1880s and the 1930s, involved encouraging women to have more children (a hopeless goal at that point) but also promoting better care of children themselves. The "child raising" or *puériculture* campaign, endlessly preached through magazines and pamphlets and directly through doctors' advice, was designed to break a number of traditional habits in children's care, judged counterproductive to sustaining a productive childhood. Given the views prevalent across the Atlantic in this very period, the result might well have been a frantic attack on real or imagined reluctant eaters. Yet exactly the reverse pattern prevailed: The *puériculturistes* uniformly and explicitly warned against excessive feeding.

Control of children's eating was not the main point of the *puériculturistes*, to be sure. Their target was infant feeding, with endless pleas for mothers to breastfeed or, if artificial feeding could not be avoided, to do so properly. Along with this came standard recommendations about inoculations and other health care issues. But it was the rare manual that did not also comment on the desirability of curbing any tendency to overeat. "It is wise to be moderate, avoiding food excess as well as insufficiency of food," noted an interwar manual that also gave calorie listings for major food types (Strauss 1901:85). Mothers had to learn that customary notions that plump children were occasions for pride were wrong, really the reverse of the truth—this from a manual of 1896. More specifically, mothers too often tried to feed children adult materials too early, which could set up patterns of overeating later on. And it was vital to turn children away from sweets and random snacks, another maternal impulse that had to be stamped out. It was in this same context that doctors worked to warn mothers that their legitimate anxiety about tubercular children should not lead them to overfeed; the problems were quite separate (ibid.).

Two standard concerns of the *puériculture* campaign helped develop the rhetoric of regulation, in addition to the overall interest in children's health past infancy. First, the zeal to attack the use of animal milk, save where there was no option, was enhanced when it could be noted that this was one of the sources of later overweight. Too many mothers, freed from the natural constraints of breast supply and perhaps a bit guilty besides, poured too much cow's milk down their children's gullets, creating later problems with fat. Second, and here particularly when breastfeeding had occurred, the issue of weaning came in for much discussion. This was a second point, still in infancy, when patterns of overeating could develop, for children often were encouraged to compensate for the denial of the breast by eating too much of other foods. Even meat, that semisacred staple of French good eating, might be overdone for children, leading later to gout and hardening of the arteries, "provoking obesity" (this from a pamphlet of 1914). Many manuals, directed to parents or for teachers to spread in the schools as ideas of *puériculture* were expanded through the curriculum, offered calorie counters and standard growth charts to help parents know when to let up on their feeding efforts. Several commentators noted, in case parents had missed the point, that children's own appetites were very bad guides; it was scientific calculation that should underlie food supply. Parents should weigh their children regularly—once a week was recommended—again, to be sure that their bodies were neither too little nor too large.

Crucial in this voluminous literature—virtually a routine item—was the insistence on establishing regular meal times and sticking to them without food in the intervals. Most authorities found this desirable even in infancy, but it certainly counted after weaning had occurred. Children should have four meals: Breakfast, lunch, *goûter* (snack time), and dinner. These meals must be scheduled; any departure from routine was very bad for children. "One can avoid overfeeding by strictly regulating mealtimes" (Comité National de l'enfance 1908:45) was a standard theme, with the added injunction of no food between meals—"forbidding any food in the intervals except water (candy, pastry, bread, and so forth)." Some advice expanded from insistence on regular timing to other disciplinary comments: "The child should eat slowly and chew well. He should get used to eating alone, sitting down, at fixed times" (Comité National de l'enfance 1942:110).

A common pattern of advice developed, along with the insistence on regularity and control, that urged some reallocation of food among the four meals. This was particularly true from the interwar period onward as the diet ideas caught on and (with exceptions for the 1930s to some extent) the abundance of food increased. Breakfasts, it was argued, were often too skimpy; lunches were all right, though some school diets were scored on nutritional grounds; but the *goûter* was often too rich and too close to dinner. Here was where indulgent mothers erred, and the frequency of comment, while doubtless unable to reverse the tendency, surely helped limit the impulse. Some experts even wondered if the *goûter* should not be abolished so that children would be able to eat proper dinners (Lacapère 1982). Other targets included the pacifier and thumb-sucking (both bound to create weak, indulgent personalities) and even having young children eat with adults—a barrier to discipline and restricting appetites. Always, even in comments on overslender, fashion-conscious girls, advice writers urged the importance of careful discipline and control, lest children overeat (Champendal no date; Stearns 1997). "There are often *gourmands* whose appetites must be restrained and who must especially learn to eat slowly" (Kriesler 1975:172).

On the whole, cautions in *puériculture* about overeating increased during the 1920s and 1930s from turn-of-the-century literature. This obviously followed from the heightened medical and popular attention being given to slenderness, while furthering the movement as well. As *puériculture* yielded to pediatrics after World War II, and certainly by the 1970s, the connections between children's eating and adult obesity were more explicitly noted, as in the United States at the same point. Doctors also were more routinely invoked: If a child seemed headed for obesity, the doctor would adjust his or her diet "to satisfy hunger while avoiding excessive *embonpoint*" (Kriesler 1975:61). "Our children have more chance of suffering from food excess . . . than from insufficiency" (Lacapère 1982:31). Any obesity was dangerous: "Very obese adults were often fat babies" (Manciaux 1971:96). The state itself stepped in from 1970 onward by requiring regular weighing of children.

But the basic message was surprisingly persistent. Too much food was bad. Children must learn to discipline their appetites and eating habits, sitting for meals regularly, chewing carefully, expecting adult supervision (Kriesler 1975; Lacapère 1982; Manciaux 1971). In dealing with food, parents should "never yield to the caprices of the child" (Benjamin and Benjamin 1975:57). This was a very different conception of childhood eating from that prevalent in the United States during the same decades, stemming from a less indulgent picture of childhood generally. In addition to the contrast in the basic message, two American staples were simply missing. First, there was no great excitement about underfed children. Infants, yes—this was the target of much of the *puériculture* campaign. And, of course, the manuals urged against too much underweight. But there was no special excitement, and the underweight warnings were always balanced by the cautions, usually wordier and more detailed, against excess in the other direction. The symbolic resonance that children's underweight had in American culture was simply absent.

There was also little concern about fussy eaters, who have to be enticed lest they somehow starve themselves. This was, of course, related to the absence of excitement about undernutrition past infancy, but it dovetailed also with the larger disciplinary ideas. Most manuals simply did not bother dealing with the issue. The few that did simply told mothers to let time solve the problem. If a child wouldn't eat one day, starvation would bring him to the table the next, and a day without food was no big deal. The same technique should be applied to particular foods: If a child refused an item, he should be given the same thing the next time. "This is the best way to teach a child to eat everything." "If he doesn't like it, it is because you haven't made him accept it. Be firm, don't yield" (Champendal, no date:50). Even infants should not be coddled; parents must be careful not to respond to every cry with food. Granted there were some nervous babies, nervous but also "badly raised" *(mal élévés)* said the editorial aside, but they were really asking for extra attention, not food, and they should be kept in their place. Children should be taught to eat everything presented to them "in reasonable quantity"; personal whims and tastes need not be indulged. This maternal teaching "is a service she is rendering them for the rest of their lives" (ibid.).

An advice literature, even with surprisingly consistent themes, is not, of course, family reality. Though aimed at the lower classes—unlike the doctors' adult diet books of the interwar years, with their references to tailors and couturiers—it is not clear how many families could take the trouble of having young children eat separately, carefully monitored (Devraigne 1928). It is certainly unlikely that all actual parents could be as blasé about fussy eaters as the manuals suggested. Personality variables aside (and some individual parents were clearly more indulgent, or more convinced that plumpness was healthy, than others), there is some evidence that by the 1970s and 1980s, maternal efforts to make sure that children ate enough, especially at breakfast, stepped up. The reason, according to one student of manners, was not nutrition but guilt on the part of French mothers, now working full-time and worried that they were not taking proper care of their offspring. Nevertheless, the clarity of the recommendations, both during the heyday of *puériculture* and later amid contemporary pediatrics, provided little extra encouragement to overfeed children, particularly by indulgence between meals. The contrast with the United States remained striking (Marence 1992).

Furthermore, aside from some very recent claims that childhood eating patterns have been changing a bit, the evidence for French distinctiveness in fact, and not just in recommendation, is strong. The relative French aversion to snacking, compared to American proclivities, is well-known, established by comparative studies during the 1970s and 1980s and probably earlier. It is highly likely that the basis for this restraint rests in the patterns of child rearing, in other words, that the recommendations did coincide with parental practice. Certainly records from French boarding schools suggest restraint. Whether this resulted only from cost considerations (clearly a leading factor in the nineteenth century) or from explicit commitment to eating discipline cannot be determined and, in a sense, does not matter too much. The prestigious French military academy, Saint Cyr, for example, provided three hundred grams of meat per day to its upper-class student clientele during the late nineteenth and early twentieth centuries (not counting bone), less than two-thirds of what was available at its American counterpart, West Point. Fat and protein content in other schools where data are available were even more constrained at all grade levels: Primary schools offered one hundred grams of meat in the main meal; *lycées* (the elite secondary schools), one hundred to two hundred. Quantities changed little from 1850 to 1940. Desserts were only added to the principal school meals in the late nineteenth century, somewhat grudgingly and in restricted amounts. The French simply did not see childhood as a time for great latitude in the range and amounts of foods offered, and this regulatory approach has applied for many decades (Aron 1973).

EXPLAINING AMERICAN EXCEPTIONALISM

Arguing that the United States differs from Europe's historical patterns is a hallowed exercise. Typically, American exceptionalism highlights features of the nation's past viewed as preferable to the tradition-bound mistakes of the Old Countries. Frequently, American distinctiveness is more assumed than explained, as if the nation were indeed God's country, even by historians who would shun invocations of the divine hand in their arsenal of causes in other circumstances. In the case of children and food, the United States is an exception, at least compared with a major European counterpart, but in this case a largely undesirable one, as greater indulgence has led and continues to lead to measurably less salutary weight patterns at all stages of life. (For comparison of American and French weight patterns, see Stearns [1997].) The real question is how the distinctiveness can be explained.

Not surprisingly, a host of factors enter in. Any larger study of American weight patterns must emphasize the extraordinary diversity of relevant subcultures. African-Americans and Hispanic-Americans carry weights well above the national average, and the distinctions begin in childhood at least in part. This means that compared to a more conformist France, somewhat less culturally divided and more accustomed to centralized cultural cues, many American groups simply did not receive, ignored, or positively resisted messages about restraining children's appetites. Hispanic-Americans, for example, recoil at traditional WASP ideas that depriving a child of a meal might be appropriate punishment; children and adequate food are too closely intertwined for this. At the same time, subgroup differences merely exacerbate an otherwise unusual pattern, for the culture of indulging children's appetites predominated in a prescriptive literature written by and primarily for a white middle class (ibid.).

French doctors held a stronger hand than their American counterparts at least until after World War II. Their research base was superior well into the twentieth century. While more solid nutritional research came from Germany and Britain than from France, the French kept pace well, and were advantageously positioned to translate research findings into standard medical practice. The United States had its scholars in the field, notably Wilbur Atwater of Yale, but their work came a bit late by European standards. More important, American training created more diversity among doctors in reacting to new findings, at least until the science-oriented reformation of medical schools in the 1920s. The greater prominence of homeopathy in French medicine may have created a more receptive climate for standards emphasizing regulation of food intake. Certainly French doctors wrote much more voluminously on diet issues between 1900 and 1945, and played a greater role in popularization as well as scientific discussion; their American counterparts moved into the field more hesitantly, in some cases reflecting as well as furthering the older beliefs in plumpness as a sign of health. A symptom was the greater role of faddists in the early stages of American weight control culture, and faddists, like Horace Fletcher or Upton Sinclair, played mainly to an adult audience that could provide the immediate attention and, in some instances, commercial support. French doctors unquestionably picked up on childhood weight issues more rapidly than Americans, in part because of the research base, and their advice more quickly informed relevant popularizations. As we have seen, when American doctors did convert more systematically to a belief that children's eating must be controlled, after World War II, they encountered an audience already comfortable with an adult-child distinction that even the increasing eminence of medical opinion could not easily erase (Chittenden 1907; LeNoir 1909; Sobal 1995; Stearns 1997).

Simple accident played some role in the American pattern. Football gained popularity long before weight control was an issue. By the 1920s, the importance of football in boyhood life, and in adult attitudes toward boys, helped justify plumpness. France had no widely popular sport in which male heaviness could be a positive advantage. Dominant sports such as bicycling and soccer put a greater premium on slender muscularity—one source of the lesser tolerance for "stockiness" in male children. Military standards loomed larger in French male culture before World War II, and these encouraged boyhood discipline in eating (Beraud 1933).

Cultural differences for girls were less great, racial subcultures aside. But France had emphasized the importance of women's fashion earlier than the United States, and the nation continued to pride itself on esthetic criteria. Training girls to accept the eating habits that would make them beautiful, or at least prevent unnecessary ugliness, won even easier acceptance among the French as a result (Delbourg-Delphis 1982; Perrot 1987).

The principal causes of unusual American indulgence of children's eating, however, derive clearly from distinctive attitudes toward food and toward childhood itself. American plenty, from the colonial era onward, helped build national beliefs in the importance of abundant food in justifying the national experiment. Whatever the nation's inferiority in formal culture, at least it had triumphed over Europe in food supply. This general notion translated readily into family values: A successful family assured more than the necessary amounts of food, just as a successful mother demonstrated her adequacy by extensive cooking that would fulfill hearty children's appetites. A thin child, in this culture, was almost a reproach, as well as a potential carrier of ill health. France, in contrast, reflected a peasant tradition in which children's eating often had to be restrained simply to preserve adequate foodstuffs. Well into the twentieth century, autobiographies recount discipline administered to children seeking an unauthorized snack, simply because there might not be enough to go around. At the other extreme, the aristocratic delight in good eating and gourmet cuisine was accompanied by belief in discipline and restraint. The gourmet foods were inappropriate for children, who must first learn the art of good eating; nature would not suffice, just as quantity must not supplant quality. The very traditions of upper-class dining helped support the notion that children must be controlled and taught—not solaced by a groaning table (Audier 1994; Brillat-Savarin 1994; Cummings 1940; Root and de Rochemont 1976).

American beliefs in the importance of justification through abundant food clearly undergirded much of the otherwise odd battle against underweight in the early decades of the twentieth century. Middle-class parents, who in fact had no worries about food supply, resonated readily to news about ill-fed immigrant children or the woes of depression-starved families. Quite simply, underfeeding seemed to be a greater issue than it actually was because so much was invested in the idea of plenty. Articles about children's hunger, directed in fact to families far removed from the problem, struck a chord because food quantity was such a measure of prosperity and parental success. Immigrant parents picked up the message readily enough: They too liked to feed their children extensively as a demonstration that the decision to come to America led to familial success. By the same token, later in the twentieth century, Americans would be far more shocked by news accounts of anorexia nervosa than would their French counterparts. The disease was hardly welcome in France, but it offered less contradiction to accepted definitions of prosperity and to ideas that parental love and adequacy were symbolized by plentiful feeding.

The commitment to abundant food predated the twentieth century. It did not lead to extensive weight problems among children earlier, however, simply because children's physical labor and extensive walking kept weight at moderate levels. Records of youth-receiving institutions like West Point suggest no increase in weight during the nineteenth century. Here, despite different food beliefs, France and the United States were similar (Cuff 1993). By 1900, however, increased school time reduced children's physical activity, and here American food expectations were more likely to lead to problems than were French. Further, building on the same expectations, American commercial companies were quick to develop and advertise snack foods, with a children's market particularly in mind. Packaged crackers and cookies began to be widely disseminated from the 1880s onward. Initially advertised to parents as a vital protection against thinness and a guarantee of appropriate childish energy, the snacks quickly became available directly to children themselves, within range of their newly acquired allowances. France, with a slower development of packaged foods but above all with different beliefs about sheer quantity and frequency of eating, was less open to these childhood temptations— and remains less open to this day. To be sure, French prescriptive literature had to advise against snacks, which meant they constituted some problem; but in point of fact there was less to advise against (Root and de Rochemont 1976).

Children themselves were viewed distinctively in the United States, and along with the commitment to food abundance this set the seal on the lag in weight discipline. Beliefs about children were particularly incompatible with a moral tone that, again distinctively, early and durably, invested American dieting advice.

French visitors, including de Tocqueville (1981), commented on the unusual latitude granted to American children in the early nineteenth century. Democratic culture and frontier conditions, they surmised, created a less hierarchical family structure. Some historians have speculated that the need for children's work, in a labor-poor economy, plus the ready availability of the frontier as an escape hatch for discontented adolescents, prompted colonial American parents to conciliate their children more than was usual in Europe at the same time—though conditions varied, in part by religious affiliation. Indeed, Puritan emphasis on children's original sin, carried on in dire warnings in the schoolbooks of the early nineteenth century, suggests a different picture, in which discipline was essential. The result of these various factors—religious culture, the frontier, and the need for labor, was an ambivalent context for children in colonial America (Greven 1991).

Far more certain is the evolution of American middle-class attitudes toward children during the nineteenth century. Increased emphasis on home and family as refuge from the outside world promoted a growing belief in childish innocence. Reduction of birth rates created greater attachment to children, even in babyhood. Shifts in religious culture progressively downplayed ideas of original sin and the need for conventionally harsh discipline. Children, or at least middle-class children, were now seen as good, their habits pure. Concomitant emphasis on beneficent motherhood enhanced an environment in which correction of certain habits might seem unnecessary, indulgence of childish pleasures being part of a happy home life. By the late nineteenth century, the intensification of what one sociological historian has called the "pricelessness" of children (Zelizer 1987) was signaled by granting allowances, lavish birthday celebrations—and increasing openness to the production of food treats, such as candy bars, ice cream sundaes (1890s), and Eskimo pies (1920s) designed disproportionately for a children's market. Finally, a growing belief in the fragility of children—the need for parental guidance and support, given new knowledge of children's frequent fears and psychological dilemmas—could spur still further adult attention. Indeed, as we have seen, advice literature frequently recommended the use of food to help children compensate for other difficulties; to counter fear of the dark, for example, a candy treat might be placed in a room to motivate a child to venture in (Stearns 1994; Stearns and Haggerty 1989; Wells 1971; Wishy 1968).

Cultural trends in the valuation of children, in other words, emphasized growing latitude and indulgence at precisely the same moment as new weight control standards emerged for adults. The latter might logically have suggested new eating discipline—and indeed some medical advice moved in this direction as early as 1914—but the values attached to children won out, having prior roots in cultural change and a deeper embeddedness in family ideology.

Further, the particular moral quality of the American approach to weight control meshed uneasily with beliefs about children. In contrast to France, where health and esthetic considerations predominated, Americans early on looked to dieting as a moral demonstration, a sign of self-control amid the temptations of consumer affluence. This approach had some perils even for adults, who might be so overwhelmed by diet failures that they ate to compensate. But it might not readily apply at all to children who, for all their fragility, were still essential innocents, with no need to reduce food intake to demonstrate virtue.

One artifact of American weight morality was particularly counterproductive. Because weight was an issue of character as well as health, in the American context, doctors and popularizers alike found it difficult to refrain from editorial comments about offenders against slenderness. Excoriating the idleness and mental disorders of fat women might or might not be useful (though French doctors, aware of American example, urged the contrary), but applied to children it offended widely held values. Thus doctors who blithely asserted that fat children and their families should be evaluated for emotional problems risked serious, if usually silent, opposition. How, given the nation's cultural history, could parents be at fault for simply feeding children abundantly? How could innocent plump children, already feeling the pressure of falling below physical standards, be subjected to further blame? As the doctors who disseminated these comments were among those who noted frequent parental denial, the vicious circle was complete (Stearns 1997).

France as a historical control case is clearly different. The French never emphasized original sin as intensely as American Puritans did. As their culture secularized and the birth rate dropped, some comparable celebration of home and family took hold in the nineteenth century. But there was no American-like emphasis on children's innocence—the cultural pendulum did not move so dramatically. Older ideas about firm discipline maintained considerable hold, which made it natural to persist in regulating children's eating and easy to respond to new advice about restricting intake. Children's impulses were not naturally good. Their emotional value was not so transcendent as to require new forms of indulgence. Indeed, children would be most valued when they looked good and behaved themselves—which meant making sure they ate properly and remained slender.

Despite some concerns that the French hold on children was relaxing a bit, amid the guilt and competing demands on adult attention associated with women's new work roles, clearly a basic disparity in approaches to children's eating persists in the late twentieth century. American children walk less (and are driven more) than their French counterparts; they face less discipline over television viewing habits; and they continue to eat more, on average. American fascination with the importance of children's self-esteem, a new expression of national cultural values that began to take hold in the 1970s, further diminished the ability to criticize overweight (Holt et al. 1953). In ways simply unimagined in France, American parents might easily prefer to praise their heavy child, burdened already with the knowledge he or she was not measuring up to conventional beauty standards, than to venture enough comment to help him or her bring daily eating under control (Ambrose and Strickland 1985; Baumeister 1993).

CONCLUSION

For a number of reasons, American cultural values facilitated weight problems among many children in the twentieth century, once affluence and sedentary school roles altered the physical demands placed on childhood. Expert pressure lagged, even as it placed new constraints on adults. Only by the 1970s did popularized advice consistently point to the need to keep children's eating under control—and by then, alternative values were deeply entrenched in many sectors of the American population (Faegre et al. 1958; Gersh 1971; Gruenberg 1958; Mack 1950; Nelson 1969). Distinctive expectations about food had merged with a new and in many ways admirable set of values applied to children—with results that made the imposition of disciplined eating difficult.

The impact of distinctive patterns of children's eating has often been discussed. A large number of American children are overweight. American adults, who put on between one and two extra pounds on average (height held constant) between the 1940s and the 1970s, contrasted with the French, who lost about a pound during the same period and whose overall obesity rates are well under half of those in the United States (Klein 1994; Kuczmarski et al. 1994; Lew 1989; Williamson 1953; Statistical Bulletin of the Metropolitan Life Insurance Company 1966). While a number of factors account for this difference, the cumulative results of childhood eating, ramifying into different degrees of reliance on snacks and different food totals even at regular meals, play the leading role. A further consequence goes beyond weight itself: Because so many Americans have to fight the burdens of childhood eating patterns and fat cells through adulthood, they are forced to think more about dieting than their French counterparts. They worry more and have less confidence in their bodies (Stearns 1997).

While American children and adults both seem to have accelerated their weight gains in the past decades (again, in contrast to the French, who remain stable), the cultural underpinnings of the gap between actual childhood eating and the standards most desirable for health go back much farther in time. They reflect, as we have seen, some important facets of American beliefs about eating, children, and family. No small part of American daily life and anxiety derives from the cultural countercurrents that shielded children from some of the obvious consequences of new findings about food consumption and from adult commitments, at least in principle, to rigorous standards of slenderness.

The rootedness of the cultural construction of children's eating has significant implications, beyond the illustration of the power of values and complexities. It serves, first, to explain the obvious: Mere invocations of doctors' authority and health goals do not suffice for change. American parents clearly agree with the idea of promoting their children's physical well-being, but they balk at exercising the control necessary to alter eating patterns. As children become more independent consumers, ready to attack the snack counters and vending machines, difficulties obviously increase. Campaigns to change behavior might of course win out over a longer term, but a better bet is to reevaluate and enhance the kinds of appeals being offered, so that the imagery attached to young children and the rewards attached to abundant food are more directly addressed. At the same time, the very importance of culture in determining the American patterns—illustrated by the chronology of the idealization of childhood and the contrast with French developments—indicates the possibility of change. Part of the American pattern, after all, results from accidents of timing—the arrival of new weight standards and potentials for weight gain right at the point when adult perceptions of the young, once held in check as inherent sinners, had shifted to make children seem most deserving of indulgence. What once changed—in this case, reactions to childish impulse and definitions of appropriate discipline—can change again. The further contribution of this particular historical finding is simply to add that the process will be difficult because the beliefs involved have otherwise seemed so serviceable.

REFERENCES

Addington, B. 1927. *Your Growing Child*. New York: Funk and Wagnalls.

Ambrose, A., and C. E. Strickland. 1985. "The Baby Boom, Prosperity, and the Changing Worlds of Children, 1945–1963." Pp. 533–85 in *American Childhood*, edited by J. Hawes and N. Hiner. Westport, CT: Greenwood.

Anderson, C. 1931. *Cultivating the Child's Appetite*. New York: Macmillan.

Aron, J. 1973. *Le Mangeur du XIXe siècle*. Paris: Presses Universitaires.

Ashmore, J. 1906. "Side-Talks with Girls." *Ladies Home Journal*, December, p. 345.

Audier, A. 1994. *Le Temps écoute: Comme on Glane le mémoire Paysanne*. Paris: Presses Universitaires.

Banner, L. 1984. *American Beauty*. Chicago, IL: University of Chicago Press.

Baumeister, R. (ed.). 1993. *Self Esteem: The Puzzle of Low Self-Regard*. New York: Plenum.

Benjamin, L. 1945. "Teen-Age Reducing." *Ladies Home Journal*, April, p. 140.

Benjamin, S., and R. Benjamin. 1975. "Le Jeune enfant et ses besoins fondamentaux." Paris: Caisse Nationale des Allocations Familiales, Fondation Pour la Recherche Sociale.

Beraud, H. 1933. *La Martyre de l'obèse*. Paris: Payot.

Bray, A. 1995. "Measurement of Body Composition: An Improving Art." *Obesity Research* 3:291–93.

Brillat-Savarin, J. 1994. *The Physiology of Taste, or Meditations on Transcendental Gastronomy*. San Francisco, CA: Arion.

Champendal, Dr. No date. *Le Petit Manuel des Mères*. Paris: Flammarion.

Child Study Association of America. 1947. *Parents' Questions*. New York: Author.

Chittenden, R. 1907. *The Nutrition of Man*. New York: F. A. Stokes.

Comité National de l'enfance. 1908. *Cours de puériculture en dix leçons*. Paris: Author.

———. 1936. *L'Alimentation de l'enfant à l'adulte*. Paris: Author.

———. 1942. *Problèmes et Aspects de la Puériculture Moderne*. Paris: Author.

Crossley, S. 1931. "When a Child Won't Eat." *Parents' Magazine*, April, p. 25.

Cuff, T. 1993. "The Body Mass Index Values of Mid Nineteenth-Century West Point Cadets." *Historical Methods* 26:171–81.

Cummings, R. 1940. *The American and His Food*. Chicago, IL: University of Chicago Press.

Delbourg-Delphis, M. 1982. *Le Chic et le Look: Histoire de la Mode Féminine et des Moeurs, de 1890 à nos jours*. Paris: Presses Universitaires.

Devraigne, L. 1928. *Vingt-cinq ans de puériculture et d'hygiène sociale*. Paris: Payot.

Dunbar, H. 1949. *Your Child's Mind and Body*. New York: Vintage.

Emerson, W. 1921. "The Overweight Child." *Women's Home Companion*, March, p. 31.

Faegre, M., J. Anderson, and D. Harris. 1958. *Child Care Training*. Minneapolis: University of Minnesota Press.

Farren, M. 1934. "Between Meals." *Nation's Schools* January, p. 256.

Fields, J. 1995. "Fighting the Corsetless Evil: Cultural Hegemony and the Corset Panic of 1921." Paper presented to the Organization of American Historians, Chicago.

Gay, L. 1936. "Feeding the Underweight Child." *Parents' Magazine*, March, p. 40.

Gersh, M. 1971. "A Fitness Program for Overweight Teen-Agers." *Parents' Magazine*, August, p. 50.

Granger, M. 1930. "Bigger and Better Children." *Parents' Magazine*, March, p. 10.

Greven, P. 1991. *Spare the Child: The Religious Roots of Punishment and the Psychological Impact of Physical Abuse*. New York: Random House.

Gruenberg, S. 1958. *The Parents' Guide to Everyday Problems of Boys and Girls*. New York: Random House.

Holt, E. 1956. "The Reluctant Eater." *Good Housekeeping*, November, p. 34.

Holt, E., R. McIntosh, and H. L. Barnett. 1953. *Pediatrics*. New York: Appleton-Century-Crofts.

Kemp, J. 1930. "When a Child Is Thin." *Good Housekeeping*, April, p. 108.

Kenyon, J. H. 1933. "The Thin Child." *Good Housekeeping*, October, p. 98.

Klein, R. 1994. "Big Country: The Roots of American Obesity." *New Republic*, September, p. 32.

Kriesler, L. 1975. *Guide de la jeune mère*. Paris: E.S.F.

Kuczmarski, R. J., K. M. Flegal, S. M. Campbell, and C. L. Johnson. 1994. "Increasing Prevalence of Overweight among U.S. Adults: The National Health and Nutrition Examination Surveys, 1960–1991." *Journal of the American Medical Association* 272:205–11.

Lacapère, S. 1982. *Le Métier des parents*. Paris: Programme 7. Diffusé par les Presses Universitaires de France.

Laurier, D., M. Guiguet, N. P. Chau, J. A. Wells, and A. Valleron. 1992. "Prevalence of Obesity: A Comparative Survey in France, the United Kingdom, and the United States." *International Journal of Obesity* 16:563–72.

LeNoir. 1909. *L'Obésité et son Traitement*. Paris: Ecole le Médicine.

Lew, E. 1989. "Mortality and Weight: Insured Lives and the American Cancer Society Studies." *Annals of Internal Medicine* 103:1024–29.

Mack, P. 1950. "Do Children Need Sweets?" *Parents' Magazine*, March, p. 51.

Manciaux, M. 1971. *Abrégé de Pédiatrie Préventive et Sociale*. Paris: Flammarion.

Marence, C. 1992. *Manières de Tables, Modèles de Moeures, 17 ème-20ème Siècle*. Paris: Presses Universitaires.

Nelson, W. 1969. *Textbook of Pediatrics*. Philadelphia, PA: Saunders.

Patten, S. 1897. *Over-Nutrition and Its Social Consequences*. Philadelphia, PA: American Academy of Political and Social Science.

Perrot, P. 1987. *Le Travail des apparences, ou les Transformations du corps féminin XVIIIe–XIXe siécles*. Paris: Presses Universitaires.

Phillips, D. 1900. "Susan Lenox: Her Fall and Rise." No place, no date included.

Richardson, F. 1930. "Your Underweight Child?" *Good Housekeeping*, January, p. 34.

Root, W., and R. de Rochemont. 1976. *Eating Well in America*. New York: Morrow.

Rorer, S. T. 1906. "Dietetic Sins and Their Penalties." *Ladies Home Journal*, January, p. 42.

Rose, M. 1955. *Feeding the Family*. New York: Macmillan.

Sobal, J. 1995. "The Medicalization and Demedicalization of Obesity." Pp. 67–90 in *Eating Agendas: Food and Nutrition as Social Problems*, edited by D. Maurer and J. Sobal. Hawthorne, NY: Aldine de Gruyter.

Spock, B., and M. E. Lowenberg. 1955. *Feeding Your Child*. New York: Pocket Books.

Statistical Bulletin of the Metropolitan Life Insurance Company. 1966. "Trends in Average Weights and Heights of Men: An Insurance Experience." 47:1–3.

———. 1970. "Trends in Average Weights and Heights of Men: An Insurance Experience." 51:6–7.

Stearns, P. 1994. *American Cool: Constructing a Twentieth-Century Emotional Style*. New York: New York University Press.

———. 1997. *Fat History: Bodies and Beauty in the Modern West*. New York: New York University Press.

Stearns, P., and T. Haggerty. 1989. "The Role of Fear: Transitions in American Emotional Standards for Children, 1850–1950." *American Historical Review* 96: 63–94.

Strauss, P. 1901. *Dépopulation et puériculture*. Paris: E. Fasquelle.

Summerville, A. 1916. *Why Be Fat?* New York: Frederick A. Stolks.

Taylor, C. 1949. "Boys Eat Too Much, or Do They?" *Parents' Magazine*, August, p. 68.

Tocqueville, A. 1981. *Democracy in America*. New York: Scribner.

Walker, E. 1904–5. "Pretty Girl Papers." *Ladies Home Journal*. June 1904, January 1905.

Way, K. 1995. "Never Too Rich . . . or Too Thin: The Role of Stigma in the Social Construction of Anorexia Nervosa." Pp. 91–116 in *Eating Agendas: Food and Nutrition as Social Problems*, edited by D. Maurer and J. Sobal. Hawthorne, NY: Aldine de Gruyter.

Wells, R. 1971. "Family Size and Fertility Control in Eighteenth-Century America: A Study of Quaker Families." *Population Studies* 25:73–82.

Williamson, D. 1953. "Descriptive Epidemiology of Body Weight and Weight Change in U.S. Adults." *Annals of Internal Medicine* 646–49.

Wishnik, S. 1935. *Feeding Your Child*. Garden City, NY: Doubleday.

Wishy, B. 1968. *The Child and the Republic: The Dawn of Modern Child Nurture*. Philadelphia: University of Pennsylvania Press.

Zelizer, V. 1987. *Pricing the Priceless Child*. New York: Basic Books.

3

Fat Boys and Goody Girls
Hilde Bruch's Work on Eating Disorders and the American Anxiety about Democracy, 1930–1960

PAULA SAUKKO

This chapter examines a contradiction. It is often said that the stigmatization of fatness has led to an epidemic of anorexia. However, commonsense and medical notions about overweight and anorexic people are strikingly similar: Both are understood to be weak and insufficiently autonomous or enslaved by modern lures such as media images or junk food. I argue that theories of obesity and anorexia—like many other theories of deviant behavior—tell more about the norms of our times, which idealize individual independence and strength, than about eating. These norms are particularly clearly articulated in the work of Hilde Bruch, the pioneer researcher on eating disorders, who is the focus of this analysis.[1]

My analysis of Bruch's work is constructionist, or to use Foucault's (1984a) term, "genealogical." This means I do not evaluate whether Bruch's theories are "right" or "wrong"; rather, I examine how her definitions of obesity and anorexia are products of their time. I want to investigate the historical contingency of Bruch's theories for two reasons. First, I want to problematize our ideas about "disordered" eating, ideas that often lead to personal agony. Because theories about eating disorders are tied not only to personal problems but also to larger historical developments, my second goal is to examine how these theories reflect and reinforce complex historical, social, and political projects.

I have chosen to examine Bruch's work because her pioneering research, her best-selling popular books, and her participation in psychiatric forums and the media have left an indelible mark on both the clinical definitions and the popular perceptions about people who are perceived to be either too fat or too thin. What makes Bruch's work particularly interesting is that she studied both obesity and anorexia, thereby highlighting the vexing connections between the definitions of the two conditions. Bruch's long career, which spanned from the thirties to the seventies, also provides a good opportunity to examine how changing historical conditions play into the notions of fatness and thinness.

To examine the historical context of Bruch's work, I will locate it within developments in world history, in the history of psychiatry, and in her personal biography. I will analyze Bruch's work against the backdrop of U.S. history from postdepression time to the cold war period. I will also situate her writing within the shifting trends in psychiatry from the thirties, when the field was still marked by hereditary theories of mental illness with their racist undertones, until the postwar psychoanalytic boom. I also discuss how Bruch's personal history as a German-Jewish exile shaped her perceptions of her patients. This historical analysis is based on Bruch's published works as well as on her reference material, correspondence, and patient files archived in the Texas Medical Center Library.[2]

The following analysis is divided into two sections. The first section examines Bruch's early research on obesity, which she conducted using poor immigrant children in New York City in the thirties and forties. The second part focuses on the postwar period, when Bruch's clientele became predominantly middle-class and her focus shifted to anorexia. I argue that in both periods Bruch's work was guided by historical anxieties about "freedom" and "democracy." The fat immigrant boys[3] Bruch studied in the postdepression era became symbols of the "authoritarian" and "backward" habits of their foreign families. The docile, middle-class anorexic girls Bruch treated later became reflections of the cold war preoccupation with the seeding of social conformism or communism in the new suburbia. Finally, I will discuss the potentially suffocating effects of making a body weight that deviates from the contemporary norm stand for a failure to meet the contemporary ideal social persona. This leads, for example, to the paradox that the anorexic who starves to escape the negative characteristics associated with fatness has the very same qualities projected upon her. These projected qualities fuel her anxiety about never being "right." Perhaps these projections fuel the anxiety of a nation.

FAT IMMIGRANT CHILDREN AND AUTHORITARIAN CHILD-REARING

Early Theories of Obesity: Weak Morals, Races, and Metabolism

Bruch began her work on eating disorders in the mid-1930s, soon after she arrived in the United States.[4] She was working at the Babies' Hospital in New York City and was asked to establish an endocrine clinic for fat children. By the 1930s heaviness, or "obesity," was firmly established as a medical and esthetic problem.[5] The idea of an endocrine clinic stemmed from the assumption that fatness was caused by slow metabolism. Other influential theories of obesity of the time—against and through which Bruch defined her ideas—traced it to a person's hereditary physical and mental "constitution" or lack of moral strength.

The moral theory of obesity saw it as a simple sign of gluttony. It depicted the fat as jolly, round hedonists devouring rich foods. An illuminating although quite late example of this theory is an ad from the early fifties for the diet pill Dexedrin.[6] It has two pictures: One of a large happily smiling woman surrounded by rich desserts and another one of a slim, sullen woman surrounded by a pile of dirty dishes, a cleaning bucket, and a baby. The ad states that Dexedrin works both as an appetite suppressant (referring to the fat woman) and as an antidepressant (referring to the overworked housewife). The juxtaposition of a happy fat woman and a depressed slim one reveals the historicity of the moral theory of obesity. Because contemporary readers are accustomed instead to understanding the obese as being sullen and depressed, the ad does not make immediate sense to us.

The early twentieth century hereditary theory of obesity was closely linked to the many speculations about the connections between body shape, personality, and intellectual endowment (e.g., Sheldon 1940, 1942). These theories often articulated racist ideas about how certain body structures corresponded with intelligence levels or particular behaviors, such as insanity or criminality. The most devastating outcome of these eugenistic ideas was the Nazi Holocaust. In the United States, speculation about body shape and character was often related to the anxiety caused by new immigrants from Southern and Eastern Europe, who were feared to be bringing bad genes to the American stock. The government started to screen immigrants according to their "appearance," to test their intelligence at the border, and later to establish stricter immigration laws (Jimenez 1993; Kraut 1994).

Not surprisingly then, obesity and the accompanying notions of a soft or "slack" personality were often associated with the new immigrant groups, such as Italians and Jews (e.g., Preble 1915). Sometimes scholars went quite far to establish a connection between a "lower" race and obesity. Angel (1949), for example, found to his surprise that the obese women he studied came from "old" American families. Yet, Angel speculated that their body shape and the higher than average frequency of German, Irish, and Italian Catholic backgrounds indicated that they represented the "alpine" and other "rugged" stocks of Europeans, who were "'survivors' of Upper Paleolithic" populations that evolved during the last glacial

period. Only a few of these women, according to Angel (1949:442–43), represented the non-Alpine, "long-headed" types that came to Europe later
and brought "farming and urban civilization" to the continent. Thus,
Angel went all the way to the Paleolithic period to establish a connection
between a robust body shape and lack of civilization.

Bruch originally followed the endocrinological theory of obesity, which
understood obesity to be caused by a slow metabolism. It was thought
that the metabolism could be accelerated by the then popular glandular
injections. Endocrinologists often diagnosed young chubby boys with
"Froehlich's syndrome," a supposed pituitary dysfunction, understood to
cause obesity, genital underdevelopment, and overall effeminate and
infantile appearance. However, the different theories were often entangled. Endocrinology was, for instance, sometimes mixed with constitutional theories to support racist and other stereotypes. An example of this
is Garrison's speculation about the metabolic origin of the "generic sexuality" of the "negroes" or the characteristic "frigidity" or "flabbiness" of
the obese (1922:70–71).

It was against this background that Bruch initiated her study of one
hundred obese two- to thirteen-year-old children in her new clinic.[7] Half
were boys and the other half were girls. As the hospital was located in
New York City and was a product of the Progressive era's public health
movement against infant mortality, the children came from relatively poor
families. The theories making connections between race and obesity were
of particular importance as most of the children came from immigrant
families of East European Jewish and to a lesser extent Italian and Irish origin (Bruch 1939a).

Bruch set out to measure the metabolism of the children, but her case
notes[8] also reflect the influence of constitutional notions of obesity. Bruch
carefully recorded the nationality and religion of the children's parents.
Besides measuring height and weight, she also noted the form of the
children's skulls, their eyes, face, hair, genitals, and general appearance.
In some cases, Bruch recorded peculiar features such as "heavy jaw"
or "coarse hair" associated with the different constitutional/racial/
endocrinological types, but she paid closest attention to the distribution of
fat within the body, as glandular disorders were understood to cause the
accumulation of fat in extraordinary places. Both IQ and the Rorschach or
ink blot tests were used to measure any abnormalities in the children's
intelligence and personality.

Although Bruch never denied the impact of heredity or metabolism on
obesity, her early studies concluded that their role was overemphasized or
misfocused. In a series of famous articles, she refuted Froehlich's syndrome and associated theories, arguing that the children's physical or genital development was not retarded (Bruch 1939a). She also argued that the

children's metabolism was normal; they simply ate too large quantities of food and were unusually inactive (Bruch 1939b). On the contrary, Bruch indicated that there seemed to be "something wrong" with the children's interaction with their mothers.

Neurotic Mothers and Claustrophobic Immigrant Quarters

After her initial studies in the thirties, Bruch became one of the pioneers who turned the attention away from constitutional, and often racist, theories of obesity and toward theories focusing on family interaction and lifestyle. As a Jew who had fled the Nazi Holocaust, it would have been difficult for Bruch to explain the obesity of Jewish children by their physical or racial constitution. Personal issues aside, Bruch's work also belonged to the wartime trend in American psychiatry away from hereditary and racial theories toward hygienic explanations that stressed the importance of environmental factors in producing social, mental, or physical deviance. This new trend criticized the harsh measures of deportation and sterilization, which were often supported by the eugenistically oriented scholarship to deal with the deviance they understood to be genetically, and thus incurably, flawed. Instead the new scholars believed in the uplifting power of education, as did the early asylum and charity activists (e.g., Grob 1984).

In her exploration of the family constellation of the obese children, Bruch noted that the families were poor.[9] They lived in small and crowded apartments, often with grandparents, which Bruch thought explained the unusual inactivity of the children as there was little room to play. Bruch also remarked that the families spent a "disproportionate" amount of their money on food and did not provide their children adequate clothing or "tools and equipment for play and athletics" (Bruch and Touraine 1940:153). Describing the parents, she noted that the fathers were "weak," lacking in "ambition" and "initiative" and unable to provide for the family (ibid.:154–55). Bruch's main focus was on the mothers, though. She observed that they had fewer children than the average, had often had several abortions, and had not wanted the obese child. The observations she made most often were about the mothers' "nervous system"; the women were described as, for example, "quiet," "upset," "unstable and impulsive," or "talkative and excitable." In the published text, they were described as "self-pitying women" who had been frustrated in their dreams of a "life of ease and luxury" (ibid.:158) in the United States and who projected their own bitterness and insecurity on the children. These women beat their children, and yet they overprotected them and stuffed them with food to pacify them and to assuage their own guilt. The resulting children were clinging, flaccid, and they ate enormously. The contempt toward the families in Bruch's depiction of them is captured in the following:

> The [child's] father is [himself] the youngest of five children. "He is the unsuccessful one of my children," says his mother, who resents the presence of his family in her overcrowded apartment. The mother . . . avoids discussion of her early life except to recount her adolescent popularity. "I never bothered with my family, I was the one having a good time." But at 42 years she displays a strong tie to her mother, which supersedes all other personal relationships. She is an immature and unreliable person who covers up real issues and facts in her life, and refuses to face realities, just as she blondines her hair and covers her wrinkles with gaudy make-up. (ibid.)

The quote above and Bruch's work as a whole manifest that, although she stressed the importance of the environment in causing obesity, her understanding of it was fairly narrow. Even as Bruch observed the families' arduous living conditions, she focused her attention on the mothers' attitudes and comportment. For example, although one interpretation of the mothers' frequent abortions and reluctance to have children could be that the immigrant women were desperately attempting to curtail their family sizes, Bruch observes this in terms of the psychological damage done to the "unwanted" obese child. These analyses and Bruch's judgmental remarks about the frivolity of the immigrants—manifested in her comments about their lack of industriousness, dreams of ease and luxury, and even their use of cosmetics—blamed the family's difficult situation and the child's obesity on the parents' lack of moral stamina. In other words, Bruch bypassed the social and economic hardships facing the immigrants in postdepression New York City.

Despite these moralizing tones, Bruch did not underwrite the moral explanation of obesity. On the contrary, she criticized the physicians and the general public for treating the fat with "unmitigated scorn," which she argued only makes them more "miserable" (Bruch 1957:36–38). Thus, Bruch represented the "therapeutic" approach. This approach, which had been typical of earlier charity- and voluntary-based social engineering enterprises, argued against the moral discourse stressing punishment and "individual responsibility" in dealing with deviance. The therapeutic stance defined the fat persons not as immoral, but as "sick"; it stressed the deviants' limited ability to perceive and pursue other modes of living and their need for care and help in doing so. Yet, although the therapeutic rhetoric and practice was more humane, it still shared with the moralizing stance the pursuit to reform the people seen as deviant and to make them fit the standard norm. These norms were defined by the historical moment and corroborated by newly invented statistical methods such as weight charts, personality tests, and intelligence tests (e.g., Miller and O'Leary 1987; Polsky 1991).

In conclusion, Bruch's psychological theory of obesity belongs to the larger body of works that marked a watershed in professions dealing with deviance. Perspectives were changing away from fatalistic hereditary and harshly judgmental moral perspectives toward new therapeutic or neohygienist approaches; yet all these views share the project of measuring and judging people against a certain norm (Rose 1985:85–86). For Bruch, the norm was not merely a certain weight: her comments on the immigrant families' home and family size, their consumption patterns, their manners, and their ways of raising children entangled body weight in a broad normative agenda for everyday life. The white middle-class family ideal, which demanded "a carefree, child-centered outlook—with relaxed methods of child discipline, separate rooms for each child, and educational toys and music lessons" (Mintz and Kellogg 1988:187), reached its apex in the fifties. In short, Bruch's agenda interpreted the immigrant families' problems as resulting from their inability to live up to that ideal.

Thus, although Bruch's work differs from the racist and violent agenda of the eugenists, it also echoes their fear that the new immigrants will erode the American social and moral order. Her critique of authoritarianism not only reflected the national anxiety about immigrants, but also fit with U.S. foreign policy at a moment when the country was entering the war against the continental fascist and Nazi countries. Furthermore, the critique of authoritarianism was also consonant with the American psychiatry's turning toward Freudianism and its antirepressive agenda as well as Bruch's own traumatic experiences as a Jew in the Germany of the 1930s. Thus Bruch's theory of obesity articulated the international, national, psychiatric, and personal historical agendas of the time, projecting them onto the immigrant children, who became symbols of the backwardness, the authoritarianism, and the adherence to tradition, to mothers, and to leaders associated with their poor, foreign-born families. In short, the fat children became the antithesis of American freedom and democracy.

THE COMPLIANT GIRLS AND THE COLD WAR
FEAR OF CONFORMITY

The Authoritarian Personality and Infant Feeding

During World War II, Bruch pursued her interest in family dynamics by specializing in psychiatry and underwent psychoanalysis with fellow

German-Jewish exile Frieda Fromm-Reichmann. Bruch soon established herself as an expert in child psychiatry and eating problems, and her clientele began to include more middle-class private patients, who were at first mostly young obese women and later young anorexic women. Bruch's turn to psychoanalysis paralleled a general interest in Freud in American psychiatry after the war. The war traumas afflicting previously healthy young men undermined intrinsic theories of mental illness and aroused the young psychiatrist's interest in the role of (childhood) traumas in forming the personality, an interest that also fit and reinforced the postwar family-centered atmosphere (Grob 1991).[10]

Bruch's new orientation and change of clientele made her gear her critique toward mainstream American child-rearing. This refocus is perhaps best illustrated by the clash between Bruch and the famous anthropologist Margaret Mead over Bruch's child care manual *Don't Be Afraid of Your Child*, published in 1952. In the book Bruch critiqued the common pop-psychological advice that led to a situation in which:

> [a]n unrelieved picture of model parental behavior, a contrived image of artificial perfection and happiness, is held up before parents who try valiantly to reach the ever receding ideal of "good parenthood," like dogs racing after a mechanical rabbit. (1952:723)

In a book review, Mead (1954:427) attacked Bruch for imposing the German ideal of "natural" child-rearing on American mothers, who were adopting more liberal ideas to train their children. Bruch was infuriated by the review, but nevertheless, the exchange exemplifies how she had gravitated toward the critical stance taken regarding American ways, which was common to many exiled European intellectuals, particularly the Marxists of the Frankfurt school. The echoes of the Frankfurt school in Bruch's work were no mere coincidence either: One of the school's early thinkers, Erich Fromm, was the ex-husband and collaborator of Bruch's analyst and teacher, Frieda Fromm-Reichmann.

Once again, Bruch turned her attention to parenting when assessing the troubles of her obese and anorexic middle-class patients, except that the setup and historical situation this time was slightly different.[11] Although anorexia had been "discovered" in the nineteenth century (see Brumberg 1988), it was a relatively rare and undefined disorder after the war. Some early doctors thought the refusal to eat was a manifestation of female capriciousness. Others understood anorexia to have endocrinological roots, and the early psychoanalysts interpreted it in terms of fear and fantasy of oral impregnation. Bruch discarded the impregnation theory as "mere analogy" (Bruch 1961a). Again, Bruch focused her psychoanalytic interest on the mothers.

The theory of eating disorders that Bruch formulated in the fifties borrowed Erich Fromm's ([1941] 1965) idea that egotism had its roots in lack of self-love. Fromm argued that this modern lack of trust in oneself resulted from people's freedom from tradition and their enslavement by capitalism, which caused people to relentlessly compete with each other and to fear losing their positions. This insecurity made people greedy, but at the same time people desperately tried to please everyone in order to get attention and affection, and the result was the increasing social conformism and authoritarianism in the whole society (ibid.:134–39). Frieda Fromm-Reichmann (1940) modified Fromm's theory and interpreted the person's lack of self-love as resulting from a domineering mother who has made the child doubt herself. Bruch (1961b) adapted Fromm-Reichmann's version of the theory and argued that eating disorders had their origin in early feeding experiences.[12] She argued that if the mother responds inappropriately to the child's hunger, for example, overstuffing the infant to silence her, the child becomes incapable of recognizing her true needs and to act in a self-directed manner (ibid.:470–71). This makes the obese and anorexic dependent and compliant, incapable of acting autonomously. The obese person reacts to this lack of self-direction by overstuffing herself to fulfill her never appropriately met needs, whereas the anorexic refuses the imposed food as a final but abortive attempt to assert her independence (Bruch 1973).

One could say that just as Bruch shifted the focus from the immigrant children's harsh living conditions to their mothers' attitudes, she reduced Fromm's critique of the psychological repercussions of the exploitative and competitive contemporary society to troubled mother-child interaction. In her therapeutic practice as well as in her writing, this meant dwelling intensively on the patient's interaction with the mother and to a lesser extent on the interaction with other family members.

Even though Bruch's theory of eating disorders tended to depend upon family interaction, it still echoed Fromm's original political agenda. The middle-class family and its central character, the mother, were a politically loaded subject in the cold war period. On one hand, the newly affluent "ranch house and refrigerator" family with its homemaker mother was used as a proof of the superiority of the American system of morals, politics, and economics. On the other hand, the suburban home became a source of cultural agony, and amidst early TV dramas embracing family values such as *Father Knows Best* there were movies such as the James Dean film *Rebel without a Cause*, which depicted the middle-class home as a loveless place reigned by passive-aggressive mothers devouring their children. The suburbs, with their "box" houses penetrated by mass products and culture, were also feared to breed a dangerous social conformism, a fascism or communism of sorts (e.g., Skolnick 1991:49–74; Susman 1989).

Thus, Bruch's critique of overpowering and frustrated mothers running like mechanical rabbits after the latest child-rearing fad was essentially the same as contemporary critiques of the suburban household as "a broken home, consisting of a father who appears as an overnight guest, a put-upon housewife with too much to do, and children necessarily brought up in a kind of communism" (Donaldson 1969:119). Just like Bruch's portrait of fat immigrant children a couple of decades earlier, her depiction of the anorexic family reflects a central political anxiety of the historical moment. While during the postdepression era the locus of her critique was the newly arrived Eastern European immigrant family that was not able to overcome its traditions and poverty, during the cold war the source of anxiety was the white middle-class suburb. Both of these theories share a criticism of "antifree" or authoritarian cultural traits.

The Anorexic as Cultural Flab: On Dependence, Abundance, and Femininity

Bruch's theory of anorexia developed in the late fifties and sixties and repeated later in her landmark book on eating disorders (Bruch 1973) and in her best-selling popular booklet on anorexia (Bruch 1978) was founded on central social agendas in cold war America. Her portrait of the anorexic as a too docile girl from an affluent family, vulnerable to peer pressure and media messages, resonated with the postwar anxieties about suburban conformity degenerating the American character, the deleterious effects of unprecedented wealth, and mass propaganda.

Bruch's description of the anorexic as a woman characterized by "cleanliness, no rough play or destructive behavior and no disobedience or talking back," who constantly worries about "not being good enough, not living up to 'expectations'" (ibid.:43) resembles the many scholarly and popular discussions in the fifties about the deterioration of the American character and the rise of the "authoritarian" (Fromm [1941] 1965; Adorno, Frenkel- Brunswik, Levinson, and Stanford [1950] 1969) or "other-directed" (Riesman [1950] 1976) personality. Bruch also explicitly linked unhealthy behavior with contemporary American culture, as exemplified in her account of her response to a reporter who asked, "What accounts for the widespread neurosis amongst our children?"

> My spontaneous answer was brief: "The pursuit of happiness and the compulsion to be popular." The interviewer was amazed, even shocked. I was myself surprised but find this brief, pragmatic statement expresses my feeling on the matter even though it needs elaboration. Actually, it is not the *pursuit of happiness* that makes for discontent and neurosis but the way this concept has been transformed into a *demand for happiness,* and the shame of having it known that one is not happy. The compulsive need for popularity

is, of course, an expression of the inner uncertainty, that one knows about one's adequacy only by finding acclaim from others. (Bruch 1961b:224, emphasis in the original)

This argument is almost identical with Riesman's thesis (which Bruch cites) that Americans have become "other-directed," people for whom "their contemporaries are the source of direction" (Riesman [1950] 1976:21) in contrast with the older American personality for whom the source of direction is "inner." Riesman's book evokes a nostalgia for the old American self-reliant personality, a nostalgia that is exemplified by his examples of typical "inner-directed characters": "The banker, the trades-man, and the small entrepreneur" (ibid.:20), mythologized as the bulwark of American liberal democracy and entrepreneurialism. Thus, the goody-goody anorexic, in trying to please everyone, becomes a symptom not only of failed infant feeding but the fear of the fall of traditional American indi-vidualism and articulates the cold war fear of fascism and communism, which pervaded the political spectrum from the right to the left.

Echoing contemporary social critics, Bruch articulated anorexia as an example of the slackening or pathologizing effects of unprecedented post-war affluence and mass culture. Like Riesman, who associates other-directedness with greater wealth and the service and consumer economy, Bruch (1978) links her patients' illness to their parents' wealth. She depicts the anorexic as feeling trapped in "a golden cage" among all the "privi-leges and benefits" and "luxuries" her parents offered her (ibid.:23–24). Furthermore, the anorexic's presumable vulnerability to peer pressure and the "fashion of slimness . . . drummed" by the mass media (ibid.:viii) fit the postwar preoccupation with the possibly dangerous effects of mass media and products, instigated by war propaganda and the spread of mass products to American homes. Thus, the anorexic—presumably fallen ill because of the excess of things and images—becomes a symbol of pop-ular and academic anxiety with the postwar consumer culture.

In a more interesting vein, Bruch also explained anorexia, which affected predominantly young women, in terms of the female experience. On one hand, Bruch embraces quite conventional notions of gender. This is evident in, for example, her disapproving notes on her patients' "tomboyish" behavior or "lesbian fantasies," but it also repeats in her pub-lished comments about the fat immigrant children's fathers, who could not provide "firm masculine guidance" (Bruch and Touraine 1940:167, 176) and her criticisms of the anorexics' mothers, who "while subservient to their husbands in many details," did not "truly respect them" (Bruch 1973:82). Bruch's assumption that mothers are naturally the children's pri-mary caretakers and are therefore the ones to be blamed if something goes wrong is also based on sexist assumptions.

Yet, what has earned Bruch's theory the label of (liberal) feminism is her consistent critique of female dependency and domesticity. Bruch argued that the problem with the anorexics' mothers, "women of superior intelligence and education," was that they had given up promising careers or other ambitions in favor of family and children. This only left them unsatisfied, neurotically focused on their children, trying to inculcate them— and especially the anorexic daughters—to live up to their own frustrated dreams (Bruch 1978:28–31, 1952:155). The anorexic herself "dreaded" the mother's confined life; yet, trained to be dependent and obedient, she also feared the new demand to "become a woman of achievement in her own right."[13] Thus, Bruch's theory, and many later feminist appropriations of it, renders the anorexic a critical symbol of the tragic nature of suffocating traditional femininity of the fifties.

As a whole, the anorexic in Bruch's theory becomes an emblem for a host of contradictory political agendas just coming to fruition in postwar America. The theory of anorexia was linked to the anxiety over social conformism, which leftist intellectuals like the scholars of the Frankfurt school associated with a new type of fascism that manifested itself in self-contemptuous intolerance and hostility toward social critique and reform. However, the fear of conformity was also associated with anticommunist paranoia and a mixed position looking back to early American culture for its pioneer spirit. During and after the war this agonizing about mass culture mobilized a small army of mainstream social scientists who investigated media effects, public opinion formation, group processes, peer pressure, and the infamous suburbs, all in the name of democracy. Yet, as Rose (1996) notes, the subsequent polling industry and social psychological experimentation served to gather knowledge to better direct people's opinions and behavior. Paradoxically, the preoccupation with people's tendency to conform to social norms then became a mechanism to guide people's attitudes and comportment to fit those norms.

In Bruch's theory the norms gather around a set of binaries such as autonomous/dependent, modern/traditional, genuine/artificial, austerity/frivolity, frugality/luxury, creativity/materiality, and public/private. These dichotomies obviously reflect the division between qualities considered "feminine" (soft, dependent, vain, material), and "masculine" (autonomous, creative, strong), and they valorize the latter. Thus, from a feminist point of view one could say that despite her liberal feminist tone, Bruch's fixation on autonomy renders her theory one-dimensional, unable to capture the complexity of norms that may suffocate people and unable to acknowledge the worth of other values and dimensions of existence, such as relationality and community.[14] But because we are talking about weight, Bruch's theory brings to mind another association. Mind-bogglingly, the binarisms embedded in her theory of anorexia articulate the pathological nature of "flab"—things soft, feminine, frivolous, excessive, and material—and our fervent fear of it.

THE SPIRAL OF NORMATIVITY

Bruch's theories are still alive in contemporary medical and popular notions about fatness and thinness. Not only have the popular ideas survived, even those theories of obesity that at some point lost their popularity have surfaced in new disguises and contexts. The association between a certain race and fatness nowadays is evoked to point at the fact that African-Americans are fatter than whites. This may be used to praise African-Americans' cultural acceptance or admiration of bigger bodies, but theories tracing fatness to race, social class, and lifestyle may mix into derogatory remarks about fat "welfare moms" as proofs of the slackness of the culture of certain groups—not unlike Bruch's comments on immigrant mothers in the thirties.

The psychological theory of obesity that Bruch advocated early on has become perhaps the most prominent way to make sense of fatness. The picture of the miserable and unpopular fat person, gulping down ice cream, candy, and delivery pizzas in front of the TV is present even in films such as *The Nutty Professor,* which apparently advocate size-acceptance. Eating too much is now becoming an official psychiatric disorder, as the American Psychiatric Association (APA) recently tentatively included a "Binge-Eating Disorder" in the fourth edition of its *Diagnostic and Statistical Manual* (APA 1994). Bruch's picture of the anorexic was of a young woman who, made overly docile and dependent by the suffocating family environment, becomes easy prey for contemporary culture's peer pressure and media imagery. This picture of the anorexic "goody girl" is present almost everywhere eating disorders are dealt with. It appears in Sunday night TV-movies such as *For the Love of Nancy* and *Dying to Be Perfect,* biographies of celebrity anorexics such as Karen Carpenter, psychiatric journals, textbooks, treatment centers, and feminist research on the condition (e.g., Orbach 1986).

However, some recent feminist works have criticized the idea that the anorexic lacks autonomy. It has been noted that thinness in our culture connotes willpower and independence and that the anorexic may be starving herself to underline her emancipation and strength (Bordo 1993). Defining the anorexic as lacking independence may just fuel her starving by positioning her as a forever "inadequate person in need of control" (Gremillion 1992:62; McNeill 1993). The self-perpetuating nature of this notion of anorexia is logical, because many of the popular notions of obesity and anorexia, notions for which Bruch and other medical scholars are responsible, are virtually the same. Thus, the anorexic who starves herself to stave off cultural notions of dependency and weakness associated with fatness ends up having those same abhorred qualities projected upon her. This spiral highlights the potentially suffocating effects of coupling the policing of contemporary strict norms for both body and personality, so that "abnormal" bodies stand for a character failure, intensifying our agonies about "right" eating, weight, and behavior.

My task in this chapter has been to examine the historical contingency of these theories of obesity and anorexia through the work of Hilde Bruch. My goal has been to show how Bruch's theorizing about fatness and thinness is intertwined with the depression era's fear of the new immigrants and the cold war period's preoccupation with suburban social conformism. Bruch's theories reveal as much about the times during which they were formulated as they reveal about the disorders themselves. This not only means that psychiatric theories of body shape parallel social and political developments, but also points to the complex ways in which the two reinforce each other (Rose 1996). The portraits of the obese and anorexic embody what is "pathological" in child-rearing, consumption, and self-decoration, and they finally propagate a certain "modern" lifestyle, personality, and society, independent of mothers, "backward" customs or ephemeral popular ideologies. Most directly this normative agenda affects people who identify themselves or are identified as having eating problems and who therefore try to or are made to modify their acts accordingly. Yet, as the psychiatric theories of pathological body/self become common sense, they start directing the thoughts and behavior of all of us.

By my genealogical journey through the history of Bruch's theory I intended to problematize the way we have become accustomed to think of certain notions of obesity and anorexia as "truths" about ourselves and/or others and to reveal the nature of these notions to be historically contingent constructions with their subsequent political agendas and blind spots (see Foucault 1984a; Dean 1994). This does not mean that Bruch's or other psychiatric theories of body weight are necessarily "bad," but to borrow Foucault's words, they are always "dangerous" (Foucault 1984b:343). My analysis has laid out the contradictory nature of Bruch's work: How it enables us to think and to do some things and, at the same time, how it hinders us from thinking and acting otherwise. For example, the liberal feminist ideal of an autonomous and emancipated woman who juggles work and is the ideal (never nervous, upset, too talkative, or too quiet) mother allows us to imagine women working outside the confines of the home. Yet, it de-emphasizes other values and dimensions of existence at the expense of autonomy and individuality and does not enable us to question the premises or exigencies of this "superwoman" ideal or to envision alternatives to it. By breaking the spell of the universality and the objectivity of these theories and pointing at their historicity, I hope to open up space to explore what they have not allowed us to be or to think or to imagine.

Yet, the gist of my analysis has been the interplay between the notions and practices surrounding such mundane and intimate issues as eating and body weight and the larger panorama of social, political, economic, racial, sexual, and even military agendas with which they are entangled. A major shortcoming of the psychiatric perspective advocated by Bruch is that it can envision change mainly in terms of changing the individual's attitudes, morals, and weight. Reading Bruch's descriptions of fat immigrant children's lives and the lives of her starving anorexic clients alongside the subsequent interpretations of the medical profession, allows one to see that changing the ways we experience ourselves and our bodies may require transformations in housing policy, treatment of ethnic minorities, health care, medical science and practice, wages, gendered labor practices, child-care, production, selling and consumption of goods, and immigration and foreign policy. In short, to effect changes in the imagery, techniques, institutions, and politics in which our bodies and our selves are enmeshed, it is not sufficient merely to reimagine or to learn to accept our individual minds and bodies; rather, it requires that we look outside ourselves and change the world.

NOTES

1. Although Hilde Bruch treated bulimics (people who binge on food and then get rid of it through, for example, vomiting or the use of laxatives), she and psychiatry in general did not consider bulimia an independent diagnostic category before the 1970s. For this reason I do not analyze theories of bulimia in this chapter.

2. Hilde Bruch's papers are archived in the McGovern Historical Research Center, Texas Medical Center Library, Houston Academy of Medicine, Houston, Texas (hereafter referred to as *The Papers of Hilde Bruch*). I thank Margaret Irwin, JoAnn Pospisil, and Beth White for their kind help at the archive and the Graduate College of the University of Illinois, Urbana-Champaign for a dissertation travel grant that enabled me to visit Houston.

3. Bruch's studies of fat immigrant children encompassed both boys and girls. However, she initially became famous for refuting so-called "Froehlich's syndrome," a supposed pituitary malfunction that was understood to cause genital maldevelopment and an overall effeminate and fat appearance in young boys.

4. Bruch was born in 1904 in Duelken to a middle-class German-Jewish family. She had just received her degree in pediatric medicine when she fled the intensifying German anti-Semitism, first to England in 1933, and then to the United States in 1934. For Bruch's biography, see Hatch-Bruch (1996) and the APA inter-

view conducted in 1974–75 by Jane Preston and Hanna Decker (*The Papers of Hilde Bruch*, Series I, Box 2).

5.   On the history of body weight as a problem, see Schwartz (1986), Sobal (1995), and Stearns (1997). My chapter has no basic disagreement with the broad contours of the history of obesity outlined in these works, although due to the specificity of my topic I focus on issues that have not been extensively dealt with in these more general histories. I find Stearns's (1997) argument that the dieting craze in the United States was a puritan reaction to the affluent consumer society particularly interesting. In my study, this middle-class ideal of genteel moderation was projected onto poor, fat immigrants, who were seen as backwards and out of bounds, with their concomitant connotations of political turmoil. Ironically, the middle-class anorexic, who refused to consume, also became symbol of the deleterious effects of consumer culture and its corruptive images and fads, befitting the ancient association between femininity and an irrational inability to control one's instincts and impulses, and evoking worries about the decay of values and the political system.

6.   I found this ad in Bruch's files. Bruch collected media articles and advertisements on obesity and anorexia throughout her career, and her clippings illuminate the changing popular perceptions of obesity and anorexia between 1930 and 1970 (see *The Papers of Hilde Bruch*, Series VII, Box 9, Folder 301, "Obesity clippings 1939–53").

7.   The extent to which the notion of "obesity" is imposed on these children becomes evident in Bruch's remarks and notes about how the mothers did not consider their children to be obese, just "big." Although some mothers became worried about the prospect of their children not being normal, their lack of concern is manifested by the fact that they often missed appointments with the research group and did not obey the diets prescribed (see Bruch and Touraine 1940).

8.   "Obese Children notes, 1939–40," Series VIII, Box 11, Folders 359–69, *The Papers of Hilde Bruch*.

9.   These observations are based on a more focused study of forty obese children and their families. This study included, for example, visits to the children's homes. For the first time the results of this study were reported in Bruch and Touraine (1940).

10.   The environmental theory of mental illness gave more hope and perhaps better treatment to patients, yet it also contributed to the trend away from public asylums to private and thus elitist outpatient care, of which Bruch's practice is an example.

11.   Bruch begins to focus on anorexia from the late 1950s onward, gradually treating fewer and fewer obese patients.

12.   Bruch also used the then popular Freudian notions of orality, Piaget's (1954) theory of development, and Bateson's famous idea of the "double bind" (Bateson, Jackson, Haley, and Weakland 1957) to argue for her theory.

13.   Stated in Bruch's letter to Judy Folkenberg, a writer with the National Institute of Mental Health who was working on an article on anorexia, July 15, 1981, *The Papers of Hilde Bruch*, Series V, Box 6, Folder 189.

14.   There is extensive feminist literature on the symbols and traits associated with femininity and motherhood. For a review of the feminist literature on moth-

erhood see Snitow (1992), and for an example of depictions of mothers and daughters see Walters (1992). On femininity as a symbol of cultural degeneracy see Felski (1995).

REFERENCES

Adorno, T., E. Frenkel-Brunswik, D. Levinson, and N. Stanford. [1950] 1969. *The Authoritarian Personality*. New York: W. W. Norton.

American Psychiatric Association. 1994. *The Diagnostic and Statistical Manual*, 4th edition. Washington, DC: Author.

Angel, L. 1949. "Constitution in Female Obesity." *American Journal of Physical Anthropology* 7:433–71.

Bateson, G., D. Jackson, J. Haley, and J. Weakland. 1956. "Toward a Theory of Schizophrenia." *Behavioral Science* 1:251–64.

Bordo, S. 1993. *Unbearable Weight: Feminism, Western Culture, and the Body*. Berkeley: University of California Press.

Bruch, H. 1939a. "Obesity in Childhood I: Physical Growth and Development of Obese Children." *American Journal of Diseases of Children* 58(3):457–84.

———. 1939b. "Obesity in Childhood II: Basal Metabolism and Serum Cholesterol of Obese Children." *American Journal of Diseases of Children* 58(4):1001–22.

———. 1952. *Don't Be Afraid of Your Child*. New York: Farrar, Strauss and Young.

———. 1957. *The Importance of Overweight*. New York: W. W. Norton.

———. 1961a. "The Effects of Modern Psychiatric Theories on Our Society: A Psychiatrist's View." *Journal of Existential Psychiatry* 2:213–32.

———. 1961b. "Transformation of Oral Impulses in Eating Disorders: A Conceptual Approach." *Psychiatric Quarterly* 35:458–81.

———. 1973. *Eating Disorders: Obesity, Anorexia and the Person Within*. New York: Basic Books.

———. 1978. *The Golden Cage: The Enigma of Anorexia Nervosa*. Cambridge, MA: Harvard University Press.

Bruch, H., and G. Touraine. 1940. "Obesity in Childhood: V. The Family Frame of Obese Children." *Psychosomatic Medicine* 11(2):141–206.

Brumberg, J. J. 1988. *Fasting Girls: The History of Anorexia Nervosa*. Cambridge, MA: Harvard University Press.

Dean, M. 1994. *Critical and Effective Histories: Foucault's Method and Historical Sociology*. London: Routledge.

Donaldson, S. 1969. *The Suburban Myth*. New York: Columbia University Press.

Felski, R. 1995. *The Gender of Modernity*. Cambridge, MA: Harvard University Press.

Foucault, M. 1984a. "Nietzsche, Genealogy, History." Pp. 76–100 in *The Foucault Reader*, edited by P. Rabinow. New York: Pantheon.

———. 1984b. "On the Genealogy of Ethics: An Overview of Work in Progress." Pp. 340–72 in *The Foucault Reader*, edited by P. Rabinow. New York: Pantheon.

Fromm, E. [1941] 1965. *Escape from Freedom*. New York: Avon.

Fromm-Reichmann, F. 1940. "Notes on the Mother Role in the Family Group." *Bulletin of the Menninger Clinic* 4(5):132–48.

Garrison, F. 1922. "History of Endocrine Doctrine." Pp. 45–74 in *Endocrinology and Metabolism*, edited by L. F. Barker. New York: D. Appleton and Co.

Gremillion, H. 1992. "Psychiatry as Social Ordering: Anorexia Nervosa, a Paradigm." *Social Science and Medicine* 35(1):57–71.

Grob, G. 1984. *Mental Illness and American Society, 1875–1940*. Princeton, NJ: Princeton University Press.

———. 1991. *From Asylum to Community: Mental Health Policy in Modern America*. Princeton, NJ: Princeton University Press.

Hatch-Bruch, J. 1996. *Unlocking the Golden Cage: An Intimate Biography of Hilde Bruch M.D.* Carlsbad, CA: Gurze.

Jimenez, M. A. 1993. "Psychiatric Conceptions of Mental Disorder among Immigrants and African-Americans in Nineteenth and Early Twentieth Century American History." *Research in Social Movements, Conflicts and Change* 16:1–33.

Kraut, A. 1994. *Silent Travelers: Germs, Genes and the "Immigrant Menace."* New York: Basic Books.

McNeill, M. 1993. "Dancing with Foucault: Feminism and Power-knowledge." Pp. 147–78 in *Up against Foucault: Explorations of Some Tensions between Foucault and Feminism*, edited by C. Ramazanoglu. New York: Routledge.

Mead, M. 1954. Book Review: "Don't Be Afraid of Your Child." *American Journal of Orthopsychiatry* 24:426–29.

Miller, P., and T. O'Leary. 1987. "Accounting and the Construction of the Governable Person." *Accounting, Organization and Society* 12(3):235–65.

Mintz, S., and S. Kellogg. 1988. *Domestic Revolutions: A Social History of American Family Life*. New York: Free Press.

Orbach, S. 1986. *Hunger Strike: The Anorectic's Struggle as a Metaphor for Our Age*. New York: Norton.

Piaget, J. 1954. *The Construction of Reality in the Child*. New York: Basic Books.

Polsky, A. 1991. *The Rise of the Therapeutic State*. Princeton, NJ: Princeton University Press.

Preble, W. 1915. "Obesity and Malnutrition." *Boston Medical and Surgical Journal* 20:740–44.

Riesman, D. [1950] 1976. *The Lonely Crowd: A Study of the Changing American Character*. New Haven, CT: Yale University Press.

Rose, N. 1985. *The Psychological Complex: Psychology, Politics and Society in England 1869–1939*. London: Routledge.

———. 1996. *Inventing Our Selves: Psychology, Power and Personhood*. Cambridge: Cambridge University Press.

Schwartz, H. 1986. *Never Satisfied: A Cultural History of Diets, Fantasies and Fat*. New York: Free Press.

Sheldon, W. 1940. *The Varieties of Human Physique: An Introduction to Constitutional Psychology*. New York: Harpers.

———. 1942. *The Varieties of Temperament: A Psychology of Constitutional Difference*. New York: Harpers.

Skolnick, A. 1991. *Embattled Paradise: The American Family in the Age of Uncertainty*. New York: Basic Books.

Snitow, A. 1992. "Feminism and Motherhood: An American Reading." *Feminist Review* 40:32–51.

Sobal, J. 1995. "The Medicalization and Demedicalization of Obesity." Pp. 67–90 in *Eating Agendas: Food and Nutrition as Social Problems*, edited by D. Maurer and J. Sobal. Hawthorne, NY: Aldine de Gruyter.

Stearns, P. 1997. *Fat History: Bodies and Beauty in the Modern West*. New York: New York University Press.

Susman, W. 1989. "Did Success Spoil the United States? Dual Representations in Post-war America." Pp. 19–37 in *Recasting America: Culture and Politics in the Age of Cold War*, edited by L. May. Chicago: University of Chicago Press.

Walters, S. 1992. *Lives Together/Worlds Apart: Mothers and Daughters in Popular Culture*. Berkeley: University of California Press.

III

MEDICAL MODELS

4

Constitutional Types, Institutional Forms

Reconfiguring Diagnostic and Therapeutic Approaches to Obesity in Early Twentieth-Century Biomedical Investigation

MARK T. HAMIN

INTRODUCTION: BODY BUILDING

The shifting, amorphous definitions of obesity across different times and places provide important evidence for historical and social variability in perspectives on disease. In an effort to discern patterns amid such variability, cultural historians and historical sociologists, much like some of the historical figures they study, have charted the complicated kinships between such popular idioms as "stout," "gross," or "fat," on the one hand, and such specialist terms as "corpulent," "obese," or "adipose," on the other (Aronson 1984; Bray 1990; Davenport 1923; Schwartz 1986; Turner 1982, 1985). Early twentieth-century biomedical researchers, for the most part, assumed a categorical distinction between the former and the latter, maintaining that "[p]opular conceptions rest on unorganized groupings" of haphazard experience, whereas scientific observation "depends on a complete, artistic, and sure schooling of the eyes" (Ernst Kretschmer, quoted in Tucker and Lessa 1940:411–112). More than most other conditions that medical researchers and practitioners have regarded as signs of illness, obesity has spanned the full breadth of theoretical and instrumental options available to professionals, past and present, for identifying or treating disorders (Ackerknecht 1973; Ayers 1958; Sigerist [1941] 1989). It has also ranged across the entire spectrum of policy initiatives, moral judgments, and personal decisions associated respectively with each of these options.

One may discern the historical legacies of these various approaches in the wide diversity of current popular-medical views regarding obesity.

Scientific accounts implicate almost every conceivable cause of disease: evolutionary lag between nature and culture in *Homo Sapiens*; genetic basis of metabolism; physiological response to environmental stimulus; hormonal impulse; acquired behavioral habit; psychodynamic motivation; cultural influence; or socioeconomic status (Beller 1977; Bloch 1987; Mayer 1972). Modes of treatment are just as diverse, ranging from basic prevention to drastic cure. The list of therapeutic recommendations, broadly speaking, includes external and internal surgeries, such as liposuction, adipectomy, gastric balloon or staple, and intestinal bypass (Payne 1980; Wurtman and Wurtman 1987); topical and mechanical therapies, including mandibular (jaw) wiring, clinical stimulus, and enema; hormonal treatments; chemical pharmacopoeia; behavior modification programs; hypnosis; psychoanalysis; voluntary lifestyle changes in diet, exercise, or social habits; and public health or social welfare policy measures, from medically insured health club membership to revised school lunch menus to proposed "sin taxes" on processed fats (Fine, Heasman, and Wright 1996; Jarmul 1993; Stacey 1994).

This range of possible diagnoses and therapies raises several questions. Does "obesity" specify a disease, or does it classify an at-risk body type? Is it best studied as one or many condition(s), with specific or diffuse cause(s)? Might it indicate not a disease, but rather some predisposing, opportunistic conditions for the incidence of other pathologies, e.g., cardiovascular, renal, or endocrine dysfunction (e.g., von Noorden 1910; Melchionda, Horwitz, and Schade 1984)? Must a biostatistical correlation between overweight and associated illnesses imply a causal relation? In which respects are obesity's "causes" internal or external to the sufferer, i.e., *endogenous* or *exogenous,* to use terms preferred by many early twentieth-century medical anthropologists? To what extent is its course determined or developed (e.g., Bray 1973; Orford 1985; von Noorden 1910)? How and when does this course take shape, especially in terms of behavioral patterns contributing to overweight: at birth, from environmental circumstances, through personal "lifestyle" choices, or by means of a complex array of factors (Kretchmer 1988; McNamara 1979)? How readily can one distinguish concepts of "disease," "symptom," "predisposition," and "alternative habitus" when classifying the diverse physiques of overweight individuals in aggregate terms, since "diverse syndromes of obesity are often grouped together . . . without further characterization" (Bray 1973:17; cf. Kretchmer 1988)?

COMMUNITY FORMATION AND TRANSFORMATION

My aim in this chapter is to trace the sources of current views on obesity back to the early decades of the twentieth century. To that end, my analysis will develop a historical and sociological model to indicate how investigators have fashioned multiple scientific identities by participating in diverse scientific communities and traditions. The guiding principles and practices of a given community or tradition stem in large part from the locations, resources, and constituencies available to and selected by its members. Finally, the account will suggest ways in which obesity investigators reconfigured their arguments with reference to wider cultural meanings and concerns.

Earlier this century, for example, various *institutional-disciplinary communities* with contending interests in the study of excess fat and overweight engaged in efforts to establish professional identities, with mixed successes. The disciplinary backgrounds and specialties of medical practitioners and researchers—e.g., gastroenterology, histology, physiological chemistry—helped to identify them with respect to their investigative peers. Each community emerged in the context of particular institutional sites, for example, clinics, hospital wards, caretaking facilities, research laboratories, government bureaus, and field outposts. At these sites, hierarchies of collaboration and skill, networks of exchange, and channels of publication organized the work conducted there (Dear 1995; Kohler 1994; Shapin and Schaffer 1986).

Many of these workers, moreover, relied on purpose-specific, often custom-designed, technical infrastructures, which embodied in their design, adaptation, and use the shared practical objectives of those institutional-disciplinary communities that selectively appropriated and deployed them. Such repertoires of technique provided the apparatus, metrics, and materials that allowed communities to coordinate and compare investigative work. In such instances, reliance on standardized equipment or indices helped to foster *technical-instrumental communities* of practitioners (e.g., users of statistical formulas, calipers, kymographs, reagents) across otherwise divergent fields. New biomedical tools proliferated in this period, among them recording instruments, measurement devices, analytic tests, and organo- or chemotherapies (Borell 1987; Cunningham and Williams 1992; Howell 1995; Reiser 1993).

Further, such communities, in adopting similar technical-instrumental means, tended to advocate their distinctively "scientific" research or treatment methods to wider constituencies, sometimes in competitive, if not combative relationship to the alleged ineffectiveness or even malpractice of rival approaches, sometimes in collaborative effort with contingent allies. Such strategic considerations encouraged participation in broad-based *public-service communities,* with the aim of translating expert debates from laboratory and clinic to boardroom, bureau, and popular forum. Among the service-oriented audiences for obesity investigations were public health officials, social welfare managers, institutional dietitians, and home economists.

Pursuant to their institutional or instrumental aims, members of professional communities in many cases oriented their work to bear directly on the development of effective policy recommendations, sometimes forming provisional coalitions across communities under broad intellectual-cultural rubrics such as "constitutional" medicine or specific pathological "mechanisms." Investigators of obesity sought in this way to maintain a precarious balance: stable support of facilities and resources in their work, but also flexible latitude to innovate, shift, or expand the direction of their activity. This crossing of intermural boundaries further tended to conflate various medical, methodological, and moral criteria defining an obese person as alternately a rehabilitating patient, research subject, or responsible agent (Brandt 1997; Lederer 1995; Lindee 1994).

The discussion to follow will outline the institutional-disciplinary, technical-instrumental, and public-service communities shaping various diagnostic and therapeutic approaches to obesity. My analytic model places these approaches within five major biomedical "traditions": *Natural-historical, biostatistical-anthropometric, psychological-behavioral, physiological-chemical,* and *surgical-mechanical.* Each tradition comprised particular views of bodily structure and function, disease etiology and symptoms, diagnostic scale and focus, therapeutic course and efficacy. From these social relations and material conditions of biomedical inquiry, each traditional community tended to develop a distinctive style or repertoire for organizing research and practice. Their scientific and clinical criteria for assessment of overweight and its health consequences often intersected with and influenced normative (social, bioethical, moral, esthetic) judgments concerning the appropriate degree of personal agency, responsibility, and consideration to accord obese people.

For example, on the basis of identification with particular communities, researchers and practitioners have tried traditionally to associate obesity with other illnesses that have been, to greater or lesser degrees, controversial, if not stigmatized. Advocates of public-health or popular-dietary reforms have compared excess body fat with other problems attributable to environmental causes, such as malnutrition or specific deficiency diseases (Mayer 1968). Vital statisticians and demographers have formulated overweight in actuarial terms, along with differential "risk" factors like age, sex, race, or occupation (Craddock 1969:9). Psychologists have grouped it with eating disorders such as anorexia or bulimia; and a related behavioral view has suggested common ground between lack of appetite control and "obsessive" habits such as sexual or hygienic compulsions. Physiological and chemical investigators have linked excess food intake to endocrinological or, more recently, molecular-genetic addiction models of "substance abuse" akin to overdependence on alcohol, narcotics, or nicotine (Orford 1985:1–5). Surgeons have favored interventive, extractive approaches to problems of obesity, analogous to bypass or removal of dysfunctional tissues or organs (Payne 1980).

A caveat here: My heuristic framework is neither exhaustive nor exact. In this account, a "tradition" includes linked paths of extended family resemblance as well as strict, uniform descent. Likewise, a "community" might have a broadly kindred more than a tightly knit membership. Though historically grounded, the five categories of biomedical tradition nevertheless allow for broad divergences within them and for exceptions, hybrids, and intermediaries at their boundaries. My account also does not pretend that all these researchers and practitioners regarded themselves as working on similar problems, or regarded obesity as their primary focus (Fujimora 1992; Galison 1997; Gieryn 1983; Leigh-Star and Griesemer 1989).

CASE HISTORIES OF COMMUNITY STANDARDS

Natural-Historical

The natural-historical tradition at the turn of the twentieth century descended from lineages dating as far back as the taxonomic observations and hygienic recommendations of physicians in the ancient world. The intellectual legacy of Hippocratic-Galenic medical philosophies remained a dominant influence well into the nineteenth century. Indeed, conceptual residues have lingered even to the recent past (Tracy 1992; Greenwood 1984:86–97). Natural-historical accounts of obesity focused on characteristic divergences from normal (i.e., ideal) forms of anatomical or physiological nature, conceived as types of temperament or constitution. In this model, variations in basic body build resulted from complex but discernible variations in environment and culture, including climate, local flora and fauna, family background, occupation, culinary practices, and so on. Advocates of this approach favored arguments from cumulative case records and schematic classifications of individuals located within particular milieus. Discussing reduction cures, Carl von Noorden (1910:Vol. IX, p. 18) argued that many "impatient" patients and physicians were:

> inclined to attribute the obesity and the lack of success in its treatment . . . to some perversion of metabolism. The deeper, however, one attempts to gain an insight into the peculiarities of each case, the more frequently will one become convinced that it is unnecessary to conjure up unknown factors, for wrong habits of life alone generally suffice to explain the pathogenesis of the obesity.

Similarly, George Draper decried the specialist who "knows nothing about these specimens of humanity—whence they came, what their individual characteristics are, and, above all, what their original health potentialities have been" (1924:21; see also Bray 1990; Williams 1926:1–29).

Many practitioners in the natural-historical tradition were classically learned physicians. Their accustomed sites of institutional-disciplinary support included the medical schools, private practices, clinics, and hospitals where doctors generally consulted. By the late nineteenth century, other institutional opportunities emerged in the context of practical service roles. Public health fieldworkers and social welfare caseworkers (Hall 1913; Thomas 1923), along with leading popular health reformers such as J. H. Kellogg and Horace Fletcher (Brown 1908; Defensive Diet League of America 1924–1928; O'Shea and Kellogg 1915), had already assimilated key elements of the natural-historical tradition, particularly those aspects stressing environmental or cultural sources of disease, in their efforts to identify and provide help for unhealthy eaters.

Operating under these institutional conditions, the traditional technical-instrumental resources for natural-historical diagnosis consisted primarily in clinical and field observation, along with basic measuring tools. Within that tradition, genres of case history, nosographic taxonomy (i.e., systematic classification of symptoms), and medical pedagogy afforded standard means of diagnosis, aids in disciplining eye and hand as skilled medical instruments. Howard Anders, for example, described methods of abdominal examination that included techniques for estimating "the proportion of *fat* and the *thickness* of the walls . . . by grasping them upward," for assessing enlargement "due in the first place to an excess of mural or omental fat, as in general obesity . . . proportionate to the bulkiness of the extremities," and for recognizing the contour and consistency of "moderate distention . . . [from] dietetic or gastro-intestinal" problems. Along similar lines, von Noorden (1910:Vol. 1, p. 19) insisted that, "In deciding whether or not a subject is to be considered excessively obese we must study more the general impression created by the patient, both as regards appearance and state of health, than the incubus of a definite number of kilos of fat" (Anders 1907:372; see also Bynum and Porter 1993).

On the basis of such diagnoses, clinical practitioners formulated therapeutic regimens that included modifications in diet, exercise, and other habits, along with their customary repertoire of drugs and *materia medica*. Public-service hygienists, on the other hand, focused on prevention and amelioration using techniques of popular health assessment and education such as pamphlets, exhibits, demonstrations, or campaigns. Genuinely "scientific" investigators could hardly be content to construct natural-historical typologies speculatively "in the armchair," but only as a practical "result of clinical experience." Such empirical detail, though, came at the cost of limited sample groups, unwieldy data, and insufficiently correlated indices, according to the more quantitatively oriented critics of natural-historical approaches (Lessa 1943:81; see also Bauer [1942] 1945:5).

Draper represents an intermediate figure in this respect. His institutional-disciplinary background situated him in a natural-historical tradition, but he also participated in a technical-instrumental community that favored systematic measurement and statistical tabulation. Draper aimed thereby to strengthen the position and authority of the clinical generalist against the growing dominance of narrowly trained specialists and technicians by introducing simplified indicators and quantitative analyses of comprehensive physical observations. He maintained that if his basic indicators, which included family and personal histories of "food idiosyncrasies," "digestion," and "bowel habit" as well as gastric juice and stool examination, were "studied and correlated in each person of a large number of individuals, one soon realizes that there is frequent repetition of certain combinations of characters. . . . Upon this basis undoubtedly has rested the unconscious skill of the older clinicians" (Draper 1924:25).

Other "iatromathematical" rivals to the clinician's art often acknowledged a continued role for what they deemed the "subjective judgments" of traditional physicians, but accorded them modest diagnostic value. Medical quantifiers placed greater confidence in the accuracy and power of "purely objective" measurements (McCloy 1936:10–11). In the interwar period, some biomedical anthropologists called for an approach that reconciled these contending values. For them, typologies structured on the basis of correlative indicators combined somascopic (qualitative observation) and somametric (quantitative mensuration) methods into a "scopometric" synthesis (Tucker and Lessa 1940:415).

Biostatistical-Anthropometric

Achieving greater prominence by the late nineteenth century, the biostatistical-anthropometric tradition represented an attempt to rectify the perceived limitations of natural-historical models. Quantifiers carried over from that antecedent tradition a taxonomic idiom of characteristic types classified according to morphological traits. In formulating a constitutional medicine of the whole patient against newer theories of specific histological, cytological, or microbiological agency, anthropometrists concurred with their naturalist predecessors (Tracy 1992; Draper 1924, 1928). They diverged, though, in devising taxonomies with greater emphasis on quantitative means of statistical aggregation and correlation, or on fine calibration of mechanical measurement, than on chiefly qualitative methods of trained inspection. Raymond Pearl, for example, claimed that "the external form of the human body has been more carefully re-studied, with the help of the exact methods of physical anthropology and the . . . bringing forward of some statistical and a great deal more clinical evidence tending to show some differential association of certain disease types with certain bodily habitus types" (1933:51).

These quantifiers, moreover, transposed natural-historical accounts of the relation between environment and constitution, moving away from more *exogenous* explanations of body habitus in terms of local, near-term conditions to more *endogenous* explanations in terms of traits adaptive to heritable, evolutionary conditions. Julius Bauer, for example, expressed skepticism "that pure exogenous obesity exists at all. What can be produced by artificial overfeeding or artificial restriction of muscular exercise is overweight or corpulence of temporary character, not obesity" ([1942] 1945:151). In the biostatistical-anthropometric tradition, investigators emphasized mathematical deviation from normal (i.e., median) anatomical-physiological type. For them, variations in body build resulted from long-range variations in lineage. They favored formalized arguments from morphological indices correlated to population and inheritance patterns (Davenport 1927; Harris and Benedict 1919; Pearl 1940).

Since advocates of biostatistical-anthropometric models were more often researchers than practitioners, they usually did not discuss therapeutic measures as such. Their agnostic if not pessimistic views regarding practical treatment options circumscribed the medical-professional opportunities available to quantitative investigators. Consequently, their institutional-disciplinary identities were more varied or unusual. Whether as biometricians, eugenists, demographers, or physical anthropologists, researchers like Pearl and Charles Davenport pursued newly established avenues of support, often making homes in interdisciplinary facilities funded by philanthropic organizations such as the Carnegie Institution of Washington (CIW) or the Rockefeller Foundation. Their policy-oriented recommendations, in more indirect and conservative ways, addressed matters of eugenics, public hygiene, or social medicine. Biostatisticians advocated policies to foster and protect favored physical traits and to reduce the incidence and perpetuation of less-than-optimal variants. Only preemptive, long-range action held any real prospects for lasting change, but even then could not vouchsafe desired outcomes. Such stark perspectives often limited public-service opportunities for anthropometrists.

Proponents argued that use of statistical techniques to tabulate actuarial or survey data, and of precision instruments to measure or record bodies— densitometric (volume), gravimetric (weight), and calorimetric (heat output) apparatus; charts; or photography, for example—afforded prospects of formal, standardized indices to refine and revise empirical judgments. Pearl argued that "there is needed some comparative or relative measure [coefficient] of variation" (1940:346) between statistical indicators measured in different kinds of units; moreover, there "would be a place of usefulness for an adequate graphical method of depicting relative variability for comparative purposes . . . for example, in respect of body-weight" (ibid.:350). As for measurement, Davenport elaborated how body girths "are taken by means of the tapes." While preferring cloth to steel tapes "because the numbers are more easily read," he mentioned that "they can not be used for more than 20 or 30 subjects" because the cloth "has a tendency to fray at its edges and . . . become entangled." Steel tapes, though prone to rust and sticking, were useful "in measuring very large people or in other emergencies" (Davenport 1927:26–29). Early twentieth-century efforts to codify international standards of biological measurement exemplified this desire for precision (Carpenter 1921, 1924, 1939; Harris and Benedict 1919; McCloy 1936:106–7).

Toward the end of the interwar period, however, social-science critics scorned application of somatic-type models to anthropological subjects, noting that "a statistical association is not to be confused with a causal relationship" (Merton and Ashley-Montagu 1940:390). Other anthropologists discerned in some of their colleagues an unbalanced, exclusionary privileging of quantitative biostatistical indicators and endogenous characters over qualitative natural-historical accounts and exogenous factors. This overstated, hypocritical contrast not only dismissed historical and conceptual continuities, but also perhaps disguised mere numerical glosses on old prejudices (Lessa 1943:85). Still another kind of criticism came from vital statisticians and human ecologists who found constitutionalist sample populations unrepresentative or misconceived in many instances, confusing static measures of physique with dynamic features of lived behavior (Craddock 1969:9; Orford 1985:75).

Psychological-Behavioral

By World War II, many naturalist and anthropometric investigators of overweight suffered guilt by association, whether well-founded or unfortunate, with "pseudosciences" such as humoral typology, physiognomy, phrenology, and racial hygiene. Many of these criticisms originated with psychologists intent on challenging suspect anthropological or hereditarian expansions onto their territory of mental development. Even sympathetic psychologist-critics remarked that the constitutionalists' evolutionary accounts of morphological and behavioral variation often retained atavistic traces of neo-Lamarckian mechanisms for environmental inheritance; structural-functional teleologies; or forces of orthogenetic recapitulation of anatomy as destiny (Wertheimer and Heskwith 1926:4–5, 12–13; Willemse 1932:265).

Earlier in the century, though, some investigators of obesity and dietary regulation had already begun to consider by means of focused, disciplined inquiries the extent to which mental condition contributed to the physical problem of excess fat. Researchers in the psychological-behavioral tradition shared with those in the biostatistical-anthropometric tradition a commitment in theory to psychosomatic interrelation and to character (personality) classification as hypotheses relevant for medical diagnosis, with inverse causal emphasis. Whereas constitutionalists tended to explain character and behavior in terms of body build and habitus, psychologists preferred to explain the latter by reference to the former. In defining obesity "as the compulsory tendency toward a marked overweight due to abnormal accumulation of fat by persons who are left to their automatic regulations, and who are not supervised so far as intake of food and expenditure of energy are concerned," Bauer ([1942] 1945:173) represented an intermediate figure between anthropometric and biobehavioral approaches.

Psychologists, however, generally reoriented their theoretical focus from the mathematics of correlation between mental and physical traits to the mechanisms and dynamics of their interaction. From this perspective, the psychological-behavioral approach placed greater stress on different kinds of interruption or disturbance to normal (i.e., stable) mental function. As such, body variations ensued from variations in formative experiences or traumas. In conceptual terms, advocates of this approach offered arguments from developmental relations and influences. They thereby reaffirmed the importance of observed individual cases against strictly aggregate models, but also initiated a transition from previous whole-patient orientations to focus on specific processes. As Henry Brosin described the transition, with "reasonable care during the physical and laboratory examinations any major organic disorders . . . can be detected if present, or ruled out if absent, so the doctor can focus his energies upon the basic emotional processes which compel his patient to overeat [, since] the preponderance of evidence is in favor of an emotional cause for the hyperphagia in most patients" (Brosin 1953; Myerson 1940; Rosenthal 1932).

Neither researchers nor practitioners in this behavioral tradition lacked for institutional-disciplinary positions, but strong family disagreements over appropriate means for identifying and treating psychological conditions foreclosed development of a unified psychosomatic approach to obesity suited for more practical applications. Experimental psychologists in their laboratories and research wards, psychotherapists of various stripes in their consulting practices, and mental hygienists in their institutes and bureaus all pursued specific behavioral bases of excessive appetite, but along widely divergent paths. Their respective technical-instrumental means of psychological assessment and treatment were also varied: physiological recording devices, hypnosis, therapeutic conversation, counseling, and standardized mental testing, among others. Of these technical-instrumental communities, only practitioners of the more routinized forms of physiological recording and mental testing managed to attract the interest of wider public-service constituencies, such as military physicians and industrial hygienists.

By these disparate means, behavioralists aimed to close the divide between exogenous and endogenous factors, between natural histories and statistical profiles of the mind's role in obesity. Experimentalist critics, however, noting the idiosyncratic qualitative criteria of constitutional as well as analytic psychologists, suggested that those putatively universal concepts of behavioral diagnosis had roots in narrower, culture-bound concerns. For those favoring physiological-chemical kinds of explanation, psychological accounts of "manias" based on compulsive actions often seemed conceptually not too far removed from antiquated systems of "temperaments" based on elemental humors. Other detractors noted the chronic propensity of mentalist researchers to translate habits deemed excessive or disordered from (moral) vices, indulgences, or morbid appetites to (medical) manias, addictions, or psychopathologies (Orford 1985:1–5). Such assessments of "abnormal" behavior hedged, if not begged, questions of distinguishing personal responsibility from pathological causality in a process of "medicalizing behavior" (Brandt 1997; Rosenberg and Golden 1992; Sobal 1995:75–76).

Physiological-Chemical

Expansion of laboratory-based life sciences on the German model had, by the end of the nineteenth century, transformed biomedical theory and practice (Coleman and Holmes 1988; Rothschuh 1973). Researchers in the psychological-behavioral tradition, especially in its more experimental aspects, shared the physiological-chemical tradition's orientation to developmental processes and functional mechanisms. Advocates for each approach looked to research in endocrine physiology and hormone biochemistry for insights into processes that contributed to obesity, though their respective areas of conceptual emphasis and investigative focus differed significantly (McNamara 1979:xii–xiii; Willemse 1932:18). Whereas some psychologists sought a biological basis for behavior or a material medium for mental activity, physiologists of gastroenterological processes, Walter Cannon (1933, 1936) and A. J. Carlson (1916), for example, investigated the effects of emotional stress on physical and chemical mechanisms of appetite inhibition and alimentary dysfunction.

To a behavioralist idiom of human volition and emotion, then, physiologists and chemists counterposed a reductive terminology of organic or even molecular forces and drives. These differences of research orientation also had theoretical dimensions. Physiologist-chemists sought to emphasize deviations from normal (i.e., regulated) anatomical and physiological functions in their explanations of obesity. In accordance with that perspective, body variations resulted from biochemical or biomolecular variations. Such a view encouraged arguments from microscale physical and chemical processes, i.e., internal functions involving specific forces and reactions (Alvarez [1922] 1928; MacLean 1925).

Clinician von Noorden and behavioralist Bauer, for example, despite opposite views regarding the prevalence of exogenous and endogenous causes for obesity, argued comparably that cases of overweight resulting from metabolic or endocrine dysfunction were "symptomatic" and thus peripheral relative to environmental or hereditary causes, respectively (von Noorden 1910:Vol. IX, p. 19; Bauer [1942] 1945:151). Some clinicians and anthropometrists, however, showed greater appreciation for physiological indicators (Cahill and Renold 1983:1). McCloy found value in "analysis of the body secretions, analysis of the body excretions, blood count, haemoglobin, basal metabolism" (1936:10). Tucker and Lessa likewise recommended "basal metabolic rate determinations; determination of the specific dynamic action of food; study of glycemia and carbohydrate tolerance" (1940:418).

In terms of institutional-disciplinary positions, the physiological-chemical tradition developed most fully among experimental physiologists, but was likewise characteristic of many medical, physiological, and biological chemists working in research institutes, university laboratories, and medical wards. They relied on technical-instrumental repertoires of biochemical analysis, respiration calorimetry, controlled feeding, and mechanical recording to identify some of these otherwise invisibly small or occluded physiological operations (e.g., Benedict and Talbot 1921; Benedict and Lee 1937; Long 1909; Poehlman and Horton 1992). Other relevant diagnostic means included microscopy, cytological and histological assay, and physiological genetics.

As for therapeutic recommendations, investigators in the physiological-chemical tradition favored research more strongly than practice, much like those in the biostatistical tradition. Their contributions to treatment were on balance more limited in scope: testing of food nutrients and pharmacological agents through experimental and clinical trial, or collaboration with dietitians, hygienists, and home economists from more natural-historical backgrounds (King 1924; McCann 1924; Russell Sage Institute 1915). Critics considered this reductive research bias a serious limitation (Orford 1985).

The experimental physiologists within this physiological-chemical cohort were among the most institutionally secure, most research discipline-oriented, and least (directly) service-oriented investigators. Perhaps because of this distinction, oddly enough, such investigators found areas of common ground with practitioners of surgical-mechanical approaches.

Indeed, the disciplinary emphases of surgeons and technicians—less occupied with theory and basic research, more focused on clinical practice and therapeutic intervention—were the obverse of physiochemists' interests and thus, in some respects, complementary to them within an intermural division of labor between laboratory-based testing and hospital-based treatment.

Surgical-Mechanical

Development and advocacy of surgical-mechanical approaches to treatment of obesity came relatively late in the period under study, achieving neither routinized technical competence nor (reluctant) acceptance until well after World War II. Although other kinds of surgery had become reliable, even standard treatments earlier in the century, it was some time before the therapeutic promise of alimentary surgery approximated the investigative prestige of experimental physiology. This was true despite the similar reliance of both activities on techniques of sectional aperture, in one case for analytical in the other for clinical purposes.

While the physiological-chemical and surgical-mechanical traditions shared inclinations toward mechanistic reduction in their approaches, surgeons aspired to move from physiochemists' modest array of indirectly acting organo- and chemotherapies toward more drastic, direct kinds of instrumental intervention. Such interventions, ranging from basic alimentary bypass to radical psychosurgery remained limited and experimental because technical developments only partially improved their record of safety and efficacy. Consequently, this bolder type of treatment continued to be a relatively peripheral latecomer to the management of obesity.

The surgical-mechanical tradition involved a conceptual emphasis on defect or deficiency in normal (i.e., reliable) physical and mental controls over food intake. Whether from inborn problems of metabolism or ingrained patterns of appetite, though, the surgical-medical tradition considered body variations the result of endogenous, intractable variations in life history. Since specialists needed to identify and isolate a distinct organic site for surgical-technical intervention, practitioners implicitly favored arguments from specific, endogenous disease locus and course over exogenous, systemic, or multifactorial etiologies (Bauer [1942] 1945:211).

Although a typical institutional location for mechanical approaches was the surgical ward of a hospital, there were also other, less-severely interventive places and practices of mechanical diagnosis or therapy. Clinical-exercise and physical therapists also worked intensively with specific regions of the body, typically on more external or readily accessible internal means, such as topical stimulus, application of heat or pressure, enema, or irrigation. Despite these differences in practical orientation, surgeons and physical therapists alike relied on diagnostic instruments such as x-rays and chemical tests to locate internal sources of organic dysfunction or pain. The former made routine use of such means, while the latter combined occasional use with a wide variety of external techniques. Modes of treatment consisted alternately of removing obstruction to waste elimination, restricting or redirecting passage of foods, and facilitating metabolism of nutrients. Such techniques, surgery especially, were vulnerable to criticism that localized interventions neglected more diffuse behavioral factors or systemic disturbances, resulting in partial, temporary solutions, often with unanticipated side-effects (Payne 1980:5–6; Orford 1985:86–87).

CONCLUDING REMARKS: PUBLIC FRAMEWORKS, POPULAR KEYWORDS

Many of the popular and expert perspectives that shape current debates about the incidence and control of obesity derived, to a large extent, from earlier patterns of professional competition and combination among various biomedical approaches to body build relative to health in the first half of the twentieth century. The panoply of present-day orientations—from exogenous to endogenous causes, from macroscopic to microscopic scales, from typical forms or norms to specific factors or processes, from complex to reductive explanations, from active to passive roles for patient or practitioner—can trace most lines of argument back to these earlier traditions. A clarification is important here. While the five biomedical "traditions" outlined above did not all emerge simultaneously, develop in parallel, or achieve success contemporaneously, neither did they stand in a relation of successive temporal stages. As this account has suggested, they often coexisted, waxing and waning relative to one another or to prevailing cultural currents (Pickstone 1993).

At the turn of the century, clinicians, dietary reformers, public health fieldworkers, and medical anthropologists sharing "constitutional" frameworks often found their institutional-disciplinary situations less stable and secure than those of their more specialized, "mechanistic" counterparts. They also had to reckon with partial consensus regarding technical-instrumental standards. As a result, these investigators proved more likely to engage in public-service debates about proper diagnosis and treatment, articulating their views in popular idioms of "wholeness," "balance," and "moderation." According to von Noorden, for example, under "normal conditions there is an automatic regulation of the output of energy and the intake of food . . . after having obtained an optimum, that is, a medium average state of nutrition, . . . a definite amount of food that constitutes for each individual the so-called 'maintenance diet'" (1910:Vol. 9, p. 13).

Use of these rhetorical-ideological "keywords" (Williams 1976), moreover, was as characteristic of their views on disciplinary relations as it was of their views on disease diagnosis and therapy. That is, they endorsed efforts to bridge division between various contending approaches and thus bring much greater flexibility to analytic techniques. The complex roots of conditions like obesity, they argued, made an integrated approach vital for greater efficacy. Even their qualitative taxonomies of forms, factors, or functions showed traces of such rhetorical influence, postulating an "intermediate" figure as the ideal or norm of moderation. They aimed thereby to round out the narrow specialists' exceedingly sharp lines of stringent oversimplification (Tucker and Lessa 1940:420–21; McNamara 1979:xi).

Research-oriented biometricians, behavioralists, physiologists, surgeons, and technicians, on the other hand, rejected the constitutionalists' eclectic criteria in favor of quantitative metrics or precise technics to isolate "simple," "uniform," and "mechanical" criteria for investigation and intervention. While this mechanistic framework perhaps contributed to effective strategies for institutional stabilization in certain cases of laboratory science and medical specialty, such perspectives also served to circumscribe possible opportunities for wider practical application (Krasnegor, Grave, and Kretchmer 1988:xi; Schemmel 1981:53). In this sense, institutional security, disciplinary focus, intensive technique, and reductive theory were complementary aspects of professional identity, analogous in their specific, localized character. For these investigators, "equilibrium" and "regulation" were precise technical terms, not popular slogans, and would thus inhibit tendencies to grandiose system-building and gross overgeneralization.

Advocates for each of these approaches often attempted to define their viewpoint in terms of a moderate position or middle ground between more extreme measures. Many of them believed that their particular tradition could lead the way in closing (perceived) gaps between theory and practice by showing how analytically precise concepts and classifications had important consequences for effective treatment (Bauer [1942] 1945:210–12; Orford 1985:2). Another key area that promised to foster disciplinary reconciliation or rationalization was the study of psychophysical interaction. Moderates claimed that scientific method required a balancing of objective and subjective assessment within a hybrid of qualitative and quantitative indicators (Graves 1937; Lessa 1943:31; McCloy 1936:99). In a related vein, other advocates of joint work called for remodeling survey sampling techniques to correlate individual case histories with statistical aggregations of behavior, or to study normal alimentary function commensurate with and symmetrical to pathological dysfunction (Craddock 1969:9; Orford 1985:75).

For many of the investigators who developed these approaches to the study and treatment of obesity, idioms of "balance" and "moderation" played an important part in establishing, for their public audiences, the coherence, credibility, and usefulness of various biomedical inquiries.

Such a rhetorical point of "equilibrium" provided a fulcrum for raising the profile and the stature of their professional claims and methodological stances. Most of these programmatic debates addressed the relative virtues and vices of multifactorial complexity as against reductive simplicity; interdisciplinary approaches as against intensively specialized expertise; and lay meanings as against technical terminology in the proper understanding of obesity as a social problem (Maurer and Sobal 1995; Mayer 1968, 1972). Much the same kind of self-analysis might well inform our current efforts as historians, sociologists, and cultural theorists of such biomedical inquiries in our efforts to address various audiences of disciplinary peers, research collaborators, and lay publics.

As a closing instance of such reflexive analysis, consider these remarks from quantifying constitutionalist Pearl (1933:63), but transposed from his discussion of human physiques to our account of cultural identities:

> Such individuals, in short, are *mixtures* or mosaics in their morphology. . . . The dysplastic individual is envisioned, by this terminology, to be badly moulded or formed, because his bodily proportions (a) depart from our ideals for the human form, and (b) are inconsistent among themselves. The euplastic individual, *par excellence*, is the exact intermediate [between types] . . . and represents the aesthetic ideals regarding human form.

My aim in this chapter has been to suggest that, through participation within particular biomedical communities and their respective traditions, researchers and practitioners investigating obesity attempted to reconfigure their intermural, hybrid, "dysplastic" identities into more stable, coherent, "euplastic" positions and service roles. Analogously, those of us with hybrid scholarly identities (e.g., history, sociology, and cultural studies of science, technology, and medicine) might better recognize and contend with the tacit esthetic and normative ideals informing our own work by means of such historical reflections.

REFERENCES

Ackerknecht, E. H. 1973. *Therapeutics from the Primitives to the 20th Century* (with "Appendix: History of Dietetics"). New York: Hafner.

Alvarez, W. C. [1922] 1928. *The Mechanics of the Digestive Tract: An Introduction to Gastroenterology*, 2nd edition. New York: Paul B. Hoeber.

Anders, H. S. 1907. *Physical Diagnosis, with Case Examples of the Inductive Method.* New York: D. Appleton.

Aronson, N. 1984. "Comment on Bryan Turner's 'The Government of the Body: . . .'" *British Journal of Sociology* 35(1):62–65.

Ayers, W. M. 1958. "Changing Attitudes toward Overweight and Reducing." *Journal of the American Dietetic Association* 34:23–29.

Bauer, J. [1942] 1945. *Constitution and Disease: Applied Constitutional Pathology*. New York: Grune and Stratton.

Beller, A. S. 1977. *Fat and Thin: A Natural History of Obesity*. New York: Farrar, Straus and Giroux.

Benedict, F. G. and R. C. Lee. 1937. *Lipogenesis in the Animal Body with Special Reference to the Physiology of the Goose*. Publ. 489. Washington, DC: Carnegie Institution of Washington.

Benedict, F. G. and F. B. Talbot. 1921. *Metabolism and Growth from Birth to Puberty*. Publ. 302. Washington, DC: Carnegie Institution of Washington.

Bloch, K. E. 1987. "Concepts and Approaches to Scientific Inquiry." *American Journal of Clinical Nutrition* 45:1054–57.

Borell, M. 1987. "Instruments and an Independent Physiology." Pp. 293–321 in *Physiology in the American Context*, edited by G. L. Geison. Baltimore: American Physiological Society.

Brandt, A. M. 1997. "'Just Say No': Risk, Behavior, and Disease in Twentieth-Century America." Pp. 82–98 in *Scientific Authority and Twentieth-Century America*, edited by R. G. Walters. Baltimore: Johns Hopkins University Press.

Bray, G. A. (ed.). 1973. *Obesity in Perspective*. DHEW Publ. No. (NHI) 75-708. Washington, DC: U.S. Government Printing Office.

———. 1990. "Obesity: Historical Development of Scientific and Cultural Ideas." *International Journal of Obesity* 14:909–26.

Brosin, H. W. 1953. "Psychology of Overeating." Pp. 52–59 in *Overeating, Overweight and Obesity*, edited by D. P. Barr, J. R. Brobeck, H. W. Brosin, L. I. Dublin, F. A. Evans, P. C. Fry, S. Gurin, P. Gyorgy, E. E. Hunt, A. Keys, P. S. Peckos, and A. W. Pennington. New York: National Vitamin Foundation.

Brown, G. 1908. *Scientific Nutrition Simplified: A Condensed Statement and Explanation for Everybody of the Discoveries of Chittenden, Fletcher, and Others*. New York: Stokes.

Bynum W. F., and R. Porter (eds.). 1993. *Medicine and the Five Senses*. Cambridge: Cambridge University Press.

Cahill, G. F., and A. E. Renold. 1983. "Adipose Tissue: A Brief History." Pp. 1–7 in *The Adipocyte and Obesity: Cellular and Molecular Mechanisms*, edited by A. Angel, C. H. Hollenberg, and D. A. K. Roncari. New York: Raven.

Cannon, W. B. 1933. *Some Modern Extensions of Beaumont's Studies on Alexis St. Martin*. Beaumont Foundation Lectures. Reprinted from *Journal of the Michigan State Medical Society* 32:307–16.

———. 1936. *Digestion and Health*. New York: W. W. Norton.

Carlson, A. J. 1916. *The Control of Hunger in Health and Disease*. Chicago: University of Chicago Press.

Carpenter, T. M. 1921. *Tables, Factors, and Formulas for Computing Respiratory Exchange and Biological Transformations*. Publ. 303. Washington, DC: Carnegie Institution of Washington. [2nd ed. Publ. 303a., 1924; 3rd ed. Publ. 303b., 1939.]

Coleman, W., and F. L. Holmes (eds.). 1988. *The Investigative Enterprise: Experimental Physiology in Nineteenth-Century Medicine*. Berkeley: University of California Press.

Craddock, D. 1969. *Obesity and Its Management*. London: E. & S. Livingstone.

Cunningham, A., and P. Williams (eds.). 1992. *The Laboratory Revolution in Medicine.* Cambridge: Cambridge University Press.

Davenport, C. B. 1923. *Body-Build and Its Inheritance.* Washington, DC: Carnegie Institute of Washington.

———. 1927. *Guide to Physical Anthropometry and Anthroposcopy.* Eugenics Research Association Handbook Series no. I. Cold Spring Harbor, NY: Carnegie Institute of Washington.

Dear, P. 1995. "Cultural History of Science: An Overview with Reflections." *Science, Technology, and Human Values* 20(2):150–70.

Defensive Diet League of America. 1924–1928. *Bulletin,* nos. 1–60, 11/24 to 10/28. Toledo, OH: Author.

Draper, G. 1924. *Human Constitution: A Consideration of Its Relationship to Disease.* Philadelphia: W. B. Saunders.

———. 1928. *Human Constitution: Its Significance in Medicine and How It May Be Studied.* Baltimore: Williams and Wilkins.

Fine, B., M. Heasman, and J. Wright. 1996. *Consumption in the Age of Affluence: The World of Food.* New York: Routledge.

Fujimora, J. H. 1992. "Crafting Science: Standardized Packages, Boundary Objects, and "Translation."" Pp. 168–211 in *Science as Practice and Culture,* edited by A. Pickering. Chicago: University of Chicago Press.

Galison, P. 1997. *Image and Logic: A Material Culture of Microphysics.* Chicago: University of Chicago Press.

Gieryn, T. 1983. "Boundary Work and the Demarcation of Science from Non-Science: Strains and Interests in Professional Ideologies of Science." *American Sociological Review* 48:781–95.

Graves, W. W. 1937. "The Age-Incidence Principle of Investigation Evaluating the Biological Significance of Inherited Variation in the Problem of Human Constitution." *American Journal of Psychiatry* 93(5):1109.

Greenwood, D. G. 1984. *The Taming of Evolution: The Persistence of Non-Evolutionary Views in the Study of Humans.* Ithaca, NY: Cornell University Press.

Hall, W. S. 1913. *Nutrition and Dietetics. A Manual for Students of Medicine, for Trained Nurses, and for Dietitians in Hospitals and Other Institutions.* New York: D. Appleton.

Harris, J. A., and F. G. Benedict. 1919. "Biometric Standards for Energy Requirements in Human Nutrition." *Science Monthly* (May):385–402). [Reprinted by Science Press.]

Howell, J. 1995. *Technology in the Hospital: Transforming Patient Care in the Early Twentieth Century.* Baltimore: Johns Hopkins University Press.

Jarmul, D. (ed.). 1993. *Headline News, Science Views II.* Washington, DC: National Academy Press. (Section 5)

King, J. T., Jr. 1924. *Basal Metabolism: Determination of the Metabolic Rate in the Practice of Medicine.* Baltimore: Williams and Wilkins.

Kohler, R. E. 1994. *Lords of the Fly: Drosophila Genetics and the Experimental Life.* Chicago: University of Chicago Press.

Krasnegor, N. A., G. D. Grave, and N. Kretchmer (eds.). 1988. *Childhood Obesity: A Biobehavioral Perspective.* Caldwell, NJ: Telford.

Kretchmer, N. 1988. "What Is Obesity?" Pp. 3–8 in *Childhood Obesity: A Biobehavioral Perspective,* edited by N. A. Krasnegor, G. D. Grave, and N. Kretchmer. Caldwell, NJ: Telford.

Lederer, S. 1995. *Subjected to Science: Human Experimentation in America before the Second World War.* Baltimore: Johns Hopkins University Press.

Leigh-Star, S., and J. Griesemer. 1989. "Institutional Ecologies, 'Translations,' and Boundary Objects: . . . " *Sociological Studies of Science* 19:387–420.

Lessa, W. A. 1943. *An Appraisal of Constitutional Typologies. American Anthropologist* 45(New Series; 4, October):Part 2.

Lindee, M. S. 1994. *Suffering Made Real: American Science and the Survivors at Hiroshima.* Chicago: University of Chicago Press.

Long, J. H. 1909. *A Textbook of Physiological Chemistry for Students of Medicine,* 2nd edition. Philadelphia: P. Blackiston's Son.

MacLean, H. 1925. *Modern Views on Digestion and Gastric Disease.* London: Constable.

Maurer, D., and J. Sobal (eds.). 1995. *Eating Agendas: Food and Nutrition as Social Problems.* Hawthorne, NY: Aldine de Gruyter.

Mayer, J. 1968. *Overweight: Causes, Costs, and Control.* Englewood Cliffs, NJ: Prentice-Hall.

———. 1972. *Human Nutrition: Its Physiological, Medical and Social Aspects.* Springfield, IL: Charles C. Thomas.

McCann, W. S. 1924. *Calorimetry in Medicine.* Medical Monographs Vol. IV. Baltimore: Williams and Wilkins.

McCloy, C. H. 1936. *Appraising Physical Status: The Selection of Measurements.* University of Iowa Studies: Studies in Child Welfare, Vol. XII, no. 2, edited by George D. Stoddard. Iowa City: University of Iowa Press.

McNamara, J. R. (ed.). 1979. *Behavioral Approaches to Medicine: Applications and Analysis.* New York: Plenum.

Melchionda, N., D. L. Horwitz, and D. S. Schade (eds.). 1984. *Recent Advances in Obesity and Diabetes Research.* New York: Raven.

Merton, R. K., and M. F. Ashley-Montagu. 1940. "Crime and the Anthropologist." *American Anthropologist* 42:385–408

Myerson, A. 1940. "Psychosomatics and Somatopsychics." *Psychiatric Quarterly* 14(4):623–41.

O'Shea, M. V., and J. H. Kellogg. 1915. *Making the Most Out of Life.* New York: Macmillan.

Orford, J. 1985. *Excessive Appetites: A Psychological View of Addictions.* New York: John Wiley.

Payne, J. H. 1980. "Surgery for Obesity: Historical Background." Pp. 1–6 in *Surgical Management of Obesity,* edited by J. D. Maxwell, J. C. Gazet, and T. R. E. Pilkington. New York: Grune and Stratton.

Pearl, R. 1933. *Constitution and Health.* London: K. Paul.

———. 1940. *Introduction to Medical Biometry and Statistics,* 3rd edition. Philadelphia: W. B. Saunders.

Pickstone, J. 1993. "Ways of Knowing: Towards a Historical Sociology of Science, Technology, and Medicine." *British Journal of the History of Science* 26:433–58.

Poehlman, E. T., and E. S. Horton. 1992. "Determinants of Body Weight Regulation." Pp. 33–48 in *Eating, Body Weight, and Performance in Athletes: Disorders of Society,* edited by K. D. Brownell, J. Rodin, and J. H. Wilmore. Philadelphia: Lea and Febiger.

Reiser, S. 1993. "Technology and the Use of the Senses in Twentieth-Century Medicine." Pp. 262–73 in *Medicine and the Five Senses,* edited by W. F. Bynum and Roy Porter. Cambridge: Cambridge University Press.

Rosenberg, C. E., and J. Golden (eds.). 1992. *Framing Disease: Studies in Cultural History.* New Brunswick, NJ: Rutgers University Press.

Rosenthal, J. S. 1932. "Typology in the Light of the Theory of Conditioned Reflexes." *Character and Personality* 1(1):66–67.

Rothschuh, K. E. 1973. *History of Physiology,* edited and translated by Guenter B. Risse. New York: Krieger.

Russell Sage Institute of Pathology and Second Medical Division of Bellevue Hospital. 1915. *Clinical Calorimetry* (May 15). Chicago: American Medical Association.

Schemmel, R. (ed.). 1981. *Nutrition, Physiology, and Obesity.* Boca Raton, FL: CRC.

Schwartz, H. 1986. *Never Satisfied: A Cultural History of Diets, Fantasies, and Fat.* New York: Doubleday.

Shapin, S., and S. Schaffer. 1986. *Leviathan and the Air Pump: Hobbes, Boyle, and the Experimental Life.* Princeton, NJ: Princeton University Press.

Sigerist, H. E. [1941] 1989. "The History of Dietetics." (Classic Article) *Gesnerus* 46(3–4):249–56.

Sobal, J. 1995. "The Medicalization and Demedicalization of Obesity." Pp 67–90 in *Eating Agendas: Food and Nutrition as Social Problems,* edited by D. Maurer and J. Sobal. Hawthorne, NY: Aldine de Gruyter.

Stacey, M. 1994. *Consumed: Why Americans Love, Hate, and Fear Food.* New York: Simon and Schuster.

Thomas, G. I. 1923. *The Dietary of Health and Disease: For the Use of Dietitians, Nurses and Instructors in the Sciences That Pertain to Nutrition.* Philadelphia: Lea & Febiger.

Tracy, S. W. 1992. "George Draper and American Constitutional Medicine, 1916–1946: Reinventing the Sick Man." *Bulletin of the History of Medicine* 66(1):53–87.

Tucker, W. B., and W. A. Lessa. 1940. "Man: A Constitutional Investigation (Concluded)." *Quarterly Review of Biology* 15:411–55.

Turner, B. S. 1982. "The Government of the Body: Medical Regimens and the Rationalization of Diet." *British Journal of Sociology* 33(2):254–69.

———. 1985. "More on 'The Government of the Body': A Reply to Naomi Aronson." *British Journal of Sociology* 36(2):151–53.

von Noorden, C. 1910. *Clinical Treatises on the Pathology and Therapy of Disorders of Metabolism and Nutrition.* New York: E. B. Treat.

Wertheimer, F. I., and F. E. Heskwith. 1926. *The Significance of the Physical Constitution in Mental Disease.* Medical Monographs, Vol. 10. Baltimore: Williams and Wilkins.

Willemse, W. A. 1932. *Constitution-Types in Delinquency: Practical Applications and Bio-Physiological Foundations of Kretschmer's Types.* London: Kegan Paul.

Williams, L. 1926. *Obesity*. New York: Oxford University Press.

Williams, R. 1976. *Keywords: A Vocabulary of Culture and Society*. New York: Oxford University Press.

Wurtman, R. J., and J. J. Wurtman (eds.). 1987. *Human Obesity. Annals of the New York Academy of Sciences* Vol. 499.

5

Defining Perfect and Not-So-Perfect Bodies

The Rise and Fall of the "Dreyer Method" for the Assessment of Physique and Fitness, 1918–26

DAVID SMITH and SALLY HORROCKS

INTRODUCTION

This chapter will consider the rise and fall of a method for the assessment of body dimensions and fitness that was put forward in Britain in the late 1910s and early 1920s by Georges Dreyer, Professor of Pathology at Oxford University (Douglas 1932–1935). According to Dreyer's method, the physical well-being of an individual could be measured by calculating the relationship between vital capacity (the maximum volume of air that the lungs can expire) and other body dimensions, specifically sitting height or stem length, and weight and chest circumference. If an individual's measured vital capacity was more than 10 percent below the expected, Dreyer suggested, then "one might have good reason to feel suspicious with regard to the present state of health" (Dreyer and Hanson 1920:16). For a brief period this method of assessing physical well-being was championed by influential figures in the field of medical science, and received significant research funding from the Medical Research Council (MRC). Ultimately, however, it was never widely applied and by the mid-1920s had been largely discredited. By exploring the construction and rejection of the "Dreyer method," this chapter shows how changes in knowledge about the relationship between body dimensions and physical well-being were a result of the conflicting aspirations of professional groups and the social and scientific context of the time.

ORIGINS AND DEVELOPMENT OF THE DREYER METHOD

During World War I, due to advances in the technology of warfare, there was an increasing demand for ways of identifying men with special characteristics (Cooter 1993). In response to the use of aircraft for military purposes, for example, the scientific and medical advisers to the British flying services began to develop special tests for assessing the physical fitness of would-be pilots. During these pioneering days of military flying the cockpits were open, making it essential to select flyers with well-developed respiratory systems able to withstand rarefied atmospheres. Such men would be able to keep their expensive machines as far away as possible from enemy guns on the ground. Prior to the war, Georges Dreyer and his colleagues at Oxford had conducted many studies of mathematical relationships between such dimensions as aorta size, body weight, and surface area in animals (Dreyer, Ray, and Walker 1912–1913). With E. W. A. Walker, a lecturer in his department, Dreyer had also worked on the effect of altitude on blood volume (Dreyer and Walker 1913). Dreyer was therefore well-equipped to consider the physiological problems of flying, and he became involved in advising on the assessment of prospective airmen, and conducting studies of the vital capacity of recruits and experienced pilots (Medical Research Committee 1917:78–79).[1] After the war, in 1919, he published an article in the *Lancet,* which argued that the systematic study of vital capacity and various other body measurements for different trades and occupations could

> afford most important information from the point of view of national health, and will throw light upon the value of such measures as may be contemplated for the improvement of the general health and well-being of the people. (Dreyer 1919:234)

Dreyer developed this article not only from his wartime experience with vital capacity measurements, but also from a study of the relationship between body weight and length in humans published by Walker (1915–1917) during the war, which in turn arose from their earlier collaborative work on animals. Walker claimed, on the basis of measurements of school children and university students, that the relationship between stem length (l) and body weight (W) conforms to the formula $l = KW^n$ and gave values for K and n for both males and females. Dreyer's *Lancet* article was based on a paper given in February 1919 at a meeting of representatives of the Allies in Rome, on medical aspects of aviation. Dreyer attended this meeting as one of three delegates of the British government. He presented formulas relating vital capacity to stem length, weight, and chest circumference, based on measurements of 16 men aged between about 13 and 52, who had been selected on the basis of their exemplary physical fitness.

The relationship of vital capacity to body dimensions had been investigated by John Hutchinson in the mid–nineteenth century. Hutchinson had claimed that there was a simple arithmetical progression with increasing height, but no definite relationship with weight, or chest measurements (Hutchinson 1846). However, Dreyer derived the following formulas linking vital capacity with each of the other variables:

$$\frac{W^{0.72}}{\text{V.C.}} = K_1 \qquad \frac{l^2}{\text{V.C.}} = K_2 \qquad \frac{Ch^2}{\text{V.C.}} = K_3$$

(Where K_1–K_3 are constants, V.C. is vital capacity, and Ch is chest circumference)

Dreyer reexamined Hutchinson's data and claimed to have identified errors accounting for Hutchinson's failure to find these relationships. Dividing 1,900 of the individuals examined by Hutchinson into occupational groups, Dreyer worked out constants using the first of the formulas (that using weight). These were then expressed as a percentage of the constant for the group that Hutchinson described as "a remarkably fine body of young men"—Chatham recruits—producing what Dreyer regarded as an index of fitness. Table 5.1 gives some of the results.

Dreyer's sixteen males had a fitness index of 108.3, seven boy scouts 105.7, twelve upper-class men 99.0, and twelve lower class men 83.6. These comparisons demonstrated how Dreyer's formulas might be used to assess, rank, and monitor the fitness of groups in the population (Dreyer 1919).

After publishing this paper, Dreyer developed a comprehensive set of tables based on his formulas and some further data, which he claimed could be used for four purposes: (1) to determine the normal proportions between weight, stem length, and chest circumference; (2) to gain evidence of underfeeding or malnutrition at different stages of life or among various classes and occupations; (3) to study physical fitness measured by vital capacity in its relationship with the other measurements, allowing

Table 5.1. Dryer's Index of Fitness Results

Group	Constant
Chatham recruits	100.0
Woolwich marines	96.9
Metropolitan police	94.8
Pressmen	91.5
Compositors	88.1
Gentlemen	84.3
Paupers	82.5

comparisons of age groups, genders, trades, occupations, and classes; and (4) to study organic diseases such as pulmonary tuberculosis, and functional disorders such as fatigue (Dreyer and Hanson 1920:11). The tables, published in book form in 1920, gave expected weight according to stem length and chest circumference, and vital capacity according to weight, stem length, and chest circumference. The vital capacities were given for three classes of fitness—perfect, medium and poor—which also corresponded to different groups of occupations. Class A included, for example, army and navy personnel, policemen, athletes, and blacksmiths. Class B included professionals such as doctors and lawyers, and railwaymen, while Class C included tailors, shopkeepers, and potters. Tables were published for both males and females (ibid.:16–18).

Dreyer's book also included detailed instructions on how to measure weight, stem length, chest circumference, and vital capacity accurately, and how to use the tables. Stem length was preferably measured using a special apparatus or, alternatively, with the subject sitting on the floor, but not on a chair. In order to assess the weight of an individual, users were advised to express the measured weight as an average of the expected weight according to stem length and chest circumference read from the tables. A difference of up to 5 percent was to be regarded as normal, between 5 and 10 percent possibly abnormal, between 10 and 15 percent as probably abnormal, and over 15 percent certainly abnormal. In order to assess the physical fitness of a normal weight individual, the measured vital capacity would then be compared with the vital capacity read from the table, giving expected vital capacity according to weight, also taking occupational group into account. For those of abnormal weight, use of the tables giving expected vital capacity according to chest circumference and stem length was recommended. Dreyer suggested that an individual's state of health might be impaired if the vital capacity was more than 10 percent below the expected level (ibid.:6, 16).

Taken together, the tables and accompanying text of Dreyer's book claimed to provide a systematic procedure for assessing and classifying the state of health of all individuals, which relied on standardized techniques rather than the vagaries of the judgment of a single physician. These two aspects of Dreyer's method—standardization and the enhancement of the role of laboratory medicine over that of the individual clinician—appealed to those such as Walter Fletcher, secretary of the Medical Research Council (MRC), who sought to reform medicine along more scientific lines. Moreover, as the following section demonstrates more fully, Dreyer's method and subject matter also fitted well into the wider intellectual and practical aims of the MRC, and offered a means by which scientists and health professionals could together contribute to the management of individual bodies on behalf of the state. This, combined with the high standing Dreyer enjoyed with Fletcher as a result of his earlier research and wartime record, ensured that he received resources from the MRC to pursue his work. This support enabled his techniques to become more widely known and incorporated into the practices of some professionals responsible for monitoring the health of large groups. Eventually, however, the basis of Dreyer's claims to provide an objective assessment of individual fitness came under attack from a group of statisticians, led by Major Greenwood, who saw this work as a threat to their own aspirations to establish professional careers on the basis of unique mathematical expertise. Faced with severe financial problems, the MRC decided to suspend support for Dreyer's anthropometric studies, which had yielded few of the results that had been promised. By the mid-1920s Dreyer's method for determining healthy bodies had been largely discredited, and the professor himself, nursing the further embarrassment of the rejection of his research into a vaccine for tuberculosis, turned his energies to the planning of new premises for his department in Oxford (Morrell 1997:182–86).

DREYER'S METHOD AND THE STRATEGIC AIMS OF THE MEDICAL RESEARCH COUNCIL

Substantial state funding of British medical research began in 1913 with the formation of the Medical Research Committee (later Medical Research Council), with Cambridge physiologist Walter Fletcher as secretary. During the war, much of the committee's initial research program was set aside to work on wartime problems (Thomson 1973). Within both the original and wartime programs, quantification was a key theme. During the war Dreyer's work came to Fletcher's attention, and Fletcher was greatly impressed. In May 1917, Fletcher remarked that he had the "highest admiration for his [Dreyer's] extraordinary skill in technique" and that pathology would be "a different science if other pathologists had his mathematical knowledge."[2]

For Fletcher, Dreyer's apparent "mathematical knowledge" also promised to further important postwar aims of the MRC. A section of the MRC *Annual Report* for 1919–20, headed "The Determination of Biological Standards and the Methods of Biological Assay and Measurement," explained that before the war it had been realized that "in many directions progress was being delayed for want of fixed standards of measurement and of means for their ready application" (Medical Research Council 1920:35). During the war the need for standards had become even more obvious, and the postwar program of research in this area included the standardization of drugs, the production of standard diagnostic sera and cultures, the formation of a national collection of type cultures, and research into pathological methods. Under this heading was also reported the establishment of an "Anthropometric Standards Committee," already responsible for a project supervised by Dreyer.

In late 1919, Dreyer carried the MRC message in favor of standardization to the United States. In a speech to the Harvey Society, he expressed a hope that

> we may soon accomplish for scientific medicine what has already been done in the field of physics, and that the time has nearly arrived when we shall see biological standard units as firmly fixed as the ampère, the volt and the ohm. (Dreyer 1919–1920:25)

In another paper entitled "Iatro-Mathematics," Dreyer explained his broader program of applying mathematics to medicine. He argued that

> in attempting to bring experimental data under the rule of mathematical law our survey must be so directed as to establish the *right* relationship where relationships are involved. In endeavoring to define new laws we must endeavor to arrive at *rational* formulae. In a word, we must seek simplicity of expression, because Nature has so continuously shown herself to be simple. (Dreyer and Walker 1919:51)

As we will see, however, Dreyer's conception of medical mathematics uncovering relatively simple mathematical relationships expressed by "rational formulae" offended the medical statisticians who were then engaged in establishing a professional niche. For pioneer medical statistician Major Greenwood, the great advantage of the "new statistical calculus" was that it allowed the researcher to unpack the wide variety of factors involved in medically and mathematically complex phenomena (Greenwood 1924:158).

Dreyer's MRC-supported anthropometric project arose from a memorandum entitled "The Normal Vital Capacity in Man in its relation to the size of the body. The importance of this measurement as a guide to physical fitness under different conditions and in different classes of individuals," which he sent to Fletcher in June 1919.[3] This summarized Dreyer's findings reported in the *Lancet,* and resulted in the award of a grant to Dreyer to expand his anthropometric studies and to continue a collaborative study of the use of vital capacity in the management of tuberculosis. When Fletcher informed Dreyer that the application had been successful, he also remarked that the MRC had long considered "the prospects of securing better anthropometric measurements and their proper study."[4] Fletcher hoped that Dreyer's work would develop into a large-scale project.

When it was decided to establish the Anthropometric Standards Committee, Fletcher explained to Dreyer that the MRC wished to obtain better knowledge of anthropometric methods with a view to their future use possibly for a wide survey, or for the use of Government Departments or private institutions employing men or women, and at least for the general service of medical science and medical practice. For better guidance in this, they desire to ask the help of a small committee in framing a program of these preliminary studies, with a view to taking later such formal steps towards the organization of anthropometric work as may seem possible and desirable.[5]

Fletcher also recorded that the Anthropometric Standards Committee was set up in case "powers and opportunities" arose for the conduct of a comprehensive anthropometric survey in Britain. The new committee would

consider and advise upon the selection and description of standard measurements of human body characters capable of easy determination and accurate record, having regard to their probable value either for practical purposes in relation to judgements of physical condition or for the purposes of scientific anthropometric survey.[6]

The "opportunities" referred to possible government responses to an analysis of physical examinations carried out upon men of military age for recruiting purposes during the later part of the war. Fletcher was a member of a committee of the Ministry of National Service that supervised this analysis, which was carried out by members of the Ministry's Medical Department. The report of this work showed that

of every nine men of military age in Great Britain, on the average three were perfectly fit and healthy; two were upon a definitely infirm plane of health and strength, whether from some disability or some failure in development; three were incapable of undergoing more than a moderate degree of physical exertion and could almost (in view of their age) be described with justice as physical wrecks; and the remaining man a chronic invalid with a precarious hold on life. (Ministry of National Service 1920:4)

The MRC's Anthropometric Standards Committee consisted of Dreyer, John Brownlee, statistician to the MRC, Colonel Lelean, professor of hygiene at the Royal Army Medical College, and Lieutenant-Colonel Martin Flack, director of medical research in the Royal Air Force, with Arthur Keith, professor of anatomy at the Royal College of Surgeons as chairman, and F. G. Hobson as secretary. Hobson, who had studied physiology in Oxford before the war, had been employed under the MRC grant to carry out the extension to Dreyer's anthropometric studies.

Keith was a powerful advocate of anthropometry. Like Fletcher he was a member of a committee that supervised the analysis of examinations of men of military age. In February 1919 he published a lecture on "Anthropometry and National Health" in the *Journal of State Medicine*, which indicated the results would show that "we . . . have a larger unfit class than any other of the leading nations" (Keith 1919:38). He argued that in order to help devise and monitor ameliorative measures it was now necessary to initiate large-scale and comprehensive surveys of health, fitness, and physical characteristics, but before such surveys could take place it was important to "agree and accept a definite and uniform British standpoint of physical or anthropometric measurements" (ibid.:40). This was the project intended the Anthropometric Standards Committee would undertake.

The work of the Anthropometric Standards Committee, and Dreyer's own work in particular, promised to help the MRC consolidate its position in the postwar period by providing the knowledge and techniques required for the study and improvement of public health as a part of reconstruction programs. However, the MRC not only faced the challenge of demonstrating how the expenditure of public money upon research promised to pay dividends in terms of public health, it was also necessary to demonstrate to skeptical clinicians the value of research for clinical practice (Lawrence 1985). Dreyer's work on vital capacity and pulmonary tuberculosis also held promise in this connection, as is clear from remarks that Fletcher made to the editor of the *Lancet* when forwarding a paper on this subject by Dreyer and a colleague in May 1920 (Dreyer and Burrell 1920). Fletcher told the editor:

> I think it is really a very striking clinical application. The coincidence between the capacity constants and the clinical condition must mean something real, I think; if so, the thing is of immediate practical value, besides being of great theoretic interest. . . . [T]here seems a *prima facie* case of this being of real value in diagnosis and especially in prognosis.[7]

The use of vital capacity in monitoring tuberculosis would not only promise to improve the management of tuberculosis for the benefit of patients. It might also be used as a method of screening applicants for disability pensions, thereby eliminating false claims and saving money. Fletcher arranged for reprints of the paper on vital capacity in tuberculosis to be distributed to members of the Disabilities Committee of the Ministry of Pensions.[8]

PROGRESS OF DREYER'S RESEARCH AND THE APPLICATION OF THE DREYER METHOD

The Anthropometric Standards Committee held three meetings between January and May 1920, at which the best methods for measuring head, face and body dimensions, hair type, eye color, lung function, and pulse rate were discussed, and hair samples, glass eyes, measuring calipers, and other instruments were examined.[9] The Committee then fell inactive, failing to meet for another eighteen months. The large-scale anthropometric survey that Keith and the MRC had thought might be established failed to materialize. This outcome was only one example of many plans that attempted to build upon wartime activities but quickly foundered due to financial stringency, and the changing priorities of recently formed government departments.[10] Nonetheless, Dreyer and Hobson's anthropometric research appeared to progress successfully for a time.

This project appears to have been originally conceived, at least by Fletcher, as a data collection exercise that would permit an assessment of the method set out in Dreyer's paper in the *Lancet*. The work appears to have proceeded, however, upon the assumption that Dreyer's method was almost certainly valid. A leaflet prepared for the authorities responsible for the subjects that Hobson wished access to encouraged this assumption. The leaflet explained that, using Dreyer's method, it seemed likely that

> definite values can be attached to the terms "good physique" and "physical fitness," two terms which have hitherto had but a vague and indefinite significance for the medical profession and for the public. There has been no standard with which an individual can be compared and his fitness and disability estimated, and the need for such a standard has been acutely realized.[11]

The survey would make good these deficiencies in existing knowledge. By October 1919, Hobson had assembled sets of apparatus and was arranging for the measurement of London policemen, firemen, and elementary school children, female medical undergraduates, and other students.[12] Later, negotiations began with secretaries of trade unions and employers, regarding access to miners, cotton and wool spinners and weavers, and operatives at the Boots Drug Factory in Nottingham.[13] Collaborators were established at various locations, some of whom, such as the Boots Welfare Department, the College of Hygiene and Physical Education at Dunfermline, and the Nottingham Schools Medical Department, acquired their own sets of measuring apparatus.[14] One of the collaborators that Dreyer and Hobson acquired was Dr. A. A. Mumford, Medical Officer of Manchester Grammar School. In July 1920, Mumford applied to the MRC, via A. V. Hill, professor of physiology at Manchester University, for a grant to buy some apparatus so that he might carry out respiratory tests along lines approved by Hill and Dreyer.[15]

By the end of July 1920, 6,000 persons had been examined, including 1,500 adults from the Metropolitan Police, the London Fire Brigade, London School of Medicine for Women, Oxford and Cambridge Universities, and physical training colleges. In addition, data had been collected on 3,000 elementary school children in London and Nottingham as well as a number from good class preparatory and public schools.[16] In May 1921 Hobson told Fletcher's assistant that he was now concentrating on working out the data on school children for the Nottingham Schools Medical Department.[17] In November 1921, the Senior Medical Officer for Nottingham wrote

> the Dreyer method enables one to estimate with striking accuracy the degree of improvement, or the reverse, in children under open-air treatment. It is of the greatest possible assistance in the early stages of pulmonary and abdominal tuberculosis as well as of other organic disease.[18]

"Open-air treatment" refers to a form of special education designed to improve the condition of children in poor health. A report on the use of Dreyer's method at Nottingham had been quoted *in extenso* in the *Annual Report of the Chief Medical Officer of the Board of Education for 1920* (Newth 1921:197).[19] A. A. E. Newth, Nottingham's senior assistant medical officer, used Dreyer's tables for assessing both nutrition and physical fitness. "Nutrition" in this sense meant body weight. As recommended by Dreyer, chest circumference and stem length were measured, and corresponding weights were read off from Dreyer's tables and averaged. This weight was then compared with the measured weight. For assessing fitness, weight was measured and the corresponding vital capacity was read off the tables. This was then compared with the measured vital capacity.[20] Hobson and Dreyer provided the Nottingham Education Committee with an analysis of the data collected at four schools in Nottingham, which they compared with data collected at four schools in London. Dreyer and Hobson's discussion was entirely in terms of the average nutrition and fitness of *schools*,[21] but Newth argued that the greatest value of the Dreyer method was in the assessment of *individuals*:

> The task of the School Medical Officer in deciding whether a child is, or is not, ill may often be by no means an easy one. . . . But he can have great help in the Dreyer assessment. These figures . . . give him a very valuable idea of the condition of the child. He sees a child who is apparently ailing. A careful examination by means of the stethoscope etc., still leaves him in doubt. Then perhaps, the Dreyer figures prove the child is markedly below normal and the doctor knows that his anxiety is justified.[22]

Newth presented a specific example of how a medical condition had come to light and appropriate action taken after a boy had been "Dreyered."

ATTACK BY MEDICAL STATISTICIANS

Despite Fletcher's initial confidence in Dreyer, and the apparent enthusiasm for the Dreyer method in Nottingham, from March 1921 Fletcher received a series of warnings from medical statistician Major Greenwood that all might not be well with the underlying basis of the project. Greenwood, who had trained in statistics under Karl Pearson, Galton Professor of Eugenics at University College, London, had successfully challenged bacteriologist Sir Almroth Wright over the correct interpretation of the results of the latter's research into vaccine therapy before the war (Rosser Matthews 1995). He became a medical officer of the newly formed Ministry of Health in 1919, and also developed close links with the MRC (Hogben 1950–1951). He acted as chair of the Industrial Statistics Committee of the Industrial Fatigue Research Board, a body administered by the MRC. The Industrial Statistics Committee, which was later renamed the Statistics Committee, became involved in scrutinizing many MRC reports. Greenwood frequently advised and warned Fletcher about happenings in the Ministry, and the two men discussed such matters as how appropriately scientifically minded medical men might be maneuvered into vacant chairs of medicine.[23] In the case of Greenwood's intervention in connection with Dreyer's work, he was apparently concerned that eventual public criticism of Dreyer would be discreditable to the MRC.

Greenwood enquired about the extent to which Dreyer's work was being supported by the MRC. He had seen Dreyer's book, but felt unable to form any opinion of the Dreyer formulas due to the lack of original data presented. However, Greenwood's concern as to the reliability of the formulas had been aroused by Walker's paper which considered the relationship between body weight and stem-length (Walker 1915–1917). This did provide some data, but Greenwood found the statistical analysis "very brief and rather crude." He was therefore anxious to have Dreyer's claims tested by a member of the medical statistics class that he had arranged at University College. With this in mind he had raised the question with Pearson. Pearson was already familiar with Dreyer's work. He thought it "grossly inaccurate" and that "all the conclusions were nonsense." Despite Fletcher's impressions of Dreyer's mathematical abilities, Dreyer fell into the category of those scientists who Pearson regarded as limited by "kindergarten arithmetic" (Pearson 1920). Greenwood commented to Fletcher:

> [L]ife is too short and we all have too much to do to waste time in mere controversy, but . . . if the discredit is ultimately to rebound to the M.R.C., I feel sure that we should endeavor to get it put straight without any public controversy. I should be sorry to see in some future number of *Biometrika* a violent onslaught by one of Karl's young women upon work for which you are paying.[24]

Greenwood suggested that if more than a few pounds were at stake, they should obtain a copy of Dreyer's data and set a member of the MRC statistical staff to test the validity of his formulas.

These suggestions seem to have made little initial impact, but in September 1921 concerns were expressed by A. V. Hill about the drift of Mumford's work in Manchester. Having examined Mumford's data, Hill told Fletcher:

> It appears . . . that any relation . . . between vital capacity and bodily efficiency including capacity for school work in general is difficult, if not impossible to find. . . . Whether the results be positive or whether they be negative is of course no crucial matter. The important thing is to know which way they are.[25]

Hill asked Fletcher's permission to submit Mumford's data to the MRC statistician, John Brownlee, and warned Fletcher that he thought Mumford's results were going to prove negative, which, he pointed out, would be "very different from what Dreyer has led us to believe."[26] Brownlee delegated this task to Matthew Young, a member of his department.

Despite the concerns of Greenwood and Hill, it seems that the fourth meeting of the Anthropometric Standards Committee, held in December 1921, was still impressed with the progress of the work that had blossomed under Dreyer's supervision. The minutes record no dissent to the view that the data collected from 5,500 children and adolescents aged 2 to 19 showed that there was no reason to modify the opinion that Dreyer's formulas gave an accurate index of physique and physical fitness for these subjects. It was even agreed "that the time had now come when an endeavor should be made to get these methods of examination introduced in a systematic way into School Medical Work."[27] It was suggested that the methods might be introduced at first in army orphan schools and the RAF school for boys.

In early January 1922 Hobson asked Fletcher for help in contacting the appropriate authorities so that the recommendations of the committee might be implemented.[28] Fletcher, however, replied that he could not act in this way until at least an interim report on the work completed to date was in hand, and urged Hobson to prepare such a report as quickly as possible.[29] Keith also urged Fletcher to assist with the arrangement of a large-scale application of Dreyer's methods among RAF recruits, but Fletcher responded:

> Before the Council can recommend the adoption of Dreyer's methods by any Government service, or indeed by anybody else, they ought to have the whole weight of the recommendations of your Committee behind them. I understand that your Committee have not yet received or considered or approved the results of the large scale trial of Dreyer's methods upon which we are still waiting for Hobson to report. No doubt you will want to have a critical examination of the method by a statistician before you are prepared to back it and to ask us to recommend it officially.[30]

The minutes of the next meeting of the Anthropometric Standards Committee, held in April 1922, suggest that the members were now conscious of doubts concerning the value of Dreyer's methods. It was now agreed that their adoption could not be recommended "until further criticism by statistical experts had been made of the necessary available material."[31]

Meanwhile Greenwood was working on an assessment of the value of the Dreyer formulas, based on an analysis of data on RAF personnel supplied by Martin Flack, rather than on data provided by Hobson. This work, in which Greenwood was assisted by MRC statistical workers Lucy Cripps and Ethel Newbold, was first presented at a meeting of the Society of Biometricians and Mathematical Statisticians held at University College, London, toward the end of October 1922. Their conclusion effectively dismissed Dreyer's claims to be able to define healthy bodies using vital capacity measurements:

> [I]t does not appear that either biometric or "rational" formulae can deduce from the non-physiological or ordinary anthropometric constants, estimates of normal vital capacity confined within sufficiently narrow limits to possess real prognostic value in individual cases. (Cripps, Greenwood, and Newbold 1923:336)

After the meeting Pearson told Fletcher that Dreyer's papers had struck him as erroneous and superficial many months ago, and he had intended writing a paper on the subject until he found that Greenwood was engaged in the task. Pearson thought that something needed to be done as Dreyer's methods were "being used by all sorts of people, who cannot possibly judge their value."[32] A paper by Cripps, Greenwood, and Newbold (1923) soon appeared in *Biometrika,* and was followed in October 1923 by a further critical paper by Mumford and Matthew Young (1923). The conclusion of the latter paper was highly critical of Dreyer's formulas and the method by which they were obtained.

> Apart from the number of observations being so relatively small, [and] that it is totally inadequate to form the basis of any general conclusion or to provide data for calculating a formula for general application, the process of selection adopted gives the formula so devised a wholly fictitious degree of accuracy as expressed in the tables by percentage error between calculated and observed values. (ibid.:133)

In their view Dreyer's claims to provide an objective, scientific, and standardized technique for assessing physical well-being rested on a base so flimsy as to render it useless for practical purposes.

THE DEMISE OF THE ANTHROPOMETRIC STANDARDS
RESEARCH PROGRAM

At the final meeting of the Anthropometric Standards Committee, which took place at the end of October 1922, a few days after the meeting at University College, it was now agreed

> when the measurements of a chance selection of the population is statistically analyzed, the relationships which can be established between physical measurements and Vital Capacity show a percentage deviation between observation and prediction so great as to render these relationships of no practical value when applied to the individual case.[33]

Dreyer effectively bowed before the claims of statisticians to greater mathematical prowess, and appears to have made little defense of his procedure of deriving "rational formulae" from measurements of the fittest specimens. The bulk of the data collected by Hobson remained both unanalyzed and undelivered to the MRC, and he lost interest in the anthropometric standards work.[34] Fletcher made several further attempts to obtain a report from Hobson, but became increasingly frustrated.[35] Greenwood formed the view that the responsibility for the unsatisfactory state of affairs lay with Dreyer,[36] but eventually Fletcher blamed Brownlee as MRC statistician and member of the Anthropometric Standards Committee. Fletcher told Brownlee:

> It is terribly depressing to realize what waste of time and money has come of this statistical work done for your Anthropometric Committee. On that Committee you were our only statistical representative. . . . [T]he work has cost the Council not much below £3000, and apparently you now agree with all the other statisticians that the suggestions under which the work was done were valueless. I had always believed that, in the opinion of your Committee, whether Dreyer's hypothesis had value or not, the accurate recording of these measurement data would produce empirical results of some value; but apparently you now think it is improbable that anything whatever can be gleaned from them, and we must write the whole thing off as a loss.[37]

DISCUSSION AND CONCLUSIONS

The story of the development of the Dreyer method serves to emphasize that techniques for assessment of the dimensions and fitness of the body may be regarded, on one level, as expressions of the aspirations of professionals involved in devising and promoting such techniques. During the first world war, scientists in Britain had been able to demonstrate clearly, for the first time, the value of scientific research to the state (Turner

1980). In the early postwar period they sought to consolidate their position by demonstrating the application of science to the problems of postwar reconstruction. The Dreyer method aimed to assist the active management of the bodies of individuals and groups in the population by scientists and health professionals, on behalf of the state.

The rise and fall of the Dreyer method depended upon the broader context in which it was put forward, and negotiations and conflicts between professionals. The development of the technique was encouraged because it initially appeared to influential people within the medical research establishment, to be a fine example of the application of mathematics to medical problems. The attraction of the method was further enhanced by its apparent ability to secure a rapid return on investment in medical research, for both public health and clinical medicine. The demise of the method was bound up with the rise of the new specialty of medical statistics, emerging from Karl Pearson's school of statistics, of which Major Greenwood was the chief and most influential representative. The new medical statisticians developed and deployed new sophisticated mathematical techniques, and regarded such efforts as those made by Dreyer as merely amateur arithmetical tinkering. But the fate of the Dreyer method was also linked to the fate of hopes that large-scale and systematic anthropometry would make major contributions to reconstruction and the improvement of public health in Britain during the period after the first world war. This, in turn, was a consequence of the rapid impact of economic realities, which ensured that the activities of the newly formed Ministry of Health were carefully controlled by the Treasury (Savage 1996). The official rudimentary anthropometric activities of school medical officers, which had been carried out as part of routine medical inspections of school children since before the war, did continue during the interwar period. However, by the 1930s, data from these inspections were used more to defend the record of the government against accusations that unemployment and government policies had led to the deterioration in the condition of children, than to plan remedial measures when areas of poor physique were identified (Harris 1995:57–58; Webster 1982).

In putting forward his system of assessing bodies, Dreyer presupposed the creation of scientific-medical-administrative machinery that would smoothly translate knowledge about poor physique and nutrition into practical action. Such aspirations were, of course, never realized. During the 1930s scientist-campaigners such as John Boyd Orr, author of *Food Health and Income* (1936), and nutrition activist Frederick le Gros Clark, secretary of the left-wing Committee Against Malnutrition, founded in 1934 (Pirie 1986), sought in vain to persuade the British government to introduce comprehensive programs to alleviate problems caused by poor diets. Such action as was undertaken by the government in the late 1930s was confined mainly to milk for school children (Webster 1997:191) and action on the wider issue of physical fitness was concerned largely with the encouragement of local voluntary efforts by the subsidy of playing fields and similar facilities (Welshman 1996).

During the interwar period the major problem concerning people such as Dreyer and others was poor development and ill-health, frequently caused by quantitative and qualitative deficiencies in diets. A comprehensive system to control food supply and distribution, administered by experts, was rapidly introduced during the second world war, but before the end of the conflict it was clear to men such as le Gros Clark that such an intervention would not be sustained. Clark began to develop a theory of dietary management of the population that relied upon nutrition education based upon the insights of sociology and psychology (Clark 1944, 1945). This vision eventually found practical expression in the "health promotion" movement of the 1980s and 1990s, which gave rise to a new group of health professionals employed by local and central government (Bunton and MacDonald 1992; Bunton, Nettleton, and Burrows 1995; Dines and Cribb 1993). By the 1980s, however, the major problem had become obesity and other problems caused by overeating.

But while the nature of the problem may have changed in this sense, it is worth comparing the systems for assessing body size and fitness put forward by Dreyer, and that which appears within modern health promotion literature. As has been observed, the Dreyer method involved the use of tests administered by experts and interpreted by means of complicated tables and calculations. The modern health promotion literature, in contrast, contains simple graphs and tables relating weight to standing height, which consumers can use, with the assistance of a set of bathroom scales, to assess themselves as "underweight," "OK," "overweight," "fat," or "very fat" (e.g., Health Education Authority 1991:8). The aim of actively managing the bodies of the population on behalf of the state appears to have given way to the provision to the public of the necessary tools for bodily self-discipline. Dreyer's encounter with the statisticians may be regarded as one episode in the process of this transition. More generally, however, the main contemporary relevance of the Dreyer episode is that it emphasizes that the rise and fall of particularly technical definitions of desirable body dimensions, and associated methods of assessment, are correlated with the efforts of experts to establish and defend particular roles in society.

ACKNOWLEDGMENTS

The authors wish to thank Bernard Harris and John Komlos, the organizers of and participants in two different research workshops at which earlier versions of this chapter were presented. David Smith also wishes to thank the Wellcome Trust for their support during the preparation of this chapter.

NOTES

1. Dreyer's wartime activities are chronicled in Public Record Office, Kew (hereafter PRO) FD5/30 and FD5/31.

2. W. Fletcher to J. L. Birley, 23 May 1917, PRO FD5/30.

3. G. Dreyer, "The Normal Vital Capacity in Man in its relation to the size of the body. The importance of this measurement as a guide to physical fitness under different conditions and in different classes of individuals," June 1919, PRO FD1/3756.

4. W. Fletcher to G. Dreyer, 30 June 1919, PRO FD1/3756.

5. W. Fletcher and G. Dreyer, 23 December 1919, PRO FD1/3762.

6. W. Fletcher, "Anthropometric Standards," 12 January 1920, PRO FD1/3762.

7. W. Fletcher to Sprigge, 19 May 1920, PRO FD1/3756.

8. A. L. Thomson to G. Dreyer, 25 June 1920; A. L. Thomson to Dr Kaye, 28 June 1920, PRO FD1/3756.

9. Anthropometric Standards Committee Minutes, 12 January; 10 February; 5 May 1920, PRO FD1/5332.

10. Another example is the fate of plans to establish a National Nutritional Laboratory to continue the work started by the Food (War) Committee of the Royal Society. See Smith (1997).

11. "Standards of Physique and Physical Fitness" (leaflet), December 1919, PRO FD1/3756.

12. F. G. Hobson to A. L. Thomson, 28 October; 4, 22 November 1919, PRO FD1/3756.

13. F. G. Hobson to W. Fletcher, 23 February 1920, PRO FD1/3756.

14. F. G. Hobson to A. L. Thomson, 3 March 1920; F. G. Hobson to W. Fletcher, 4 July 1920, PRO FD1/3756.

15. A. A. Mumford to MRC, 17 July 1920, A. V. Hill to W. Fletcher, 17 July 1920 PRO FD1/3764.

16. F G. Hobson to A. L. Thomson, 26 July 1920, PRO FD1/3756.

17. F. G. Hobson to A. L. Thomson, 25 May 1921, FD1/3762.

18. Senior Medical Officer, Nottingham, to A. L. Thomson, 16 November 1921, PRO FD1/3756.

19. A. A. E. Newth (1921).

20. "Special Report by Dr. A. A. E. Newth." n.d., PRO FD1/3756.

21. G. Dreyer and F. G. Hobson, "Report from the Department of Pathology, University of Oxford," n.d., PRO FD1/3756.

22. "Special Report by Dr A. A. E. Newth." n.d., PRO FD1/3756.

23. M. Greenwood to W. Fletcher, 22 January; 25 July 1920, PRO FD5/91.

24. M. Greenwood to W. Fletcher, 21 March 1921, PRO FD5/91. *Biometrika* had been established in 1901, primarily by Karl Pearson, who was also its editor. It was

one of the first journals devoted to statistical theory, and became the major vehicle for publication by Pearson, his students, and collaborators (MacKenzie 1981:9–10).

25. A. V. Hill to W. Fletcher, PRO FD1/3764.

26. A. V. Hill to W. Fletcher, PRO FD1/3764.

27. Anthropometric Standards Committee Minutes, 19 December 1921, PRO FD1/5332.

28. F. G. Hobson to W. Fletcher, 4 January 1922, PRO FD1/3762.

29. Fletcher refers to his response to Hobson's letter on 4 January 1922 in W. Fletcher to A. Keith, 1 April 1922, PRO FD1/3762.

30. W. Fletcher to A. Keith, 1 April 1922, PRO FD1/3762.

31. Anthropometric Standards Committee Minutes, 19 April 1922, PRO FD1/5332.

32. K. Pearson to W. Fletcher, PRO FD1/3763.

33. Anthropometric Standards Committee Minutes, 31 October 1922, PRO FD1/5332.

34. F. G. Hobson to W. Fletcher, 12 March 1923, PRO/3756.

35. W. Fletcher to F. G. Hobson, 24 October 1923, FD1/3756.

36. M. Greenwood to W. Fletcher, 5 March 1924, PRO FD1/3763.

37. W. Fletcher to J. Brownlee, 23 June 1924, PRO FD1/3763.

REFERENCES

Bunton, R., and G. MacDonald (eds.). 1992. *Health Promotion: Disciplines and Diversity.* London: Routledge.

Bunton, R., S. Nettleton, and R. Burrows (eds.). 1995. *The Sociology of Health Promotion.* London: Routledge.

Clark, F. le Gros. 1944. "Preamble to Post-War Food Education." *British Medical Journal* 2:763–65.

———. 1945. "'Food Advice' in a Post-War World." *Health Education Journal* 3:75–78.

Cooter, R. 1993. "War and Modern Medicine." Pp. 1536–73 in *Companion Encyclopedia of the History of Medicine,* edited by W. F. Bynum and R. Porter. London: Routledge.

Cripps, L. D., M. Greenwood, and E. M. Newbold. 1923. "A Biometric Study of the Inter-Relations of 'Vital Capacity,' Stature, and Weight in a Sample of Healthy Male Adults." *Biometrika* 14:316–36.

Dines, A., and A. Cribb (eds.). 1993. *Health Promotion: Concepts and Practice.* Oxford: Blackwell.

Douglas, S. R. 1932–1935. "Georges Dreyer 1831–1934." *Royal Society Obituary Notices* 1:569–76.

Dreyer, G. 1919. "Investigation on the Normal Vital Capacity in Man and Its Relation to Size of the Body." *Lancet* 2:227–34.

———. 1919–1920. "Biological Standards and their Application in Medicine." *Harvey Society Lectures* 20:21–25.

Dreyer, G., and L. S. T. Burrell. 1920. "The Vital Capacity Constants Applied to the Study of Pulmonary Tuberculosis. The Importance of these Constants as a

Guide to the Classification and as a Means of Ascertaining the Results of Treatment." *Lancet* 1:1212–16.

Dreyer, G., and G. F. Hanson. 1920. *The Assessment of Physical Fitness*. London: Cassell.

Dreyer G., W. Ray, and E. W. A. Walker. 1912–1913. "The Size of the Aorta in Warm-Blooded Animals and Its Relationship to the Body Weight and to the Surface Area Expressed in a Formula." *Proceedings of the Royal Society, Ser. B* 86:56–65.

Dreyer, G., and E. W. A. Walker. 1913. "The Effect of Altitude on Blood Volume, Together with Further Observations on the Blood of Warm-Blooded and Cold-Blooded Animals." *Lancet* 2:1175–77.

———. 1919. "'Iatro-Mathematics,' A Plea for a More General Application of the Value of Applied Mathematics and Exact Quantitative Methods in Biological Science." *New York* 1:40–51.

Greenwood, M. 1924. "Is the Statistical Method of Any Value in Medical Research." *Lancet* 2:153–58.

Harris, B. 1995. *The Health of the Schoolchild: A History of the School Medical Service in England and Wales*. Buckingham: Open University Press.

Health Education Authority. 1991. *Beating Heart Disease*. London: Health Education Authority.

Hogben, L. 1950–1951. "Major Greenwood." *Obituary Notices of Fellows of the Royal Society* 7:139–54.

Hutchinson, J. 1846. "On the Capacity of the Lungs and on the Respiratory Functions." *Lancet* 1:630–32.

Keith, A. 1919. "Anthropometry and National Health." *Journal of State Medicine* 27(2):33–42.

Lawrence, C. 1985. "Incommunicable Knowledge: Science, Technology and the Clinical Art in Britain 1850–1914." *Journal of Contemporary History* 20:503–29.

MacKenzie, D. 1981. *Statistics in Britain 1865–1930: The Social Construction of Scientific Knowledge*. Edinburgh: Edinburgh University Press.

Medical Research Committee. 1917. *Report of the Medical Research Committee 1916–17*. London: HMSO.

Medical Research Council. 1920. *Report of the Medical Research Council 1919–20*. London: HMSO.

Ministry of National Service. 1920. *Report upon the Physical Examination of Men of Military Age by National Service Medical Boards from November 1st 1917–October 31st 1918*. London: HMSO.

Morrell, J. 1997. *Science at Oxford 1914–1939: Transforming an Arts University*. Oxford: Oxford University Press.

Mumford, A., and M. Young. 1923. "The Interrelationships of the Physical Measurements and the Vital Capacity." *Biometrika* 1923:109–33.

Newth, A. A. E. 1921. "Appendix C." P. 197 in *Annual Report of the Chief Medical Officer of the Board of Education for 1920*. London: HMSO.

Orr, J. B. 1936. *Food Health and Income: Report on a Survey of Diet in Relation to Income*. London: Macmillan.

Pearson, K. 1920. "On the Need for a New Technique in Anthropology." *Lancet* 2:697.

Pirie, N. W. 1986. "Frederick le Gros Clark." Pp. 149–50 in *Dictionary of National*

Biography, edited by Lord Blake and C. S. Nicholls. Oxford: Oxford University Press.

Rosser Matthews, J. 1995. "Major Greenwood versus Almroth Wright: Contrasting Visions of 'Scientific' Medicine in Edwardian Britain." *Bulletin of the History of Medicine* 69:30–43.

Savage, G. 1996. "The Ministry of Health: Fiscal versus Social Responsibility." Pp. 158–78 in *The Social Construction of Expertise: The English Civil Service and its Influence 1919–1939,* edited by G. Savage. Pittsburgh, PA: University of Pittsburgh Press.

Smith, D. F. 1997. "Nutrition Science and the Two World Wars." Pp. 142–65 in *Nutrition in Britain: Science, Scientists and Politics in the Twentieth Century,* edited by D. F. Smith. London: Routledge.

Thomson, A. L. 1973. *Half a Century of Medical Research.* Volume 1: *Origins and Policy of the Medical Research Council (UK).* London: HMSO.

Turner, F. M. 1980. "Public Science in Britain, 1880–1918." *Isis* 71:589–608.

Walker, E. W. A. 1915–1917. "The Growth of the Body in Man—The Relationship between the Body-Weight and the Body-Length (Stem-Length)." *Proceedings of the Royal Society, Ser. B* 89:157–73.

Webster, C. 1982. "Healthy or Hungry Thirties." *History Workshop* 13:110–29.

———. 1997. "Government Policy on School Meals and Welfare Foods 1939–1970." Pp. 190–213 in *Nutrition in Britain: Science, Scientists and Politics in the Twentieth Century,* edited by D. F. Smith. London: Routledge.

Welshman, J. 1996. "Physical Education and the School Medical Service in England and Wales, 1907–1939." *Social History of Medicine* 9:31–48.

IV

GENDERED DIMENSIONS

6

Ideal Weight/Ideal Women
Society Constructs the Female

NITA MARY MCKINLEY

Historically, social constructions of the ideal woman have been conspicuously connected with weight. For example, in the latter part of the nineteenth century, when the ideal woman of the emerging middle class was both an ornamental and maternal object, *Harper's Bazaar* was advising women to exercise infrequently and to eat more cream and butter in order to preserve their womanly curves (Dorenkamp, McClymer, Moynihan, and Vadum 1985). After the turn of the century, the ideal middle-class woman was becoming more active and independent and, in growing numbers, working outside the domestic sphere (Seid 1989). At this time, fashion and medical authorities began exhorting her to shed excess flesh. More recently, *ideal weight* has come into popular culture with the introduction of the Metropolitan Life Insurance Company weight charts in the 1940s (ibid.). This narrow range of sizes has been constructed to be a sign not only of health, but also of a wide array of behaviors from how much a woman cares about herself to how much control she has of her appetites (both nutritional and sexual). In this chapter, I will demonstrate how the ideologies of weight closely parallel ideologies of womanhood, how fat stigmatization enforces conformity to the requirements of the ideal woman, as well as to ideal weight, and how being fat may function as a form of resistance to gender ideologies for women.

IDEAL WEIGHT AS GENDERED

Whether they call it "ideal weight," "desirable weight," or "healthy weight," public health officials have designated a narrow range of weights at which we are supposedly most healthy, that is, have the lowest levels of disease and the longest life expectancy (Seid 1989). The first "ideal weight" charts, published in 1942 for men and in 1943 for women by the Metropolitan Life Insurance Company, were determined from the weight of the longest-lived policyholders at the time they took out their insurance policies and were below the average weight for Americans at the time. These ideals have gone up and down over the succeeding decades, so that the number of overweight Americans has fluctuated (usually upward) by definitional fiat (ibid.). By the 1970s, officials were claiming that any level of thinness was healthier than being fat and that the thinner a person was, the healthier she or he was.

There have been few official challenges to the claim "fat equals unhealthy, thinness equals healthy" (Mayer 1983a).[1] For example, the current Shape Up America Program (Shape Up America! 1997) counsels readers, "If you are at or below the 'Healthy Weight,' your goal is to maintain this weight for the remainder of your life." In other advice, the only reasons given for not losing weight are pregnancy, certain medical conditions, and if one has anorexia nervosa or a terminal illness. So there is no low end for healthy weight and no weight for which the advice is to *gain* weight in order to "shape up." The medicalization and stigmatization of anorexia nervosa serves to create social distance from the sufferers of this eating disorder and lessens its impact as a social problem (Way 1995). At the same time, it constructs two categories—thinness that is healthy and thinness that is not healthy—allowing us to conceive of thinness that is healthy. This in turn reinforces the construction of ideal, healthy weight as being as thin as possible and conflates ideal weight with extremes of thinness that are typically portrayed in women's magazines.

Although ideal weight may be pursued through drugs or surgery, more generally experts claim that ideal weight must be achieved through a combination of healthy eating, increased physical activity, and adopting an appropriate "lifestyle" (Shape Up America! 1997). In a circular argument, experts also claim that a person's weight provides the evidence that a person's lifestyle is correct and that he or she is eating in a healthy manner and exercising sufficiently (Mayer 1983a; Seid 1989), and thus "ideal weight" becomes not only a number on a scale, but the definition of "proper lifestyle," "healthy eating," and "sufficient exercise." In addition to these presumptions, dominant culture associates fatness with everything from being ugly to being weak-willed and morally impaired (Crandall 1994), so being thin provides evidence that we are attractive, in control, and morally upright. This ideology depends on the assumption that weight can successfully be controlled, a claim that is not well supported by empirical evidence (Berg 1995; Ernsberger 1997).

Both women and men are evaluated by their weight, but weight has special meaning for women. Several theorists (for example, Bartky 1988;

Spitzack 1990) have noted how dominant culture constructs the feminine body as an object to be watched. Psychological research shows that from the day they are identified as female, girls learn that others evaluate them in terms of their appearance, whereas boys are evaluated on other bases such as strength, coordination, and alertness (Rubin, Provenzano, and Luria 1974; Stern and Karraker 1989). Girls internalize this view of themselves, learning to watch their own bodies as an outside observer and to regulate their "body size and contours, its appetite, posture, gestures and general comportment in space, and the appearance of each of its visible parts" (Bartky 1988:80). The social construction of the female body as an object to be watched makes the definition and evaluation of women in terms of appearance seem "natural." Because women themselves, as well as dominant culture, define women by their appearance, women are particularly susceptible to public claims related to appearance and weight. So although officials report that weight is a grave national problem and more men than women are overweight (National Academy of Sciences, National Research Council 1989), more women than men are dieting at any given time, women are more likely than men to use diet drugs, and women are more likely to use more drastic means such as surgery to lose weight (Berg 1995; Wolf 1991).

Also because women are defined primarily in terms of their appearance and weight, ideologies about weight and ideologies about womanhood are intimately connected. For example, as we have seen, ideal weight is being as thin as one can possibly be. Being small and taking up little space is part of the traditional female gender role (Henley 1977; Schur 1984). In achieving or working toward ideal weight, women can become as small as they can possibly be. Again, there is no downward limit either to the space allotted to women or to ideal weight, which is evidenced by the decreasing size of women portrayed in the popular media (Garner, Garfinkel, Schwartz, and Thompson 1980; Wiseman, Gray, Mosimann, and Ahrens 1992) and the extensive documentation of women's desire to lose weight, often when they are thinner than supposedly "healthy weight" (see Rodin, Silberstein, and Striegel-Moore 1985). In contrast, the traditional male gender role stresses physical strength and aggression (Pleck 1981). Being as thin as possible is not consistent with this role. Thus, in this case, the construction of ideal weight parallels the construction of the traditional ideal woman and ideal weight becomes gendered.

IDEAL WOMEN AND IDEAL WEIGHT

Gender is one of the major organizing categories in human societies (Lorber 1994). The dominant culture's gender roles crystallize an extensive discourse of normative behavior for women. We can infer the content of these gender roles by observing the gendered nature of people's behavior and the sanctions that society imposes when roles are transgressed (Schur 1984). Other theorists have inferred gender roles by examining the cultural messages implicit in media such as advertisements and movies (for example, Bordo 1993; Kilbourne 1994). These cultural roles are also inscribed in academic discourse and can be inferred from examining theories about gender and gendered behavior.

The construction of the ideal woman is not monolithic, however, and within U.S. culture, there are multiple competing meanings. The ideal woman has been constructed as both passive and active, as mother and sex object. Even within a given discourse, the prescribed roles for the ideal woman may be contradictory. For example, the "superwoman" of popular culture must be both feminine and masculine, two mutually exclusive categories (Bordo 1990). The construct of ideal weight also encodes multiple, conflicting meanings. The thin body can be simultaneously feminine, that is, small, fragile, and vulnerable, and masculine, that is, lacking in female breasts and hips (ibid.). In this section, I identify some of the important components of the cultural constructions of the ideal woman, including those dealing with femininity norms, presentation norms, maternity norms, and sexual norms, utilizing examples from popular culture, various psychological and sociobiological theories of gender, and feminist writings on gender. Each of these multiple and sometimes conflicting constructions of the ideal woman has parallels in the cultural constructions of ideal weight.

Femininity Norms

Norms of femininity encompass presentation, maternal, and sexual norms. However, "femininity" is itself a dimension that appears to be useful for understanding gender within dominant culture (Hyde 1991). Psychologists define "femininity" and "masculinity" in terms of whatever traits and behaviors distinguish reliably between women and men, and then those identified traits and behaviors become a requirement for women's "normal" behavior (Constantinople 1973). Women who do not follow the norms and roles for femininity have been defined as deviant both within psychology and popular culture and even labeled mentally ill (Chesler 1972; Schur 1984). Culture also constructs ideal weight as normal. Rather than being normally distributed as other attributes, such as height, "normal weight" is "ideal weight." Those whose weights vary even slightly from ideal are deviant (Seid 1989). Thus, femininity and ideal weight are both categories that have been useful for defining people as deviant.

Beginning with the 1970s wave of feminism, "androgyny" replaced "femininity" as the norm for the ideal woman in dominant culture. Within psychological discourse, the dichotomous "feminine" and "masculine" categories were challenged and the ideal woman was reconstructed as an androgynous mix of "expressive" and "instrumental" (see Bem 1974). The popular representations of this androgynous woman might be expressive, but more typically, she rejected traditional roles and was assertive and strong. She was in control of her life and ready to enter the masculine public sphere (Bordo 1993). The construction of ideal weight parallels this construction. Ideal weight symbolizes a rejection of traditional domestic roles for women (Bordo 1990; Rodin et al. 1985). The fit, fat-free body that popular media portrays as ideal in weight is rare in women, and is more typical of the bodies of men (Seid 1989), and is therefore the perfect body for the male sphere.

More recently, the ideal woman of popular culture is both feminine and masculine, and neither. She constructs herself with ease, embracing multiplicity and "a construction of life as plastic possibility and weightless choice, undetermined by history, social location, or even individual biography" (Bordo 1993:251). Bordo analyzed the actress Madonna as an example of this postmodern woman who refuses definition, and simultaneously embraces and defies traditional gender definitions.[2] The dexterity with which the postmodern woman can put on one identity or another is matched by the fluidity of the constructions of ideal weight. Ideal weight can be both masculine and feminine, both rejecting traditional roles, as well as encompassing them.

Presentation Norms

Presentation norms refer to the wide range of behaviors and visual norms for the presentation of self that establish the gendered base of routine interactions within dominant culture (Schur 1984). I will discuss the presentation of the ideal woman in terms of passivity/control and physical attractiveness, and show how these constructions parallel constructions of ideal weight.

Passivity/Control. The dichotomy of male-as-active, female-as-passive permeates Western constructions of the world and of the self (Bordo 1993). Freud's (1962) psychoanalytic theory exemplifies this cultural construction of the female as passive; he argued that female sexuality is passive, waiting to be impregnated, and this becomes a trait of her personality. Sociobiologists, who argue that gendered traits evolved because of the differing reproductive strategies for women and men, define the ideal woman as one who attracts and then chooses (Buss 1987); she does not actively pursue. Ideal weight can also be connected to passivity in two ways. First of all, dieting discourse suggests that we can achieve ideal weight when we quit fighting our bodies and thus become passive (Spitzack 1990). Second, weight loss advocates, such as Jenny Craig, Inc. (1997), have insisted on the necessity of relying on experts to tell people how to achieve and maintain ideal weight, again placing the individual in a passive position.

Feminist constructions of the ideal woman have rejected passivity and emphasized personal freedom and control, and empowerment. This ideal woman can achieve anything she wants. "'This year,' Betty [Friedan] proclaimed, 'women will make policy, not coffee!'" (Cohen 1988:338). Constructions of ideal weight parallel these feminist constructions of the ideal woman. For example, imagery in advertising associates the norms of control and freedom with ideal weight. Shaping the body is equated with the ability to shape one's life (Bordo 1993) and products designed to help women attain ideal weight offer women a "taste of freedom" (Kilbourne 1994). At the same time, dominant culture constructs weight loss as a significant achievement, especially for women (Rodin et al. 1985).

Dominant social discourse has adopted and transformed this feminist construction of the active, empowered woman. The ideal woman must now remain "feminine" while she is in control, that is, she must not appear to transgress traditional gender roles even as she transgresses them. While she "Seal[s] the Deal! (and Make[s] Him Commit 100%)" (which is supposedly tougher than closing a media merger), she must let her male partner do the pursing in the relationship, as an article in *Cosmopolitan* claimed (Fein and Schneider 1997:209). Contestants in the 1997 Miss America pageant were encouraged to express their individuality by "choosing" whether to wear a one-piece or two-piece swim suit (Miss America Organization 1997). In fact, the only control the ideal woman is allowed is usually self-control. The "empowerment" offered to women is "a certain state of mind (feeling powerful, competent, worthy of esteem, able to make free choices and influence their world), *while leaving structural conditions unchanged*" (Kitzinger and Perkins 1993:43, emphasis in the original). Constructions of ideal weight also emphasize simultaneous freedom and self-control. For example, Weight Watchers, which claims to teach people how to change their lifestyle so that they can achieve and maintain healthy weight, has a "Freedom Plan," which "combines the freedom you want with the control you need" (Weight Watchers Interactive 1997). Ideal weight also offers women empowerment (Spitzack 1990). However, working to achieve an ideal weight allows women to be active and empowered in a way that does not challenge gender roles (Kilbourne 1994; Rodin et al. 1985).

Attractiveness. Dominant culture requires that the ideal woman be attractive (Brownmiller 1984; Wolf 1991). Beauty is not so much esthetically important as it is a sign that the woman is fulfilled in her role as a woman (Spitzack 1990). But beauty is a subjective state that requires approval from someone else, so that "attractive" carries the meaning "attractive *to someone*" (Wolf 1991). The attractive ideal woman is clearly heterosexual,[3] that is, attractive to men (Spitzack 1990). Being attractive demonstrates that a woman cares about how she looks to others, particularly men. Constructions of ideal weight and attractiveness are closely related. More than any other standard of beauty, thinness is a major component of the current standard of attractiveness for women (Rodin et al. 1985). Ideal weight is constructed as attractive, and particularly attractive to men. Ideal weight and weight management also demonstrate that a woman cares about her appearance and *wants* to be attractive (Spitzack 1990).

The mass media's long history of accusing feminists of being ugly demonstrates the importance of feminism in challenging cultural requirements for attractiveness in women (Rothblum 1994). However, as feminist ideas have permeated popular culture and women's independence has been emphasized, attractiveness continues to be important for the ideal woman. The focus, however, changes from standards of frailty to an "action beauty," that is, beauty based on athleticism and health (Faludi 1991). This is a "natural beauty," supposedly not characterized by artifice (although one may have to use the right kind of makeup to achieve this look!). Constructions of ideal weight have undergone similar metamorphoses. Since experts have changed their prescriptions for the ideal body from "thinness" to "fitness," prescriptions for achieving ideal weight no longer include simple dietary restriction, but also exercise (see Shape Up America! 1997). Additionally, ideal weight is achieved by changing the body directly and thus appears more natural than cosmetics or fashion (Seid 1989). An article in *First for Women* magazine illustrates the "naturalness" of ideal weight: "Your body was designed for 'perfect eating,' a completely unconscious process that automatically adjusts calorie and nutrition intake to produce your ideal weight" (1997:32).

Maternity Norms

Social constructions of the female as maternal include the understanding that women will be literally reproductive, but also nurturers. Whether women's maternal personality is attributed to her biology, her socialization, or to her role as caretaker of children, this construction is prevalent in cultural discourses. One might expect that ample breasts and hips would be important to these constructions of ideal womanhood, given that

women have been assigned to maternal roles (both as nurturer and repro-
ducer) because of their biological bodies (see Ortner 1974). However, in
this section I will show how construction of the ideal woman as maternal
parallels construction of ideal weight, so that thinness, not a lush body, is
associated with maternity norms.

Woman as Nurturer.   Dominant discourse constructs the ideal woman
as a nurturer, but she only nurtures others, not herself. Women's needs for
nurturing are constructed as excessive and dangerous, that is, too "needy"
(Bordo 1993). On the other hand, some feminist psychologists have challenged this construction. For example, Gilligan (1982) described the highest level of functioning for women as taking care of both themselves and
others. Ideal weight can carry both these disparate views of ideal womanhood.

Psychoanalytic theory constructs fatness as being caused by a longing
for love or emotional warmth (Seid 1989). Ideal weight, then, shows that a
woman has her own neediness under control. In addition, she both literally and figuratively does not feed herself more than is absolutely necessary. However, ideal weight also carries the contradictory meaning that a
woman cares about herself and takes care of herself (Spitzack 1990).

Reproduction.   In addition to nurturing others, dominant culture associates the ideal woman with motherhood and reproduction. According to
sociobiological discourse, for a woman to be reproductively successful,
she must attract a mate by demonstrating her reproductive value through
cues to her health and age (Buss 1987). Thus, the ideal reproductive
woman must appear healthy and young. We have seen that dominant culture associates ideal weight with health. Thinness is also a sign of youth.
Humans fatten as they age and managing weight often represents an
attempt to control aging (Bordo 1993). Rather than displaying a "maternal
body" with ample breasts and hips, women can demonstrate their reproductive value by signaling their health and youth through ideal weight.

Feminist reconstructions of maternity norms for the ideal woman center
on choice. This ideal woman chooses when and whether she will use her
biological ability to reproduce. As de Beauvoir (1952) argued, a woman's
physiology does not have to control her destiny. This ideally maternal
woman is evident in the feminist framing of the abortion debate in terms of
choice. The construction of ideal weight fits within this construction of
choice as well. Weight can presumably be chosen by the way one eats and
exercises. More importantly perhaps, when a woman controls her weight
and thus her body, she graphically illustrates the idea that biology is not
destiny (Bordo 1993).

Sexual Norms

Cultural constructions of female sexuality are ambivalent, including both fear and desire (Schur 1984). Dominant constructions of the ideal woman's sexuality have two aspects: Female desire must be to give pleasure to one's male partner and female desire in its own right must be controlled, although feminist revisions of women's sexuality have emphasized desire. Perhaps because of cultural ambivalence toward female desire, female sexuality also is closely connected to issues of morality. In this section, I will describe how these sexual norms parallel constructions of ideal weight.

Male Pleasure and Female Desire.   MacKinnon argues that within dominant culture, sexuality is "the gaze that constructs women as objects for male pleasure" (1987:53). Freud's psychoanalytic theory is consistent with this construction of female sexuality in terms of male pleasure: To achieve maturity, a woman must transfer her erotic feelings from her clitoris to her vagina (Ehrenreich and English 1978). Thus the only acceptable "mature" pleasure for a woman is that sexual act which is most accommodating to the male sexual organ, rather than her own. We have seen that ideal weight is constructed as attractive to men. Thinness itself has become highly eroticized, with 69 percent of *Playboy* centerfolds from 1979 to 1988 having weights 15 percent or more below the expected weight for their height (Wiseman et al. 1992).

The ideal woman must be sexual, but not too sexual (Schur 1984). The "frigid" woman threatens male pleasure; the "oversexed" woman threatens male virility. In dominant culture, female desire for its own sake is often portrayed as dangerous and loathsome (Bordo 1993; Schur 1984). Fatness represents bodily desire out of control and thus ideal weight represents properly controlled desire. To demonstrate this, Bordo (1993) deconstructed the underlying sexual messages in advertisements for food to illustrate the differences in acceptable desire for women and men. Voracious appetites are acceptable only for men. (Can we even imagine a "Hungry Woman" TV dinner, except as humor?) Women's desire is to be contained and the only "indulgence" allowed is a low-calorie product. Thus, a woman who is fat is doubly sexually deviant: she must be engaging in sex (eating) for her own pleasure and she presumably displays a voracious appetite. A woman with ideal weight, on the other hand, has more appropriate controlled her appetites.

Feminists have challenged these constructions of female desire; the ideal woman may choose to pursue sexual pleasure as an end in itself. Books like Brown's (1962) *Sex and the Single Girl* proclaimed women were sexual beings with their own desires (Ehrenreich and English 1978). Ideal weight has been constructed as a necessity for a sexual life, both psychologically and interpersonally. In contradiction to the previously mentioned "voracious appetites" of fat women, experts have also claimed that fat people are lacking in sexual desire (Seid 1989) and so ideal weight is constructed as a sign of psychological sexual desire. Additionally, we believe that the body that comes with ideal weight has become a necessity for pursuing an active sex life (Bordo 1993).

Female Sexuality and Morality. Dominant culture links morality particularly with women's sexuality, with the ideal woman demonstrating her pureness by her sexual behavior. "Going all the way" was the traditional measure of whether girls were "good" or "bad" and despite some changes in which acts are acceptable, female goodness is still judged on the basis of sexual behavior (Thompson 1995). Through her sexual behavior, then, a woman demonstrates her moral character. Ideal weight has also been connected with moral behavior (Sobal 1995). Fatness is "bad" and "sinful" and so conversely, thin is "good." The woman who watches her weight and works to achieve ideal weight has willpower and self-control and this sort of self-control often becomes more important than sexual self-control. Nowadays when a woman says she was "bad," we understand that to mean she has gone off her diet, not that she been involved in a sexual liaison (Kilbourne 1994). Thus, body weight presumably demonstrates moral character even more so than sex.

Summary

The constructions of the ideal woman discussed above are multiple and contradictory, as are the constructions of ideal weight, and there are extensive parallels between these two constructions. Because of the ability of ideal weight to embody these multiple contradictory meanings, it becomes the sine qua non of ideal womanhood, able to encompass the multiple meanings of disparate ideologies. Ironically, because "ideal weight" embodies contradictory meanings, it is endorsed by competing ideological factions, such as feminist and dominant discourses.[4] In the following section, I will examine how women's discontent with their weight, which is encouraged by these connections between ideal womanhood and ideal weight, controls women's behavior.

WEIGHT AND WOMEN: THE NORMALIZING DISCONTENT

Weight dissatisfaction is so common among women that it is called "normative" (see Rodin et al. 1985). Foucault (1978) argued that through the articulation of what is normal and what is not, the social scientist brings the body under social control through the creation of desire, rather than through more direct control. Through the positive construction of ideal weight, the stigmatization of fatness, and the connection of ideal weight with ideal womanhood, dominant culture creates the desire for thinness, especially in women, and simultaneously controls women's behavior. Thus, we can understand this ubiquitous female discontent as *normalizing, rather than normative*.

Discipline of the female body cuts across age, race, class, and sexual orientation (Bordo 1990). As a TV commercial for Equal® brand of nutrasweet, an artificial sweetener sold as a means to control weight, says in an unconsciously ironic message, "We [women] are all different, but we're all Equal." Regardless of her race, ethnicity, age, or sexual orientation, if she wants to be acceptable within dominant culture, a woman must watch her body and control her weight.[5] When a woman internalizes dominant cultural meanings that judge her in terms of her appearance, she feels deep shame when her body does not measure up (Bartky 1988). Rodin et al. (1985) argued that shame is a common emotion women feel in relation to their bodies and that this often keeps them from challenging this judgment based on weight.

The stigmatization of fat women ensures that all women understand the consequences of not watching their bodies. According to dominant culture, fat women are not only physically unhealthy, but also mentally unhealthy, ugly, out of control, and sexually deviant. A fat woman can ameliorate these judgements by confessing her "excess," that is, professing her unhappiness and her desire to achieve ideal weight (Spitzack 1990). Women who do not do this are targets for humiliation and hostility. "If the rest of us are struggling to be acceptable and 'normal,' we cannot allow them [those who are fat and happy] to get away with it; they must be put in their place, be humiliated and defeated" (Bordo 1993:203). A woman who works to achieve ideal weight (or at least says she does), regardless of size, supports the gendered political system that constructs ideal weight (Rodin et al. 1985; Spitzack 1990).

So what are the lessons of femininity inherent in ideal weight? One important feature that many of the multiple conflicting constructions of femininity hold in common is a focus on the body. Working to achieve and maintain ideal weight keeps women focused on their bodies and reinforces the construction of women as primarily bodies. At the same time, while women's attention is focused inward, they presumably will not be focused on challenging external constraints to their lives. A second feature common to many of these constructions of the ideal woman is the demand for containment and control. Women must take up little space both physically and symbolically as they contain their desires and control themselves and their bodies. As she works to achieve and maintain ideal weight, a woman willingly takes up less space in the world (Bordo 1990).

A third feature of these constructions is the difficulty of achieving the norms for ideal women. A woman must feed others, but not herself. She must also beware that she displays just the "right" amount of sexuality. She especially must not age! Some of the requirements for the ideal woman are paradoxical in nature, such as the requirement to be both masculine and feminine or the requirement to be in control, but in a "ladylike" (that is, passive) manner. Constructions of ideal weight appear to resolve some of these dilemmas for women and contain many of the paradoxical meanings of ideal womanhood. However, ideal weight as represented in the popular media has become farther and farther away from the average weight of women and thus harder and harder to achieve (Garner et al. 1980; Wiseman et al. 1992). Schur (1984) has noted how gender norms for women are so stringent that most women can be labeled deviant. Ideal weight, then, provides an additional means for labeling most women deviant.

Constructions of gender as difference and endless debate over whether women are "naturally" emotional, or nurturers, or concerned with their bodies, conceals the social institution of gender as a status variable and as a category for the assignment of resources and power in social relations (Hare-Mustin and Marecek 1990; Lorber 1994). Women have less access than men to resources, including money (Rix 1990), time (Hochschild 1989), and institutional power (Wolf 1991). Male dominance depends on female subordination (Schur 1984). Consistent with women's subordinate position in society, working to achieve ideal weight deprives women of time, energy, and economic resources (Wolf 1991). Women spend their incomes on weight loss programs and use their precious leisure time and energy to exercise and count calories. At the same time, working to achieve illusive ideal weight deprives women of self-esteem and keeps their energies directed toward personal change rather than political change.

Chesler argued that psychotherapy and marriage are similar in that they both "isolate women from each other; both emphasize individual rather than collective solutions to women's unhappiness; both are based on woman's helplessness and dependence on a stronger male authority figure" (1972:108). These "safe havens" encourage women to talk endlessly, rather than to act. In pursuing ideal weight, women also become isolated from each other as they compete for scarce approval of their bodies; they pursue individual solutions, such as obsessively watching and controlling their bodies, rather than collective solutions to their discontent; and they depend on health experts who tell them that *this* diet at last will help them achieve the often unattainable ideal weight [as well as depending on individual men for approval (Mayer 1983b)]. They work endlessly at dieting and exercising, hoping to finally reach that mirage of acceptability that is ideal weight, rather than acting directly on the sources of their discontent (Wolf 1991).

FAT WOMEN AS RESISTERS TO NORMALIZING DISCOURSES

Fatness has alternatively been constructed as a moral problem, a medical problem, and a political problem within U.S. culture (Sobal 1995). The political discourse of fatness highlights the use of fatness as a status variable through which certain groups of people can be stigmatized and exploited. Feminist theorists have argued that the discrimination against fat people is not gender neutral (Rothblum 1994). I have documented the extensive parallels between the constructions of ideal weight and ideal women and argued that the construction of ideal weight and the stigmatization of fatness is a means of social control that ensures women's conformity to gender norms. In this section, I argue that fat women have the potential to challenge both constructions of ideal weight and especially constructions of ideal women.

Fat women have challenged dominant ideologies of ideal weight through the construction of fatness as healthy, beautiful, and sexual. Constructing ideal weight as "healthy" makes claims about weight appear scientific and objective and thus hard to challenge. Whenever I present papers on how standards of thinness oppress women, the first question my usually sympathetic listeners ask is, "But what about health?" Although "health" often appears to be a empirical category, it is itself socially constructed and often means "behaving in a socially acceptable manner" (Chesler 1972; Spitzack 1990). Many of the behaviors required to achieve ideal weight are those associated with eating disorders, including obsessive eating behaviors (Bruch 1976) and obsessive exercise (Blumenthal, O'Toole, and Chang 1984). The recent furor over the diet drug fenfluramine is another example of the strange relationship between weight and health. Beginning around 1992, doctors began prescribing a combination of fenfluramine and phentermine (fen-phen) to help patients lose weight, even though these drugs were never approved for combined use (Golden 1997). As the FDA told drug companies to recall fenfluramine in September 1997 after finding that 30 percent of users had developed heart valve problems, an official of the American Obesity Association claimed that the drug might still be useful for the "obese" (Fox 1997)! Fat women have challenged the "fat equals unhealthy" equation through their creation and participation in fat fitness programs (for example, Lyons and Burgard 1990; Women at Large 1987), through public claims regarding fatness and health (see Burke 1998), and through sharing their experiences of health and ill health (see Schoenfielder and Wieser 1983).

Fat women also have challenged the connection between body size and attractiveness. Constructing ideal weight as attractive and sexual is powerful because it threatens fat women with the loss of relationships. Because attractiveness to men is supposedly required for women to have relationships, the message is: Women must be thin to be loved. However, fat women have argued that their body size is sensual and attractive to men. One respondent to a survey I conducted with fat acceptance activists wrote, "I would not be nearly so sexy in a size 10. I am much more attractive, sexual and sensually responsive." Roseanne, star of the long-running sit-com by that name, is surrounded by loving friends and family, especially in her TV persona. She is also openly sexual. In addition, magazines like *Radiance: The Magazine for Large Women*, *BBW* (Big Beautiful Woman), and *Mode*, have published images of fat women, showing them to be both sensual and attractive and involved in romantic relationships (see Evans 1998).

Challenging these constructions of ideal weight may be an important political tactic for dealing with the stigmatization of fatness, but arguing that fat women can be healthy, attractive, and sexual does not necessarily challenge constructions of the ideal woman, especially the construction that women should be watched and judged by their bodies. However, just as anorexia nervosa may be an embodiment of female protest against the strictures in a woman's life (Bordo 1993), a fat body, especially when the woman refuses to apologize for her size, can also embody protest against the control and limitations of the female gender role. However, while we hold a somewhat ambivalent attitude toward the woman with anorexia nervosa, being both repulsed by her emaciated appearance and amazed by her iron will, our attitudes toward fat women are clearly unambiguously hostile (ibid.). Perhaps the anorexic woman is acceptable because her protest is self-limiting; in the end, she will self-destruct. The fat woman is not so limited.

The hostility that is directed toward fat women who do not "confess excess" is evidence for the challenge that the fat woman presents to dominant cultural discourse, especially those of the ideal woman. For example, Roseanne is not only fat, but loud and otherwise "unfeminine." "[Roseanne] Barr personifies everything about women that women have been told is unacceptable to men" (Dresner 1993:41). In 1997, readers of *Esquire* voted Roseanne "the scariest woman alive" (*Esquire* 1997). The bumper sticker NO FAT CHICKS also reflects this hostility and succinctly illustrates the connection between ideal weight and ideal women. A "chick," that is an appropriately feminine woman, must be simultaneously attractive and nonthreatening (that is, immature); she must also be small. A "fat chick" would be an oxymoron.

Rather than arguing that fatness can be attractive or sexual or healthy, when a fat woman refuses to watch her body and refuses to apologize for her nonconformity to ideal weight, she challenges constructions of the ideal women as bodies, as contained, and as subject to male approval. She also resists labeling herself and other women as deviant. When asked about the benefits of a large body size, fat acceptance activists wrote on my survey that they were stronger both physically and psychologically, more noticeable, and less focused on themselves as bodies (McKinley 1995). These responses demonstrate the challenges fat women present to dominant culture's construction of the ideal woman.

CONCLUSIONS

A social constructionist perspective is particularly useful for demonstrating how modern social control operates through the creation of meaning and desire. In this chapter, I have demonstrated the parallels between constructions of ideal women and ideal weight and argued that these connections normalize women's behavior, enforcing conformity to the requirements of the ideal woman, as well as to ideal weight. Fat women can embody resistance to ideologies of weight and, more importantly, to ideologies of gender. However, Bordo (1993) has warned against our inclination to celebrate resistance. We should neither construct resistive forms of subjectivity as equal in power to dominant discourse nor turn our attention away from continued patterns of normalization. For example, fashion magazines featuring fat women may continue to create and prey on women's anxieties in order to sell products, even while they purportedly relieve anxieties about being fat. The purpose of advertising in a capitalist culture is to make objects of consumers and women have traditionally been the targets (and thus objects) of advertising (Barthel 1988). Changing the size of the models in the magazine does not change this relationship. Also, while refusing to try to change her weight may have positive material consequences for a fat women by giving her more money, time, and energy, it does not change the discrimination she may face.[6] Effectively changing women's "discontent" with their weight will require a challenge to current cultural power structures.

ACKNOWLEDGMENTS

The author thanks Mareena McKinley Wright and Brandy Dolan Maszka for comments.

NOTES

1.   Ernsberger and Haskew (1987) demonstrated that "ideal weight" is not the weight of the longest-lived participants in several long-term epidemiological studies and argued that health experts have ignored the health benefits of obesity. This counterclaim has received very little official attention.

2.   Bordo critiqued this stance and argued that regardless of what conventions Madonna flouts, she never disrupts the meaning of femininity as existing to receive the gaze of others.

3.   Norms of attractiveness are also ethnocentric and class- and age-specific (Brownmiller 1984; Bordo 1993).

4.   While there is a body of feminist critique of ideologies, ideal weight, and fat discrimination, see Rothblum (1994) for a discussion of why mainstream feminism has often ignored society's disparagement of fatness.

5. By this argument, I do not mean to ignore competing meanings of fatness for women of color, lesbians, and working-class women. Psychological research, for example, has shown that for some groups of African-American women, body image may be more positive (Cash and Henry 1995) and concepts of beauty more flexible (Parker et al. 1995) than for some groups of European-American women. On the other hand, to be acceptable *within dominant culture* and to gain access to the resources controlled by those who hold these values, women must conform to the ideologies of weight and gender of that culture.

6.   See Rothblum (1994) for a description of discrimination against fat women.

REFERENCES

Barthel, D. 1988. *Putting on Appearances: Gender and Advertising*. Philadelphia, PA: Temple University Press.

Bartky, S. L. 1988. "Foucault, Femininity, and the Modernization of Patriarchal Power." Pp. 61–86 in *Feminism and Foucault: Reflections on Resistance,* edited by I. Diamond and L. Quinby. Boston: Northeastern University Press.

Bem, S. L. 1974. "The Measurement of Psychological Androgyny." *Journal of Consulting and Clinical Psychology* 42:155–62.

Berg, F. M. 1995. *The Health Risks of Weight Loss*. Hettinger, ND: Healthy Weight Journal.

Blumenthal, J. A., L. G. O'Toole, and J. L. Chang. 1984. "Is Running an Analogue of Anorexia Nervosa?" *Journal of the American Medical Association* 252:520–23.

Bordo, S. R. 1990. "The Body and the Reproduction of Femininity: A Feminist Appropriation of Foucault." Pp. 13–33 in *Gender/Body/Knowledge: Feminist Reconstructions of Being and Knowing,* edited by A. M. Jaggar and S. R. Bordo. New Brunswick, NJ: Rutgers University Press.

———. 1993. *Unbearable Weight: Feminism, Western Culture, and the Body*. Berkeley: University of California Press.

Brown, H. G. 1962. *Sex and the Single Girl*. New York: Bernard Geis.

Brownmiller, S. 1984. *Femininity*. New York: Fawcett Columbine.

Bruch, H. 1976. "The Treatment of Eating Disorders." *Mayo Clinic Proceedings* 51:266–72.

Burke, A. 1998. "Fat and Proud." *Chicago Tribune,* 2 January 2, p. 7.

Buss, D. M. 1987. "Sex Differences in Human Mate Selection Criteria: An Evolutionary Perspective." Pp. 335–51 in *Sociobiology and Psychology: Ideas, Issues, and Applications,* edited by C. Crawford, M. Smith, and D. Kreks. Hillsdale, NJ: Lawrence Erlbaum.

Cash, T. F., and P. E. Henry. 1995. "Women's Body Images: The Results of a National Survey in the U.S.A." *Sex Roles* 33:19–28.

Chesler, P. 1972. *Women and Madness.* New York: Avon.

Cohen, M. 1988. *The Sisterhood: The Inside Story of the Women's Movement and the Leaders Who Made It Happen.* New York: Fawcett Columbine.

Constantinople, A. 1973. "Masculinity-Femininity: An Exception to a Famous Dictum?" *Psychological Bulletin* 80:389–407.

Crandall, C. S. 1994. "Prejudice Against Fat People: Ideology and Self-interest." *Journal of Personality and Social Psychology* 66:882–94.

de Beauvoir, S. 1952. *The Second Sex,* translated/edited by H. M. Parshley. New York: Vintage.

Dorenkamp, A. G., J. F. McClymer, M. M. Moynihan, and A. C. Vadum. 1985. *Images of Women in American Popular Culture.* San Diego, CA: Harcourt Brace Jovanovich.

Dresner, Z. Z. 1993. "Roseanne Barr: Goddess or She-Devil." *Journal of American Culture* 16:37–43

Ehrenreich, B., and D. English. 1978. *For Her Own Good: 150 Years of Experts' Advice to Women.* New York: Anchor.

Ernsberger, P. 1997. "Why a Nondiet Approach? Summarizing the Research on Diet and Obesity." Paper presented at the annual meeting of the American Psychological Association, Chicago.

Ernsberger, P., and P. Haskew. 1987. "Rethinking Obesity: An Alternative View of Its Health Implications." *Journal of Obesity and Weight Reduction* 6:58–137.

Esquire. 1997. "And the Women You Love." August:58–59.

Evans, M. 1998. "Clowning Around with Vanessa." *BBW,* May, pp. 28–43.

Faludi, S. 1991. *Backlash: The Undeclared War against American Women.* New York: Anchor.

Fein, E., and S. Schneider. 1997. "Seal the Deal! (And Make Him Commit 100%)." *Cosmopolitan,* October, pp. 209–11.

First For Women. 1997. "The New Science of 'Perfect Eating.'" 29 September, pp. 32–35.

Foucault, M. 1978. *The History of Sexuality,* Vol. 1: *An Introduction,* translated by R. Hurley. New York: Vintage. (Original work published 1976.)

Fox, M. 1997. "Experts: Dangerous Diet Drugs Can Help Some." Reuters News Service, 16 September.

Freud, S. 1962. *Three Contributions to the Theory of Sex,* translated by A. A. Brill. New York: E. P. Dutton.

Garner, D. M., P. E. Garfinkel, D. Schwartz, and M. Thompson. 1980. "Cultural Expectations of Thinness in Women." *Psychological Reports* 47:483–91.

Gilligan, C. 1982. *In a Different Voice: Psychological Theory and Women's Development.* Cambridge, MA: Harvard University Press.

Golden, F. 1997. "Who's to Blame for Redux and Fenfluramine?" *Time* 150:78–79.

Hare-Mustin, R. T., and J. Marecek. 1990. "Gender and the Meaning of Difference: Postmodernism and Psychology." Pp. 150–83 in *Making a Difference: Psychology and the Construction of Gender,* edited by R. T. Hare-Mustin and J. Marecek. New Haven, CT: Yale University Press.

Henley, N. 1977. *Body Politics: Power, Sex, and Nonverbal Communications.* New York: Simon and Schuster.

Hochschild, A. 1989. *The Second Shift.* New York: Avon.

Hyde, J. S. 1991. *Half the Human Experience,* 4th edition. Lexington, MA: D. C. Heath.

Jenny Craig, Inc. 1997. *The Leaning of America.* Available on-line: http://www.jennycraig.com/ns/WhitePaper/WhitePaper.htm.

Kilbourne, J. 1994. "Still Killing Us Softly: Advertising and the Obsession with Thinness." Pp. 395–418 in *Feminist Perspectives on Eating Disorders,* edited by P. Fallon, M. A. Katzman, and S. C. Wooley. New York: Guilford.

Kitzinger, C., and R. Perkins. 1993. *Changing Our Minds: Lesbian Feminism and Psychology.* New York: New York University Press.

Lorber, J. 1994. *Paradoxes of Gender.* New Haven, CT: Yale University Press.

Lyons, P., and D. Burgard. 1990. *Great Shape: The First Fitness Guide for Large Women.* Palo Alto, CA: Bull.

MacKinnon, C. A. 1987. *Feminism Unmodified: Discourses on Life and Law.* Cambridge, MA: Harvard University Press.

Mayer, V. F. 1983a. "The Questions People Ask." Pp. 23–36 in *Shadow on a Tightrope: Writings by Women on Fat Oppression,* edited by L. Schoenfielder and B. Wieser. San Francisco: Spinsters/Aunt Lute.

———. 1983b. "The Fat Illusion." Pp. 3–14 in *Shadow on Tightrope: Writings by Women on Fat Oppression,* edited by L. Schoenfielder and B. Wieser. San Francisco: Spinsters/Aunt Lute.

McKinley, N. M. 1995. "Practicing Resistance: Fat Women Write about Their Body Experience." Paper presented at the annual meeting of the Association of Women in Psychology, Indianapolis, Indiana.

Miss America Organization. 1997. "Miss America Pageant Returns to ABC Television Network with Bold New Look, Focus on Individuality." *The Latest News.* Available online: http://www.missamerica.org/news/072197.html.

National Academy of Sciences, National Research Council. 1989. *Diet and Health: Implications for Reducing Chronic Disease Risk.* Washington, DC: National Academy Press.

Ortner, S. B. 1974. "Is Female to Male as Nature Is to Culture?" Pp. 67–87 in *Women, Culture, and Society,* edited by M. Z. Rosaldo and L. Lamphere. Stanford, CA: Stanford University Press.

Parker, S., M. Nichter, M. Nichter, N. Vuckovic, C. Sims, and C. Ritenbaugh. 1995. "Body Image and Weight Concerns among African American and White Adolescent Females: Differences that Make a Difference." *Human Organization* 54(2):103–14.

Pleck, J. H. 1981. *The Myth of Masculinity.* Cambridge, MA: MIT Press.

Rix, S. E. (ed.). 1990. *The American Woman 1990–91: A Status Report*. New York: Norton.

Rodin, J., L. Silberstein, and R. Striegel-Moore. 1985. "Women and Weight: A Normative Discontent." Pp. 267–307 in *Psychology and Gender: Nebraska Symposium on Motivation*, edited by T. Sonderegger. Lincoln: University of Nebraska Press.

Rothblum, E. 1994. "I'll Die for the Revolution but Don't Ask Me Not to Diet." Pp. 53–76 in *Feminist Perspectives on Eating Disorders*, edited by P. Fallon, M. A. Katzman, and S. C. Wooley. New York: Guilford.

Rubin, J. Z., F. J. Provenzano, and A. Luria. 1974. "The Eye of the Beholder: Parents' Views on Sex of Newborns." *American Journal of Orthopsychiatry*, 43:720–31.

Schoenfielder, L., and B. Wieser (eds.). 1983. *Shadow on a Tightrope: Writings by Women on Fat Oppression*. San Francisco, CA: Spinsters/Aunt Lute.

Schur, E. M. 1984. *Labeling Women Deviant: Gender, Stigma, and Social Control*. New York: Random House.

Seid, R. P. 1989. *Never Too Thin: Why Women Are at War with Their Bodies*. New York: Prentice Hall.

Shape Up America! 1997. "Healthy Weight, Healthy Living." Available on-line: http://www2.shapeup.org/sua/

Sobal, J. 1995. "The Medicalization and Demedicalization of Obesity." Pp. 67–90 in *Eating Agendas: Food and Nutrition as Social Problems*, edited by D. Maurer and J. Sobal. Hawthorne, NY: Aldine de Gruyter.

Spitzack, C. 1990. *Confessing Excess: Women and the Politics of Body Reduction*. Albany: State University of New York Press.

Stern, M., and K. H. Karraker. 1989. "Sex Stereotyping of Infants: A Review of Gender Labeling Studies." *Sex Roles* 20:501–22.

Thompson, S. 1995. *Going All the Way: Teenage Girls' Tales of Sex, Romance, and Pregnancy*. New York: Hill and Wang.

Way, K. 1995. "Never Too Rich . . . Or Too Thin: The Role of Stigma in the Social Construction of Anorexia Nervosa." Pp. 91–113 in *Eating Agendas: Food and Nutrition as Social Problems*, edited by D. Maurer and J. Sobal. Hawthorne, NY: Aldine de Gruyter.

Weight Watchers Interactive. 1997. "The Freedom Plan with the Weekend Option." Available on-line: http://wwgroup.metroguide.com/freedom.html.

Wiseman, C. V., J. J. Gray, J. E. Mosimann, and A. G. Ahrens. 1992. "Cultural Expectations of Thinness in Women: An Update." *International Journal of Eating Disorders* 11:85–89.

Wolf, N. 1991. *The Beauty Myth: How Images of Beauty Are Used Against Women*. New York: Anchor.

Women at Large. 1987. *Women At Large: Breakout*. Video. Van Nuys, CA: Weller Productions.

7

Dieting Women
Self-Surveillance and the Body Panopticon

JOHN GERMOV and LAUREN WILLIAMS

INTRODUCTION: TOWARD A SOCIOLOGY OF DIETING

Dieting to control weight has become so common in developed countries that its "taken for granted" nature obscures the sexual division of dieting: dieting is primarily a female act. A number of studies report that women are more likely to be dissatisfied with their body shape than men and perceive the need to lose weight even when within the medically defined "healthy weight range" (Grogan and Wainwright 1996; Tiggemann and Pennington 1990). This body dissatisfaction can result in dieting behavior, irrespective of actual body weight, so that for many women it is now "normal" to limit their fat and energy intake in a state of restrained eating (Herman and Mack 1975). This dissatisfaction with body image and the unsuccessful nature of many diets facilitates a cycle of "yo-yo" dieting or weight cycling, which can have detrimental physiological and psychological consequences (Brownell and Rodin 1994).

In studying body issues and dieting in women, a sociological approach recasts the focus away from medical concerns about weight, toward the social construction of the body (Sobal 1991, 1992; Turner 1992). Therefore, this chapter focuses on the behavior of dieting, and the beliefs and environmental influences that drive that behavior, outside the context of actual body weight, its measurement, and classification. Women perceive the need to diet in the context of a cult of slimness—the "thin ideal"—as represented in the media, fashion, and fitness industries (among others) in developed countries. The discourse of the "beauty myth" and the thin ideal portrayed by fashion models and other celebrities is often cited as *prima facie* evidence of the patriarchal social control of women (see Bordo 1993; Charles and Kerr 1988; Wolf 1990). Such traditional explanations of why

women succumb to the pressure to conform to the thin ideal rely on patronizing and simplistic formulations that posit women as "brainwashed" subjects of a patriarchal society. Explanations that suggest dieting women are
simply the victims of patriarchal culture, capitalist interests, and male
oppression ignore *resistance* to the thin ideal. This chapter seeks to explain
why women adopt *or* reject the thin ideal and how this affects dieting
behavior by analyzing the social construction of the thin ideal and how
women respond to it through the following questions:

- How are women pressured to conform to the thin ideal?
- How do women respond to that pressure?
- If there is resistance to the thin ideal, how is it expressed?

Exploration of these questions requires a renewed focus on the role
women play in the processes that shape their lives. A number of feminist
poststructuralist authors stress the importance of theorizing female subjectivity and agency (Barrett and Phillips 1992; Bartky 1990; Pringle 1995;
Weedon 1987). These authors attempt to deal with the complex and subtle
facets of women's lived experience of the social construction of the female
body. Recent Australian research conducted by the authors used this
approach to investigate the experiences of dieting women (see Germov
and Williams 1996a). The research used qualitative focus group methodology to investigate women's experiences of food, eating, and dieting. Six
focus groups were conducted over two studies, with a total of forty pre-
menopausal adult women participating. Selected quotes by self-selected
pseudonym of the focus group participants are used throughout this chapter to illustrate the argument that women play a prominent role in the
reproduction of, *and* resistance to, the thin ideal.

THE SOCIAL CONSTRUCTION OF THE THIN
IDEAL FOR WOMEN

To understand how women are pressured to conform to the thin ideal
we first need to examine the gendered nature of women's bodies. Douglas
and Sontag view the body as a symbolic metaphor for society; the "social
body constrains the way the physical body is perceived" (quoted by Crawford 1984:61). Yet the social body is a "gendered body," with significant
differences in the normative expectations of female and male bodies as
reflected in cultural esthetic ideals. Gendered bodies are produced and
reproduced through discourses of beauty, health, food, cosmetics, fashion,
and exercise. The social construction of the female body is based on a thin
ideal, which has become the symbol of youth, beauty, vitality, success, and

health—representing the social pressure to discipline the surface body, where "fat" is perceived as unfeminine, unattractive, and a sign of a body "out of control." This involves connotations of deprivation and denial of women's natural body diversity. Wolf (1990) argues the thin ideal should be viewed as a preemptive strike at women because "fat" is inherently feminine—women naturally have breasts, buttocks, rounded abdomens, and hips—and thus to deny fat is misogynist. The thin ideal represented by fashion models today reflect the thinnest 5-10 percent of the population, but this "statistical deviation has been normalized, leading millions of women to believe that they are abnormal" (Seid 1994:8). Schur argues that "definitions of female deviance are, in fact, so extensive that virtually every woman becomes a perceived offender of some kind" (1983:37). The social construction of thinness has resulted in an epidemic of female body dissatisfaction and consequent dieting as women attempt to conform to "female appearance norms" (Rodin, Silberstein, and Striegel-Moore 1985; Rothblum 1994).

The regulation of the female body is not a new phenomenon—with many examples such as foot binding, corsets, and most recently cosmetic surgery (see Corrigan and Meredyth 1994). Turner (1992) outlines the historical role of dietary management in producing a docile and disciplined body by punishment and penance to purge oneself of excess. Various authors have discussed the links between religion and the self-starvation diet regimen in relation to eating disorders (Bell 1985; Brumberg 1988; Bynum 1987). In modern society, the regulation of women's bodies through dieting practices is no longer about religious spirituality, but sexuality. The thin body is an "ideal type" to which women aspire to avoid the stigma of overweight and to conform to cultural notions of female attractiveness. As Sternhell states, "[W]hen I hear people talking about temptation and sin, guilt and shame, I know they're referring to food rather than sex" (quoted in Rothblum 1994:53). Seid notes the parallel between Victorian attitudes to sex and modern attitudes to food, where for women "food rules have become as dour and inhibitory as the sex rules of the 19th century" (1994:8). In many nonindustrialized societies, a large body size often reflects a sign of luxury and wealth and is perceived as voluptuous and attractive (Bordo 1993). This is certainly not the case in developed countries today, where being overweight is considered as a loss of self-control, a "risk" for ill-health, and a "problem" to be corrected. Overweight is an ascribed status, but the point at which the label and stigma apply varies over time and among cultures (Sobal 1991).

Focus group research conducted by the authors found that women perceived gender differences in social expectations of body weight and shape. It appears to be acceptable for men to vary within a wide range of body shape and weight, while women have a far narrower "acceptable" body range. As the following quotes indicate, this also applied to executive-level women who, while supposedly equal to men in a work role, were expected to conform to the thin ideal while men were not.

> I've had people ask me whether my senior manager [female] is going to lose weight and it totally astounds me, because people would never think of asking about the CEO [who is male and very overweight] whether he'll lose weight. . . . [I]t's quite acceptable for him, but it's not acceptable for her. . . . Since she's been promoted more questions have arisen about her weight. Because she is successful, they think she should be more in control of her diet. (Mitzy)

> Even in the corporate world with female executives, the first thing people talk about is "look at her, she's put on weight." (Scarlett)

Therefore, "success" for a woman is still measured by her appearance, where economic success needs to be matched with "body success." Seid (1994) argues that feminism initially embraced the slender, superfit ideal because health and strength were seen as positive symbols of femininity—in contrast to previous centuries, which conceptualized women as invalids. Rothblum (1994:72) argues that "women's gains have required more sophisticated and subtle techniques to induce conformity." Since women's bodies are regulated to within narrower boundaries than in the past, the intensity required to discipline the "exposed" body is extremely rigid. As Bartky (1990:81) puts it: "A tighter control of the body has gained a new kind of hold over the mind." Faludi (1991) and Wolf (1990) make cogent arguments linking the rise of female sexual liberation with the rise of the thin ideal, where part of the backlash against the gains of the feminist movement have been the increasing emphasis on women's appearance. Schur (1983:68) argues that

> physical appearance is much more central to evaluations of women than it is to evaluations of men; this emphasis implicitly devalues women's other qualities and accomplishments; women's "looks" thereby become a commodity and a key determinant of their "success" or "failure"; the beauty norms used in evaluating women are excessively narrow and quite unrealistic; cultural reinforcement of such norms conveys to the ordinary women a sense of perpetual deficiency.

It is probably not by accident that women's appearance norms have intensified with the political and economic gains made by women in advanced industrialized society. Gendered bodies and the production of the thin ideal can be perceived as an attempt to neutralize these gains.

Structural Interests

The thin ideal is primarily produced and reproduced by various structural interests, or industries, that profit from its promotion, such as the fashion, dieting, fitness, and media industries. These industries have developed a "sure-fire" formula for success: Standardize a thin ideal of beauty that the majority of women can never attain, but make it look so appealing that they actually seek it out. The pursuit of thinness and the subsequent failure of most women in this pursuit construct an infinite market of consumers. Although it is likely that most women self-select diets, many also seek the services of the commercial weight loss industry. In America, it is estimated that the diet industry is worth $55 billion, with over 65 million Americans on a diet (Brownell 1993). Similarly, over 500 million dollars is spent on commercial weight loss programs in Australia each year (Lester 1994).

Fewer women seek the services of health professionals than commercial programs, but the discourses of medicine, public health, and fitness generally equate slimness with health. The thin ideal is reinforced through health promotion campaigns that promote weight control on the premise that it will promote health (Germov and Williams 1996b). However, Wooley and Garner (1991) argue that the well-intentioned actions of health professionals still reflect cultural biases and are partly responsible for treating overweight as a form of deviance. Weight discrimination or "fatism," particularly against women, has been documented, with studies in the United States showing that some health professionals view overweight women as less successful and less intelligent than women of "normal" weight; where the key assumption is that thin is always better than fat (Maddox, Back, and Leiderman 1968; Maiman et al. 1979; Najman and Monroe 1982). According to Lupton (1996:137), the increasing link between health and diet has led to increasing rationalization, surveillance, and regulation of people's food habits and bodies through what she terms the "food/health/beauty triplex." Featherstone, Hepworth, and Turner (1991) conceptualize two social bodies subject to regulation: The "inner body" refers to body management based on a concern for health, and the "outer body" refers to the concern for appearance. They suggest that consumer culture joins the inner and outer body into one so that "the prime purpose of the maintenance of the inner body becomes the enhancement of the appearance of the outer body" (ibid.:171). While we clearly view structural factors as important, for the remainder of the chapter our focus will be on the subjective experience of dieting and the thin ideal to understand how women respond to the social construction of gendered bodies.

DIETING AS A RATIONAL RESPONSE TO THE THIN IDEAL:
CONFORMING TO THE PRESSURE

Many women diet due to dissatisfaction with their body size or shape mediated by the cult of slimness discussed above. Dieting is used as a tool in the quest for slimness and the desire for a socially acceptable body. Dieting is thus one response to the pressure to conform to the thin ideal. The subjective experiences of women who diet can be characterized in women's contradictory relationship with food, where they derive both "pleasure and pain" from food and dieting. Dieting is often perceived as a negative experience, although for some women it can be a source of pleasure, resulting in enhanced satisfaction with appearance, social recognition, and acceptance through compliments from others and the achievement of personal goals of self-discipline (Orbach 1986; Chernin 1981). The women who participated in our focus group research reflected these two states, but Maxine summed up the feeling of many of the participants: "I hate the thought of dieting, I hate it!" Audrey agreed, saying that dieting was "restricted and boring. Deprived!" Many women also felt that dieting induced guilt and depression. This was either due to succumbing to the temptation to eat nondiet foods, or the failure to lose weight and achieve the ideal body shape

> As soon as I eat something that's not on my diet, I do feel guilty, I feel really bad. As soon as I stop a diet, I'll go virtually the opposite way, I'll just about eat anything and I know I shouldn't do it but I just can't help myself. . . . It's depressing when you reach the plateau because you're still dieting and you're sticking to the diet perfectly, you're not doing anything wrong and you're still not losing any weight. (Helga)

The plateau effect Helga describes resulted in the phenomenon another participant called the "vicious cycle," referring to the never-ending process of dieting, failure to maintain "control," and returning to eating "bad" foods, gaining weight, feeling "unhappy with weight," only to once again enter the diet cycle. Such yo-yo dieting can alter body metabolism to make weight loss even more difficult to achieve (Brownell and Rodin 1994).

For some participants early dieting behavior was initiated in response to pressure to conform to the thin ideal mediated by family:

> I can still remember my mother saying when I was sixteen that "You cannot wear those shorts, you look like an elephant," and that's when I was only seven and one-half stone [105 pounds]. (Audrey)

> I am a bigger build than my sister who's a lot thinner. . . . People have always compared me to her and used to say that my sister was the slim one. (Claudia)

The peer group played a significant role in reinforcing cultural notions of female attractiveness for other participants:

> Dieting was never an issue in my house . . . until when I discovered boys. . . . I wanted to look good. (Maxine)

> A boy [at school] told me that I had a big bum and that embarrassed me so much that I went on a diet. (Di)

These responses emphasize that conforming to the thin ideal is important for social acceptance and therefore trying to conform is a rational response to this pressure. This attempt at conformity was reinforced by positive reactions and direct compliments when women lost weight, such as "You look great," "Have you lost weight?" "You look so much better." The reward is linked to "regaining control" over one's body and this reinforces the "beauty myth" (Wolf 1990) based on the notion that there is only one acceptable form of female beauty and all women should strive to achieve it. The pressure to conform and thereby gain social acceptance, in addition to wanting to be attractive to the opposite sex, are potent examples of the internalization of social norms and power relations. In her analysis of women who undergo cosmetic surgery, Davis concludes, "Cosmetic surgery is not simply the expression of the cultural constraints of femininity, nor is it a straightforward expression of women's oppression or the normalization of the female body through the beauty system. . . . [It] can enable some women to alleviate unbearable suffering, [and] reappropriate formerly hated bodies" (1996:116). While women are objectified in a patriarchal social order, as participants in such a society, they also come to "view themselves as the objects of the intentions and manipulations of others" (ibid.:115). Women learn to "compare their appearance with that of the patriarchal feminine ideal and thus become objects for their own gaze" (Duncan 1994:50). Some women experience intrinsic pleasure in the process of dieting, for reasons such as the ability to realize personal goals through self-discipline, the compliments of others, and the attainment of culturally prescribed norms of attractiveness and femininity. For example:

> If you get the reward, there can be a lot of positive feelings—if you lose weight and people comment on your appearance. (Abigail)

> I just get really excited about losing weight. . . . I live for the excitement of losing weight each week. (Claudia)

Some of the research participants acknowledged that they used weight loss methods that were detrimental to their health. The focus group research found that women who were of a medically defined "healthy weight" were engaging in weight loss practices with health risks:

> I'm willing to trade off health for weight loss in the short term. I even do it when I'm not on a diet, so I'll definitely do it . . . when I want to lose weight. (Clara)

One participant had become so addicted to dieting that she did not fear the development of the life-threatening disease anorexia nervosa:

> I think that no matter how light I am, that I'll always want to be lighter, that I'll have to keep going and going and going. If I could get to that anorexic state, I would, yeah if I could, I would! . . . I'd rather be thin than worry about my health. It doesn't scare me to have anorexia . . . but I know that I like food too much to be anorexic, but I know I could probably border on anorexia! Like I've tried laxatives and stuff but I know it doesn't last. (Claudia)

The apparent irrationality of such beliefs and actions actually have a rational basis. Dieting and pursuit of the thin ideal "at any cost" can be viewed as a rational response by women striving for acceptance in the context of dominant ideals of beauty, sexuality, and femininity. Other authors have noted that women who diet to lose weight place the value of actual weight loss above all other aspects of their lives, such as success in work or love (Charles and Kerr 1988; Wolf 1990). The thin female body has become an integral part of women's lives and identity in modern society. This helps to explain why many women themselves partake in the patriarchal construction of the female body. The rewards of compliance to the thin ideal can be a greater (or at least easier) lure than acts of defiance. As Bartky argues, the thin ideal is so entwined with cultural prescriptions of femininity that:

> any political project which aims to dismantle the machinery that turns a female body into a feminine one may well be apprehended by a woman as something that threatens her with desexualization. (1990:77)

Bartky (1990) argues that the internalization of patriarchal norms, rather than external coercion, is the dominant form of power relations that result in regulation and disciplining of female bodies in the pursuit of the thin ideal. The dispersion and anonymity of patriarchal power relations through internalization makes the aim of overturning the thin ideal a difficult task; social control is exercised through and by the very individuals who are the subjects. While agreeing that the norms are internalized, we assert that such self-regulation does not occur in a vacuum and is externally reinforced by structural interests such as the fashion, weight loss, fitness, health, and cosmetic industries. Women also actively play a part in constructing "the forms of femininity through which they are also controlled: They are never merely victims" (Pringle 1995:207).

THE ROLE OF WOMEN IN PERPETUATING THE THIN IDEAL

One aspect of the social construction of the thin ideal is the role women play in actively perpetuating this ideal. They do this in two main ways: women reinforce the thin ideal on themselves through constant self-surveillance of their bodies; and women place other women under body-surveillance to ensure they comply or at least attempt to conform to the thin ideal as well. These findings arose from the focus group research:

> Women are too hard on themselves. I know I am, it depresses me. It makes me go on a diet. I look in the mirror and go "Oh no." (Frances)

> Society is the biggest enemy, it's made up of women as well. . . . Women make comments. It's the pressure from other women. It's like, how can you walk around like that, don't you feel uncomfortable? (Naomi)

> Women are their own worst enemy, they strive to look better. (Cindy)

> Women are bad at putting crap on other women. I know the media has a lot to do with it but I think women put pressure on themselves. Women are the worst judges. (Carolyn)

Such comments illustrate the view that some women place themselves and other women under a form of body-surveillance. Therefore, the social control over women's appearance was perpetuated not just by men, or by external factors like the media, but by women as well. There was even recognition that the women themselves expected the highest standards of body control. For some women this related to seeking social acceptance. As Marcia said:

> I don't like people because of their body size, but I think others are going to like me because of *my* body size. It's self-pressure I think.

Therefore, women themselves become the ultimate "body police" by internalizing the cultural imperatives of the thin ideal. Women are encouraged to modify and monitor themselves and other women in a never-ending process of body-surveillance to conform to the culturally acceptable body image, even at the expense of their health. The adages, "Women dress for other women," and "Women are the harshest judges of other women," were expressed by the focus group participants. The practice of being critical of the bodies of other women (especially thin women) boosted their own self-esteem:

> It makes you feel better if she's got something wrong, it makes you realize she's not perfect. (Ethel)

Gyrtle agreed:

> You see flaws in yourself and you concentrate on your own flaws, [but] if
> you can pick on someone else for a while it makes you feel better.

The Body Panopticon: Surveillance of
Women's Bodies

The "political anatomy" of the body, to use Foucault's (1979) phrase,
entails the constant surveillance of the human body as a form of social control. According to Foucault, the social control of a disciplining society consisted primarily of "biopolitics"—through the definition and regulation of
actual bodies. However, the political anatomy is gendered since the social
construction of the thin ideal is primarily aimed at regulating women's
bodies (Bartky 1990; Weedon 1987). The regulation of women's bodies is
achieved through indirect coercion from the structural interests discussed
earlier and often with the consent of women themselves. The participation
of women in the reinforcement of the thin ideal can be explained by adopting Foucault's conceptualization of the panopticon. Foucault (1979) used
the panopticon as a metaphor for how social control could be administered without recourse to coercion. The panopticon (all-seeing place) was
developed by Jeremy Bentham in the eighteenth century as an architectural design of a prison with a central observation tower that was surrounded by concentric cells. The design allowed the guards to potentially
observe all cells simultaneously, thereby enhancing control of the inmates,
who had to assume they were under constant surveillance. Hence, the
panopticon induced conformity through self-policing behavior. The
"body panopticon" refers to women's constant monitoring of their own
bodies and those of other women. Thus, women who themselves seek to
conform to the thin ideal actively participate in stigmatizing women who
do not exhibit body conformity. Therefore, pressure to conform to the thin
ideal not only stems from cultural dictates and material interests, but also
from women acting as the "body police" for themselves and other women.
The body panopticon conceptualizes the social construction of the thin
ideal by explaining that women—in Foucault's words—are in a power situation of which they are themselves the "bearers of their own surveillance" (ibid.:201).

The prison analogy of the body panopticon metaphor can imply there
is no escape for women from the disciplinary power of the thin ideal.
While Foucault is famous for stating that power is everywhere, and where
there is power there is resistance, it remains difficult to conceptualize how
resistance emerges or can be effective in such a schema. For example, even
though Bordo (1993) stresses "female praxis," she ultimately sees no
escape from the dominant thin ideal discourse. The irony of such a pes-

simistic conclusion is that it leaves us where we started—with women as "cultural dupes" of the "patriarchal system." The acknowledgment that some women reinforce patriarchal discourses on other women does little to liberate feminist theory of the fatalistic language of oppression and subordination (Barrett 1992; Barrett and Phillips 1992). It would be easy to misinterpret Foucault's metaphor as implying total control so that women are still conceptualized as victims—in this sense as "active" rather than passive victims—since women are constructed as actively participating in a "female gaze." As "bearers of their own surveillance" through the internalization of sociocultural discourses, women are conceptualized as colluding in the production of "docile bodies" (Foucault 1979). However, we assert that not all bodies are so "docile" and that the concept of the body panopticon does not preclude the potential for some women to reject the thin ideal and resist the disciplining gaze. Resistance to the thin ideal through female agency can create the "social spaces" where alternative discourses form and challenge the dominant discourse. To continue the prison metaphor, the possibility exists for women to break free from the "social" bars that constrain and construct them.

RESISTING THE PRESSURE OF THE THIN IDEAL: THE ALTERNATIVE DISCOURSE OF SIZE ACCEPTANCE

The concept of the body panopticon provides a comprehensive account of why some women conform to the thin ideal and partake in enforcing conformity on themselves and other women through a disciplining "female gaze." However, focusing on women's agency also allows the possibility of resistance to patriarchal panoptic power. The focus group research uncovered an alternative discourse of size acceptance by participants who had rejected the thin ideal and ceased dieting. The development of a size acceptance identity poses the analytical question of how some women are able to manage the consequences of rebelling against the thin ideal. For example, both Audrey (who had a long history of dieting) and Scarlett (who had only dieted in her late teenage years) no longer dieted to lose weight and accepted their body shape:

> It's taken me thirty years to accept myself. (Audrey)

> I've realized I'll never be a size 10 and so it really doesn't bother me, and my shape doesn't worry me. (Scarlett)

While some women had stopped dieting and become size accepting, others such as Gyrtle and Abigail were trying to be size accepting, but occasionally lapsed and sporadically dieted:

I'm happy with myself. . . . I don't worry about how big I am, but other people worry for me and that's what makes me feel guilty. (Gyrtle)

I guess now I've accepted the fact that I either want to be happy with the size that I am and just have a healthier eating pattern and if in the process of that, it helps me to lose weight, well that's great, and if it doesn't, well this is the shape that I am. (Abigail)

Mitzy and Marilyn had only recently accepted their size and stopped dieting due to the support of their partners (neither of whom were overweight):

Actually having a boyfriend who appreciated my body because it looked like a woman, which made me think that these curves are all me and that's how I am supposed to look. (Mitzy)

When I was with my ex-boyfriend he used to say how fat I was . . . and now I've got a new boyfriend and he always tells me that I'm voluptuous and sexy and I think I feel heaps better so I think it depends on who you're with sometimes. (Marilyn)

The comments of the above women who were size accepting indicate there can be various reasons underlying the adoption of such an identity. For Mitzy and Marilyn, in particular, it could be argued that their size-accepting identity was developed in a patriarchal context of conforming to their male partners' preferences. However, for other women, size acceptance was the result of a history of failing to lose weight; or it was based on the decision to end the pain of the dieting process and the obsession with their bodies. These responses indicate a potential mechanism by which women may reject the thin ideal: they become self-accepting rather than requiring social acceptance. Therefore, the notion of female agency incorporates the possibility to effectively resist the female gaze and the body panopticon. Such a conceptualization requires that a more complex and subtle form of feminism and femininity be developed. We acknowledge there are multiple forms of femininities, splintered by individual, class, ethnic, and racial factors (Connell 1987; Pyke 1996; Walby 1990). As Poovey states:

All women may currently occupy the position "woman" . . . but they do not occupy it in the same way. Women of color in a white ruled society face different obstacles than do white women, and they may share more important problems with men of color than with their white "sisters." . . . [C]onsolidating all women into a falsely unified "woman" has helped mask the operations of power that actually divide women's interests as much as unite them. (1988:59)

The construction of femininity in developed societies means that "being a woman" is inherently linked to the perpetuation of the thin ideal. Yet the fact that *femininities* exist and are constantly constructed or reconstructed in interactional situations recognizes the importance of female agency, where notions of gender are no longer fixed or static (Pyke 1996). The discourse of size acceptance is one example of the dynamic nature of femininity. While such a discourse is marginalized at present, it nonetheless represents a competing discourse that may gather momentum, just as other minority movements have in the past. In Weedon's terms, such "reverse discourses" lead to the "production of alternative forms of knowledge [which may result in] winning individuals over to these discourses and gradually increasing their social power" (1987:111). Brownell (1993) notes the emergence of an antidieting movement in the United States lead by the National Association to Advance Fat Acceptance (NAAFA), which addresses fat prejudice and exposes the ineffectiveness and detrimental effects of weight loss programs. In advanced industrialized countries, antidieting, size acceptance, and "fat rights" groups are emerging and modeling themselves on previous civil rights movements. It is important to note that such movements are social, rather than health movements, in reflection of the social construction of the thin ideal (see Chrisler 1996). These movements provide an alternative form of social acceptance and therefore facilitate rejection of the thin ideal by creating a subculture that values body diversity.

Therefore, it would be a mistake to classify the social pressure exerted on women to conform to the thin ideal as all-encompassing or all-determining. As Weedon states, there is a need to avoid "the reductionism of single-cause analyses" (1987:122). Women are not an undifferentiated mass and clearly react to and resist "patriarchal discourses" in varied ways. Alternative discourses such as size acceptance offer hope for body diversity and a dismantling of the thin female ideal. By gaining an understanding of the process of attaining size acceptance, it may be possible to promote it as a viable option for women, so that women's resistance to the thin ideal develops into a "critical mass." The resistance to dieting through size acceptance is a field that qualitative, sociological inquiry has yet to fully explore. Further research is needed to clarify the processes by which women become size accepting—a topic that will be the next stage of our research (see Germov and Williams 1999).

CONCLUSION: CHALLENGING THE THIN IDEAL

In addressing questions of the social construction of the thin ideal and women's responses to it, we need to move away from individualistic psychological explanations of dieting, to focus on the public sphere (see Wolf 1990; Zdrodowski 1996). The eating patterns of women are a public issue because they reflect the social construction of femininity and female beauty. However, as we have argued in this chapter, we need to move beyond overly deterministic accounts that posit women as victims and puppets of commercial and cultural imperatives, toward explanations that incorporate the varied ways women respond to the pressure to conform to the thin ideal. The notion of women as victims of patriarchal subordination has been successfully critiqued by feminist poststructuralist theorists through a renewed focus on women's agency and subjective experiences of femininity (Bartky 1990; Weedon 1987). Such a perspective, combined with a qualitative research methodology, revealed the complexity of the responses to the thin ideal. The results of the focus group research reported throughout this chapter clearly show that women react to the thin ideal in a myriad of ways: accepting, reinforcing, and resisting the dominant discourse.

The concept of the body panopticon is a useful metaphor to explain how women participate in the reinforcement of the thin ideal by placing themselves and other women under constant body-surveillance. Women can act as agents of their own "oppression," but they can also resist patriarchal social control through the construction of alternative discourses such as size acceptance. While poststructuralism has placed renewed focus on agency in the production and reproduction of patriarchy, we agree with Walby (1990, 1992) that such an emphasis may be overstated if the important role played by material interests and identifiable holders of power is ignored. An examination of the discourse of dieting exposes the social construction of women's bodies, the structural interests involved, and women's struggle to reconstruct their own identities and femininities beyond the narrow, misogynistic conception of the thin ideal.

REFERENCES

Barrett, M. 1992. "Words and Things: Materialism and Method in Contemporary Feminist Analysis." Pp. 201–19 in *Destabilizing Theory: Contemporary Feminist Debates*, edited by M. Barrett and A. Phillips. Cambridge: Polity.

Barrett, M., and A. Phillips (eds.). 1992. *Destabilizing Theory: Contemporary Feminist Debates*. Cambridge: Polity.

Bartky, S. L. 1990. *Femininity and Domination: Studies in the Phenomenology of Oppression*. New York: Routledge.

Bell, R. 1985. *Holy Anorexia*. Chicago: University of Chicago Press.

Bordo, S. 1993. *Unbearable Weight: Feminism, Western Culture and the Body*. Berkeley: University of California Press.

Brownell, K. D. 1993. "Whether Obesity Should Be Treated." *Health Psychology* 12(5):339–41.

Brownell, K. D., and J. Rodin. 1994. "The Dieting Maelstrom: Is It Possible and Advisable to Lose Weight?" *American Psychologist* 49(9):781–91.

Brumberg, J. J. 1988. *Fasting Girls: The Emergence of Anorexia Nervosa as a Modern Disease.* Cambridge, MA: Harvard University Press.

Bynum, C. W. 1987. *Holy Feast and Holy Fast: The Religious Significance of Food to Medieval Women.* Berkeley: University of California Press.

Charles, N., and M. Kerr. 1988. *Women, Food and Families.* Manchester: Manchester University Press.

Chernin, K. 1981. *The Obsession: Reflections on the Tyranny of Slenderness.* New York: Harper.

Chrisler, J. C. 1996. "Politics and Women's Weight." *Feminism and Psychology* 6(2):181–84.

Connell, R. W. 1987. *Gender and Power.* Cambridge: Polity.

Corrigan, A., and D. Meredyth. 1994. "The Body Politic." Pp. 30–51 in *Contemporary Australian Feminism,* edited by K. Pritchard Hughs. Melbourne: Longman.

Crawford, R. 1984. "A Cultural Account of 'Health' Control, Release, and the Social Body." Pp. 60–103 in *Issues in the Political Economy of Health Care,* edited by J. B. McKinlay. New York: Tavistock.

Davis, K. 1996. "From Objectified Body to Embodied Subject: A Biographical Approach to Cosmetic Surgery." Pp. 104–18 in *Feminist Social Psychologies: International Perspectives,* edited by S. Wilkinson. Buckingham: Open University Press.

Duncan, M. C. 1994. "The Politics of Women's Body Images and Practices: Foucault, the Panopticon and Shape Magazine." *Journal of Sport and Social Issues* 18(1):48–65.

Faludi, S. 1991. *Backlash: The Undeclared War Against Women.* United Kingdom: Chatto and Windus.

Featherstone, M., M. Hepworth, and B. S. Turner (eds.). 1991. *The Body: Social Process and Cultural Theory.* London: Newbury Park.

Foucault, M. 1979. *Discipline and Punish.* Harmonsworth: Penguin.

Germov, J., and W. Williams. 1996a. "The Sexual Division of Dieting: Women's Voices." *Sociological Review* 44(4):630–47.

——— . 1996b. "The Epidemic of Dieting Women: The Need for a Sociological Approach to Food and Nutrition." *Appetite* 27:97–108.

——— (eds.). 1999. *A Sociology of Food and Nutrition: The Social Appetite.* Melbourne: Oxford University Press.

Grogan, S., and N. Wainwright. 1996. "Growing Up in the Culture of Slenderness: Girls' Expectations of Body Dissatisfaction." *Women's Studies International* 19(6):665–73.

Herman, C. P., and D. Mack. 1975. "Restrained and Unrestrained Eating." *Journal of Personality* 43:647–60.

Lester, I. H. 1994. *Australia's Food and Nutrition.* Canberra: AGPS.

Lupton, D. 1996. *Food, the Body and the Self.* London: Sage.

Maddox, G. L., K. W. Back, and V. R. Leiderman. 1968. "Overweight as Social Deviance and Disability." *Journal of Health and Social Behavior* 9:287–98.

Maiman, L. A., V. L. Wang, M. H. Becker, T. Finlay, and M. Simonson. 1979. "Attitudes Toward Obesity and the Obese among Professionals." *Journal of the American Dietetic Association* 74:331–36.

Najman, J., and C. Monroe. 1982. "Patient Characteristics Negatively Stereotyped by Doctors." *Social Science and Medicine* 16:1781–89.

Orbach, S. 1986. *Hunger Strike*. London: Faber and Faber.

Poovey, M. 1988. "Feminism and Deconstruction." *Feminist Studies* 14(1):51–65.

Pringle, R. 1995. "Destabilizing Patriarchy." Pp. 198–211 in *Transitions: New Australian Feminisms*, edited by B. Caine and R. Pringle. Sydney: Allen and Unwin.

Pyke, K. D. 1996. "Class-based Masculinities: The Interdependence of Gender, Class and Interpersonal Power." *Gender & Society* 10(5):527–49.

Rodin, J., L. Silberstein, and R. Striegel-Moore. 1985. "Women and Weight: A Normative Discontent." Pp. 267–306 in *Psychology and Gender: Nebraska Symposium on Motivation*, edited by T. Sonderegger. Lincoln: University of Nebraska Press.

Rothblum, E. D. 1994. "'I'll Die for the Revolution But Don't Ask Me Not to Diet': Feminism and the Continuing Stigmatization of Obesity." Pp. 53–76 in *Feminist Perspectives on Eating Disorders*, edited by P. Fallon, M. A. Katzman, and S. C. Wooley. New York: Guilford.

Schur, E. 1983. *Labelling Women Deviant: Gender, Stigma, and Social Control*. Philadelphia: Temple University Press.

Seid, R. P. 1994. "Too 'Close to the Bone': The Historical Context for Women's Obsession with Slenderness." Pp. 3–16 in *Feminist Perspectives on Eating Disorders*, edited by P. Fallon, M. A. Katzman, and S. A. Wooley. New York: Guilford.

Sobal, J. 1991. "Obesity and Nutritional Sociology: A Model for Coping with the Stigma of Obesity." *Clinical Sociology Review* 9:125–41.

———. 1992. "The Practice of Nutritional Sociology." *Sociological Practice Review* 3(1):23–31.

Tiggemann, M., and B. Pennington. 1990. "The Development of Gender Differences in Body Dissatisfaction." *Australian Psychology* 25:306–13.

Turner, B. S. 1992. *Regulating Bodies*. London: Routledge.

Walby, S. 1990. *Theorizing Patriarchy*. Oxford: Blackwell.

———. 1992. "Post-Post-Modernism? Theorizing Social Complexity." Pp. 31–52 in *Destabilizing Theory: Contemporary Feminist Debates*, edited by M. Barrett and A. Phillips. Cambridge: Polity.

Weedon, C. 1987. *Feminist Practice and Poststructuralist Theory*. Oxford: Blackwell.

Wolf, N. 1990. *The Beauty Myth*. London: Vintage.

Wooley, S. C., and D. M. Garner. 1991. "Obesity Treatment: The High Cost of False Hope." *Journal of the American Dietetic Association* 91:1248–51.

Zdrodowski, D. 1996. "Eating Out: The Experience of Eating in Public for the 'Overweight' Women." *Women's Studies International* 19(6):655–64.

8

Fleshing Out the Discomforts of Femininity
The Parallel Cases of Female Anorexia and Male Compulsive Bodybuilding

MARTHA MCCAUGHEY

INTRODUCTION

Self-starvation appears to be the antithesis of bodybuilding. The anorexic eats one meal a day (if that), reluctantly ingesting five hundred calories, while the compulsive bodybuilder eats seven meals, devouring five thousand calories daily. One looks frail and weak, the other monstrous. One seems to shrink from the world while the other seems to impose himself on it. That the former is usually female and the latter usually male is probably the main reason that anorexia and compulsive bodybuilding have been viewed differently and theorized independently. Yet there are striking similarities. Both the anorexic and the compulsive bodybuilder are consumed with wacky, rewarding, freakish, and often deadly body projects. Both spend an incredible amount of time reflecting on their bodies, critically appraising their physiques. Both take drugs and various diet supplements to help with their body projects. Both, as a consequence of those drugs, risk serious illness and death. Both have so transformed their bodies that they look like freaks and, if they live, will have permanently altered metabolisms and muscle-to-fat ratios. As this chapter will illustrate, both feel mentally strong, proud of their discipline, will power, control, and mastery of their bodies. And both find in their body projects protection from feelings of vulnerability.

The word "anorexia" already distinguishes between someone obsessively caught up with self-starvation and someone simply on a diet. "Anorexia," in other words, is already the name of a disease. Bodybuilding has not been theorized or pathologized that way, and thus no popular term distinguishes a man who lifts weights from a man whose life is

133

wrapped up with, and sometimes jeopardized by, bodybuilding. Within bodybuilding culture, however, lifters refer to such men as "bigorexic" or as having "the disease." Recently, the medical labels "reverse anorexia" (Pope, Katz, and Hudson 1993) and "muscle dysmorphia" (Phillips, O'Sullivan, and Pope 1997) have begun to position the obsessive pursuit of muscles as a pathology. Until now, however, the disease label has most often been used by bodybuilders for themselves and their peers, while such a label is more often imposed on anorexics by family members and clinical authorities.

Although my goal is not to pathologize bodybuilding (or anorexia, for that matter), it is important to note that both projects are equally obsessive and physically damaging, and offer similar psychic and social security. Both bodybuilders and anorexics can be seen as trying to escape feelings of vulnerability—a sense of boundarylessness and susceptibility to remarks, harassment, or worse, primarily from men. It is this parallel discomfort with femininity I wish to flesh out, in order to emphasize what forms an important component of the social context of women's eating problems. When anorexia and bodybuilding are theorized together, we might begin to understand anorexics in a new way. My main concern, then, is anorexic women and the feminist analysis of their condition. Far more women than men are afflicted with feelings of vulnerability. Far more women have, and are dying from, an obsessive bodily regime. But we are so accustomed to positioning women as passive dupes of a sexist culture, and men as willful agents who gain meaning and material rewards from their activities, that we have missed the parallels between the two body projects.

My aim is not to declare the definitive causes of the relentless pursuit of thinness or muscles for everyone so vexed, but rather to point toward a set of interpretive *possibilities* that feminists, cultural theorists, therapists, and medical professionals have not emphasized. Instead of positioning the anorexic as the embodiment of heterosexual femininity *writ large*, as most feminists do, I argue that many anorexics can be understood as particularly entitled girls and women engaged in a desperate attempt to ward off oppressive impositions of heterosexual femininity. The attempt to situate anorexia in a cultural context of compulsory heterosexuality and rape culture might complement, rather than deny, the importance of other studies that highlight, for instance, the anorexic's family dynamics or the therapeutic treatment of anorexics. In demonstrating the psychic and social parallels between women's anorexia and men's bigorexia, I hope to show that female anorexia can be more fruitfully read neither as an obsession with getting men's sexual attention, the striving for heterosexual femininity gone fanatical, nor an unentitled abstinence from "sexuality," but as a resistance to men's sexual objectification by women who grew up expecting more, yet find no other means of protesting[1] the meager rewards of heterosexual womanhood.[2]

IS GENDER CONFORMITY REALLY THE GOAL OF ANOREXIA AND BIGOREXIA?

Hilde Bruch's (1978) ground-breaking work and subsequent feminist interpretations have challenged the individual, medical model of anorexia in Western culture and instead understand it as a gendered disorder in which unentitled women with low self-esteem are caught up in an attempt, encouraged by a patriarchal capitalist "beauty ideal," to achieve feminine bodies that are pleasing to men and are, paradoxically, afraid of "sexuality" (defined as having a feminine body pleasing to men). Social expectations for women to be thin, perpetuated and glamorized in the media, are routinely identified as the web in which anorexics are caught. Analysts suggest that anorexics fear rejection, feel unentitled to exist, and strive to embody society's ideal of beauty and slenderness (Bartky 1988; Bordo 1993; Bruch 1978; Giddens 1991; Gilday 1991; Lowe 1995; Orbach 1986; Székely 1988; Wolf 1991). For instance, Wolf suggests that anorexics are engaged in an attempt to make themselves sexual and valuable: "Beauty pornography makes an eating disease seem inevitable, even desirable, if a young woman is to consider herself sexual and valuable" (1991:213). Giddens (1991:105) suggests that anorexics display "shame anxiety" over their bodies because of the unrealistic level of attractiveness they are supposed to achieve. Lowe (1995:165–66) argues that anorexia is a late-capitalist sociopathology, the anorexic being particularly consumed with dieting fads and thinness-promoting advertisements aimed at females. Others have claimed that the anorexic gets caught up with a drive to be attractive to men, and yet avoids sexuality (Bordo 1988; Hiltmann and Clauser 1961, quoted in Aronson 1993:51).

These interpretations of anorexia commonly take the afflicted individual as evidence of something that everyone of her gender experiences to a lesser degree:

> The anorexic's attempts to change her body are in essence an exaggeration of the activities of all women who must enter a society in which they are told that not only is their role specifically delineated, but success in that role relates in large part to the physical image they can create and project. (Orbach 1986:126)

Such interpretations assume that the more obsessive and disciplined the pursuit, the more such endeavors represent, in extreme form, that which is pursued by everyone. Bordo notes the cultural requirements that women be thin and suggests that "the anorexic does not 'misperceive' her body; rather, she has learned all too well the dominant cultural standards of *how* to perceive" (1993:57). Thus the anorexic is construed as quite aware of, and rigorously pursuing, cultural requirements for women.

Even psychotherapist Susie Orbach (1986), known for claiming that anorexics are engaged in a protest, suggests that anorexics strive to embody the gendered beauty ideal. Orbach does not think anorexics are entitled females who "protest" the meager rewards of heterosexual womanhood. Orbach argues that women are not allowed to initiate, and are taught to fear their own desires and appetites. Hence, anorexics' self-deprivation, an exaggerated version of all women's, exposes this horrible circumstance of womanhood. The protest, for Orbach, is that the very extreme to which anorexics lack entitlement constitutes a parody, which then exposes the horrible crime of a world in which women do not get to feel entitled. The anorexic's emaciated body is the sign of her subjective position as least entitled of all. The anorexic is seen as not allowing herself food, self-esteem, sexuality, femininity, freedom, and security in the world.

Bordo (1993), Heywood (1996), and Wolf (1991) argue that anorexia is simply a symptom of everywoman's participation in modern logic, which pits the body against the mind. Since women are associated with the body side of this dualism, the framework pits womanhood against individuality. This perspective dignifies the anorexic's pursuit somewhat, by suggesting that she is interested in achieving a social status normally reserved for privileged men. But each theorist continues to suggest that, even while the anorexic engages in "male" modernist logic, she engages in the feminine project of striving to have the body of sexist beauty culture:

> The anorexic . . . is usually a male-identified woman who has accepted white male philosophical ideals and standards. . . . Paradoxically, part of the "achievement" that is required of her if she is to accord with the dominant culture is the physical appearance of an acceptable feminine beauty usually defined as white. (Heywood 1996:29)

Anorexia has become the example par excellence of the damaging effects of sexist beauty standards. In essence, feminists rightly critical of sexist media images have wrongly made the anorexic their poster-child.

What do we make of the embodied sense of empowerment and agency the anorexic characteristically experiences? I shall show that she, much like the mammoth iron-pumping, carbo-loading man in the gym, gains an empowering sense of control over her body and a safe distance from those who threaten to control her. Of course, to study the parallels between anorexia and bigorexia, I shall have to contend with the common misperception that compulsive bodybuilding is itself a project of simple gender conformity.

Bodybuilding has been construed as an arena for men who are insecure in their masculinity and who wish to establish themselves as unquestionably, essentially male. In his ethnographic study of Southern California bodybuilding subculture, Klein states: "It seems almost tautological to claim that bodybuilding is hypermasculine. No matter what we can say in rationalizing the style and content of the subculture, it is preoccupied precisely with inflating and exaggerating male physical traits" (1993:221). Just as Giddens (1991:191) regards anorexics as relentless conformists, Klein (1993) regards bodybuilders as hopelessly committed to the achievement of heterosexual masculinity. According to Klein, compulsive bodybuilders play out a pathology of late modernity: authoritarian conformity to gender construction. The authoritarian individual only feels secure while others recognize his behavior as appropriate or reasonable. Bigorexics, therefore, are assumed to have an even greater need than most men to live and be seen as masculine.

Just as theorists of anorexia have claimed anorexics want to please men and then note the irony that they look terrible, Klein performs the same interpretive number to see male bodybuilders as pursuing "hypermasculinity." He insists that bodybuilding is "a subculture preoccupied with attaining hegemonic masculinity, but individuals within it who, because of the psychological baggage they carry with them, are only partially successful in accomplishing their goals" (ibid.:240). Interpretations of both anorexics and bodybuilders first claim that they are rigorously pursuing naturalized gender ideals, and then catch them in a contradiction by noting that the anorexic actually becomes less attractive and the bodybuilder gets less macho. I take this contradiction, as well as the similarities between anorexia and bigorexia, to indicate the need for an alternative interpretation.

Klein (1993) applies Lasch's (1979) theory of narcissism to claim that male bodybuilders are simply exhibiting our cultural preoccupation with youth, health, and vigor, and a narcissistic fear of aging to an obsessive degree. The evidence he provides to support this claim is what bodybuilding magazines declare (for instance, articles and advertisements that promise vigor, vitality, and virility to those who lead the bodybuilding lifestyle and use bodybuilding nutritional supplements). But the narratives of the body business, which promotes products by claiming that their consumers are getting more attention from the opposite sex, cannot count as evidence that in real life anorexics or bodybuilders seek, or are getting relatively more, attention from the opposite sex.

The claims in magazines cannot be taken as evidence supporting claims about the things with which bodybuilders or anorexics are preoccupied.

While bodybuilding magazines do emphasize youth, beauty, and health, bodybuilders are not necessarily in it for that. In his autobiography, *Muscle*, former bigorexic Samuel Fussell (1991:193) recalls his bodybuilding compatriots telling him as he complained of sickness before a competition: "What, do you think this has anything to do with health?" (1991:224). Laschian claims that anorexic women are obsessively engaged in that same narcissistic pursuit, simply because fashion magazines display such a narrative logic, are similarly erroneous.[3] It is a mistake to conflate the psychic motivations of anorexics and bodybuilders with the narratives provided by the capitalist institutions that benefit from these "diseases." To argue that anorexics and bodybuilders are victims of consumerism concedes too much to capitalism and refuses to recognize any other possible desire.

Both the anorexic and the bodybuilder have *asceticized* their projects and, further, both projects involve the body. The media glamorizes such self-defeating body projects, and people make money from them. Bodybuilders and anorexics buy diet pills, vitamins, diuretics, growth hormones, gym memberships, gym equipment for their homes, and other products. Indeed, the body business is big, and the magazines and related body products rarely mention the problems many of their consumers have. However, these facts can cause confusion over how the body projects are gendered, leading many to assume that they are about conformity to, rather than defiance of, sexed embodiment.

The facts that anorexics and bigorexics have asceticized their projects and that the media have estheticized their projects does not mean that they have estheticized the culturally popular gender ideals.[4] There is scarcely evidence of that. Both experience a reduction in sexual attention. It is common knowledge that few find sexually appealing a female skeleton with no breasts, brittle hair, and bones protruding from her back, shoulders, and ribs, or a man with muscles so large and body fat so low that his limbs bulging with veins resemble the ground meat at a butcher's shop. Anorexia and bodybuilding involve bodies, but this should not be conflated with projects of attractiveness or heterosexual attention-seeking.

Turner states (citing MacLeod 1981) that "the conscious aim of much anorexic behavior is to subordinate female sexuality, to deny the gender-specific characteristics of personality and to withdraw from any sexual contact with men." (Later in the chapter I will suggest that we consider what is commonly meant by "female sexuality" and why someone would want to "subordinate" it.) Some anorexic patients recall enjoying the maneuverability that their appearance gave them and enjoying being "uncharacterizable in conventional feminine terms" (Orbach 1986:100). From afar, the anorexic might not even be taken as a woman, and up close she is a subject for scrutiny, for her shapelessness removes her from the immediate categorization of conventional femininity. She is oddly desexualized and degendered. She demands to be related to originally. Reflexive responses—for example, flirtatious or patronizing ones from men, or the "once over" from another woman who needs to position herself vis-à-vis this woman—are confounded. (ibid.:102)

One significant difference between interpretations of anorexics and bodybuilders is that only the former are construed as victims. While cultural theorists often consider male bodybuilders in a judgmental tone (see, e.g., Simpson 1994), as though they are culpable subjects who desire the rewards of a masculine subject position, they consider anorexics to be comparatively innocent victims of a sexist culture who pathetically desire a feminine subject position or who are victimized by the hegemony of masculine modes of thought (see, e.g., Heywood 1996). Bigorexics are seen as having a certain agency that scholars seem hesitant to attribute to anorexics. Yet anorexics exercise a will over their bodies the same way bodybuilders do, often for the same psychic ends.

Perhaps because men's body projects are pathologized less often than women's, the self-talk of bodybuilders displays a more entitled version of the angst and desires that anorexics share. Rape culture and compulsory heterosexuality, along with other forms of violence that tell women of their second-class status, provide good reason for women to feel anxious about inhabiting female bodies and to desire control over their own bodies. Men find invulnerability easier to attain and embody; men may also feel more entitled to a powerful, safe, secure social position (which I argue is sought by both bodybuilding men and anorexic women) than women. Indeed, the male body in Western culture is defined as impenetrable and invulnerable, whereas the female body is construed as a violable, ownable complement to that male body. Such culturally constructed forms of sexed embodiment are overdetermined in women's real experiences of heterosexism and violent physical intrusion.

ACHIEVING INVULNERABILITY IN A PREDATORY ENVIRONMENT

A formerly anorexic woman explains the moment that spurred her weight-loss regimen: "[An old male acquaintance] remarked on my weight loss and said that it suited me; in fact, he said, I looked much more attractive. I reduced my intake of food, considerably, from that moment on" (Giddens 1991:103). Giddens reads this woman's remark as an indication that receiving the sexual attention of men is important. But if her physical form was already pleasing to men, why would she change that form, deny that form, and exercise that form down to almost nothing? If we reject the implicit premise that anorexics are conforming to heterosexual gender norms, then we might reconsider the meaning of her weight loss. Before anorexia, this same woman went through another phase of femininity that was not of the proper, glamorized sort: "I started to wear old clothes; from jumble sales and of my own making. And make-up—strange make-up—white or black lips; dark, violent-coloured eyelids. I plucked my eyebrows away and back-combed my hair. . . . I looked at photographs in magazines: There the girls were beautiful and thin" (ibid.:103). This young woman's make-up habits constitute less an imitation of fashion magazines' construction of femininity than a rebellion against it.

Often anorexia comes on after an objectifying comment or after the onset of menstruation, breasts, and hips (i.e., a womanly shape) (Orbach 1986)—which are then almost inevitably followed by objectifying comments and an overall sense of oneself as prey to heterosexual men (see Lee 1994). This sense of oneself turns the body into an enemy of one's will to freedom. I sustained the condition of anorexia for two years in the 1980s. In my case, the anorexia appeared after being picked up (literally) and handled by several young men on a Fort Lauderdale beach, who then carried me into the ocean proclaiming, "You've got curves in all the right places." I had to get away from their hold on me and walk back from the water to my place on the beach, aware of the stares of all the men sitting on the beach. The "shame anxiety" [as Giddens (1991:105) calls it] I experienced didn't have to do with thinking that I didn't measure up but rather with how they saw me as someone who did measure up. Given our cultural assumptions that women are supposed to like feeling objectified by men—indeed, it defines femininity—it has been difficult for analysts to imagine that young women might be shamed precisely because their bodies are "appreciated," that is, objectified. Harassment is disparaging for an entitled young woman who discovers that men often experience their sexual interest in women to the exclusion of intellectual, collegial, respectful interest. Anorexics may very well be women who are forestalling heterosexual femininity. What anorexics can teach the experts is how debilitating sexual objectification is, not because anorexics naively try to make themselves objectifiable, but because they go to such traumatic lengths to avoid it.

One anorexic woman explained: "I want to avoid curves—I always avoided looking like a woman. . . . I do not want to have the kind of body females have. From childhood on I had a negative association, felt it was not nice to look like a woman" (Bruch 1988:120). I interpret testimony from anorexics in light of a feminist critique of male violence and compulsory heterosexuality. Examining the parallel character traits of anorexics and bigorexics shows that anorexia is an extreme, but not of femininity. Instead, anorexia is an extreme form of the body control projects bestowed to us by late modernity in a political context of male violence and compulsory heterosexuality.

Feelings of vulnerability and insignificance initiate the path toward anorexia and bodybuilding. The discipline required by such pursuits provides some feelings of security. "The tightly controlled body is an emblem of a safe existence in an open social environment" (Giddens 1991:107). Former Mr. Universe Joe DeAngelis (Hellwarth 1992) explained that he began weightlifting at age fifteen after being teased by both boys and girls: "I was an egghead. I was overweight, and shy and quiet. Usually whenever I had a problem at school I would just buy a book or get a magazine, and instead of figuring out how to fix the problem, I'd go to the library." Before his bodybuilding endeavor, DeAngelis was "ashamed to walk down the beach, or ashamed to take a shower with the lights on because of the way [he] looked" (ibid.). After he got skinny, he still got picked on, and so spent the next decade working his way to titles like Mr. USA and Mr. Universe. Steve Michalik, another famous bodybuilder, had grown up skinny, and endured a violent alcoholic father whose idea of fun was to smash little Steve's face into a plate of mashed potatoes (Solotaroff 1991). Former competitive bodybuilder Sam Fussell (1991:20–21) was not only skinny (a gaunt six feet four and 170 pounds) but also in poor health. The problem, Fussell explains, was what his friends called "urban dissonance" combined with his inadequate public demeanor in the crowded and confusing New York City. As Fussell explains, "Jerry [a man representing Jews for Jesus who regularly approached Fussell on the subway] was just one of many 'friends' drawn to me through the course of the day like slivers of steel to a magnet. Something about me seemed to appeal to every deadbeat, con artist, and self-proclaimed philosopher of the city. No matter where I turned, confidence tricksters hounded my path" (ibid.:21). This wasn't all. Fussell recalls an early experience in New York City where he watched a business man being beaten by a homeless man. Fussell's fear came from identifying with the business man and realizing that "it could just as easily have been me" (ibid.:22). His fears widened to include the possibilities of air conditioners falling from buildings, a snapping bridge cable, etc. This man's journey into bodybuilding was prompted by feeling out of control, and the fear and shame of vulnerability: "I'd experience whatever physical pain was necessary to cauterize my real pain, the pain I felt in being so vulnerable, so assailable" (ibid.:75).

If modern life in Western culture can make Fussell—a six-foot-four-inch, white, heterosexual, economically privileged, Oxford University–educated, employed, young man—feel assailable and vulnerable, then it should not be difficult to understand the average young woman's feelings of vulnerability. After Fussell saw a photograph of Arnold Schwarzenegger and thought, "[N]othing could disturb this man," he knew that body-building was the answer (ibid.:24). As he puts it: "Why couldn't I use muscles as insurance, as certain indemnity amidst the uncertainty of urban strife? And if the price was high, as a quick glance at the tortured faces in the training photos suggested, well, wouldn't four hours a day of private pain be worth a lifetime of public safety?" (ibid.). It is perhaps the men who found themselves without the means, either by virtue of interpersonal skills or of social position, to gain the respect they grew up feeling entitled to who are most likely to catch the bodybuilding "disease." Thus it becomes clear that bodybuilders feel a certain distance from other people and, by extension, control. Despite common cultural presumptions that women are not interested in invulnerability or other things deemed masculine, anorexics are engaged in a parallel pursuit through self-starvation.

Both anorexics and bodybuilders become freaks, intimidating and turning people off. Most people aren't sexually attracted to them, and neither wants to date the opposite sex. Anorexics and bodybuilders, then, may start out less as successes at their gender roles than as failures. (But of course by "failure" I don't mean to imply anything bad, deficient, or amoral.) Both the anorexic and the bodybuilder defy simple gender categorization. This is part and parcel of the achievement of feelings of heroic invincibility and control. While bodybuilders have been seen as hyper-masculine, they do not neatly fit common cultural constructions of "normal" masculinity. They are seen as freaks (Klein 1993). Bodybuilding has failed to become an Olympic sport, and bodybuilders are not recognized or respected as athletes.[5] In fact, they often hear jabs such as, "He couldn't even run around the block." Bodybuilders, like anorexics, maintain their obsessions in the face of opposition from loved ones and despite others' blatant displays of disgust with their appearance. Most of Fussell's friends regarded his huge muscles not with respect or admiration for masculinity successfully displayed, but as an obvious sign that he had "gone queer" (Fussell 1991:146).

Just as the bodybuilder becomes less angular, more curvy, with little elbows, tiny ankles, and "tits," the anorexic becomes increasingly androgynous as she loses weight—she loses menses, curves, breasts, and body fat. This is typically accompanied by an avoidance of heterosexual encounters. About sexuality, Fussell explains: "The prospect of dating terrified me. It ran counter to my life's work, bodybuilding. To date meant to admit frailty, to acknowledge the fact that I was less than complete" (ibid.:157). Klein found that "the rigors of dieting, training, and, more importantly, excessive steroid use severely curb the capacity and will for sex" (1993:229). Simpson confirms this: "With prolonged steroid use testicles atrophy, penises shrink and erections become infrequent or cease altogether" (1994:41). Anorexics avoid sex as well. What is perhaps most empowering for both anorexics and bigorexics is their new social position in the public world: Nobody bugs them.

Anorexics are typically socially and intellectually precocious and dread subjugation to men (see Aronson 1993:129–30). What is empowering in anorexia is that the woman regains a status of integrity in the public world that women lose when they get the body fat, curves, and other signs of womanly (disempowered, ownable) status. If health were defined from a feminist standpoint, the only thing unhealthy about anorexia would be the way of handling that dread. Anorexics are pathologized for fears of sexuality getting out of control. Such fears are rarely interpreted as wishes for the control over their own sexuality that most heterosexual men take for granted.

Orbach (1986) and Giddens (1991) emphasize the active nature of the anorexic's pursuit. (Indeed, it is as active as that of the bodybuilder, whose exertion has always been obvious to everyone.) Because anorexics and bigorexics feel incapable of boundary-setting with strangers in public and often with people more familiar as well, their bodies come to feel like the only things under their control. In contemporary Western culture, the body is a site of self-reflection and construction. We no longer live in a world where our body sizes and shapes are the result of our occupation; nor do we adorn our bodies according to traditional ritual (Giddens 1991). That the body has become a primary target for the performance of choice and self-construction is evidenced by the increasing popularity of tattooing, body piercing, exercise, meditation, and getting to know your sexuality. Everyone is on some sort of reflected-upon diet, and everyone must come to terms with or make some choices amid the barrage of information about foods, additives, vitamins, herbs, medicines, bodily therapies, exercises, etc. (ibid.). For the economically privileged, such choices also include electrolysis, liposuction, breast implants, chest and calf implants, hair transplants, colored contact lenses, face lifts and nose jobs, fat camps and spa vacations. Even our genitals are now technologically up for grabs. The disciplined control of the body offers a structure to one's existence in a way that feels empowering, even heroic, in a world of crumbling truth regimes and moral fixities. It is in this context that intense bodily discipline can become the route to the invulnerability and control sought by anorexics and bodybuilders.

Anorexics and bigorexics are consumed by the same quest for bodily mastery and perfection. Body mastery is gendered in this culture. Women's control issues usually have to do with controlling the percentage of body fat, which is large relative to men's. Given that young men are more likely to look skinny than fat, their bodily control issues are more likely to concern musculature. Both anorexics and bodybuilders constantly criticize themselves and strive for ultimate control, as in the anorexic's infamous statement, "But my stomach is still fat" or the bodybuilder's, "My back just won't grow."

The commitment to strive for ultimate control is expressed through intense daily discipline. Consider the anorexic's diet. Audrey, a patient of Orbach, eats "a roll of sugar-free mints, 100g cottage cheese or yoghurt, two iceberg lettuces, 500g carrots, three teaspoons of bran, half the white of a small egg, unlimited amounts of Diet Coke and black coffee, and a quarter or a half of an English muffin" (1986:137). Further, the anorexic "becomes susceptible to all manner of unsubstantiated 'truths' about the 'fattening' capacities of food" (ibid.:121). The dieting discipline of body-builders is quite parallel. Joe DeAngelis begins his day with at least six egg whites, two cups of oatmeal, and a tall glass of iced tea. He then has a two-hour morning workout in the gym, and then lunch, which consists of two broiled chicken breasts and plain pasta. Nothing can have much fat. By 5:00 he repeats the lunch meal, sometimes with tuna instead of chicken. He works out after dinner for two hours, then has more egg whites, more tuna or chicken, and a salad or plain baked potato (Hellwarth 1992). Not only do bodybuilders exhibit the same kind of discipline over their time and diets that anorexics do, but they also exalt the same kind of mental disci-pline. Bodybuilders commonly describe the mental focus their workouts require for maximum physical benefit. They feel a high of endorphins run-ning through their bodies, often called "the pump." This is similar to the anorexic's hunger high, often affected by intense exercise and drugs (caf-feine and amphetamines).

Further, both anorexics and bodybuilders engage expert knowledge about the body: "You have to be so in tune with your body, you have to be so up on physiology and exercise physiology, and nutrition. You've almost got to be an expert in each of those fields in order to get this look. . . . It takes a lot of thought. It's a science and a discipline, too" (DeAngelis, quoted in Hellwarth 1992). Michalik became an expert in steroids and was described as

> a self-taught sorcerer whose laboratory was his body. From the age of 11, he'd read voraciously in biochemistry, obsessed about finding out what made people big. . . . And years later he scoured the *Physician's Desk Refer-ence* from cover to cover, searching not for steroids but for other classes of drugs whose secondary function was to grow muscle. (Solotaroff 1991)

He also got things on the black market, such as the skulls of monkeys, which he and his compatriots would crack open with bare hands to drink the hormone-rich fluid in the monkey's hypothalamus gland (ibid.).

Diuretics, which cause heart attacks by draining the body of potassium and magnesium, are the number one death risk for both bodybuilders and anorexics. Michalik had been shooting anabolic steroids—"juicing"—for ten years, taking speed to get through his workouts and taking downers at night to get some sleep: "Every system in my body was shot, my testicles had shrunk to the size of cocktail peanuts. It was only a question of which organ was going to explode on me first" (quoted in Solotaroff 1991). In parallel fashion, anorexics often memorize the contents of calorie and fat counting books, study nutrition and exercise physiology in college, and use various drugs.

The severe restrictions around diet and exercise, along with the intense thought that goes into such restrictions, make such projects thoroughly absorbing. A moment feels wasted if it is not serving the disciplinary project. Anorexics commonly do leg lifts to burn calories while standing in line at the supermarket, while bodybuilders may do calf flexes while waiting in lines or lying in bed. Fussell (1991:122) confesses that this whole process overtook him: "I couldn't stop. Seventeen-inch arms were not enough; I wanted 20. And when I got 20, I was sure that I'd want 22. My retreat to the weight room was a retreat into the simple world of numbers." And Michalik went from skinny kiddom to Mr. America to, "at age 34, years after he'd forgotten where he put all his trophies, he was still crawling out of bed at two in the morning to eat his eighth meal of the day because he *still* wasn't big enough" (Solotaroff 1991). In a similar fashion, the anorexic might stay up all night exercising for fear that she will not burn enough calories sleeping. The discipline required by these body projects provides a sense of mastery and empowerment, and enables the avoidance of social interactions with others.

In his review essay of Fussell's autobiography, Wacquant (1994:85) suggests that the pursuit of extreme muscularity expands the body's powers and offers a sense of agency. The discipline of the endeavor effects a process of heroization:

> Indeed, one of the attractions of competitive weightlifting, as of other sportive activities that demand a thorough subjugation of the organism and the colonization of the self, lies in the *heroization of everyday life* it effects. By turning the most mundane ingredients of ordinary existence, including nutrition, sexuality and sleep, emotional and social relations, into obstacles to be vanquished, dangers to be thwarted, and forces to be domesticated, the commandments of the bodybuilding ethic transform life into an endless series of tests of moral will and excellence through which a transcendent self may be constructed. Crucially, this process of heroization is simultaneously a process of masculinization since, as cultural history and comparative ethnology abundantly reveal, the heroic moral is the manly moral par excellence.

Wacquant's analysis of masculine heroization must be extended to anorexia. For the discipline that anorexia requires is similar, as are the psychic rewards of the sense of invincibility and control.

One anorexic explained, "I want to stay slender because I look more like a man. I push myself to do as much as any man can do" (quoted in Bruch 1988:125). Orbach suggests this sentiment is typical of anorexic patients:

> Although she looks extremely frail, she feels herself to be strong, to have defeated the exigencies of the body, to have overcome its human limits. Her 70-pound body can run eight miles a day and work out for hours on the exercise machines. She doesn't need food, she doesn't need to respond to the unseemly appetites of the ordinary female body. . . . [H]er self-image is one of which she is proud. She feels strong and impenetrable. (quoted in Glassner 1992:90–91)

Both the committed self-starvation of the anorexic and the committed self-enlargement of the bodybuilder involve a desire for mastery that reaches a will to immortality. The extreme physical risks incurred by a bigorexic amount to a playing with fate and a challenging of mortality. As one bodybuilder explained: "It's like how far can I push myself without dying? If you walk the line and don't die, well, man, it's a helluva rush" (quoted in Hedegaard 1993:192). They do not think death can happen to them. As bodybuilder Mike Matarazzo admitted after being hospitalized from taking diuretics and drinking almost no water in three days, "I didn't think it could happen to me" (quoted in Hedegaard 1993:142). Of course, they all know of the many bodybuilders who have died or who have been repeatedly hospitalized with serious ailments. Anorexics' apparent lack of concern when they are told they might die and refusal of intravenous feedings once hospitalized display the same will to immortality. The control anorexics and bodybuilders have over themselves provides them with protection against the vulnerability that began the endeavor.

The new bodily appearance and sense of personal control gives both anorexics and bodybuilders the armor they feel they need to contend with the public world. One anorexic recounts how her sense of helplessness decreased with her weight:

> Anorexia provided me with the illusion that I was in control, not only of my body and my own status within the community, but of that community itself and, finally, of the biological processes which others around me were powerless to influence. In short, I became convinced of my own omnipotence. The conviction started from my body and the discovery that no one could prevent me—if I were determined enough—from treating it as I wished (MacLeod 1982, quoted in Aronson 1993:169).

Fussell describes the way that bodybuilding gave him a kind of confidence he had heretofore lacked. Indeed, he became a bully. About his speech, Fussell says that it "had been too tame before, too timid. No wonder I never got my way in life. I went from answering the phone meekly to shrieking 'SPEAK!' into the receiver on the first ring" (1991:68). His walk changed, and everything else as he began to lose his sense of passivity and gentleness: "Gone was the cautious, passive, tolerant student, the gentle soul who had urged departing friends to 'take care' and actually meant it. The new me was a builder" (ibid.).

The anorexic is engaged in a disciplinary pursuit that is not the extreme of femininity but rather every bit as "macho" as that of the bodybuilder. It is not that heroism is gendered so much as the form such heroics take. One anorexic patient told her therapist that she was raised by her wealthy family to be one of those big colorful birds in a cage, and that she wanted to be more like a sparrow, inconspicuous, energetic, and free to fly in the wild (Bruch 1978:24). This is a common way for anorexics to express themselves (ibid.).

For both anorexics and bodybuilders, something about being an average human being is too vulnerable. Bodybuilders do not want to be normal men—they want to defy the human condition. As one bodybuilder put it, "I'm no *man*! You'd think I was, like, a race horse, yeah, one of those gleaming thoroughbreds with my blond mane whistling in the wind. I don't look like no *guy*. I don't want to look like no guy" (quoted in Fussell 1991:137). As Fussell himself admits, "I hated the flawed, weak, vulnerable nature of being human as much as I hated the Adam's apple which bobbed beneath my chin. The attempt at physical perfection grew from seeds of self-disgust" (ibid.:138).

Anorexics characteristically do not want to grow up and become the women their mothers are (characteristically intelligent and talented women whose talent was sacrificed for the family). They reject food and a womanly figure and status, in much the same way that the bodybuilder denies himself a normal man's body and thus a normal man's status. (Here we can begin to see how the popularization of slenderness and muscles for women and men, respectively, may fuel the "addictions" of these people trying so hard to look like freaks. The more other people approximate them, the greater the lengths to which they must go to distinguish themselves.) Bodybuilding and anorexia accomplish this exalted display of self-mastery, not heterosexual attractiveness or essentialized gender identity.

One former anorexic comments: "When I was anorexic I had only dim feelings of resentment as to how my body was destined to be used, and the thought of anything as positive and specific as penetration never entered my mind. . . . I think I was afraid that, once I recognized it, it too might get out of control—just like my body in general" (MacLeod 1982, quoted in Aronson 1993:169). While Bordo notes that anorexics are "avoiding sexuality," the words of two anorexics she quoted put it more precisely: they said they wanted to be "androgynous" and to avoid being a "'temptation' to men" (1988:95). This indicates that anorexics do not necessarily avoid sexuality per se, but avoid a certain kind of sexuality—perhaps a rigid, gender-polarized, heterosexual, predatory male sexuality. While Bordo's (1993) work involves what is unpleasant about womanhood, her reading of the anorexic's abstinence from heterosex as guilt, fear, or lack of entitlement makes her unable to see the anorexic as refusing to be valued in relation to a body that measures up. Most analyses of anorexia treat the anorexic's fear of sexuality being or getting out of control as, a priori, pathological rather than as a reasonable fear of sexuality getting out of the anorexic's own control. But given many men's view of penetration as the aggressive intrusion on someone else's boundaries (see Bersani 1991; Dworkin 1987; MacKinnon 1989), and the frequency with which they try to force it on unwilling women (MacKinnon 1989), pathologizing the anorexic's failure to see "sexuality" as an unquestioned good is highly problematic. Heterosexual gender prescriptions, and the subjugation they entail, may be just what anorexics, for good reason, fear.

Anorexics avoid the sexual encounters "healthy" young women are expected to seek (Bruch 1978). Anorexics commonly explain that they felt excluded from their female peers because those peers were interested only in boys (ibid.). One anorexic said that she was pleased at the disappearance of her breasts (ibid.:131). Another admits feeling disgust with her breasts: "I grab my breasts, pinching them until they hurt. If only I could eliminate them, cut them off if need be, to become as flat-chested as a child again" (Liu 1979:79). Moreover, for many athletic girls, the onset of menstruation, like the development of sizable breasts, can be an unbearable handicap (see Lee 1994). Some anorexics experience their weight to be inversely proportional to their feelings of power, as though in becoming anorexic they finally (re?)gain a core to their personality (Bruch 1978).

It seems plausible, then, that the dieting starts not because anorexics begin to hate the way their bodies look (as if they do not measure up to the feminine ideal), but because they hate the way others begin to look at their bodies. These women become "prudish" when their weight increases, but when skeletal feel that they can unshamefully display their bodies. Clearly, then, this is not a disease characterized by the desire to be attractive to others. When these women have bodies that fit the cultural standard of beauty, they hide them. Getting thin enough to repel men may be, at least in some cases of anorexia, the point. Women live in a predatory culture that they are supposed to, especially if "sexually liberated," enjoy. I do not mean to argue that feminists' ideals of the sexual liberation of women entailed embracing more of the heterosexuality women were supposed to enjoy but did not. Unfortunately, though, during the "sexual revolution," feminism and the "sexual liberation" of women came to be defined as women's availability to service men's sexual desires (Jeffreys 1990:103). As Sheila Jeffreys declares:

> The sexual revolution completed the sexualization of women. Both married and unmarried women were expected now to become experts in sexually servicing men, and to get over their own tastes and interests in order to become efficient at this task. Where once a large group of single women might have escaped the destiny of servicing men and concentrated upon their own life work, they were now conscripted into compulsory heterosexuality. (ibid.:110)

This "liberated" sexuality, then, under the pretense of feminism, has arguably affected young women profoundly. Many now define women's own sexual freedom in terms of men's desires. Anorexics may very well sense that "sexual liberation" is *not* sex on their own terms, but more sex on men's terms. Indeed, single women used to have a social space within which not to be sexual for men (ibid.). Anorexia may be evidence that there is no such space left. In this light, perhaps a degree of "prudishness" is understandable. As Dworkin tells us of Joan of Arc, such women may hang on to virginity as "a fuller experience of selfhood and identity" (1987:113). Anorexics may be modern-day Joans of Arc, not modern-day hysterics. The desire to stay a little girl could be affirmed in a way that is responsible to and empowering for these women. Girlhood is arguably much more peaceful, secure, and self-respecting than womanhood—at least for the women who become anorexic.

Bartky contends that "in the regime of heterosexuality, woman must make herself 'object and prey' for the man" (1988:72), suggesting that anorexics seek to embody this status. I am suggesting that anorexics are not the women who have most internalized that heterosexual ideology. In fact, they may be the ones most uncomfortable with it, most unwilling to incorporate it into their hearts and bodies, least "successful" at it. If anorexics hate their female bodies then, it is not because they hate themselves or feel insufficiently entitled. Rather than assuming that love of self and love of sex are the same, or that self-esteem and femininity are codeterminous, it is possible to see anorexics as entitled and, precisely for that reason, as hating their bodies. Anorexics' engagement in a body project, and ability to eat less than most women who try to emulate *Vogue* models, cannot constitute unproblematic evidence that anorexics have a stronger than average desire for their bodies to resemble popular representations of them. Bartky's statement that many women become "the docile and compliant companions of men" (ibid.:75) is certainly true; but the extremely disciplined life of anorexia does not imply that anorexics are the extremely compliant companions of men. Evidence indicates quite the contrary.

Bruch mentions that "girls are expected to begin dating or to have het-erosexual experiences at a much earlier age than before. . . . Often the anorexia appears after a film or lecture on sex education which empha-sizes what she should be doing but is not ready to do" (1978:ix). These sex education films, in which women are told of their role as menstruating baby-bearers whose sexuality involves an essential penis-centered procre-ative impulse, are enough to make self-respecting young women weary of womanhood. Sometimes the anorexia begins after a profound perception of one's lack of freedom—for instance, after a rape, as in the following case:

> [A]t sixteen, I was raped by my track coach. For a long time after, I screamed in silence, displacing anger onto the body that had made me vulnerable to attack, and declaring myself separate from it. I was at war with that body, starving it, punishing it by running intervals on the track every evening until I couldn't stand, running ten miles hard each morning and doing half an hour of situps on the back lawn under the apricot trees before breakfast, then making it vomit anything taken in. (Heywood 1996:4)

Rape, like any bodily trauma, tends to change a person's relationship to her body. Where once a woman may have deployed her body in ways that were not self-conscious, bodily trauma turns the body into an object for reflection and, due to a rape culture that blames the victim for assault, possibly blame as well. Thompson's (1994) life-history interviews with women coping with chronic eating problems confirms that sexual violence quite often prompts a change in one's view of one's body and eating pat-terns. One woman told Thompson that she began to diet (and, subse-quently, binge and purge) at age eleven, the year she was sexually abused by her sister's husband. Recalling adults' remarks that men who harass women like chubby girls, she associated fat with men's violation: "I asso-ciated fat with holding back by dreams" (ibid.:73–74). Another woman, now an out lesbian, told Thompson that her eating problem began when she felt uncomfortable being pushed into heterosexual femininity. "At puberty she was told to wear dresses, stop participating in sports, eat 'like a lady,' and show interest in boys" (Thompson 1994:82). "At some point someone said, 'Okay, now you have to be a girl.' And that means you have to go to the Jewish community center on Sundays. I was not into this at all. I wanted to be riding my bike. I wanted to be out playing. I was not into boys from day one" (ibid.).[6] As Thompson remarks, "[W]hile many women link eating problems to physical intrusions, others relate them to the psychic invasions of heterosexism, poverty, the stress of acculturation, racism, and emotional abuse. A combination of physical and psychic assaults leaves many women vulnerable to bingeing, purging, and dieting" (ibid.:94).

Thus anorexics are not tragically emulating the gender ideals so much as they are refusing to be evaluated in relation to them. The feminists I have cited here all lament the confines of heterosexual femininity, but see anorexics as the most caught up with it. Sexual violence and compulsory heterosexuality are parts of the context of the sexual objectification of women, which could motivate a self-respecting woman to get rid of the characteristics that make her objectified and, by extension, prey to violence.

Eating disorders make perfect sense not because women don't get to learn their sexual value, but because many women do not want to be valued for their sexuality. Beauty ideals do not simply brainwash women to become deathly skinny. This might explain the many women who are careful to keep nice figures, but anorexic women may be the very women who at some level resist such brainwashing and insist on being related to originally. Bordo (1993) has criticized specifically Freudian interpretations of eating disorders, arguing that the anxieties about the dangers of sexual involvement might be based on a realistic apprehension of domestic violence and sexual abuse. She notes that many anorexics, like many women in the population at large, may have been sexually abused. However, suggesting that the sexually abused, rather than entitled women more generally, would be apprehensive about heterosexual involvement comes dangerously close to what Bordo usually tries to avoid. Pathologizing women who are disinterested or apprehensive through an invocation of the abusive background only reestablishes feminine heterosexuality as normative.[7] A self-respecting girl or woman need not have been abused to be wary of heterosexual relations.

Anorexics are the women who refuse to engage in the masochistic sexuality that the culture of beauty pornography insists upon. Indeed, many women say how sexually alive they felt during anorexia, perhaps precisely because they were not what men wanted but were instead sexual on their own terms. As Mary Daly (1978) pointed out in *Gyn/Ecology*, women have always been pathologized for not doing what patriarchal society requires of them. One formerly anorexic woman recalls:

> The psychiatrist told me I was doing this because I didn't want to have sex with my boyfriend. He may have been right, in that I certainly wasn't having sex. But the odd thing was I've never in my life felt more passionate. Not toward men, but within myself. I felt that I was really alive and beautiful, that I was becoming a whole new person, someone I could admire. (Glassner 1992:97–98)

Anorexics' abstinence from "sexuality" is "sick" only when healthy femininity is presumed to include a desire for intercourse with men.

CONCLUSION

That anorexics usually approximate the beauty ideal at the onset of symptoms and are commonly high-achieving young women who would be upset to be placed in an inferior or objectified social position demand both alternative interpretations and therapeutic treatments. The cultural beauty ideal is significant but, I have argued, not in the way suggested by previous commentary on anorexia. Starving oneself enables a woman to escape from offensive male attention, which is in part a result of the commodification of a very particular form of the young woman's body.

While feminists have thus far argued that women are trained, anorexics even more than the others, to value the slender ideal, I have argued that anorexics retreat from it. The "unattainable goal" in this body project, as in the bigorexic project, is not thinness but invulnerability in a predatory culture. Both anorexics and bigorexics need help acquiring the boundary-setting skills that would keep them from making physically destroying projects the more viable options. Of course, it is not difficult to understand why far more females are afflicted with anorexia than males are with bigorexia: Women have far more reason to feel assailable and to erect a posture of self-containment.

As attempts at control, both anorexia and bigorexia are inevitably unsuccessful. Surviving anorexics finally notice the irony that they are controlled by their desire to control, and surviving bodybuilders ultimately admit that they never achieved the happiness and security they thought their pursuit would bring them. The triumph of "mind over body" becomes one of body over mind. What begins as a project of reflexivity turns into just the opposite, where the number of choices that once seemed overwhelming diminishes drastically: They become robots. As Michalik describes: "Those 10 years, it was like I was trapped inside a robot body, watching myself do horrible things, and yelling, 'Stop! Stop!' but I couldn't even slow down. . . . For 10 years, I was just an animal on stimulus-response" (quoted in Solotaroff 1991:33). It seems that the striving for control over our futures is all anyone can ever have. The work, the striving for control, is all there is—which is why there is no reason to stop engaging in it, or put differently, why it becomes "addictive."[8] Addiction feels like free will, and vice versa. The obsession with bodily control becomes a self-defeating downward spiral in which the subject has less and less chance of gaining a perspective or acting in a conscious political way on her situation. The wild sparrow who longed to fly free contrives a new kind of cage. The room of one's own winds up an inescapable self-torture chamber.

ACKNOWLEDGMENTS

Thanks to Madelyn Detloff, Sarah Fenstermaker, Barbara Franz, Laura Grindstaff, and Patricia Ingham for comments on an earlier draft of this chapter. A special thanks goes to Neal King, who provided comments and discussions of several drafts. Thanks also go to my mother, who got me out of anorexia by threatening my pursuit of education.

NOTES

1.   Some female bodybuilders might also fit in this analysis. But since most anorexics are women and most bodybuilders are men, I focus here on that pattern. Bordo (1988:98–99) argues briefly that female bodybuilders have the same willpower, bodily control, and self-discipline issues as anorexics. Heywood (1996:34–40) suggests that female bodybuilders, despite their own claims that they understand and experience their projects to be "liberating," have the same desires to be attractive to men as anorexics.

2.   This is not to say that anorexic behavior is resistance in the humanist sense—as though anorexics are thoroughly conscious individuals who, having all the information, decide to wage a protest. Further, in pursuing the parallels with bodybuilding, I do not wish to argue that anorexia is about masculinity rather than a rejection of femininity or incomplete femininity. Both anorexics and bodybuilders avoid vulnerability. Thus I argue that anorexia is resistance to feminine identification (not unachieved feminine identification); this does not result in masculine identification but rather exceeds phallic definition. As de Lauretis (1990:126) points out, this psychoanalytic understanding of resistance moves beyond traditional feminist notions that allow for resistance only as unachieved femininity.

3.   Some cases of obesity may have the same psychosocial roots as anorexia. Some women might get fat because of male harassment, and many young women are overweight. Those women who reject body discipline may simply be playing out the other side of the same control coin. Furthermore, many anorexics wind up overweight for a large portion of their lives. Binge-purgers (also known as bulimics) and binge-dieters (those women who are caught in a vicious cycle of bingeing followed by fasting) constantly teeter back and forth between the two sides of that coin. Thompson's (1994) research suggests that serious eating problems of all sorts often begin as a reaction against problems of sexist, racist, and heterosexist violence against women.

4.   Anorexics are self-absorbed, but this is a result, not a cause, of starvation. Psychological changes such as a preoccupation with food, a keenness of the senses, narcissistic self-absorption, and infantile regression occur in cases of both self-induced and forced starvation (Bruch 1978). Seltzer notes that anorexia is an exam-

ple of "an aesthetic purified of the interestedness of pleasure itself" (1992:125). Bodybuilding may be seen the same way. Bodybuilders can get away with such obsessions because people fail to notice as obsessive precisely those culturally valued health and fitness activities.

5. Contrary to popular belief, bodybuilders make very little money. Winning one of the biggest contests of all, the Arnold Schwarzenegger Classic, pays a mere $80,000 to the winner. Considering the costs of airfare, hotel, drugs, lotions, etc., they are not getting rich from this sport. Similarly, it would be misguided to assume that anorexics stand to make millions as top fashion models.

6. This woman's response was to binge eat, not starve herself. As stated earlier in note 2, compulsive overeating may achieve some of the same results as anorexia.

7. While some studies have shown that a great many anorexics and bulimics had been sexually abused as children (Glassner 1992), it has never been clearly established that the ratio is greater than in the female population as a whole.

8. A lengthy discussion of the politics of deciding what counts as "addiction" and when a feminist might force the treatment of a unwilling addict (for instance, hospitalize and intravenously force-feed an anorexic woman) is beyond the scope of this chapter. Since I want a world with these women in it, and since starvation itself changes one's perceptions, I do favor force-feeding and other treatments that may be against their will. But it is true that this forfeits the feminist commitment to letting women define their own experiences. Yet, the assumption that a woman is willfully starving is as precarious as the assumption that she is addicted to starvation. For an interesting discussion of addiction-attribution and its dependence on a notion of free will, see Sedgwick (1992).

REFERENCES

Aronson, J. K. (ed.). 1993. *Insights in the Dynamic Psychotherapy of Anorexia and Bulimia: An Introduction to the Literature.* Northvale, NJ: Jason Aronson.

Bartky, S. L. 1988. "Foucault, Femininity, and the Modernization of Patriarchal Power." Pp. 61–86 in *Feminism and Foucault: Reflections on Resistance,* edited by I. Diamond and L. Quinby. Boston: Northeastern University Press.

Bersani, L. 1991. "Is the Rectum a Grave?" Pp. 197–222 in *AIDS: Cultural Analysis, Cultural Activism,* edited by D. Crimp. Cambridge, MA: MIT Press.

Bordo, S. 1988. "Anorexia Nervosa: Psychopathology as the Crystallization of Culture." Pp. 87–117 in *Feminism and Foucault: Reflections on Resistance,* edited by I. Diamond and L. Quinby. Boston: Northeastern University Press.

——— . 1993. *Unbearable Weight: Feminism, Western Culture, and the Body.* Berkeley: University of California Press.

Bruch, H. 1978. *The Golden Cage: The Enigma of Anorexia Nervosa.* New York: Vintage.

——— . 1988. *Conversations with Anorexics,* edited by D. Czyzewski and M. A. Suhr. New York: Basic Books.

Daly, M. 1978. *Gyn/Ecology: The Metaethics of Radical Feminism.* Boston: Beacon.

de Lauretis, T. 1990. "Eccentric Subjects: Feminist Theory and Historical Consciousness." *Feminist Studies* 16(1):115–50.

Dworkin, A. 1987. *Intercourse.* New York: Free Press.

Fussell, S. 1991. *Muscle: Confessions of An Unlikely Bodybuilder.* New York: Avon.

Giddens, A. 1991. *Modernity and Self-Identity: Self and Society in the Late Modern Age.* Stanford, CA: Stanford University Press.

Gilday, K. 1991. *The Famine Within.* Santa Monica, CA: Direct Cinema, Ltd.

Glassner, B. 1992. *Bodies: Overcoming the Tyranny of Perfection.* Los Angeles, CA: Lowell House.

Hedegaard, E. 1993. "Making It Big." *Details* (October):136.

Hellwarth, B. 1992. "Pump You Up." *Santa Barbara News-Press,* 30 August, p. D1.

Heywood, L. 1996. *Dedication to Hunger: The Anorexic Aesthetic in Modern Culture.* Berkeley: University of California Press.

Jeffreys, S. 1990. *Anticlimax: A Feminist Perspective on the Sexual Revolution.* New York: New York University Press.

Klein, A. M. 1993. *Little Big Men: Bodybuilding Subculture and Gender Construction.* Albany: State University of New York Press.

Lasch, C. 1979. *The Culture of Narcissism.* New York: W. W. Norton.

Lee, J. 1994. "Menarche and the (Hetero)Sexualization of the Female Body." *Gender and Society* 8(3):343–77.

Liu, A. E. 1979. *Solitaire: A Narrative.* New York: Harper and Row.

Lowe, D. M. 1995. *The Body in Late-Capitalist USA.* Durham, NC: Duke University Press.

MacKinnon, C. A. 1989. *Toward a Feminist Theory of the State.* Cambridge, MA: Harvard University Press.

MacLeod, S. 1981. *The Art of Starvation.* London: Virago.

Orbach, S. 1986. *Hunger Strike: The Anorexic's Struggle as a Metaphor for Our Age.* New York: Avon.

Phillips, K., R. L. O'Sullivan, and H. G. Pope, Jr. 1997. "Muscle Dysmorphia." *Journal of Clinical Psychiatry* 58(8):361.

Pope, H. G., Jr., D. L. Katz, and J. I. Hudson. 1993. "Anorexia Nervosa and 'Reverse Anorexia' among 108 Male Bodybuilders." *Comparative Psychiatry* 150:302–8.

Sedgwick, E. K. 1992. "Epidemics of the Will." Pp. 582–95 in *Incorporations,* edited by J. Crary and S. Kwinter. New York: Zone.

Seltzer, M. 1992. *Bodies and Machines.* New York: Routledge.

Simpson, M. 1994. *Male Impersonations: Men Performing Masculinities.* New York: Routledge.

Solotaroff, P. 1991. "The Power and the Gory." *Village Voice* 29 October, p. 20.

Székely, É. 1988. *Never Too Thin.* Toronto, Ontario: Women's Press.

Thompson, B. W. 1994. *A Hunger So Wide and So Deep: American Women Speak Out on Eating Problems.* Minneapolis: University of Minnesota Press.

Turner, B. S. 1992. *Regulating Bodies: Essays in Medical Sociology.* New York: Routledge.

Wacquant, L. J. D. 1994. "A Body Too Big to Feel" (Review Essay). *Masculinities* 2(1):78–86.

Wolf, N. 1991. *The Beauty Myth: How Images of Beauty Are Used Against Women.* New York: William Morrow.

V

INSTITUTIONAL COMPONENTS

9

Commodity Knowledge in Consumer Culture

The Role of Nutritional Health Promotion in the Making of the Diet Industry

S. BRYN AUSTIN

As far as I can tell, the commercial side of health is both legitimate and socially beneficial. After all, medical care has always been a business and a profitable one at that. So let's not get upset that money is being made in the health biz. Climb aboard. (Levin 1987:60)

Some may consider these words from Yale professor of public health Lowell Levin to be a voice of pragmatism: Profit-making is a given in our capitalist society, so public health professionals should not waste efforts resisting and instead should come along for the ride. Levin invokes the persuasive power of ahistoricity to bolster his stance: After all, how can we resist the inevitability of something that has "always been?" But has the entanglement of public health with the marketplace that we experience today in fact always existed? This linkage may appear normative, but by what standard have we established its social or health benefits?

These are questions that must be asked about the commodification of health. Some authors have begun to do so, taking steps to lay a broad, theoretical framework for examining the interplay of health promotion and industry (e.g., Bunton and Burrows 1995; Featherstone 1982; Grace 1991; Lupton 1995; McKnight 1986). Sociologist Victoria Grace has articulately critiqued the ways in which health promotion "effectively constructs the individual subject as a 'health consumer' in accordance with the model of consumer capitalism" (1991:329). Grace questions the uncritical acceptance of the tie binding consumerism and health promotion. Building upon Grace's generalized theoretical groundwork, I extend consideration of this alliance to its everyday manifestations in the contested world of food. My chief interest is in the industry built on diet foods and the public health subspecialty of nutritional health promotion.

My aim is to delineate the structure of the industry–health promotion linkage, the historical timeline of its invention, and its consequences today for both commercial profits and societal patterns of health risk. The first section of this chapter will discuss the roots of commodity culture, analyzing the development of the contemporary diet industry and the coterminous expansion of nutritional health promotion. Drawing chiefly on the work of historian Stuart Ewen and anthropologist Arjun Appadurai, I will present a historical and theoretical discussion of consumer education and commodity knowledge as they relate to the creation and proliferation of markets, particularly diet food markets. Then I will provide a framework from economic theory to situate the diet food industry in its broader context of contemporary economic change and advanced capitalist expansion. Following this historical and theoretical grounding, I will present two low-fat campaigns as case examples: one originating from nutritional public health's Project Lean intended to promote consumption of low-fat foods, and the other from food processing giant ConAgra designed to promote its Healthy Choice product line. The synchronicity of these two campaigns exemplifies the profound interdependence of nutritional health promotion and the diet food industry, a relationship that has been forged in no small part from the privileging of social marketing and the lifestyle model as the axiomatic praxis and theory of nutritional health promotion. The end result of this pairing, I will argue, has been far more salubrious for the diet industry's bottom line than the public's health.

HISTORICAL ROOTS OF CONTEMPORARY CONSUMERISM

In the first decades of this century, unprecedented efficiency of mass production techniques created a tension between the profit-seeking imperative of capitalism and the long-standing Protestant values of parsimony and thrift. While industrialism was founded on a Protestant ethic valuing work and restraint of gratification as ends in themselves, the survival of capitalism through extension and accumulation creates a conflicting demand for mass consumption and excess. This "disjunction between the norms of the culture and the norms of the social structure," Daniel Bell (1978:71) argues, created "an extraordinary contradiction within the social structure itself." The economic system at once demanded denial and excess. "Its values derive from the traditionalist past, and its language is the archaism of the Protestant ethic. Its technology and dynamism, however, derive from the spirit of modernity—the spirit of perpetual innovation and of the creation of new 'needs'" (ibid.:78). Industrialists sought to redress this conflict by promoting new norms for commodity relations. A distinctive modern-day consumerism, which Stuart Ewen defines as "the mass participation in the values of the mass-industrial market," emerged in the 1920s, not as a seamless progression from prior consumption trends, but rather "as an aggressive device of corporate survival" (1976:54). Through a new partnership with advertising and marketing, industrialists devoted concerted effort to forging a transformed and decidedly non-Puritan ideology of consumption, where commodity purchasing and product "choice" were framed as the democratic expressions of individualism. In his 1934 manifesto *The Consumer's Dollar,* industry leader Edward Filene was explicit in his advocacy of a modern culture built on consumerism. It was time, he asserted, to teach "the masses not what to think but *how to think*" (as cited in Ewen 1976:55, emphasis Ewen's).

Marketers made it their mission to denormalize the self-sufficiency of the preindustrial family structures, which required very little consumption outside what could be produced in the home, and instead instill a new set of values that supported extensive involvement in the marketplace. Excess and learned wastefulness became the chief lessons. Industry's educational efforts were pursued not only through mass media advertising but also through multiple other channels including magazine contests and parades and collaborations with film producers, 4-H clubs, and schools. For instance, in the mid-1930s, both Westinghouse Electric and General Electric established culinary schools chiefly to acclimate women to use a multitude of newly available electric gadgets in the kitchen (Ewen 1976:172). Ewen argues that a priority for industrialists such as Filene and others was to institutionalize "a selective education which limited the concept of social change and betterment to those commodified answers rolling off American conveyor belts" (ibid.:54). Importantly, the chief purpose of this education was to accustom people to seeking out commodity solutions to all types of dilemmas, regardless of whether they were social, emotional, health-related, etc., in nature. The explicitness of this goal in the writings of industrialists and their marketers is illuminating when considered in the context of the contemporary relationship between the commodity world and public health. I will return to this point in my discussion of social marketing.

Extending Ewen's historical account, anthropologist Arjun Appadurai analyzes the function of education in a consumer economy. Appadurai (1986) describes a dual knowledge in the "career" of a commodity, informing production at one pole and consumption at the other, with knowledge at either pole having a reciprocal interaction with the other. Potential gaps in communication that may exist between producer and consumer are bridged by overlapping spheres of knowledge. Fashion represents a critical sphere linking production and consumption in capitalist societies.

Consumption, in fact, is dependent on people possessing the skill and knowledge required to read continually shifting fashion messages. This knowledge, Appadurai argues, "is not principally targeted to the production of commodities but is directed at producing the conditions of consciousness in which *buying* can occur" (1993:31, emphasis in original).

A parallel can be drawn between the position of fashion bridging the gap between the production and consumption of clothing and the position of nutritional health promotion linking diet food producers and consumers. Product differentiation for many processed foods depends on the consumer possessing a highly specific knowledge about fat, calories, cholesterol, and fiber. When a product is advertised as having a particular characteristic, marketers expect it to be meaningful for consumers, signifying an important quality that distinguishes the product from others. Saturated fat provides a clear example. Fifty years ago, if a product had been advertised as low in saturated fat, consumers most likely would have been unimpressed by the claim because the term carried virtually no meaning in the consumer vernacular at the time. Today, however, *saturated fat* is highly charged, carrying definitively negative connotations for consumers. The semiotic transformation of *saturated fat* and other terms formerly sequestered in the discourse of nutritional science should not be viewed facilely as a natural evolution of lay parlance. Rather the transition represents a historically specific and complex process of creation and dissemination of knowledge that links public health to consumer and producer. Like knowledge of fashion, knowledge falling within the rubric of nutritional health promotion produces "the conditions of consciousness" with which the purchasing of diet and reduced-negative-ingredient[1] foods can occur.

Public health promotion, I would argue, does not simply bridge the knowledge gap between processors and consumers. It is essential to the production and dissemination of the forms of knowledge used in both food processing and consumption. In a most direct and active way, public health promotion has been instrumental in creating a quantitative language of diet, the social meaning of nutritional knowledge, and the context of dietary and bodily self-consciousness and surveillance that serve to buttress the diet industry's complicated project.

The Challenge of Market Expansion.   Despite capitalism's massive success in consumer education, a conflict of values has remained, and expansion in the modern consumer economy has at times been "trapped" by our culture's simultaneous privileging of excess and restraint (Bell 1978). In this respect, the diet industry is exceptional. Dietary restraint has long been considered a virtue in our culture, and—especially for women and girls—consuming *less* ranks high in the expression of socially sanctioned gendered behavior (Brumberg 1988; Schwartz 1986). But unlike the products and services of other industries (e.g., automobiles, clothing, tourism), those of the diet food industry make possible innovation and accumulation along an axis of asceticism. The diet food industry paradoxically harnesses restraint and denial in the service of capitalist expansion.

The case of ice cream and frozen yogurt provides a simple illustration. In our contemporary society, few would quibble with the observation that the consumption of a high-fat brand of ice cream such as Häagen-Dazs carries the social meaning of indulgence and excess (connotations that are particularly apparent when the consumer is a woman). If high-fat ice cream were the only type of frozen dairy dessert on the market, then the consumer would be presented with an indulgence/restraint duality in which a display of indulgence is achieved through purchasing ice cream and a display of restraint is achieved through *not* purchasing. The diet food industry provides consumers with a way out of the indulgence (purchase)/restraint (no purchase) duality: In the form of low-fat frozen yogurt, an alternative is presented to consumers by which they may simultaneously display restraint *and* make a commodity purchase. It should be noted, however, that capitalism's harnessing of restraint has always been a tenuous one, particularly under conditions of intensified expansion in the contemporary era. At this juncture nutritional science becomes essential to produce consumption at the frenetic pace demanded by industry in what one theorist has dubbed the era of flexible accumulation (Harvey 1995).

David Harvey (1995) posits that a shift has occurred in the structure of advanced capitalism since the transnational financial crisis of the early 1970s. His thesis provides a framework for situating the contemporary expansion in the diet industry within the larger context of economic change. Harvey argues that following the postwar economic boom, generally regarded to have lasted from 1945 to 1973, capitalism made a transition into a period he terms the "flexible regime of accumulation." This regime, he argues, has demanded "an acceleration in the pace of product innovation together with the exploration of highly specialized and small-scale market niches. Under conditions of recession and heightened competition, the drive to explore such possibilities became fundamental to survival" (ibid.:156). The intensification in product innovation has necessitated a parallel acceleration in the turnover time of commodity consumption (ibid.:156–57). The emphasis on the invention and aggressive pursuit of highly specific market niches described by Harvey represents a departure from the goal of creating a unified market in the early decades of commodity expansion in this country. Though Harvey does not address the diet industry, diet products exemplify the type of innovations required by flexible accumulation as he defines it. In the decades that Harvey is most concerned with, the industry has created an enormous and extremely lucrative market niche for its innovations. Processed food, in fact, which lasts only as long as it takes a person to chew and swallow, represents a near ideal in terms of accelerated commodity turnover time.

LIGHT FOOD AND NEGATIVE NUTRITION

Until the late 1960s, food manufacturers maintained a small niche market for dietetic foods, but attempts at expansion—with products such as Meisterbrau—were largely unsuccessful because of negative associations with dietetics. Manufacturers had a problem with market positioning. At that time, a dietary counterculture—or "Countercuisine" (Belasco 1984)— garnered a small but enthusiastic following. The movement shared characteristics with its predecessors over the previous half-century, such as adherence to ascetic ideals of dietary restraint and casting of obesity as a symbol of overconsumption. The movement was distinguished, however, by its opposition to processed foods and food additives and its promotion of chemical-free (so-called organic) and small-scale, decentralized farming. Warren Belasco argues that the Countercuisine movement's association of "light" foods with health and holistic living gave manufacturers the foothold they needed to reposition diet foods and broaden appeal. In the process, however, the Countercuisine meaning of "light" was stripped of its more subversive sentiments unfriendly to the requisites of mass production (e.g., preservatives, additives, and packaging). Belasco explains:

> [T]he public perceived lightness to be healthier; industry thought it to be profitable. The former perception was questionable, the latter indisputable. While purporting to promote health, most light foods simply allowed food processors and fast food franchisors to go on doing what they had been doing since the 1920s: converting inexpensive raw commodities into elaborately refined, preserved, packaged, and promoted brand-name products. (ibid.:255)

The concept of "light" food was first made popular with a mass audience with the 1975 introduction of the low-calorie beer Miller Lite on the national market. The term then took on a broader definition by the early 1980s to include any processed foods that had less of an ingredient that was perceived as negative (Belasco 1984).

By recasting the formerly unsavory image of dietetic products, manufacturers were able to increase profits appreciably with new lines of light foods, charging more for these specialized "health" foods and expanding their market—originally targeting primarily middle-class, educated, white consumers, especially women. But more importantly, by offering less in the way of calories and fat, manufacturers were able to solve a unique biological dilemma facing the food industry: The typical adult can eat no more than 1,400 to 1,500 pounds of food per year (ibid.:272). Light products facilitated increased consumption, particularly of highly profitable snack foods, by circumventing biological constraints.

From the late 1960s through the 1970s, diet products steadily proliferated, and grocers began to mainstream the low-calorie foods that for decades had been cordoned off in special dietetics sections (Schwartz 1986:253). But in the 1980s the industry boomed. In that decade, the diet soda market grew at a 20 percent annual rate, and G.D. Searle and Company earned $585 million in 1984 from its newly approved artificial sweetener, aspartame. Nonprescription weight control drug sales exceeded a 20 percent annual growth rate in the same decade, after the FDA approved phenylpropanolamine as an appetite suppressant. The first diet fast food chain—D'lites—opened in 1981 (ibid.:242). Light foods made up more than 40 percent of the $10 billion market in snack foods in 1982 (Belasco 1984:272). Through the 1980s, frozen low-calorie dinners were the fastest growing segment of the food industry. Nearly nonexistent in 1980, they represented 21 percent of the frozen market by middecade, earning over $800 million annually (Kleinfield 1986).

SOCIAL MARKETING, LIFESTYLE, AND THE HEALTH CONSUMER

During this boom period for the diet industry, public health campaigns focused increasing attention on diet and obesity and widened the reach of promotional messages through the mass media (Contento et al. 1995). These campaigns helped create the "conditions of consciousness," as defined by Appadurai (1993), necessary to make diet product differentiation coherent and salient to potential consumers being groomed for the emerging market. Not unlike the schools, community organizations, and myriad other institutions described by Ewen (1976) and other scholars, public health took on the task of consumer education. This task was executed through the field's practice of social marketing and theoretical orientation toward the lifestyle model.

Since the late 1960s, social marketing has been enthusiastically adopted in the field of public health. Nutritional public health efforts have relied heavily on social marketing—an approach to media education that borrows extensively from commercial marketing techniques—as its promotional strategy. The field has likewise been guided by a theoretical dependence on the lifestyle model of health and risk (Coreil, Levin, and Jaco 1985). Emulating commercial marketers, government agencies and nonprofit organizations have sought to adapt industry techniques to the "sale" of social and health issues (Novelli 1990; Solomon 1989).

Commercial marketing historically is founded on the exchange model of consumer behavior, which holds that individuals will exchange money or other resources for something deemed valuable or beneficial. Integral to commercial marketing is the notion of the individual as a free agent in the marketplace. William Novelli, a champion of social marketing in public health, is passionate about the promise he sees in bringing marketing to health: "The health consumer must be at the center of health education programs and efforts. This intense concentration on the consumer is marketing's greatest asset. It is the most significant contribution that the marketing discipline can bring to any social program" (1990:346).

Social marketers generally have not been explicit about the theory underlying their campaigns (Contento et al. 1995; Glanz, Hewitt, and Rudd 1992), but the individualist notion of the free agent consumer at the core of exchange theory has clearly predominated in health promotion efforts, chiefly in the form of the lifestyle model of health behavior. Tracing the history of the lifestyle concept from scholarly writings of last century to the present day, Coreil et al. discuss how the model is premised on "the notion that personal habits are discrete and independently modifiable, and that individuals can voluntarily choose to alter such behaviors" (1985:428). Several early reports from Great Britain, Canada, New Zealand, the United States, and the World Health Organization helped bring the lifestyle model into prominence in public health (Grace 1991). Appearing in 1974 and published by a former minister of the Canadian National Health and Welfare department, *A New Perspective on the Health of Canadians: A Working Document* was among the first of these pivotal pro-lifestyle reports (Lalonde 1974). By the late 1970s, the lifestyle model had become the leading framework in health promotion and continued to hold this position through the 1980s and 1990s, especially in nutritional health promotion (Coreil et al. 1985).

A small but vocal minority in public health has inveighed against the preeminence of the lifestyle model and social marketing in health promotion efforts (Anonymous 1980; Buchanan, Reddy, and Hossain 1994; Coreil et al. 1985; Grace 1991). Critics have pointed out the tendency to decontextualize health, ignoring significant social and economic forces shaping patterns of risk, and to focus instead on individual responsibility.[2] I would add that not only does this framework ignore systemic influences on health and disease, but it also elides influences on health promotion strategies and their consequences.

The volume of publications from the federal government and major health organizations proffering nutritional recommendations has ballooned since the 1960s. In 1969 the National Academy of Sciences warned that recommended levels of daily calorie intake be lowered by between 100 and 300 calories, and in 1974 the American Heart Association raised the pitch of its anti-dietary cholesterol crusade. In 1977, the Senate's Select Committee on Nutrition and Human Needs advised that Americans should cut fat intake by 10 percent or more (Levenstein 1993:203; Schwartz 1986:254), a recommendation that presaged the public health community's and the nation's impending obsession with dietary fat. In 1980, Americans saw the first edition of Dietary Guidelines, issued jointly from the U.S. Department of Health and Human Services and the U.S. Department of Agriculture, which instructed people to avoid dietary fat, especially saturated fat and cholesterol. It is important to note that it was not until a decade later that fruits and vegetables received a level of attention in the guidelines commensurate with that of fat, a point to which I will return shortly (Kennedy, Meyers, and Layden 1996).

In a special issue of the *Journal of Nutrition Education,* Contento et al. (1995) review national and regional nutritional health promotion programs that have been launched in the United States over the past two decades in response to the evolving nutritional guidelines. Many of the programs reviewed are social-marketing-based and a number involve supermarket and vending machine point-of-purchase campaigns. The authors describe health promotion campaigns that identify specific brands and are located in grocery stores and restaurants—strategies that target individuals as consumers—as "highly effective" because they maximize effect on "purchase intention and behavior." An earlier review also published in the *Journal of Nutrition Education* documents a number of studies finding increased product sales following nutrition education interventions (Glanz et al. 1992).

THE AGE OF LOW-FAT

The editors of the trade journal *New Product News* declared 1989 a turning point for introduction of low-fat and other "nutritionally" positioned products: 626 reduced-fat foods were launched that year, an increase of 127 percent over 1988, and 962 calorie-reduced products were introduced, more than double those of the previous year (Best 1990). One-tenth of the 9,192 new food products introduced were reduced fat or calorie. In a survey of over four hundred food processors, research and development leaders listed reduced fat and calories, reduced cholesterol, and reduced sodium as three of the top five objectives (ibid.). Numerous industry experts pronounced the beginning of a new low-fat age. "'Healthy'—controlled for fat, cholesterol, sodium and calories," declared *Supermarket Business*, "has replaced 'low calorie' as what the consumer of the '90s is looking for in diet foods" (Papazian 1990:49).

The industry journal *Lowfat/Low Cholesterol Monitor* saw its inception in 1989. Published by the New York consulting agency Find/SVP Inc., an annual subscription to the journal, which catered to an exclusive client base of forty to fifty strategic planners with major pharmaceutical and food processing firms, cost $2,700 per year. After several years, the journal dropped "low cholesterol" from its name because of the nutrient's shrinking currency among food marketers and then in 1993 cut the price down to $395 and expanded the subscriber base to three hundred. Designed as a compendium of food science, medical, and public health research news for nonscientist readers, *Lowfat Monitor* reported on new drugs, food products, taste test results, and other related topics and included interviews with leaders in low-fat food processing and decision-makers at health agencies, including the Food and Drug Administration.[3] Other industry publications routinely reported on the latest news from medical and public health research. A technical article in a 1989 issue of *Prepared Foods*, titled "Processors Pursue the Perfect Nutritional Profile," proclaimed, "Food processors are hitching their fortunes to nutritional breakthroughs in the understanding of coronary heart disease. New ingredient technologies will help consumers redefine what is healthy, and what is not" (Best 1989a:79).

While the opprobrium for dietary fat was—and is still—consistently endorsed by government agencies, national health associations, and the food industry, one intractable problem remains: The scientific evidence is far from clear about what health risks are associated with dietary fat and exactly which of the many types of fat can be blamed. The 30 percent calories from fat and 10 percent from saturated fat guidelines are largely arbitrary, and there is very little medical or epidemiologic significance to the popularized cutoffs (Ascherio, Rimm, et al. 1996; Ascherio and Willett 1995; Campbell and O'Connor 1988; Willett et al. 1992). The cutoffs were chosen chiefly because they were modestly below the nation's estimated mean dietary intake and, therefore, considered reasonable goals for change. They are not representative of any type of threshold above which the risk of disease or obesity increases appreciably. While the absence of a threshold does not in principle negate the merit of recommending safe limits for risk exposures, the insistence on specific values—such as the 30 and 10 percent limits—does invoke the assumed authority of scientific precision in a situation where there is none.

A more important issue is that the sizable health risks associated with dietary fat that were inferred from animal and ecological studies have not been borne out in epidemiological research. After animal studies had found evidence of an association between tumor growth and fat intake, some researchers took center stage in the scientific community by making international comparisons of human cancer rates and per capita fat consumption and claiming a causal relationship (Armstrong and Doll 1975;

Prentice et al. 1988). These studies, based on what is referred to as ecological analyses, have been widely challenged on methodological grounds. More analytically rigorous epidemiological studies have not corroborated the assertions of a clear increased risk of breast, colon, prostate, or other cancers posed by dietary fat (Giovannucci et al. 1994; Graham et al. 1982; Willett, Stampfer, Colditz, Rosner, and Speizer 1990; Willett et al. 1992).

For obesity research, the story unfolded similarly. Following up on some plausible hypotheses generated from metabolic and animal studies, international comparisons were made using ecological data on per capita fat consumption and prevalence of obesity. When nonindustrialized nations were compared with industrialized nations, where both dietary fat intake and obesity prevalence tend to be higher, researchers inferred a causal relationship. Again, these conclusions have been critiqued for their serious methodological weaknesses. Reviews of decades of epidemiological and experimental studies have found results to be inconsistent at best, with no indication that fat consumption is a cause of the increasing prevalence of obesity in the United States (Lissner and Heitmann 1995; Willett 1998).

Results from studies on coronary heart disease (CHD) and dietary fat are more suggestive of a relationship, though again the evidence is not clear-cut. Epidemiological studies through the 1980s were largely conflicting (Gordon et al. 1981; Kromhout and de Lezenne Coulander 1984; Kushi et al. 1985; McGee, Reed, Yano, Kagan, and Tillotson 1984; Shekelle et al. 1981; Scott, Gorry, and Gotto 1981), and studies from the current decade have found only mild or no association between total dietary fat or saturated fat intake and CHD (Ascherio, Rimm, et al. 1996a; Hu et al. 1997; Pietinen et al. 1997).

The dilemma of the dearth of evidence was not a secret to food processors. In a 1989 issue of *Prepared Foods,* writer and technical editor Daniel Best (1989b) acknowledges that the scientific evidence on the relationship between dietary fat and illness is far from conclusive, yet he remarks that food processors Kellogg, Procter and Gamble, and Campbell "probably served their short-term interests" in terms of public relations by reformulating their product lines to adhere to the low-fat agenda. Nor was it unknown to nutritional researchers. A 1980 National Academy of Sciences (NAS 1980) publication on dietary guidelines for the nation asserted that based on the scientific evidence of the day, there was no need for healthy people to lower their intake of cholesterol or fat. By 1989 NAS had changed its recommendations to be more in line with the dominant public health opinion on dietary fat, but it nevertheless acknowledged that the supporting evidence was less than conclusive. While recommending that all Americans reduce their fat intake to 30 percent and saturated fat intake to 10 percent of calories, the NAS report explicitly states, "No studies in humans have yet examined the benefits of changing to low-fat diets" (NAS 1989:144). The latest edition of federal Dietary Guidelines, published in

1995, still promotes the 30 percent of calories from fat and 10 percent of calories from saturated fat recommendations (Kennedy et al. 1996).

In contrast to the case of dietary fat, epidemiologic evidence has fairly consistently shown that a diet high in whole fruits and vegetables is inversely associated with cancers of the colon, lung, stomach, and other sites and coronary heart disease (Ascherio, Hennekens, et al. 1996b; Block, Patterson, and Subar 1992; Giovannucci and Willett 1994; Steinmetz and Potter 1991; Willett 1996; Ziegler 1991). Promotion of the consumption of fruits and vegetables, however, has not been emphasized in public health campaigns until relatively recently. It was not until 1992 that a national fruit and vegetable promotion project—the Five a Day for Better Health program sponsored by the National Cancer Institute—was initiated (Contento et al. 1995; Crawford 1988; Office of Cancer Communications 1993; Patterson, Block, Rosenberger, Pee, Kahle 1990). Not coincidentally, raw fruits and vegetables in most cases do not present a profit potential for producers anywhere near that of processed foods (Belasco 1984). Some state departments of food and agriculture, in fact, offer technical assistance to growers and producers to help them identify opportunities to convert raw fruits and vegetables into more profitable "value-added foods," as these processed foods are called in the industry.[4] Importantly, while national nutrition surveys have documented a downward trend in total fat and saturated fat consumption by Americans in recent decades, there has been no evidence of a coterminous increase in consumption of fruits and vegetables (CDC 1994; Heini and Weinsier 1997; Patterson et al. 1990; Peterkin and Rizek 1986; Popkin, Siega-Riz, and Haines 1996; Stephen and Wald 1990; USHHS and USDA 1989).

After a decade of mounting animosity toward dietary fat, the crescendo culminated in 1989 with the arrival of an unprecedented and ambitious social marketing campaign and an unexpectedly profitable line of low-fat frozen dinners. In early 1989 Project LEAN, a national nutrition education campaign initiated by the Henry J. Kaiser Family Foundation, kicked off its first major media drive. In January of that year, ConAgra Inc., a food manufacturer based in Omaha, Nebraska, launched its Healthy Choice brand of low-fat and low-cholesterol frozen dinners and entrees. The timing of the two events could not have been more fortuitous for ConAgra.

Project LEAN. "The latest effort to get Americans to cut down on their biggest edible vice" is how one *Washington Post* reporter chose to describe Project LEAN, a national social marketing initiative dedicated to the mission of persuading Americans to cut dietary fat intake from a national average of 37 percent to 30 percent of daily calories by 1998 (Sugarman 1988). The term *edible vice*—with connotations of a moral crusade more than an informed health campaign—seems apropos given the lack of strong evidence as to the risk of disease or obesity posed by dietary fat or the benefits of dietary fat reduction.

With a $3.5 million grant from the Kaiser Foundation, Project LEAN, an acronym for Low-Fat Eating for America Now, was up and running in the fall of 1988 with plans for a major national media drive beginning in early 1989. The project acronym no doubt was meant to tap into the connection in most people's minds by that time between lean *food* and lean *bodies*. Through public service advertising, print and broadcast press publicity, and point-of-purchase programs in stores, restaurants, and cafeterias, the national nutrition education campaign targeted consumers, government, and the food industry. Ten regional projects also were set up to intensify efforts in some areas. Local programs worked closely with grocery chains such as Sloan's Supermarkets in New York and Safeway in California (Ostroff 1989; Taylor 1990).

From its inception, Project LEAN was established as a partnership with the food industry and stated that part of its mission was to increase availability of and consumer demand for low-fat products (McNeil 1988). In addition to the grant from Kaiser, Project LEAN received nearly $100,000 in the first three years from corporate sponsors, including funds from food giants Procter and Gamble, Kraft General Foods, and Campbell Soup Company. The project's advisory board, called Partners for Better Health, was a coalition of thirty-four public agencies and private associations and industry groups. The members included the American Cancer Society, U.S. Department of Agriculture, American Public Health Association, American Dietetic Association, Centers for Disease Control, and American Heart Association, alongside industry groups such as the Food Marketing Institute, National Fisheries Institute, National Food Processors Association, and National Turkey Federation (Samuels 1993). The Food Professionals Working Group, made up of forty chefs, nutritionists, and journalists, advised the project on low-fat recipes (Tougas 1992).

Although the project began with a policy not to allow product endorsements (Samuels 1993), the Project LEAN instructional manual for health educators, "Tips, Tools, and Techniques for Promoting Low-Fat Lifestyles," was paid for by a grant from Nestle's Stouffer's Lean Cuisine division and comes with a cover letter cosigned by representatives from the American Dietetic Association and Stouffer's (American Dietetic Association 1995). The project's educational video kit "Lean 'n Easy: Preparing Meat With Less Fat and More Taste" was coproduced with the National Cattlemen's Beef Association.

Project LEAN ran its public service announcements through the Advertising Council (an agency most known for its "This is your brain on drugs" frying pan ad from its clever but dismally ineffectual national war on drugs advertising campaign). In 1990 alone, Project LEAN estimates that it garnered $36 million in donated advertising media time, reached half of the nation's television-viewing households and 16.5 million print readers, and earned spots on over 2,800 radio stations. Media publicity for the project was handled by Porter/Novelli, a public relations agency cofounded by social marketing proponent William Novelli. From October 1989 to June 1990, the campaign generated almost 300 articles in print publications with a combined circulation of over 35 million. In the same period, radio and TV publicity was estimated to have reached more than 27 million people (Samuels 1993). Through its 1-800-EAT-LEAN hot line, the project distributed a free booklet—*LEAN Toward Health*—that offered advice on how to cut down on dietary fat while shopping, cooking, and eating out (*PR Newswire* 1990). Almost 300,000 calls were logged to the 1-800-EAT-LEAN hot line in the first year. In fact, the enormous hot line response was so financially overwhelming that the line was disbanded after a year and a half (Samuels 1993). In 1991, Kaiser awarded the National Center for Nutrition and Dietetics, the education arm of the American Dietetic Association, which receives funding from the food industry, $240,000 to take over and expand the project (Tougas 1992).

Healthy Choice.   ConAgra chairman and CEO Charles Harper astutely predicted in the late 1980s that low-fat foods would be a lasting trend, and in January 1989 launched a new brand of frozen meals. The company announced that any products under the Healthy Choice label would be low in calories, cholesterol, and sodium, and—plainly linking the new product profile to the *de rigueur* health promotion language—the products would contain no more than 30 percent of calories from fat or 10 percent from saturated fat (Wollenberg 1995). The early Healthy Choice television marketing campaign included an ad featuring a testimonial from Con-Agra's Harper, describing how his own heart attack had inspired him to create the new food line (Wellman 1992).

Within months Healthy Choice had taken nearly a quarter of the $700 million market in frozen dinners, earning an estimated $150 million in sales in the first year. Earnings more than doubled in 1990, making Healthy Choice the top selling brand (Ellis-Simons 1990; Liesse 1990; Major 1991). Healthy Choice became one of the most successful upstart food brands in recent decades, according to *Food and Beverage Marketing* (Wellman 1992). Within the industry, the success of Healthy Choice was credited with pushing competitors to reposition diet food products as "nutritional" (Ellis-Simons 1990; Major 1991). For instance, in the spring of 1991, Campbell changed the name of its Le Menu LightStyle to Le Menu Healthy (Dagnoli and Liesse 1991).

For the fiscal year beginning June 1992, ConAgra slated $200 million to promote its expanding Healthy Choice brand. Healthy Choice entree and dinner sales alone were $341 million in the year ending April 1992 (Liesse 1992). Within four years of its launch date, Healthy Choice had taken a 40 percent share of the market in frozen dinners and entrees (Driben, Kelley, Szathmary, Wisendanger, and Rottenberger 1992). The success of Healthy Choice earned Harper and ConAgra both the Adman of the Year award from *Advertising Age* and the Marketing Achievement Award from *Sales and Marketing Management* (Driben et al. 1992; Liesse 1991).

The heavy promotion and profitability of Healthy Choice has continued. In the spring of 1994, ConAgra began publishing a quarterly lifestyle magazine called *Healthy Choices*, designed "to find and bond with loyal buyers" of its food products, according to *Adweek* (Heitzman 1994). The corporation also disseminates the newsletter "Healthy Choice Hotline" to promote products to retailers (*Lowfat Monitor* 1995). ConAgra started leasing out its Healthy Choice brand name to other food giants, and in the summer of 1994, Kellogg's negotiated terms to introduce three cereals under the Healthy Choice moniker. By this time, *Advertising Age* was calling Healthy Choice a "$1 billion megabrand" with over 300 products under the label, drawing in over $1.3 billion in sales in 1994 (Heitzman 1994; Liesse 1994; Wollenberg 1995). The next year, ConAgra made its second brand-name leasing deal, this time with Nabisco, allowing the U.S. cookie market leader to introduce new snacks under the Healthy Choice label (Wollenberg 1995). *Frozen Food Age* reported in July 1995 that Healthy Choice entree sales had grown 33 percent over the previous year, and in the fall of 1996, the corporation prepared for another major product relaunch and promotional boost (Thayer 1995, 1996).

ConAgra's decision to parrot the much publicized public health nutrition goals—no more than 30 percent of daily calories from fat and 10 percent from saturated fat—clearly paid off for the corporation, just as *Prepared Foods* writer and editor Best had observed. ConAgra consistently emphasized the image of its products with concern for the public's health. A new line of Healthy Choice entrees was introduced just weeks after a major report, reiterating the recommendation that all Americans reduce dietary fat and cholesterol, was issued in February 1990 from the National Cholesterol Education Program and endorsed by Project LEAN (Papazian 1990). The brand name and Harper's television testimonial explicitly associated the products with "health" and reaffirmed notions that health is a personal choice, a lifestyle choice, and that health concerns should be addressed through commodity solutions compatible with the marketplace.

Low-fat processed food sales for the industry as a whole had reached $29 billion in 1990 and rose to $32 billion in 1991. In the following year, 519 new products claiming low fat or low cholesterol were introduced, a 39 percent increase over 1991. By the mid-1990s, the market in light food products had expanded to $35.8 billion and accounted for more than half

of the so-called health foods sector, according to the market research firm
Datamonitor (Calorie Control Council 1997).

The Food Marketing Institute's annual surveys of household shop-
pers documented an upward trend in consumer concerns with dietary fat
throughout the 1980s. It was during the period of Project LEAN's and
Healthy Choice's intensive campaigns, however, that the trend shot up
most precipitously. In 1983, 9 percent of consumers reported concern
about dietary fat, and in 1988, the number rose to 27 percent. But by 1990
and 1991, fully 42 percent of those surveyed reported dietary fat as a major
concern (Food Marketing Institute 1983, 1988, 1990, 1991). A series of surveys conducted for the Calorie Control Council, a food industry group,
found that in 1986, 45 percent of adults consumed low-calorie, reduced-
fat, and other light food products. By 1993 the percentage had almost doubled, rising to 81 percent. And within three more years, consumption of
these products by adults was virtually universal, rising to 92 percent—a
figure representing 179 million Americans (Calorie Control Council 1996;
Mancini 1993).

"[A]t the heart of the lo-cal economy," writes historian Hillel Schwartz,
"was long-term shift in fundamental eating patterns, habits of exercise,
and manners of speech. To become a national way of life, weight control
had to be built into the culture as if it had always been there. Diet food had
to seem to be basic foods" (1986:255). In the decade since Schwartz's
observation, the light foods economy has continued its expansion, extending its domain, by means of campaigns such as those of Project LEAN and
Healthy Choice, from low-calorie to low-fat markets with a corresponding
shift in dietary patterns. The transformation of specialized dietetic products into staples signifies a tremendous commodity marketing achievement accomplished within the time line of Harvey's period of flexible
accumulation and made possible by nutritional health promotion.

CONCLUSION

Some critics of health promotion and social marketing, while raising
questions about the entanglement of public health with the marketplace,
have concluded that the relationship ultimately furthers the aims of public
health practitioners (Levin 1987; Lupton 1995). Others have argued
that health promotion messages have either been diluted and rendered
ineffectual by bonds with consumer culture or appropriated by commercial interests (Bunton and Burrows 1995; Featherstone 1982). As I have
attempted to demonstrate, however, public health is far more than an ineffectual or co-opted pawn of consumer culture. Nutritional health promotion plays an integral role in the production and dissemination of the req-

uisite knowledge and ultimately the social conditions in which the diet food producer and consumer can coexist. From this perspective, nutritional health promotion—dominated by a particular combination of practice and theory that is uniquely linked with our consumer economy—is essential to the commodity relations of food and diet in contemporary American society.

In open partnership with the food industry, nutritional health promotion has privileged a conception of health that is compatible with the exigencies of the marketplace and educated a modern cadre of consumers about how to seek commodity solutions to real and anticipated health problems, not unlike industry's explicit consumer education in the formative decades of consumer capitalism as documented by Ewen (1976) and others. The stalking of dietary fat in public health promotion has been pursued with a zeal well beyond that justified by the field's own scientific research. The near unanimous endorsement of the fat reduction guidelines among public health opinion leaders is unprecedented in the contentious history of nutrition research (Levenstein 1993). This unprecedented consolidation of "expert" opinion has been buttressed, I maintain, by the logic of the marketplace when a logic of scientific evidence alone would not have proven sufficient.

The uncritical promotion of a dietary fat reduction message and comparative neglect of fruits and vegetables should serve as an object lesson regarding the consequences of the presumption of commodity logic over alternative ways of conceiving of illness and health. But my objective here has not been to posit a theoretical critique of simply the fact of the accumulation of profits by the diet industry. Rather, my goal has been to examine the economic context of health promotion, to make plain the ways that public health has served an essential and *productive* role within the system of accumulation—productive in the sense of the generation of commodity knowledge and consumer markets—and what this has meant in terms of the everyday details of matters of health, illness, and the practice of public health. By documenting the historical development and enormous economic leverage of the diet food industry in a period of massive market proliferation and flexible accumulation and the links in theory and practice between industry and public health, I hope to make obvious the importance of striving to be cognizant of how particular "solutions" become standard and at what expense.

ACKNOWLEDGMENTS

The author is grateful to Kirstin Austin, Daphne Berdahl, and Arthur Kleinman for their insights on earlier drafts of this manuscript.

NOTES

1.   Warren Belasco has aptly dubbed the expansion of the diet industry into the creation of product lines based on the absence of nutrients deemed undesirable as "negative nutrition" (Belasco 1989).

2.   An official statement from Louis Sullivan, secretary of the U.S. Department of Health and Human Services under President Bush, lauds the kickoff of Healthy People 2000, the preeminent federal health promotion crusade, from a decidedly lifestyle model perspective. Published in 1990 in the *American Journal of Health Promotion*, the two-page editorial repeatedly uses catch phrases such as "freedom of choice" and "personal responsibility" to describe the mission of Healthy People 2000. "We need a nationwide priority placed on personal responsibility and choices," Sullivan intones, "[to] enhance our individual independence. . . . We need a clear, serious, and *constant* acceptance of personal responsibility" (Sullivan 1990:6; emphasis his).

3.   *Lowfat Monitor* ended publication in October 1996 for financial reasons.

4.   Rick LeBlanc, marketing specialist, Massachusetts Department of Food and Agriculture, personal communication, 1998.

REFERENCES

American Dietetic Association. 1995. *Project LEAN Resource Kit: Tips, Tools, and Techniques for Promoting Low-Fat Lifestyles*. Chicago: American Dietetic Association.

Anonymous. 1980. "The Lifestyle Approach to Prevention" (editorial). *Journal of Public Health Policy* 1(1):6–9.

Appadurai, A. 1986. "Introduction: Commodities and the Politics of Value." Pp. 3–63 in *The Social Life of Things: Commodities in Cultural Perspective*, edited by A. Appadurai. Cambridge: Cambridge University Press.

———. 1993. "Consumption, Duration, and History." *Stanford Literature Review* 10(1–2):11–33.

Armstrong, B., and R. Doll. 1975. "Environmental Factors and Cancer Incidence and Mortality in Different Countries, with Special Reference to Dietary Practices." *International Journal of Cancer* 15:617–31.

Ascherio, A., C. Hennekens, W. C. Willett, F. Sacks, B. Rosner, J. Manson, J. Witteman, and M. J. Stampfer. 1996. "Prospective Study of Nutritional Factors, Blood Pressure, and Hypertension Among US Women." *Hypertension* 27(5):1065–72.

Ascherio, A., and W. C. Willett. 1995. "New Directions in Dietary Studies of Coronary Heart Disease." *Journal of Nutrition* 125(3 suppl.):647S–55S.

Ascherio, A., E. B. Rimm, E. L. Giovannucci, D. Spiegelman, M. J. Stampfer, and W. C. Willett. 1996. "Dietary Fat and Risk of Coronary Heart Disease in Men: Cohort Follow Up Study in the United States." *British Medical Journal* 313(7049):84–90.

Belasco, W. 1984. "'Lite' Economics: Less Food, More Profit." *Radical History Review* 28–30:254–78.

———. 1989. *Appetite for Change*. New York: Pantheon.

Bell, D. 1978. *The Cultural Contradictions of Capitalism*. New York: Basic Books.

Best, D. 1989a. "Processors Pursue the Perfect Nutritional Profile." *Prepared Foods* March:79–84.

———. 1989b. "Unsaturated Fats: Know Your Source Well." *Prepared Foods* March:87–89.

———. 1990. "Health Perceptions Preoccupy Product Developers." *New Product News* Oct. 7:8.

Block, G., B. Patterson, and A. Subar. 1992. "Fruits, Vegetables, and Cancer Prevention: A Review of the Epidemiological Evidence." *Nutrition and Cancer* 18:1–29.

Brumberg, J. J. 1988. *Fasting Girls: The Emergence of Anorexia Nervosa as a Modern Disease*. Cambridge, MA: Harvard University Press.

Buchanan, D. R., S. Reddy, and Z. Hossain. 1994. "Social Marketing: A Critical Appraisal." *Health Promotion International* 9(1):49–57.

Bunton, R., and R. Burrows. 1995. "Consumption and Health in the 'Epidemiological' Clinic of Late Modern Medicine." Pp. 202–6 in *The Sociology of Health Promotion: Critical Analyses of Consumption, Lifestyle and Risk*, edited by R. Bunton, S. Nettleton, and R. Burrows. London: Routledge.

Calorie Control Council. 1996. "Light Foods and Beverages Soar to New Levels of Popularity." *Calorie Control Commentary* 18(1):1, 3.

———. 1997. "Low-Calorie/Low-Fat Bulletin." *Calorie Control Commentary* 19(1):3.

Campbell, T. C., and T. O'Connor. 1988. "Scientific Evidence and Explicit Health Claims in Food Advertisements." *Journal of Nutrition Education* 20(2):87–92.

Centers for Disease Control. 1994. "Daily Dietary Fat and Total Food-Energy Intakes—Third National Health and Nutrition Examination Survey, Phase 1, 1988–91." *Morbidity and Mortality Weekly Report* 43(7):116–17,123–25.

Contento, I., G. I. Balch, Y. L. Bronner, D. M. Paige, S. M. Gross, L. Bisignani, L. A. Lytle, S. K. Maloney, S. L. White, C. M. Olson, and S. S. Swadener. 1995. "Nutrition Education for Adults." *Journal of Nutrition Education* 27(6):312–28.

Coreil, J., J. S. Levin, and E. G. Jaco. 1985. "Life Style—An Emergent Concept in the Sociomedical Sciences." *Culture, Medicine and Psychiatry* 9:423–37.

Crawford, P. 1988. "The Nutrition Connection: Why Doesn't the Public Know?" (editorial). *American Journal of Public Health* 78(9):1147–48.

Dagnoli, J., and J. Liesse. 1991. "'Healthy' Frozen Foods Launch Offensive: ConAgra, KGF Face Off in Pizza; Le Menu Offers Taste Guarantee." *Advertising Age* 62(36):1, 45.

Driben, L. I., B. Kelley, R. Szathmary, B. Wisendanger, and K. Rottenberger. 1992. "Sales & Marketing Management's 1992 Marketing Achievement Awards." *Sales and Marketing Management* 144(9):40–47.

Ellis-Simons, P. 1990. "The Marketing Successes of 1989—Prepared Foods: One from the Heart." *Marketing and Media Decisions* 25(3):32–36.

Ewen, S. 1976. *Captains of Consciousness: Advertising and the Social Roots of the Consumer Culture*. New York: McGraw-Hill.

Featherstone, M. 1982. "The Body in Consumer Culture." *Theory, Culture and Society* 1(2):18–33.

Food Marketing Institute. 1983. *Trends: Consumer Attitudes and the Supermarket.* Washington, DC: Food Marketing Institute.

———. 1988. *Trends: Consumer Attitudes and the Supermarket.* Washington, DC: Food Marketing Institute.

———. 1990. *Trends: Consumer Attitudes and the Supermarket.* Washington, DC: Food Marketing Institute.

———. 1991. *Trends: Consumer Attitudes and the Supermarket.* Washington, DC: Food Marketing Institute.

Giovannucci, E., E. B. Rimm, M. J. Stampfer, G. A. Colditz, A. Ascherio, and W. C. Willett. 1994. "Intake of Fat, Meat, and Fiber in Relation to Risk of Colon Cancer in Men." *Cancer Research* 54:2390–97.

Giovannucci, E., and W. C. Willett. 1994. "Dietary Factors and Risk of Colon Cancer." *Annals of Medicine* 26:443–52.

Glanz, K., A. M. Hewitt, and J. Rudd. 1992. "Consumer Behavior and Nutrition Education: An Integrative Review." *Journal of Nutrition Education* 24:267–77.

Gordon, T., A. Kagan, M. Garcia-Palmieri, W. B. Kannel, W. J. Zukel, J. Tillotson, P. Sorlie, and M. Hjortland. 1981. "Diet and Its Relation to Coronary Heart Disease and Death in Three Populations." *Circulation* 63(3):500–15.

Grace, V. M. 1991. "The Marketing of Empowerment and the Construction of the Health Consumer: A Critique of Health Promotion." *International Journal of Health Services* 21(2):329–43.

Graham, S., J. Marshall, C. Mettlin, T. Rzepka, T. Nemoto, and T. Byers. 1982. "Diet in the Epidemiology of Breast Cancer." *American Journal of Epidemiology* 116:68–75.

Harvey, D. 1995. *The Condition of Postmodernity: An Enquiry into the Origins of Cultural Change.* Cambridge, MA: Blackwell.

Heini, A. F., and R. L. Weinsier. 1997. "Divergent Trends in Obesity and Fat Intake Patterns: The American Paradox." *American Journal of Medicine* 102:259–64.

Heitzman, B. 1994. "Food for Thought." *Adweek* 35(11):3.

Hu, F. B., M. J. Stampfer, J. E. Manson, E. Rimm, G. A. Colditz, B. A. Rosner, C. H. Hennekens, and W. C. Willett. 1997. "Dietary Fat Intake and the Risk of Coronary Heart Disease in Women." *New England Journal of Medicine* 337(21): 1491–99.

Kennedy, E., L. Meyers, and W. Layden. 1996. "The 1995 Dietary Guidelines for Americans: An Overview." *Journal of the American Dietetic Association* 96(3): 234–37.

Kleinfield, N. R. 1986. "The Ever-Fatter Business of Thinness." *New York Times,* 7 September, Section 3, p. 1.

Kromhout, D., and C. de Lezenne Coulander. 1984. "Diet, Prevalence and 10-Year Mortality from Coronary Heart Disease in 871 Middle-Aged Men: The Zutphen Study." *American Journal of Epidemiology* 119(5):733–41.

Kushi, L. H., R. A. Lew, F. J. Stare, C. R. Ellison, M. el Lozy, G. Bourke, L. Daly, I. Graham, N. Hickey, R. Mulcahy, and J. Kevaney. 1985. "Diet and 20-Year Mortality from Coronary Heart Disease: The Ireland-Boston Diet-Heart Study." *New England Journal of Medicine* 312(13):811–18.

Lalonde, M. 1974. *A New Perspective on the Health of Canadians: A Working Document.* Ottawa: Government of Canada.

Levenstein, H. 1993. *Paradox of Plenty: A Social History of Eating in Modern America.* New York: Oxford University Press.

Levin, L. S. 1987. "Every Silver Lining Has a Cloud: The Limits of Health Promotion." *Social Policy* 18(1):57–60.

Liesse, J. 1990. "ConAgra Expands Healthy Choice." *Advertising Age* 61(48): 3, 21.

———. 1991. "Harper: ConAgra's Healthy Choice." *Advertising Age* 62(1):1, 16, 38.

———. 1992. "Health Choice Growing Pains." *Advertising Age* 63(34):3, 23.

———. 1994. "Kellogg Is ConAgra's New Healthy Choice." *Advertising Age* 65(11):3, 42.

Lissner, L., and B. L. Heitmann. 1995. "Dietary Fat and Obesity: Evidence from Epidemiology." *European Journal of Clinical Nutrition* 49:79–90.

Lowfat Monitor. 1995. "Highlights." 5(6):1.

Lupton, D. 1995. *The Imperative of Health: Public Health and the Regulated Body.* London: Sage.

Major, B. 1991. "Consumer Expenditures Study: Diet." *Supermarket Business* 46(9): 167, 121–22.

Mancini, L. 1993. "Low Fat Comes of Age." *Food Engineering* (June):149.

McGee, D. L., D. M. Reed, K. Yano, A. Kagan, and J. Tillotson. 1984. "Ten-Year Incidence of Coronary Heart Disease in the Honolulu Heart Program: Relationship to Nutrient Intake." *American Journal of Epidemiology* 119(5):667–76.

McKnight, J. L. 1986. "Well-being: The New Threshold to the Old Medicine." *Health Promotion* 1(1):77–80.

McNeil, M. 1988. "National Campaign Announced to Cut U.S. Fat Consumption." Reuters, 27 September.

National Academy of Sciences. 1980. *Toward Healthful Diets.* Washington, DC: National Academy of Sciences.

———. 1989. "National Academy of Sciences Report on Diet and Health." *Nutrition Reviews* 47(5):142–49.

Novelli, W. D. 1990. "Applying Social Marketing to Health Promotion and Disease Prevention." Pp. 342–69 in *Health Behavior and Health Education: Theory, Research, and Practice,* edited by K. Glanz, F. M. Lewis, and B. K. Rimer. San Francisco: Jossey-Bass.

Office of Cancer Communications. 1993. *Five a Day for Better Health: NCI Media Campaign Strategy.* Bethesda, MD: National Cancer Institute.

Ostroff, J. 1989. "Project LEAN to Educate Consumers on Fat; Low-Fat Diet Education Program Sponsored by the Henry J. Kaiser Family Foundation." *Supermarket News* 23 October.

Papazian, R. 1990. "Diet Foods: Counting Fat Instead of Calories." *Supermarket Business* 45(10):49–52.

Patterson, B. H., G. Block, W. F. Rosenberger, D. Pee, and L. L. Kahle. 1990. "Fruit and Vegetables in the American Diet: Data from the NHANES II Survey." *American Journal of Public Health* 80:1443–49.

Peterkin, B. B., and R. L. Rizek. 1986. "Diets of American Women: Looking Back Nearly a Decade." *National Food Review* Summer:12–15 (NFR-34).

Pietinen, P., A. Ascherio, P. Korhonen, A. M. Hartman, W. C. Willett, D. Albanes, and J. Virtamo. 1997. "Intake of Fatty Acids and Risk of Coronary Heart Disease in a Cohort of Finnish Men: The Alpha-Tocopherol, Beta-Carotene Cancer Prevention Study." *American Journal of Epidemiology* 145:876–87.

Popkin, B. M., A. M. Siega-Riz, and P. S. Haines. 1996. "A Comparison of Dietary Trends among Racial and Socioeconomic Groups in the United States." *New England Journal of Medicine* 335:716–20.

PR Newswire. 1990. "Project LEAN Releases Statement on National Cholesterol Education Program Report." February 28.

Prentice, R. L., F. Kakar, S. Hursting, L. Sheppard, R. Klein, and L. H. Kushi. 1988. "Aspects of the Rationale for the Women's Health Trial." *Journal of the National Cancer Institute* 80:802–14.

Samuels, S. E. 1993. "Project LEAN—Lessons Learned from a National Social Marketing Campaign." *Public Health Reports* 108(1):45–53.

Schwartz, H. 1986. *Never Satisfied: A Cultural History of Diets, Fantasies and Fat*. New York: Free Press.

Scott, D. W., G. A. Gorry, and A. M. Gotto. 1981. "Diet and Coronary Heart Disease: The Statistical Analysis of Risk" (editorial). *Circulation* 63(3):516–18.

Shekelle, R. B., A. M. Shryock, O. Paul, M. Lepper, J. Stamler, S. Liu, and W. J. Raynor. 1981. "Diet, Serum Cholesterol, and Death from Coronary Heart Disease: The Western Electric Study." *New England Journal of Medicine* 304(2):65–70.

Solomon, D. S. 1989. "A Social Marketing Perspective on Communication Campaigns." Pp. 87–104 in *Public Communication Campaigns*, 2nd edition, edited by R. E. Rice and C. K. Atkin. Newbury Park, CA: Sage.

Steinmetz, K. A., and J. D. Potter. 1991. "Vegetables, Fruits and Cancer: I. Epidemiology." *Cancer Causes and Control* 2:325–57.

Stephen, A. M., and N. J. Wald. 1990. "Trends in Individual Consumption of Dietary Fat in the United States, 1920–1984." *American Journal of Clinical Nutrition* 52:457–69.

Sugarman, C. 1988. "The Lean, Clean Machine: A New Program Targeted to Help Americans Reduce Fat Consumption." *Washington Post*, 5 October, p. E3.

Sullivan, L. W. 1990. "Healthy People 2000: Promoting Health and Building a Culture of Character." *American Journal of Health Promotion* 5(1):5–6.

Taylor, M. 1990. "State Starts Campaign against Fatty Food." *San Francisco Chronicle*, 6 September, p. A8.

Thayer, W. 1995. "Share Points Change Hands in Dinner/Entree Shakeout." *Frozen Food Age* 43(12):1, 16.

———. 1996. "ConAgra Ups Support 30–40% for Relaunch of Healthy Choice." *Frozen Food Age* 45(3):8, 39.

Tougas, J. G. 1992. "Project LEAN Seeks to Educate Consumers." *Restaurant Hospitality* 76(2):72.

U.S. Department of Health and Human Services and U.S. Department of Agriculture. 1989. *Nutrition Monitoring in the United States: An Update Report on Nutrition Monitoring*. Hyattsville, MD: USDHHS (DHHS Publication No. PHS 89-1255).

Wellman, D. 1992. "Low-Cal Vs. Healthy." *Food and Beverage Marketing* 11(2):18.

Willett, W. C. 1996. "Diet and Nutrition." Pp. 438–61 in *Cancer Epidemiology and Prevention*, 2nd edition, edited by D. Schottenfeld and J. F. Fraumei. New York: Oxford University Press.

——— . 1998. "Is Dietary Fat a Major Determinant of Body Fat?" *American Journal of Clinical Nutrition* 67(suppl.):556S–62S.

Willett, W. C., D. J. Hunter, M. J. Stampfer, G. Colditz, J. E. Manson, D. Spiegelman, B. Rosner, C. H. Hennekens, and F. E. Speizer. 1992. "Dietary Fat and Fiber in Relation to Risk of Breast Cancer. An 8-Year Follow-up." *Journal of the American Medical Association* 268(15):2037–44.

Willett, W. C., M. J. Stampfer, G. A. Colditz, B. A. Rosner, and F. E. Speizer. 1990. "Relation of Meat, Fat, and Fiber Intake to the Risk of Colon Cancer in a Prospective Study among Women." *New England Journal of Medicine* 323: 1664–72.

Wollenberg, S. 1995. "What Has Less Fat But Expands? Nabisco Licenses Healthy Choice." Associated Press, 13 September.

Ziegler, R. G. 1991. "Vegetables, Fruits, and Carotenoids and the Risk of Cancer." *American Journal of Clinical Nutrition* 53(suppl.):251S–59S.

10

Meanings of Weight among Dietitians and Nutritionists

ELLEN S. PARHAM

INTRODUCTION

For almost a hundred years, dietitians and nutritionists have advised Americans about how to manage their weights. In a culture where being the ideal weight is interpreted as visible evidence of personal worth, dietitians and nutritionists have been sought out to assist in weight loss for esthetic as well as health reasons. Unfortunately, permanent weight loss is extremely difficult to achieve. In spite of recommendations by these professionals for changes in eating behavior that according to the laws of thermodynamics could be expected to lead to long-term weight losses, the prevalence of obesity continues to increase. This paradoxical situation creates a dilemma about how to deal with obesity when the best approaches have not performed as expected. This dilemma affects all those who work with weight management, whether from a medical, commercial, educational, or other perspective. Dietitians and nutritionists are, however, unique in the extent to which being experts in weight management is a part of their professional identity.

This chapter will explore how the weight paradox came to be and how dietitians and related health professionals have dealt with the resulting dilemma, as well as the attitudes these professionals have toward obesity and the attitudes that members of the public have toward dietitians and their work with weight management. Although there are issues related to weight all along the continuum from emaciation to superobesity, the focus of this chapter will be on the aspect of greatest concern to both lay persons and professionals: excessive fatness.

WHO ARE DIETITIANS AND NUTRITIONISTS?

According to most dictionary definitions, *dietitian* and *nutritionist* are synonymous, that is, professionals who advise individuals and groups on matters of food and nutrition. While this definition is accurate for nutritionists, who may be anyone who styles him- or herself as a nutrition expert, *dietitian* is more formally defined by the process of dietetic registration and, in some states, licensure. Registration requires completion of a didactic baccalaureate program in dietetics plus a supervised practice experience, followed by passing the registration examination in dietetics (American Dietetic Association 1997). When the term *dietitian* is used in this chapter, the reference will be specifically to registered dietitians.

Although registration does not require membership in the American Dietetic Association, it is by far the largest professional society in dietetics. In 1997, there were 69,100 members, including not only registered dietitians, but also students and dietary technicians (*ADA Courier* 1998). According to a 1995 survey of the registered dietitians in the association, 98 percent were female and 91 percent were white, not Hispanic (Bryk and Soto 1997). Most dietitians have a strong health-care orientation, with over 70 percent working in a health-care setting (ibid.). Although the majority of these clinical dietitians worked in hospitals, the proportion working in health care facilities other than hospitals has increased since 1990, whereas the percentage employed by hospitals has declined over that period. Forecasts for the year 2005 indicate that the trend of movement out of hospitals will continue and that the rate of employment will rise rapidly in sectors not directly health-care related (Kornblum 1994). These employment changes are relevant to the focus of this chapter because they will increase the visibility and accessibility of dietitians, as well as demand more diversity of services.

In addition to dietitians and dietetic technicians, there are thousands of other individuals who, having completed undergraduate and/or advanced degrees in nutrition, pursue nutrition-related careers and can be referred to generally as nutritionists. In this chapter, the term *nutritionist* will refer to these professionals and not to the self-styled nutritionist, who may have no formal study of nutrition. Even with this more limited definition, nutritionists are a heterogeneous group that includes both researchers and practitioners. There is no single professional organization that represents nutritionists in the way the American Dietetic Association does dietitians. The American Society for Clinical Nutrition attracts nutrition scholars whose research has a clinical focus. Both nutrition researchers and practitioners seeking a broader perspective may belong to the Society for Nutrition Education. For the most part, dietitians and nutritionists[1] make their living by telling other people how to eat, and how to choose or modify their diet.

Although the talents of dietitians are directed toward using food to influence a wide variety of health conditions, the most universal concern is weight management. This chapter focuses on dietitians because they are the more easily defined group and because they work directly with patients and clients on weight issues. Certainly dietitians are not the only group of professionals involved with weight management. Much of the research and commentary about weight in the professional literature has come from physicians, psychologists, exercise physiologists, educators, and others. The perspectives of these other professionals have influenced dietitians and have been influenced by dietitians.

Several histories of diet, weight, and obesity published in recent decades (Beller 1977; Levenstein 1988; Schwartz 1986; Stearns 1997; Wyden 1965) have discussed the role of physicians in developing the meanings of weight in the United States, but have not addressed the impact of dietitians and nutritionists. Stearns (1997) does mention dietitians and home economists but does not directly explore their influence. Likewise, Levenstein (1988) comments upon the dietary advice of dietitians and nutritionists, but does not consider their impact on the meanings of weight. Possibly these omissions reflect an understanding of these professionals as mere extensions of physicians. Mayer, writing about overweight thirty years ago, certainly projected this view in saying, "The physician and his auxiliary, the dietitian, in addition to their medical and nutritional knowledge, are well-informed about the psychology of becoming obese, being obese, and doing something to correct the obesity" (1968:164). Apparently if we want to examine how the meanings of weight dietitians and nutritionists have developed, we shall have to consider the history of dietetics directly.

HISTORICAL FOUNDATIONS LED TO
DUAL PERSPECTIVES

Dietetics is a relatively young profession, being about a hundred years old. It began at a time when the knowledge of nutrition was largely limited to the role of the energy nutrients and when the American public was turning to a rejection of fatness (Stearns 1997). This new public preference for thinness created a demand in medical care for attention to weight loss, as well as to treatment of illness through diet. Sarah Tyson Rorer, usually cited as the first American dietitian, started teaching, writing, and lecturing in the 1870s. Mrs. Rorer was a practical woman who believed that exercise, proper food, and fresh air were the keys to good health, as well as to "perfect beauty" (Weigley 1980). Rorer and others of her time practiced a dualism that has continued through the present day: a major concern with adequacy of food intake even while advocating dietary restriction as treatment for disease. In contrast to Rorer's emphasis on carefully chosen and well-cooked foods as health promotion factors, the approach of the diet therapy of her day was largely one of deprivation.

It is not surprising that the early practice of dietetics emphasized greatly restricted diets. When body systems were compromised, there were few options other than avoidance of problematic foods. Until insulin became available, diabetes usually was treated by periods of fasting. The more severe the diabetes, the longer and more frequent the fasts. Even as late as the 1920s, Blum (1924) advocated withdrawing for one to four days all food except coffee and whiskey or cognac, spirits that he reported were usually unnecessary. Between fasts diabetics were maintained on diets extremely limited in carbohydrates and generally low in calories. Blum noted that under this treatment obese diabetics would experience a beneficial weight loss of five to ten pounds.

According to Ohlson (1976), the association of food intake and weight change was widely understood before the last turn of the century and advice on weight loss was freely given. In Britain, Banting wrote in 1869 describing how his own food habits, which featured large quantities of bread and butter, had led to gross overweight. Repenting that generous diet, Banting put himself on a restricted regime that severely limited bread, butter, and milk and that led to a sustained weight loss (ibid.). Similarly in the mid-1880s, Bennet advocated eating less and exercising more as means to avoid corpulence (ibid.). Noting that implementing his advice required sacrifice and self-control, he predicted that few would follow it. Thus Bennet made dietary recommendations that would endure for more than a hundred years and generalized about how these recommendations would be received.

Although the earliest dietitians were trained only through brief courses of study in cooking schools such as that headed by Rorer, soon professional preparation was extended and standardized. Education for dietitians emphasized practical experience from the beginning. Courses of study were expanded in the 1920s, and in 1927 preparation included a baccalaureate degree followed by a supervised internship (Commission on Accreditation/Approval for Dietetics Education 1987). In the early 1970s the curriculum offered eligibility to sit for the registration examination in dietetics (Study Commission on Dietetics 1985).

To observe the meanings of weight conveyed to young dietitians during their professional education over the past century, I examined a series of dietetics textbooks. Textbooks, interpreted by instructors and studied by students, constitute an important part of the socialization of dietetics students to their profession. Examining the books' messages about weight reveals how weight was viewed in the profession throughout the century. Thirteen textbooks reviewed here included at least one for each decade of this century plus additional books from the current decade (Hutchison 1903; Pattee 1917; Blum 1924; Sansum, Hare, and Bowden 1936; Sherman and Lanford [1943] 1950; Proudfit and Robinson 1955; Pattison, Barbour, and Eppright 1957; Guthrie 1971; Whitney and Hamilton 1981; Mahan and Arlin 1992; Nieman, Butterworth, and Nieman 1992; Katch and McArdle 1993; Nelson 1994). The books were all published in the United States and designated by their authors as designed for use in educating dietitians, nutritionists, and related health professionals. Content analysis involved scanning the sections identified by the indexes as related to weight and examining what these sections said about the importance of overweight and underweight, their relationship to health, their etiology, recommended interventions, and statements about the success of the interventions.

The earliest text reviewed, Hutchison (1903:52), included more concern for underfeeding than overfeeding, stating that "a moderate excess of food is probably harmless." Other than concern about mobility, little or no connection was made between excessive weight and illness. The reader was advised to judge the appropriateness of weight by the general appearance of the patient. Several highly structured reducing diets were presented without any discussion of the likelihood of their long-term success. The text mentioned that some persons, especially the very young and the very old, seem predisposed to fatness and for those people attempts at weight loss might be ill advised.

Pattee (1917) wrote a dietetics text that reflected the dual attention to dietary adequacy and therapeutic restriction found in earlier messages. Most of the book's five hundred pages were devoted to general nutrition, with the eighty pages on diet in disease including dietary treatment of obesity and diabetes. Treatment of obesity was referred to as one of the most important features of dietetic therapy. The author noted that obesity implied "advanced years" and was therefore considered unattractive. She ascribed no adverse health effects to obesity and stated that the recognition of the importance of obesity had to do with its relationship to athletic performance. Increased exercise as well as restricting the fat and carbohydrate sources in the diet were emphasized as treatment for obesity.

Rigidly restricted diets were not limited to diabetes and obesity. Dietary interventions described by physicians early in this century were extremely didactic in the kind and amount of foods allowed (Ohlson 1976). Ohlson credits early dietitians with the skill and flexibility to translate these early diets into more tolerable plans. In spite of this commitment to flexibility, it may well have been this somewhat desperate attempt to help patients survive devastating disease that led to dietitians' reputation as "diet police" who punish through deprivation. Even today, dietitians chide each other for delivering negative messages that tell people what not to eat.

OVERWEIGHT IS TAKEN MORE SERIOUSLY

Nutrition textbooks published in the mid-1930s provided a changing view of weight. In contrast to Pattee's rather relaxed attitude, Sansum et al. quoted life insurance data as showing that "for each pound a person is overweight or underweight, excepting possibly only a very few pounds variation from the average, the expectancy of life is decreased by one per cent" (1936:136). Although this text recognized some minor influence of genetics upon body size, it attributed excessive weight gain to overindulgence in food, especially fats and alcohol. Readers were reminded that weight is not fixed, but rather a plastic characteristic that can be regulated. This theme of the malleability of weight has been sustained up to the present, where it is currently an issue of considerable debate among dietitians.

Ayers (1958) characterized the weight management approach of the health professional of the 1930s as "ardent missionary work." Working from a perception that obesity was always the direct result of overeating, the routine therapeutic approach was to force the patient to recall his food intake "in guilt-making detail." Armed with this evidence, the dietitian attempted to impress the patient with the "enormity of his intake." It was assumed that once convinced that his intake was, indeed, grossly excessive, the patient would proceed to correct the situation.

On the other hand, Sherman and Lanford ([1943] 1950) reflected concerns about underfeeding. In contrast to contemporary books that tend to mention underweight only in connection with eating disorders, this mid-century book devoted equal attention to over- and underweight. It recognized that some people have more of a tendency toward obesity than others and questioned the extent that body weight is a health problem as opposed to a matter of style. Observing that college women tended to keep themselves thinner than is best for health, happiness, efficiency, and longevity, the authors suggested that these women would feel better if they gained weight.

Consistent with the medicalization of obesity (Sobal 1995), the Proudfit and Robinson textbook took a stronger stand on the health implications of obesity, stating, "The greatest problem of preventive medicine today is obesity" (1955:347), and "Many cases of diabetes are, no doubt, preventable if individuals will avoid overeating and its consequent adverse effects" (ibid.:425). Although the authors mentioned that weight reduction is difficult to achieve and maintain, they were quite definite in stating that "obesity can be overcome by strict adherence to a low calorie diet" (ibid.:356–57). The health professional was charged with the responsibility of giving patients the motivation to lose weight, but they noted that the patient must have the capacity for self-discipline, patience, and perseverance.

Although the textbooks of the 1950s were still optimistically advocating low-calorie diets, there was increasing evidence that instruction in calorie restriction was not producing the desired results. For example, a paper by McCann and Trulson (1955) reported that three years after individual nutrition counseling or group therapy, there was no evidence that either treatment was effective for sustained weight reduction. Although these authors recommended that obesity prevention be given priority, they did note that with more information and motivation their patients might have fared better. Young, Moore, Berresford, Einset, and Waldner (1955) reported modest weight loss success, but later Young confided to Wyden (1965) that it seemed that all the losses had been regained.

It was in the climate of such reports that Stunkard and McLaren-Hume (1959) reviewed the success of various programs and concluded that most overweight persons would not stay in treatment, and of those who did, most would not lose weight, and if they were lucky enough to lose weight, they would regain it. Following this stark observation about the failure of weight loss treatments, a succession of new therapies was introduced in the second half of the century, including starvation (Gries, Berger, and Berchtold 1978), very low calorie diets (Kirschner, Schneider, Ertel, and Gorman 1987), surgery (Kral 1985), medications (Bray 1979), behavior modification (Brownell and Wadden 1986; Stunkard 1978), and aerobic exercise (Stern, Titchenal, and Johnson 1987).

Most interventions at first appeared to offer significant advantages. Long-term evaluations, however, revealed that none were able to reverse the dismal outcome statistics (Holmes, Zysow, and Delbanco 1989). Some innovations were soon abandoned. On the other hand, behavior modification passed through several evolutionary generations and became a component of many combined programs (Wadden and Stunkard 1986). Most of these new approaches involved continuation of dietary restriction of some sort. In 1983 a panel organized through the International Congress of Obesity prepared therapeutic guidelines recommended for professional weight control programs that identified diet modification as the major therapeutic modality for weight control (Weinsier, Wadden, Ritenbaugh, Harrison, Johnson, and Wilmore 1984). Even though new and varied approaches to weight loss were being introduced, dietitians were primarily involved in helping patients implement the diets that accompanied the other therapies.

A popular textbook of the 1970s (Guthrie 1971) acknowledged the complexity of obesity and noted that the prognosis for weight management was more successful in some groups than others. A persuasive review of the health, social, economic, and psychological disadvantages of obesity implied that even though the process of weight loss might be difficult, it was imperative.

Whitney and Hamilton (1981) is a good example of a somewhat revised orientation in the weight management content of textbooks. It included a lengthy discussion of factors contributing to obesity. Although the authors stated that only a third of those losing weight were able to maintain their losses, they still presented an expectation of universal (though individualized) intervention. In striking contrast to Sherman and Lanford's ([1943] 1950) urging of young women to relax about their weight, these authors state, "Inside of every fat person a thin person is struggling to be freed. Get in touch with—reach out your hand to—your thin self, and help that self to feel welcome in the light of day" (Whitney and Hamilton 1981:299).

Nutrition and dietetics textbooks of the 1990s no longer reflect wholehearted confidence in the power of the diet, recognizing the complexity of factors contributing to fatness levels. Restricted diets are still recommended, but there is increased recognition of the limited effectiveness of dieting or other weight loss interventions to lead to weight losses that can be sustained for periods beyond a few months. Parham, Flynn, Frigo, and Perkins (1991) revealed some of this discouragement when they compared the opinions of dietitians, fitness instructors, and dieters about weight control and its outcomes. All three groups concurred in a strong feeling that weight control is difficult and requires a chronic effort. Dietitians, however, were significantly less optimistic than the other two groups about permanent solutions to weight problems. Although dietitians rated behavior modification, self-understanding, diet, exercise, and willpower as very important components of weight control, their ratings did not show the extreme confidence expressed by the fitness instructors.

COPING WITH THE WEIGHT DILEMMA

Recognition of the health consequences of obesity and the ineffectiveness of weight loss treatments creates a weight dilemma. Obesity is associated with health impairments, and dietitians and other health professionals are committed to health promotion and disease prevention. However, the interventions that can be employed do not work well enough. Faced with disappointing outcomes of dieting and other weight loss interventions, dietitians have resorted to various ways of conceptualizing the weight dilemma so as to reduce the dissonance: victim blaming, denial, reframing goals, paradigm change, and prevention. Although all the strategies appear to be currently in use, there has been movement away from the more negative ones in recent years.

Victim Blaming. A long-standing strategy for dealing with the weight dilemma has been to blame the patient. Writers as early as 1880 observed that few people have the self-control to follow a restricted diet for long. Stunkard and McLaren-Hume observed that professionals faced with the failure of their treatments resorted to "moralizing, indifference, and despair" (1959:84). The extreme of this reaction is disgust, but a more common response is to describe the patient as "not ready" to make the commitment and sacrifices required to stick to a strict diet and exercise regimen.

A variation on the strategy of blaming the patient is to declare that success is possible if the patient stays in treatment long enough, works hard enough, and incorporates enough lifestyle changes. The National Institutes of Health (NIH 1998) report on clinical guidelines for work with obesity recommends that a weight maintenance program should continue indefinitely. Kirschenbaum and Fitzgibbon (1995) advocate an intensive two-year program with the goal of helping participants achieve obsessive-compulsive self-regulation. The program stresses acceptance of a lifestyle involving "supernormal" eating and exercise behaviors. Although Kirschenbaum may be unique in the extreme statement of his goals, he is not alone in his emphasis on the importance of inducing restraint, a common theme to many dietitians.

Denial. Another coping strategy has been to deny the existence of the weight dilemma. A very few individuals are successful at losing weight and sustaining the loss; these exceptions confuse the issue and maintain hopes for weight control. Brownell and Rodin (1994) observe that some modern approaches show somewhat more favorable outcomes than the programs on which Stunkard and McLaren-Hume (1959) based their gloomy summary. Further, Brownell and Rodin (1994) point out that most of the data on weight loss failure come from clinical trials in university settings. These programs tend to attract a high proportion of binge eaters and otherwise resistant patients who are atypical in their weight loss failures. If adequate data on the weight loss experiences of ordinary people were available, Brownell and Rodin suggest, dieting would be seen as more successful and weight management less of a problem. It is difficult to reconcile that interpretation with the increasing prevalence of obesity in this country (Kuczmarski, Flegal, Campbell, and Johnson 1994). Neither is it possible to explain the weight dilemma by assuming that the obese people neither care about their fatness nor try to do anything about it. Numerous reports of widespread dieting clearly indicate much weight loss concern and effort.

A related perspective is to view the limited success in long-term weight loss maintenance as a situation to be expected when the data on which to base interventions are inadequate. Some dietitians and other health professionals have dealt with the weight dilemma by noting that there is much that is not understood about obesity. They call for new interventions and urge expansion of research efforts. While more understanding of obesity would be helpful, dietitians still face the issue of what to do with their current patients. The response seems to be to continue doing what they have always done and hope that they are not making matters worse.

Another variation on denial of the weight dilemma is to blame the problem on a failure to match the patient with the right approach. Bushman (1996) surveyed clinical dietitians about beliefs regarding various weight loss interventions. Although 90 percent thought effective weight loss methods existed, there was very little agreement about which methods were effective. The greatest consensus (33 percent) was that an individualized approach was the most effective.

Several years ago there was a movement to develop a system of characterizing obesity that would provide guidance in matching patients to a treatment modality that best suited their needs. The goal was ambitious, involving a number of factors. Unfortunately, this goal was not fulfilled. Current systems often assign patients to treatments solely on the basis of the extent of their obesity and the presence of co-morbid conditions that increase risk (Bray 1992, NIH 1998). The manual published by the Shape Up America! campaign and the American Obesity Association (1996) continues giving primary attention to the extent of obesity and health risks, but expands the factors used to select treatment to include patient interest, risk-benefit ratio, and treatment history.

A weight dilemma can be denied by observing that even if patients do not lose or regain what they have lost, they still may have benefited from the program (Kolasa 1996). These benefits might include increased nutrition knowledge, acquisition of exercise skills, making new friends, or the support of caring health professionals. Yet, as Satter (1997) pointed out, it is difficult for someone to feel successful about an effort when they have failed at the main goal.

Dietitians have discussed the ethics of encouraging participation in a weight loss program by predicting significant losses. Some assert that to promise to all what only a few will achieve is quackery. Others counter that such predictions are essential marketing strategies and that participants who fail to achieve the promised losses have only their own limited motivation to blame. Still others note that the apparent immediate failure of an intervention does not mean that the learning may not be applied in the future. While official and unofficial statements emphasize the ethical responsibility to truthfully inform clients of probable outcomes (ADA 1997; Pace, Bolton, and Reeves 1991), dietitians continue to debate the issue.

Reframing Goals.   Another way of coping with the weight dilemma is to revise the outcome goals. Minor weight losses often produce health-significant improvements in symptoms of the risk factors associated with obesity: blood pressure moderates, blood glucose control improves, and serum lipid levels are lowered (Brownell and Rodin 1994). Apparently slenderness does not have to be achieved to reap these rewards. Although the literature is vague about whether the improvements are sustained for long periods in obese persons without further weight loss, there is widespread enthusiasm for the immediate benefits. Practitioners embracing an approach that focuses on these relatively small losses speak not of healthy weights, but rather of healthier weights, weights that may be well above the range usually identified as healthy, but are low enough to have induced positive health changes (ADA 1997).

The concept of health improvements resulting from small amounts of weight loss is so pervasive that the Institute of Medicine (1995) stated that the criterion of success in a weight management program should be a weight loss of at least 5 percent of body weight [or one or more Body Mass Index (BMI) units] that is sustained for at least one year. The institute's other criteria included improvement in obesity-related comorbidities, improved health practices, and monitoring of adverse effects that might result from the program. The sustained loss of 5 percent is considered success regardless of the magnitude of the original loss. Thus, a person originally weighing 200 pounds could have lost 50 pounds, regained 40 of them, and still be considered successful if a year later he or she is 10 pounds below the initial weight. However, it is not clear how successful this individual feels.

The goals recommended in the recent National Institutes of Health clinical guidelines are more ambitious: a weight loss of 10 percent of initial weight over six months of treatment (NIH 1998). Successful maintenance is defined as regaining less than 6.6 pounds and less than 4 cm in waist circumference over two years. Depending on the initial weight, individuals meeting those goals would have gained back less than half of their losses and presumably would be more satisfied. Unfortunately, the evidence cited in these recommendations supports the challenge of maintenance, not that the maintenance goals are realistic.

Framing the loss of relatively small amounts of weight as success requires that concern be limited exclusively to the medical aspects of obesity. Dietitians who use this approach of dealing with the weight dilemma may find that their clients have different agendas. Surveys of consumer motivations for losing weight usually show that health is a distant second to social or appearance factors (Germov and Williams 1996). A 5 percent weight loss will not produce a body size consistent with the extreme slenderness that seems to be the American ideal.

Some dietitians have coped with this problem by viewing weight management as a long-term process broken down into segments in which clients never attempt to lose more than 5 to 10 percent of their weight in a single weight loss effort, with maintenance periods of at least six months interspersed among dieting periods (ADA 1997; NIH 1998). Unfortunately, there is no evidence that most heavy persons are any more able to achieve this sequential loss pattern than they are to succeed at more traditional programs.

Paradigm Change. Recently there has been discussion of a new weight paradigm. This paradigm recognizes the limited success of weight loss interventions, questions the medicalization of obesity, advocates acceptance of one's self, body size, and shape, and may recommend abandonment of all attempts to lose weight (Parham 1996). Many refer to this new weight paradigm as the nondiet approach. In spite of the obvious limitations of the term *nondieting,* there is currently no consensus about a better label. Some alternatives that have been advanced include normalized eating (Miller 1997), intuitive eating (Tribole and Resch 1995), purposeful eating (Siegel 1997), healthy enjoyable eating (Omichinski 1993), and flexible control (Stuart 1997).

Acceptance of a nondiet approach constitutes a challenge for some dietitians, although many have endorsed the concept. The programs for the American Dietetic Association annual meetings in recent years have included presentations and workshops emphasizing less restrictive approaches to weight management. In 1995 the Society for Nutrition Education chartered a new division named Nutrition and Weight Realities. This division describes itself as supporting a new weight paradigm that opposes fat phobia, deals honestly with the difficulties of long-term maintenance of weight loss, accepts the goal of health promotion and quality of life rather than slenderness at any cost, and recognizes the rights of heavy persons to make decisions about their own goals and behaviors.

How do dietitians function within a paradigm that views dieting as an inappropriate intervention? One school of thought advocates total abandonment of advice about eating. More typical among dietitians, however, is an approach that recognizes the importance of balance and moderation in food intake and relies more on the individual's own control systems to achieve those conditions. Critics of the new weight paradigm point out the dearth of data to demonstrate that the approach will achieve the objectives that the public and the health care industry demand in an approach to weight management.

Prevention. Another way of coping with the discrepancy between the goals and outcomes of weight control interventions is to direct attention to the prevention of obesity and eating disorders. Clearly if treatments are less than effective, then prevention is especially important. Prevention may involve avoidance of weight gain by adults, but the major attention has focused upon children's weight gain. Although dietitians and nutritionists enthusiastically endorse the need for prevention, they face two barriers: One barrier is that dietitians usually approach weight as an individual, rather than societal concern. Primary and universal prevention of obesity involves widespread changes, including such diverse components as cultural attitudes toward eating and exercise, acceptance of individual differences, increased availability of affordable and acceptable nutrient-dense foods, and access to safe places to exercise. Considering the need for these changes, dietitians and nutritionists trained in clinical work with individuals may feel poorly equipped to contribute to prevention efforts.

Another barrier to prevention is the concern that efforts initiated with the goal of preventing obesity and eating disorders may actually exacerbate the problems. This is dramatically illustrated in the accounts of heavy adults who tell of the attempts by their parents and health care professionals to prevent a chubby child from becoming an obese adult. The feelings of deprivation induced by restricted diets, mandatory exercise, and special schools or camps contributed to a sense of being unacceptable, unloved, and unlovable. These negative feelings often led either to seeking comfort from food or to extreme efforts to become thin and therefore lovable. One woman confided that as a preteen she became discouraged that in spite of her use of prescribed amphetamines, she still hadn't become thin enough. So she took the remainder of the bottle in a frantic attempt to become instantly slender. She became so ill that she was convinced that she would die, but shame kept her from telling anyone what was happening.

It would be misleading to imply that the prevention efforts of contemporary dietitians are necessarily characterized by such negative outcomes. Today it is more typical for dietitians to work with parents to value their children irrespective of their level of fatness. Nevertheless, prevention of obesity has proved to be difficult.

Consistent with typical prevention strategies, dietitians and other health care professionals warn their clients about the dangers of obesity. Given the extreme stigma of obesity, however, this warning is hardly needed. Yet emphasizing the connection between food intake and fatness may have the effect of encouraging unnecessary dieting. Some of this dieting by slender persons may be a successful attempt to prevent unhealthy weight gain. Nevertheless, many Americans view dieting as an all-purpose way to improve their lives. This may be especially true of young girls who, driven by a need to be "all right" in a very demanding world, turn to dieting (Czajka-Narins and Parham 1990; Pipher 1994).

Do dietitians contribute to unnecessary dieting? While there is a lack of data relevant to the question, compared to the impact of the media in promoting fat phobia the influence of dietitians is surely minor. If dietitians play a role, it is not so much to convince the public that it needs to diet as it is to facilitate dieting among those who have made a decision to do so. Routine protocol for responding to a request for a weight-reducing diet would involve objective assessment by the dietitian of the client's level of fatness and physiological need to lose weight. The typically brief clinical encounters with clients, however, do not provide an opportunity to explore the meanings of food and weight in any depth. Dietitians who have worked with eating disorders often are quite adamant about the potential harm of indiscriminate weight loss advice.

WHAT DOES WEIGHT MEAN TO CONTEMPORARY DIETITIANS?

Health professionals often view obese persons as childlike, foolish, lazy, and lacking self-control, overall being undesirable patients from whom a professional would want to withdraw (Blumberg and Mellis 1985; Price, Desmond, Krol, Snyder, and O'Connell 1987). Lazare (1987) has interpreted such negative attitudes as responses to the frustration of limited effectiveness in treating obesity and to identification within oneself of the same personal characteristics that interfere with success for the patient. It is encouraging, however, that there is some recent evidence of success in reducing obesity stigmatization among medical students (Wiese, Wilson, Jones, and Neises 1992).

Do dietitians share these negative attitudes found among some other health professionals? Given the centrality of weight management to the practice of dietetics, it is odd that there has been relatively little research focused specifically upon dietitians' attitudes about obese clients. An early study (Maiman, Wang, Becker, Finlay, and Simonson 1979) reported attitudes like those found among physicians and nurses: A full 87 percent agreed that obese persons are self-indulgent. Emotional problems were considered important causative factors, with the majority of dietitians believing that family problems, emotional problems, and eating as compensation were associated with obesity. Even though 33 percent agreed that "sometimes no matter what one does, one can't lose" and 53 percent indicated that obesity was the price we pay for affluence, a full 88 percent advocated firm counseling as a means to lose weight.

The limited data available from more recent studies suggest a trend toward somewhat more positive attitudes of dietitians toward obese people. Parham et al. (1991) found that, compared to fitness instructors and dieters, dietitians had more moderate views about the importance of ideal weight to health, attractiveness, and happiness. Nevertheless, dietitians still attached great importance to weight, reporting that not being at an ideal weight should make someone feel more guilty than proud. Oberrieder, Walker, Monroe, and Adeyanju (1995) compared attitudes of dietetics students and registered dietitians about obesity. Both displayed slightly negative attitudes, with those who reported lower body weights being slightly more negative than those whose weights were higher. McArthur and Ross (1997) found that dietitians involved with weight management had relatively positive feelings about overweight people. Strong majorities agreed that overweight clients were competent employees, trustworthy, and easy to get along with. They were less positive about the abilities of overweight clients to implement and stick with various strategies for weight management. Most importantly, however, the vast majority enjoyed counseling overweight clients. The handful of available studies are inadequate to draw firm conclusions about the attitudes of contemporary dietitians toward obesity and overweight clients. However, they suggest more positive attitudes than have been previously reported for other health professionals.

OVERWEIGHT DIETITIANS[2]

At dietetics conferences speakers often chastise members of the audience for being overweight and thereby failing to "practice what they preach." The need to serve as a role model is a concern for any health professional. When the issue is weight, the evidence is in plain sight. A test of the meanings of weight to nutritionists and dietitians is the attitudes toward members of their profession whose bodies fail to conform to recommended fatness levels. The professional literature includes little direct examination of this topic, although there are some indirect indicators. Two studies of the attitudes of dietitians toward obesity (McArthur and Ross 1997; Oberrieder et al. 1995) examined the respondents' perceived and actual weight status. In both studies, considerably more dietitians considered themselves overweight than the number who would be classified as overweight based on their self-reported weights. Apparently dietitians are susceptible to the cultural obsession with slenderness, even to the point of making an incongruent assessment of their own weight status. Marchessault (1993) has suggested that health professionals, in general, are affected by culture as much as by science.

McArthur (1995) studied opinions of nutrition majors and other college students by asking parallel questions about attitudes toward overweight people and attitudes toward oneself when one is overweight. There was a positive correlation between the attitudes toward "self when overweight" and overweight others. Both groups of majors were much harder on themselves than they were on other overweight people. The differences between ratings applied to self and those given others were particularly striking in the items relating weight to guilt, ease in social relationships, attractiveness, and health.

McArthur and Ross (1997) assessed the attitudes of dietitians who counsel overweight clients toward the dietitians' own (perceived) excessive weight. Dietitians displayed negative weight attitudes similar to the "normative discontent" that Rodin, Siberstein, and Striegel-Moore (1984) described as characteristic of contemporary American women. More interesting, however, were the four items that related to the dietitians' personal and professional functioning when they were overweight. Dietitians overwhelming agreed that they were trustworthy and competent employees when overweight, and denied that they were hard to get along with when they were heavy. However, they gave mixed reports about their confidence in social situations.

There is increasing evidence that dietitians recognize the limitations of their efforts to assist patients in sustaining long-term weight losses (American Dietetic Association 1997). This has led to an acceptance of the inevitability of some degree of obesity among many of their patients. Yet this acceptance has not been extended to the members of the profession. Some dietitians evidently interpret "role model" to mean modeling that slenderness is achievable by all. Apparently no consideration is given to the possibility that there are many positive roles that a dietitian might model (Parham 1993). For example, a heavy dietitian might model the health payoffs of a sustained loss of no more than 5 percent of her original weight, the possibility of size acceptance and high self-esteem, or the benefits of healthy eating and exercise behaviors (without weight loss).

Grassi (1997) conducted an electronic mail survey of the directors of dietetic internships in the United States, posing three questions: Does a dietitian's size affect his/her effectiveness? If so, why? and Is the effect of being overweight different from the effect of being underweight? The directors expressed concern that being overweight would affect a dietitian's effectiveness. Although some observed that a heavy dietitian might have trouble securing a position, more indicated that being overweight would cause a dietitian to lose credibility and would compromise her ability to serve as a role model. A minority stated that how a dietitian felt about herself was more important than her size. A few noted that a heavy dietitian might be better able to establish rapport with a heavy client. All respondents agreed that having an active eating disorder would compromise the dietitian's effectiveness. There was less consensus, however, that just being thin would be a problem.

Older dietitians described being in internships where they were weighed weekly and punished if the scale did not show progress toward a weight goal. Other heavy dietitians told of being advised to enter food-service rather than clinical dietetics, or to choose an entirely different field. One dietitian reported staying in the field as a nutrition professor. She sadly recounted her practice of including in each class a disclaimer about doing as she said rather than as she did. The wisdom of preventing what you can't treat is sometimes interpreted as advising heavy students to choose a major other than dietetics.

PATIENTS REFLECT ABOUT DIETITIANS

Many studies have explored the sources that consumers consult for information about nutrition and health. Typically, the media are a widely used source, followed by physicians, and eventually by dietitians. While consumers consider dietitians as an important source of information about weight and weight management, there is a lack of investigation of patients' attitudes toward dietitians in matters of weight. To fill this void about experiences of overweight individuals with dietitians, I gathered information from personal accounts published in lay and professional literature, interviews with current and former students and clients, and electronic interviews. Some involved responses to questions posed on computerized electronic list servers, including a size acceptance list, and spontaneous exchanges on such list servers. These interviews and dialogues may not be representative of the population of clients or dietitians. Three themes were encountered repeatedly, although there is no assurance of the extent to which each theme occurred among the general public.

The most frequent theme was a medical interpretation of weight. Almost all former patients indicated that the dietitians who had advised them consistently emphasized that fatness was incompatible with health. There were many accounts of seeking medical treatment for a problem unrelated to weight, only to find oneself facing a dietitian for instruction about the importance of weight loss to health. One woman described feeling disgusted when, as part of a media event featuring children's clothes in large sizes, a pediatric nutritionist warned that although pretty, stylish clothes may be good for self-esteem, being heavy was "not desirable." On the other hand, the few people who had worked with a dietitian who entertained the possibility of a healthy obese person expressed amazement.

Another theme dealt with the importance of dietitians as a source of understanding and empathy. Some individuals had very positive encounters with dietitians and appreciated their willingness to listen and accept the patient's values and perspectives. One professional woman reported that her dietitian asked her what her goals were for her health. "I told her and she seemed to find them acceptable. She was willing to talk about what I wanted to do to meet those goals." On the other hand, others reported encounters with dietitians who seemed rushed, applied stereotypical thinking, or were unwilling to consider perspectives about weight other than their own (or that of their institution). One woman lost faith in dietitians because those who had worked with her "took it upon themselves to believe every cliche about fat people and their eating habits." Another woman explained to her dietitian that she worked a constantly changing shift and ate "according to when I was awake." When the dietitian replied "Oh, you graze your way through the day," the woman was indignant that the dietitian had not listened to what she had said but nevertheless had formed negative conclusions about her behavior.

The size acceptance list serve included people searching for a dietitian who would be sensitive and nonjudgmental. When one individual identified such a dietitian, several others suggested that they were willing to travel several hours to consult with her. Both negative and positive accounts revealed that patients/clients viewed dietitians as potential sources of understanding, possibly as people who might bridge the gap between rather impersonal medical recommendations and the realities of the individual's life. When this happens, the client feels empowered. When it doesn't happen, he or she feels cheated or insulted.

A third theme considered dietitians as secondary actors. When asked about their experiences with dietitians, many people responded that even though they were heavy and had received medical advice to lose weight, they had never seen a dietitian. Some expressed regret about this: "Does everyone get a consult with a dietitian [when they become a fat diabetic]? I have had nothing, nada, zip, zilch, zero. I even changed doctors because of this, but the new one isn't better." One woman was indignant about the restricted diet a dietitian provided, but another person responded "If you were automatically placed on a reduced-calorie diet, it is likely that the doctor ordered it." The executive director of the size acceptance organization NAAFA (National Association to Advance Fat Acceptance), Sally Smith, reported "The last thing we need is for doctors to encourage health care providers to further harass their patients about their weight" (Berg 1997). Although some patients see dietitians as the enforcer of the physician's dictates, most people simply do not view dietitians as primary forces in the various battles with weight. Undoubtedly, both the relatively low number of dietitians in the United States and the limited availability of third-party payment for the services of dietitians are significant factors in this limited role.

CONCLUSIONS

Dietetics originated at a time of strong popular interest in slenderness, when dietary restriction was often the sole means to prolong life in certain disease states. The profession has matured during the era when obesity became medicalized. These influences, plus the emphasis on the role of food intake in body composition, have led to the widespread use of restricted diets as weight management tools. The extremely limited long-term success of dieting has created a weight dilemma for dietitians. Dietitians have employed various means of coping with the weight dilemma without reaching any consensus as to how best to proceed.

The recent ADA position paper on weight management (ADA 1997) masterfully recognizes the weight dilemma so subtly that the casual reader may miss its presence. The temporary nature of weight loss outcomes is recognized, and there is a call for promotion of healthy lifestyles as an alternative to diets. The ADA paper goes on to recommend moderate, holistic approaches that contrast with the rigid diets of earlier times. The paper does not, however, provide strong guidance for dietitians about how to respond to the public association between slenderness and attractiveness, or to the health care industry's assertion that obesity is incompatible with health. The weight dilemma remains unresolved.

NOTES

1.   Dietitians and nutritionists include both men and women, but because the women far outnumber the men, this chapter will use female pronouns.

2.   Although dietitians' commitment to health indicates concern with excessive thinness as well as fatness, other than concern with eating disorders, there is no evidence that most dietitians seriously consider the possibility of being too thin.

REFERENCES

ADA Courier. 1998. "Growth Trend Is Steady." 37(2):1.

American Dietetic Association. 1997. "Position Paper: Weight Management." *Journal of the American Dietetic Association* 97:71–74.

Ayers, W. M. 1958. "Changing Attitudes toward Overweight and Reducing." *Journal of the American Dietetic Association* 34:23–29.

Beller, A. S. 1977. *Fat and Thin: A Natural History of Obesity*. New York: Farrar, Straus, Giroux.

Berg, F. M. 1997. "Industry Gives 'Guidance' to Doctors." *Healthy Weight Journal* 11:54–55.

Blum, S. 1924. *Practical Dietetics for Adults and Children in Health and Disease*. Philadelphia: F. A. Davis.

Blumberg, P., and L. P. Mellis. 1985. "Medical Students' Attitudes toward the Obese and the Morbidly Obese." *International Journal of Eating Disorders* 4:169–75.

Bray, G. A. 1979. "Treatment of Obesity with Drugs and Invasive Procedures." Pp. 179–205 in *Obesity in America*, edited by G. A. Bray. NIH Publication No. 79-359. Washington: National Institutes of Health.

———. 1992. "An Approach to the Classification and Evaluation of Obesity." Pp. 294–308 in *Obesity*, edited by P. Bjorntorp and B. N. Brodnoff. New York: Lippincott.

Brownell, K. D., and J. Rodin. 1994. "The Dieting Maelstrom: Is It Possible and Advisable to Lose Weight?" *American Psychologist* 49:781–91.

Brownell, K. D., and T. A. Wadden. 1986. "Behavior Therapy for Obesity—Modern Approaches to Better Results." In *Handbook for Eating Disorders*, edited by K. D. Brownell and J. P. Foreyt. New York: Basic Books.

Bryk, J. A., and T. K. Soto. 1997. "Report on the 1995 Membership Database of the American Dietetic Association." *Journal of the American Dietetic Association* 97:197–203.

Bushman, C. C. 1996. *Attitudes of Registered Dietitians toward Two Weight Management Approaches: Very-low-calorie Diets and the Non-diet Approach*. Unpublished master's thesis, Northern Illinois University, DeKalb.

Commission on Accreditation/Approval for Dietetics Education. 1994. *Accreditation/Approval Manual for Dietetics Education Programs*. Chicago: American Dietetic Association.

Czajka-Narins, D. M., and E. S. Parham. 1990. "Fear of Fat: Attitudes toward Obesity." *Nutrition Today* 25:26–32.

Germov, J., and L. Williams. 1996. "The Sexual Division of Dieting: Women's Voices." *Sociological Review* 44:630–47.

Grassi, A. 1997. "Electronic-Mail Survey of Directors of Dietetic Internship Programs in the United States." Unpublished data, Northern Illinois University, Dekalb.

Gries, F. A., M. Berger, and P. Berchtold. 1978. "Clinical Results with Starvation and Semistarvation." Pp. 359–69 in *Recent Advances in Obesity Research: II*, edited by G. A. Bray. Westport, CT: Technomic.

Guthrie, H. A. 1971. *Introductory Nutrition*, 2nd edition. St. Louis: C. V. Mosby.

Holmes, M. D., B. Zysow, and T. L. Delbanco. 1989. "An Analytic Review of Current Therapies for Obesity." *Journal of Family Practice* 28:610–16.

Hutchison, R. 1903. *Food and the Principles of Dietetics*, 4th edition. New York: William Wood.

Institute of Medicine. 1995. *Weighing the Options: Criteria for Evaluating Weight-management Programs*, edited by P. R. Thomas. Washington, DC: National Academy Press.

Katch, F., and W. McArdle. 1993. *Introduction to Nutrition, Health, and Exercise,* 4th edition. Philadelphia: Lea & Febiger.

Kirschenbaum, D. S., and M. L. Fitzgibbon. 1995. "Controversy about the Treatment of Obesity: Criticisms or Challenges." *Behavior Therapy* 26:43–68.

Kirschner, M. A., G. Schneider, N. Ertel, and J. Gorman. 1987. "A Very-low-calorie Formula Diet Program for Control of Major Obesity: An 8-year Experience." Pp. 342–46 in *Recent Advances in Obesity Research: V,* edited by E. M. Berry, S. H. Blondheim, H. E. Eliahou, and E. Shafrir. London: John Libbey.

Kolasa, K. 1996. "Letter to the Editor: Treatment Outcomes." *Healthy Weight Journal* 10:115.

Kornblum, T. H. 1994. "Professional Demand for Dietitians and Nutritionists in the Year 2005." *Journal of the American Dietetic Association* 94:21–22.

Kral, J. G. 1985. "Obesity Surgery: State of the Art." Pp. 237–46 in *Recent Advances in Obesity Research: IV,* edited by J. Hirsch and T. B. van Itallie. London: John Libbey.

Kuczmarski, R. J., K. M. Flegal, S. M. Campbell, and C. L. Johnson. 1994. "Increasing Prevalence of Over-weight among U.S. Adults: The National Health and Nutrition Examination Surveys 1960–1991." *Journal of the American Medical Association* 272:205–11.

Lazare, A. 1987. "Shame and Humiliation in the Medical Encounter." *Archives of Internal Medicine* 147:1653–58.

Levenstein, H. A. 1988. *Revolution at the Table: The Transformation of the American Diet.* New York: Oxford University Press.

Mahan, L. K., and M. T. Arlin. 1992. *Krause's Food, Nutrition, and Diet Therapy,* 8th edition. Philadelphia: W. B. Saunders.

Maiman, L. A., V. L. Wang, M. H. Becker, J. Finlay, and M. Simonson. 1979. "Attitudes toward Obesity and the Obese among Professionals." *Journal of the American Dietetic Association* 74:331–36.

Marchessault, G. D. M. 1993. "Weight Preoccupation in North American Culture." *Journal of the Canadian Dietetic Association* 54:138–42.

Mayer, J. 1968. *Overweight: Causes, Costs, and Control.* Englewood Cliffs, NJ: Prentice Hall.

McArthur, L. H. 1995. "Nutrition and Nonnutrition Majors Have More Favorable Attitudes toward Overweight People Than Personal Overweight." *Journal of the American Dietetic Association* 95:593–96.

McArthur, L. H., and J. K. Ross. 1997. "Attitudes of Registered Dietitians toward Personal Overweight and Overweight Clients." *Journal of the American Dietetic Association* 97:63–66.

McCann, M., and M. F. Trulson. 1955. "Long-term Effect of Weight-reducing Programs." *Journal of the American Dietetic Association* 31:1108–10.

Miller, W. C. 1997. "Health Promotion Strategies for Obese Patients." *Healthy Weight Journal* 11:47–48.

National Institutes of Health. 1998. *Clinical Guidelines on the Identification, Evaluation, and Treatment of Overweight and Obesity in Adults: An Evidence Report.* Bethesda, MD: Author.

Nelson, J. K. 1994. *Mayo Clinic Diet Manual: A Handbook of Nutrition Practices,* 7th edition. St. Louis: Mosby.

Nieman, D., D. Butterworth, and C. Nieman. 1992. *Nutrition*, revised 1st edition. Dubuque, IA: Wm. C. Brown.

Oberrieder, H., R. Walker, D. Monroe, and M. Adeyanju. 1995. "Attitude of Dietetics Students and Registered Dietitians Toward Obesity." *Journal of the American Dietetic Association* 95:914–16.

Ohlson, M. A. 1976. "Diet Therapy in the U.S. in the Past 200 Years." *Journal of the American Dietetic Association* 69:490–96.

Omichinski, L. 1993. *You Count, Calories Don't*. Winnipeg, Manitoba: TAMOS.

Pace, P. W., M. P. Bolton, and R. S. Reeves. 1991. "Ethics of Obesity treatments: Implications for Dietitians." *Journal of the American Dietetic Association* 91:1259–60.

Parham, E. S. 1993. "What Should Nutrition Educators Model?" *Journal of Nutrition Education* 25:89–90.

———. 1996. "Is There a New Weight Paradigm?" *Nutrition Today* 31:155–61.

Parham, E. S., M. J. Flynn, V. L. Frigo, and A. H. Perkins. 1991. "Weight Control: Attitudes of Dieters and Change Agents." *Journal of Home Economics* 83:6–12.

Pattee, A. F. 1917. *Practical Dietetics with Reference to Diet in Health and Disease*, 11th edition. Mount Vernon, NY: A. F. Pattee.

Pattison, M., H. Barbour, and E. Eppright. 1957. *Teaching Nutrition*. Ames: Iowa State University Press.

Pipher, M. 1994. *Reviving Ophelia: Saving the Selves of Adolescent Girls*. New York: Ballantine.

Price, J. H., S. M. Desmond, R. A. Krol, F. F. Snyder, and J. K. O'Connell. 1987. "Family Practice Physicians' Beliefs, Attitudes, and Practices Regarding Obesity." *American Journal of Preventive Medicine* 3:339–45.

Proudfit, F. T., and C. H. Robinson. 1955. *Nutrition and Diet Therapy*, 11th edition. New York: Macmillan.

Rodin, J., L. Siberstein, and R. Striegel-Moore. 1984. "Women and Weight: A Normative Discontent." Pp. 267–303 in *Nebraska Symposium on Motivation*. Lincoln: University of Nebraska Press.

Sansum, W. D., R. A. Hare, and R. Bowden. 1936. *The Normal Diet and Healthful Living*. New York: Macmillan.

Satter, E. 1997. "Letter to the Editor: Treatment Successes." *Healthy Weight Journal* 11:17.

Schwartz, H. 1986. *Never Satisfied: A Cultural History of Diets, Fantasies, and Fat*. New York: Free Press.

Shape Up America! and the American Obesity Association. 1996. *Guidance for the Treatment of Obesity*. Bethesda, MD: Shape Up America!

Sherman, H., and C. Lanford. [1943] 1950. *Essentials of Nutrition*, 2nd edition. New York: Macmillan.

Siegel, K. 1997. "Purposeful Eating in the Nondiet Approach." *Healthy Weight Journal* 11:52.

Sobal, J. 1995. "The Medicalization and Demedicalization of Obesity." Pp. 67–90 in *Eating Agendas: Food and Nutrition as Social Problems*, edited by D. Maurer and J. Sobal. Hawthorne, NY: Aldine de Gruyter.

Stearns, P. N. 1997. *Fat History: Bodies and Beauty in the Modern West*. New York: New York University Press.

Stern, J. S., C. A. Titchenal, and P. R. Johnson. 1987. "Obesity: Does Exercise Make a Difference?" Pp. 352–64 in *Recent Advances in Obesity Research: V,* edited by E. M. Berry, S. H. Blondheim, H. E. Eliahou, and E. Shafrir. London: John Libbey.

Stuart, J. 1997. "Restrained Eaters Rigidly Control Their Food Intake." *Healthy Weight Journal* 11:49–51.

Study Commission on Dietetics. 1985. *A New Look at the Profession of Dietetics.* Chicago: American Dietetic Association.

Stunkard, A. J. 1978. "Behavioral Treatment of Obesity: The First Ten Years." Pp. 295–306 in *Recent Advances in Obesity Research: II,* edited by G. A. Bray. Westport, CT: Technomic.

Stunkard, A., and M. McLaren-Hume. 1959. "The Results of Treatment of Obesity." *Archives of Internal Medicine* 103:79–85.

Tribole, E., and E. Resch. 1995. *Intuitive Eating.* New York: St. Martin's.

Wadden, T. A., and A. J. Stunkard. 1986. "Controlled Trial of Very Low Calorie Diets, Behavior Therapy, and their Combination in the Treatment of Obesity." *Journal of Consulting and Clinical Psychology* 54:482–88.

Weigley, E. S. 1980. "Sarah Tyson Rorer: First American Dietitian?" *Journal of the American Dietetic Association* 77:11–15.

Weinsier, R. L., T. A. Wadden, C. Ritenbaugh, G. G. Harrison, F. S. Johnson, and J. H. Wilmore. 1984. "Recommended Therapeutic Guidelines for Professional Weight Control." *American Journal of Clinical Nutrition* 40:865–72.

Whitney, E., and E. M. Hamilton. 1981. *Understanding Nutrition,* 2nd edition. St. Paul, MN: West.

Wiese, H. J. C., J. F. Wilson, R. A. Jones, and M. Neises. 1992. "Obesity Stigma Reduction in Medical Students." *International Journal of Obesity* 16:859–68.

Wyden, P. 1965. *The Overweight Society.* New York: William Morrow.

Young, C. M., N. S. Moore, K. Berresford, B. M. Einset, and B. G. Waldner. 1955. "The Problem of the Obese Patient." *Journal of the American Dietetic Association* 31:1111–15.

VI

COLLECTIVE PROCESSES

11

Too Skinny or Vibrant and Healthy?
Weight Management in the Vegetarian Movement

DONNA MAURER

Successful social movements, those that attract adherents and attain their goals, continually respond to the social and cultural contexts within which they operate. They take advantage of available cultural opportunities, drawing out the connections between public concerns and the movements' activities (Gamson 1988; Williams 1995). In addition, social movements sometimes *react* to negative messages put forth by the popular press, scientific professionals and other experts, and counter-movements. A successful movement operates as an ongoing, complex discourse (Brulle 1996), propagating positive messages that resonate with current cultural concerns and repudiating negative messages spread by its detractors.

Most social movements try to manage their public images in ways that heighten their credibility, emphasize their relevance to public concerns, and diminish what outsiders may perceive as radical or extreme aspects of their activities and beliefs. Studies of individual social movement organizations suggest that these groups engage in impression management strategies in order to compete on the social movement "stage." For example, a study of a local environmental advocacy group in Illinois found that the organization expressed one set of messages to the general public and the media ("frontstage"), and a more radical set of messages within the organization itself ("backstage") (Kubal 1998). Social movement organizations tend to filter their more extreme ideological tenets when trying to attract new constituents (Lipsky 1968).

This chapter extends previous research on the dramaturgical aspects of social movement activities by explaining how one social movement constructs its public image in response to popular and profession constructions of the body weight of its members. In the case of the vegetarian movement, both professional and popular discourses construct the vegetarian body type as thinner than average, underweight, or "skinny." The vegetarian movement typically responds by de-emphasizing the potential weight loss aspect of following vegetarian diets, focusing on the lightness and health-giving properties of vegetarian foods, and using current vegetarian constituents as healthful, moral exemplars, regardless of body type. This chapter contributes to sociological understanding about how social movements negotiate their images in the public sphere by neutralizing negative stereotypes perpetuated by outsiders.

This chapter is based on a broader study that examines the links between social movement culture and organizational strategies in the vegetarian movement (Maurer 1997). In this study, I used a multifaceted research design that included (1) a review of mainstream popular press literature about vegetarians; (2) a review of printed matter from nine national vegetarian organizations; (3) a review of other vegetarian movement literature, products, and services; (4) tape-recorded and transcribed depth interviews with thirty movement leaders and spokespersons; (5) a qualitative survey of local vegetarian organizations ($n = 97$) in the United States and Canada; (6) ethnographic fieldwork at several national and regional vegetarian conferences. As my research methodology suggests, I chose to analyze the North American vegetarian movement at its broadest scope to better understand the trends, patterns, and inconsistencies in the movement as a whole, as it operates in its cultural and structural environments. The interpretations expressed in this chapter are grounded in a complex, yet integrated set of data resources.

Defining Vegetarian and Vegan

Vegetarians, people who do not consume meat, poultry, or seafood, comprise between 0.5 and 2 percent of the Canadian and U.S. populations (Dietz, Frisch, Lalof, Stern, and Guagnano 1995; Stahler 1994; Toronto Vegetarian Association 1995). The term *vegetarian* typically connotes what also is known as an "ovo-lacto-vegetarian." An ovo-lacto-vegetarian eats some dairy products and eggs. Following this, a lacto-vegetarian eats dairy products and not eggs, and an ovo-vegetarian consumes eggs but not dairy products. While a small percentage of the population practices some form of ovo-lacto-vegetarian or vegan (see below) diet, many more people are "semivegetarians." Between 7 and 12 million people in the United States occasionally eat meat and/or seafood yet *claim* to be vegetarians (Dietz et al. 1995; Krizmanic 1992; Robeznieks 1986).

Dietary vegans (sometimes called "complete vegetarians" or "pure vegetarians") not only follow ovo-lacto-vegetarian proscriptions; they also do not eat eggs and dairy products and avoid the use of animal by-products in foods, such as whey and casein. In addition to these food proscriptions, many vegans do not wear leather, wool, or silk, or use health or cleaning products that contain animal by-products or that have been tested on animals. Many vegans do not eat honey and also eschew products such as sugar and wine that sometimes are processed with animal by-products. Hence, a wide continuum of avoidances and preferences characterizes the eating practices of semivegetarians, ovo-lacto-vegetarians, and vegans (see Beardsworth and Keil 1992).

VEGETARIAN BODY WEIGHT IN PROFESSIONAL AND POPULAR DISCOURSES

During the early rise of vegetarian diets in mid-nineteenth-century North America, advocates of conventional ("regular") medicine disparaged their alternative health counterparts, often labeling them as "quacks" (Friedson 1970). "Fun was poked at the vegetarians on the printed page, in comic opera and in the newspapers" (Roe 1986:1361). According to historian James Whorton, the regulars "had much merriment at vegetarians' expense," characterizing vegetarian women as "mummies preserved in saffron" and vegetarian men as "lean-visaged cadaverous disciples [of Sylvester Graham]" (1977:121–22). Vegetarians often were portrayed as sallow, wan, and emaciated. The notion that vegetarians—and especially vegetarian children and adolescents—should be concerned about low weight persists today in nutritional science, psychological, and popular discourses about food and weight. These discourses contribute to the cultural environment in which vegetarian advocacy and activism take place.

Nutritional Science Discourse on Vegetarian Diets

In the latter half of the twentieth century, nutritional scientists have paid significant attention to vegetarian diets. Nutritional scientists began to use the term "new vegetarians" in the 1970s to indicate converts to vegetarianism, distinguishing them from others who grew up eating vegetarian as part of a religious doctrine (e.g., Seventh Day Adventist, Hindu, or Jain). In some of the 1970s nutritional science literature, writers used "new vegetarian" interchangeably with "food cultist" and "food faddist," the two predominant, disparaging terms that nutritional scientists had used previously to describe vegetarians (Erhard 1973, 1974; Roberts, West, Ogilvie, and Dillon 1979; Todhunter 1973; Varner 1994:35–37). In 1975, the American Dietetic Association (ADA) conveyed its stance on vegetarian diets in its "Position Paper on Food and Nutrition Misinformation on Selected Topics":

> The American Dietetic Association recognizes the quality of vegetable pro-
> tein is less than animal protein, but the careful selection of foods for vege-
> tarian diets can insure adequate nutrition for adults. . . . Infants and children
> two to five years of age need more protein for growth and development than
> is likely to be available from pure vegetarian [vegan] diets. (1975:279)

In the 1970s, many nutritional scientists characterized vegetarian diets
as a *medical problem*. A substantial amount of research focused on the problem of underweight vegetarian children in particular (e.g., American
Academy of Pediatrics 1977; Burke and Huse 1979; Zmora, Gorodischer,
and Bar-Ziv 1979), with some researchers labeling the feeding of vegan
diets to children a form of child abuse (Roberts et al. 1979). For example, a
section of a *Nutrition Today* article bears the subtitle, "A Starved Child of
the New Vegetarians" (Erhard 1973:10). The opening paragraph suggests
that this particular case history typifies the problems that a medical professional is likely to encounter with a "new vegetarian":

> Recently an infant was admitted to the San Francisco General Hospital rep-
> resenting all the problems one faces in dealing with the children of the new
> vegetarians. There was the deplorable condition of the child itself, the diffi-
> culty of convincing a reluctant mother of the staff's benevolent intentions
> and the downright opposition of an elusive father. It's an instructive case his-
> tory. (ibid.)

Erhard's portrayal of vegetarianism exemplifies the nutrition profession's
concerns about children becoming emaciated by following vegetarian
(and, in particular, vegan) diets in the 1970s.

More recently, many nutritional scientists changed their assessment of
vegetarian diets (see Messina and Messina 1996), exemplified by the
American Dietetic Association's first position paper on "the vegetarian
approach to eating," which states that "well planned vegetarian diets are
consistent with good nutritional status" (ADA 1980:61). Subsequent, periodic ADA position papers on vegetarian diets reinforced the potential
healthfulness of vegetarian diets and minimized the risk of vegetarian
diets for growing children (see ADA 1988, 1993, 1997).

Still, concerns about serving vegetarian diets to children persist, particularly among medical professionals. For example, when physician Benjamin Spock's (Spock and Parker 1998) revised edition of *Baby and Child
Care* (the second best-selling book ever, next to the *Bible*) announced that,
ideally, parents should provide a vegan diet for the children after age two,
pediatrician T. Berry Brazelton

> called his new dietary recommendations "absolutely insane. . . . A vegetar-
> ian diet doesn't make any sense. Meat is an excellent source of the iron and

protein children need, and to take milk away from children—I think that's really dangerous. Milk is needed for calcium and vitamin D." (cited in Brody 1998)

Despite the ADA's (1997) position that calcium and vitamin D deficiencies are unlikely when a child's diet is well-planned, many physicians and nutritionists still regard vegetarian (and especially vegan) diets as dangerous. Such appeals to concerns about risks to innocent and vulnerable children are particularly likely to generate social concern (Best 1994).

While concerns about malnutrition problems among vegetarian children linger, recent nutrition research has focused more on the lower prevalence of obesity among vegetarians than among nonvegetarians (e.g., Appleby, Thorogood, Mann, and Key 1998; Key and Davey 1996; Janelle and Barr 1995; Knutsen 1994; Messina and Messina 1996:45–46; Ossipow 1995), with the lowest average body mass index found among vegans (Key and Davey 1996). Despite scientific confirmation of this seemingly desirable aspect of following vegetarian diets, the vegetarian movement tends to de-emphasize the vegetarian diet/weight loss connection, as I shall discuss later.

Psychological Discourse on Vegetarian Diets

Like nutritional scientists, psychologists also have expressed concerns about thinness, yet these concerns have focused on one social group following vegetarian diets—adolescent females. Many psychologists describe an association between following a vegetarian diet and developing anorexia nervosa, a disease characterized in part by thinness and emaciation (Bakan, Birmingham, Aeberhardt, and Goldner 1993; Kadambari, Gowers, and Crisp 1986; Kalucy 1987; O'Connor, Touyz, Dunn, and Beumont 1987). While psychological comparison studies have found no significant differences between vegetarian and nonvegetarian populations regarding mental health (Cooper, Wise, and Mann 1985; West 1972), some psychologists view a young woman's adherence to a vegetarian diet as a "warning sign" that may be masking an eating disorder (e.g., Worsley and Skrzypiec 1997). "Vegetarian practice, widely acclaimed as healthy, is adopted, often with deleterious consequences such as the development of eating disorders, by increasing numbers of young women as a means of losing or controlling weight" (Bakan et al. 1993:232).

At the same time, according to Monika M. Woolsey (1997), a vegetarian eating-disordered patient (VED) may use her diet to express a very wide range of psychological disturbances. For example, a VED may use her vegetarianism as a form of "meat transference." If "she is angry at her father for his verbal abuse of her mother," she may avoid roast beef because "it was her father's favorite food" (ibid.:33). Or, following a vegetarian diet may mask hidden sexual abuse issues or a posttraumatic stress disorder. Some VEDs may be vegetarians because

> [i]t takes longer to digest meat than it does other foods. Victims of sexual abuse often describe the sensation of prolonged fullness as a "dirty" feeling, suggesting that feeling full is a retraumatization of an undesired trespassing across the individual's physical boundaries. (ibid.)

> [t]he hypersensory function in post-traumatic stress disorder triggers numerous food aversions. Because of their fat content, meat's [sic] sensory characteristics (and graphic memory-enhancing potential) are greater than other foods. A PTSD vegetarian is easily identified by her complaints of nausea at the mere smell of cooking meat. (ibid.:34)

Not all psychologists view following a vegetarian diet as causing or masking an eating disorder or other deeply seated psychological problem. Rather, many psychologists view vegetarian diets and anorexia nervosa as simply correlated, with many young women adopting a vegetarian or partial vegetarian diet *after* the onset of other symptoms (O'Connor et al. 1987). Still, some psychologists' associations between vegetarian diets and anorexia nervosa suggest that such diets may be linked to undesirable thinness, as well as other possible psychological problems. This may evoke public concern, especially among parents of adolescent girls.

Media Discourse on Vegetarian Diets

The popular print media have strengthened the tie between vegetarian diets, thinness, and malnourishment with media reports, like nutritional scientists, often focusing on children. For example, in one case of heightened vegetarian news coverage in the 1980s, eight *Washington Post* articles provided ongoing reportage of six children who were removed from their home by a local social service agency, which charged that the children were malnourished on the vegetarian diet their guardians provided for them (Hill 1984a, 1984b). Five of the children were hospitalized because they weighed approximately half the normal weight for their respective ages. Prior to their hospitalization, the children lived with the leader of a defunct local conservative religious group (the Assembly of Yehowah) and another devotee, the mother of two of the children. The guardians then charged that the county authorities had removed their children because of their dietary and religious practices, not because the children were unhealthy (Hill 1984c). While one article quoted the children's pediatrician, who testified in court that "vegetarianism normally is a safe diet for children, as well as for adults" (Hill 1984a), the prominence of the ongoing story and its focus on malnourished vegetarian children reinforced the belief that vegetarian diets may lead to malnourishment. Similar cases of vegetarian parents accused of neglectful feeding of their children (i.e., feeding them vegetarian diets) have continued in the 1990s (see Attwood 1996).

The preceding examples of professional and popular discourses on vegetarian diets focus on vegetarians as thinner than the "average" person. Even though much attention has been paid to vegetarian children and adolescents, these concerns may resonate with other social groups as well. Certainly, many females wish to lose weight (Hesse-Biber 1996), but associations with weakness and anorexia nervosa may make vegetarian-derived "skinniness" less desirable to many women. Also, fears that vegetarian diets may cause one to lose weight and possibly become emaciated or malnourished may be of particular concern to males who risk becoming "feminized" if they adopt vegetarian diets. "Real men don't eat quiche," as the saying goes, while consuming bloody red meats is the epitome of masculinity, according to Westernized cultural definitions (Twigg 1983). More males than females wish to gain weight (Hesse-Biber 1996; Garner 1997); popular and professional discourses on vegetarian diets, then, could make vegetarian diets particularly unappealing to men. A male's resistance to vegetarianism also may become a barrier to his spouse's adoption of a vegetarian diet, as a husband's preferences often dictate which foods are served in a household (Beardsworth and Keil 1992:279; Charles and Kerr 1988; Zey and McIntosh 1992).

The discourses discussed in this section are an important aspect of the cultural environment in which the vegetarian movement operates. Negative connotations associated with vegetarian diets are barriers to the movement recruiting new adherents. Consequently, the vegetarian movement manages these connotations to create a more positive public presentation.

WEIGHT MANAGEMENT IN THE VEGETARIAN MOVEMENT

Social movements are ongoing constructions, negotiated through the actions of movement leaders, participants, opponents, "experts," bystanders, and the media. Social movements are particularly concerned with challenging generally accepted definitions of the existing social order. In large part, social movements engage in *public presentations* to convince bystanders that the existing social order should be changed and that they need to act.

A dramaturgical perspective views a social movement as a collection of continuous, multiple performances directed toward numerous audiences. This perspective can be used as the basis for studying a variety of social movement processes, "including formulating roles and characterizations, managing performance regions, controlling information, sustaining dramatic tensions, and orchestrating emotions" (Benford and Hunt 1992:37). Just as an individual engages in impression management to effect a particular presentation of self (Goffman 1959), a social movement manages the public performance of a collective self, albeit with a multitude of sometimes very disparate perspectives.

In the vegetarian movement, leaders seek to generate public interest in vegetarianism, motivate people to become vegetarians, and effect cultural changes to make a vegetarian lifestyle easier and more pleasurable. In other words, vegetarian leaders want to both attract newcomers to vegetarianism and help to create an environment in which people find it easy to maintain their new dietary practices (see Jabs, Devine, and Sobal 1998a). The vegetarian *movement* includes activities intended to effect personal, cultural, and sometimes, structural changes. The movement includes local and national social movement organizations (SMOs), a body of movement literature, an identifiable set of rhetorical arguments (see Maurer 1995), and a range of products and services (e.g., cookbooks, t-shirts, dating services). In North America, several national organizations, over one hundred local groups, and many "one-person" operations contribute to cultural change activities, and encourage people to become vegetarians in a variety of ways.

The vegetarian movement addresses two distinct audiences: current vegetarians and potential adherents. The movement reaches current vegetarians through its many organizational publications, mass-marketed magazines, such as *Vegetarian Times,* and regional and national conferences. Through these venues, vegetarians learn not only about how to prepare vegetarian foods, but also how to become a positive exemplar in order to attract new adherents. The movement primarily reaches potential adherents *indirectly,* by publishing books and magazines directed toward a more general audience and by relying on people's social networks to draw new movement participants. Similarly, the vegetarian movement manages negative images related to vegetarians' body weight *indirectly,* by downplaying the issue and focusing instead on other positive aspects of following vegetarian diets.

Vegetarian leaders and organizations sometimes engage in techniques of neutralization (Sykes and Matza 1957) to deflect negative body stereotypes about vegetarian adherents, and to create the most positive impression of vegetarians, the vegetarian movement, and the vegetarian philosophy. Movement leaders and organizations manage the image of vegetarians by de-emphasizing the weight loss aspects of vegetarian diets; focusing on the lightness and health-giving properties of vegetarian foods; and using current vegetarian constituents as healthful, moral exemplars.

De-Emphasizing the Weight Loss Aspects of Vegetarian Diets

A predominant way that the vegetarian movement neutralizes negative stereotypes about skinniness is to minimize discussions about body weight. When vegetarian organizations discuss body weight in their publications, they often do not focus exclusively on the weight loss aspect of following vegetarian diets; instead, they emphasize that a person could lose or *gain* weight as a vegetarian, depending on what foods he or she eats. (For an autobiographical account, see Gregory 1973:11–19.) For example, in a "true or false" quiz at the end of *Meatless Meals for Working People*, Vegetarian Resource Group co-founders and directors Debra Wasserman and Charles Stahler include the statement, "Becoming a vegetarian will help me lose weight" (1996:92–94). In the "Answers" section, they state:

> FALSE. Again, a vegetarian diet is like any other diet. Fat has twice as many calories as carbohydrates and proteins. If you have a normal metabolism, and overconsume high-fat foods such as high-fat dairy products, peanut butter, avocados, or cook with too much oil, and do not burn up or eliminate these excess calories, you will probably gain weight no matter what the sources of these calories.

Another organization, the North American Vegetarian Society (NAVS), publishes a sixteen-page guide for prospective vegetarians entitled: "Vegetarianism: Answers to the Most Commonly Asked Questions." The guide provides an answer to the question, "How come vegetarians sometimes seem to eat more and yet are not overweight?": "Some vegetarians do gain weight, but most keep a stable weight even though they eat a greater volume of food than meat-eaters" (NAVS, no date:6).

Similarly, Howard Lyman, president of the International Vegetarian Union, who describes having lost 130 pounds on a vegan diet, writes that it is possible to gain weight on a vegan diet:

> Even a vegan diet may not help you lose weight, or lower your blood cholesterol levels, if you replace meats with large helpings of guacamole, peanut butter, fried vegetables, white bread smothered in margarine, pasta soaked in olive oil, doughnuts, and potato chips. It is unusual but certainly possible to gain weight on a vegan diet, and oils (which are 100 percent fat) and nuts (which are all extremely high fat) tend to be the prime culprits when this occurs. (1998:169–70)

Vegetarian leaders and the publications of their respective organizations emphasize that following a vegetarian or vegan diet will not *necessarily* lead to weight loss; a person's food choices within the diet (along with exercise and metabolism) will to a large extent affect a person's body weight. Importantly, vegetarian organizations do not make weight loss promises in their publications, even though, as discussed earlier, many vegetarians weigh less than meat-eaters. Avoiding such claims helps to neutralize the impression that vegetarians are doomed to become skinny and emaciated.

Even though leaders in the vegetarian movement downplay the vegetarian diet–weight loss connection, vegetarians often cite desirable weight loss as an outcome of their dietary changes (Dwyer, Kandel, Mayer, and Mayer 1974; Jabs et al. 1998a), and many people adopt semivegetarian and vegetarian diets to lose weight (Hurlburt and Nouri 1998). For example, Worsley and Skrzypiec (1997) report that teenaged female vegetarians are more likely than nonvegetarian teens to be dieting. Beef, in particular, is associated with hindering weight loss efforts. Many women avoid eating beef when they are trying to lose weight, and as Zey and McIntosh conclude: "[A]ttitudes concerning the relationship between weight control and beef may affect intentions to consume beef" (1992:254).

Also, some physicians promote vegetarian weight loss plans (e.g., see Barnard 1992; Ornish 1993), and many nonvegetarians may associate vegetarian diets with weight loss efforts (e.g., see Sadalla and Burroughs 1981:52). For example, in a study of "overweight" women's experiences of public eating, Zdrodowski (1996:662) summarizes: "Eating a salad or a plate full of mainly vegetables conveys the message that something is being done about being 'overweight.'" As one of her respondents stated about eating in public places:

> I have vegetarian meals because they look healthier. . . . I'd rather have steak or chicken etc. but they often come with chips and I feel as if everyone is looking at me. (ibid.:661)

Although nonvegetarians may view following a vegetarian diet as a potential weight loss strategy, little attention is paid to this in the vegetarian movement. One way of neutralizing the image of the skinny vegetarian simply has been to downplay it and instead to focus on the positive qualities of vegetarian foods and vegetarian advocates, as discussed in the next two sections.

Focusing on the Lightness and Health-Giving Properties of Vegetarian Foods

The vegetarian movement also attempts to neutralize negative connotations by focusing on the positive qualities of vegetarian foods. Claims about the healthfulness of vegetarian diets date back to Pythagorean philosophy (sixth century B.C.), which stressed vegetarianism's life-giving properties (Spencer 1995:33–68). Vegetarian discourse often focuses on the life-giving vitality of consuming plants, as well as the deadening quality of eating meat (see Beardsworth and Keil 1992; Twigg 1979; Maurer 1995:154–56). The term "vegetarian" is not a condensation of "vegetable eater," but derives from the Latin *vegetus,* meaning "whole, sound, fresh, and lively" (Bargen 1979:4). As Ossipow (1995:133) notes in his ethnographic study, many vegetarians

> qualify their food as "light" [and] they compare it to "rich," "fat," "heavy," and "dead" food used by "carnivores." . . . Vegetarian food is considered "light" because it is characterised by a fluid and rapid intestinal transit.

Vegetarians characterize plants as life-giving and meat as dead matter or decaying flesh. For example, one vegetarian author writes:

> Many plants retain their life-giving energy for many days after they remain still capable of sprouting and growing. Meat, on the other hand, has been in the process of decay for several days. (Parham 1979:57)

Also, meat takes longer to pass through the intestinal tract than most vegetarian foods, leaving the consumer feeling heavy (see ibid.:25–26); and a high-meat, low-fiber diet may lead to constipation, another source of heaviness, as described in an NAVS publication:

> You may be less constipated. People who eat a typical American diet may be constipated and not realize it. . . . Most new vegetarians report that they feel great! Some say they've never felt better in their lives. For some people, there is a very brief adjustment period where they may feel weak or tired. . . . Many do not experience this adjustment at all and most find after they adjust that they have more energy and feel better than ever. (Sapon, Berg, and Campanile 1993:6)

Focusing on the positive, enlivening qualities of vegetarian foods helps to neutralize the any negative connotations associated with skinniness.

Along the same lines, some leaders emphasize that people often can eat larger quantities of food on a vegetarian diet than on a meat-based one and not gain weight. Interestingly, vegetarians managing their image do not mention that if people eat the *same* quantity of food as they did on omnivorous diets, an *undesired* consequence may be that they may lose weight. For example,

> You'll find that the volume of food that you eat on a vegetarian diet will often be greater than it was on a meat-based diet. Fibrous vegetarian food is naturally lower in calories and higher in nutrients than animal-based food. So you may find yourself eating more and losing weight, *if you need to,* at the same time. (Lyman 1998:173, emphasis added)

Here Lyman claims that undesirable weight loss is not a likely outcome of following vegetarian diets; at the same time he suggests that vegetarians have the *benefit* of consuming larger quantities of food. Emphasizing all of these positive aspects of vegetarian diets helps to neutralize people's negative perceptions.

Use of Current Vegetarian Constituents as Healthful, Moral Exemplars

The vegetarian movement also attempts to neutralize negative connotations about vegetarian diets by promoting their advocates as healthful, moral exemplars, regardless of their body weight. Like most other social movements (McAdam, McCarthy, and Zald 1988; Snow, Zurcher, and Ekland-Olson 1980), vegetarian mobilization occurs primarily within social networks (Amato and Partridge 1989; Powell 1992:91–113). Vegetarian leaders regard interpersonal relationships as the most effective way to attract new adherents, for example:

> I personally believe that survival for us is going to be one-on-one: talking to our friends, our parents, our business associates about why it is we ought to change what we're putting at the end of our fork [*sic*]. (Lyman, no date)

> I want to show that one person can do many things, and it's not hopeless. And, matter of fact, that's the reason why vegetarianism is where it is at the moment—because of individuals. Organizations . . . have their place and they're helpful. But it is basically because of people talking to other people, and their families and over the back fence. (personal interview with local group leader)

Leaders consider each vegetarian to be a potential advocate for attracting new adherents; they encourage vegetarians to "use lifestyle daily to confront what is accepted as the status quo" (Powell 1992:4). Therefore, every vegetarian is a walking advertisement for the potential benefits and hazards of following a vegetarian diet, and leaders encourage vegetarian advocates to become exemplars that others would want to emulate.

While some social movements call on participants to change in order to benefit a collective good, others—like the vegetarian movement—encourage people to change for their own self-improvement (see Maurer 1997:73–80). An essay from Max Weber's *The Sociology of Religion* ([1922] 1963:55) provides the language and theoretical basis for this dichotomy. Weber described two kinds of religious prophets: the "ethical" prophet, who demands obedience to god as a moral, or ethical duty, and the "exemplary" prophet, who appeals to the seeker's self-interest, and offers his life as an example of religious salvation for others to follow. Leaving the religious terms and applications aside, we can use the same concepts to describe social movements. An ethical movement admonishes its adherents to follow an abstract set of rules prescribed for the appropriation of some collective good, and an exemplary movement offers recommendations and examples for the adherent to follow, to the degree that he or she chooses, for his or her self-benefit. Ethical movements offer *prescriptions* for moral attitudes, whereas exemplary movements offer suggestions and general direction. In an ethical movement, adherence to prescribed rules is viewed as a *duty,* a moral obligation, whereas in an exemplary movement, this adherence is more processual than absolute, a path.

The vegetarian movement is a good example of an exemplary movement. Its leaders rely on advocates to portray positive examples to others, so that newcomers will be inspired to try a vegetarian diet. Interestingly, although the vegetarian movement focuses on providing exemplars to potential adherents for their education, it pays little attention to the body weight of these exemplars. Instead, in vegetarian writings and at organizationally sponsored events, leaders emphasize that vegetarian advocates should be morally consistent, personally likeable, and physically healthy. For example, a local vegetarian group leader admonishes advocates:

> Don't give off negative vibes. Be someone that others would want to emulate. Look good, smile, and be confident and positive. . . . You may not notice, but you can be sure that others are watching you. Sooner than you think they will start asking you about your diet and why you made your choice. (Brown 1995)

Most vegetarians are motivated by a desire for improved personal health (Krizmanic 1992), so it is not difficult for them to display this quality to others. Other vegetarians, many of those primarily motivated by animal rights issues, are not particularly concerned about their own health. This type of exemplar may have a difficult time attracting newcomers to vegetarian diets, as the president of a national organization and the leader of an organization of vegetarian nutritionists both state:

> Someone who is a "junk food vegetarian," who doesn't take good care for their health and mainly eats junk food is not a good advertisement for vegetarianism. Strategically, it's not a good thing. (personal interview, national organization leader)

> [T]here are many "junk food" vegetarians who abstain from eating animal flesh for humanitarian reasons . . . rather than for hygienic concerns. Yet if these people suffer ill health, they are not only handicapped in the efforts to create a gentler, more just world, but they also set a poor example for those who may be considering changing their diet in a similar direction. (Eisman 1994:11)

Although exemplifying good health is regarded as important, the *body weight* of vegetarian exemplars is rarely discussed publicly. This does concern some leaders, however, as a former executive director of a national organization reported in a personal interview:

> I think there's one problem the movement does have—and that is that a lot of people in the movement are very thin. And the general public perceives that as being unhealthy. . . . And it is something that we aren't going to change because as people do take on a vegan diet they do lose a lot of weight. . . . John Robbins [founder of EarthSave International] is a very thin person. And he used to eat tons of Baskin Robbins ice cream, and he was still a thin person. But people maybe see him . . . and some people consider it unhealthy. But, you know, he's one of the healthiest, most robust people I've ever met.

In my fieldwork observations, I also noted that many vegetarian leaders (particularly the males) are very thin by cultural standards. This fact may be problematic for promoting vegetarianism, but, again, this point is not openly discussed at vegetarian events nor in vegetarian publications. Instead, vegetarian advocates are admonished to exemplify positive personal characteristics and a healthy outlook.

Interestingly, the current most public vegetarian figure in the United States, Howard Lyman, defies the image of the skinny, weak, and feminized vegetarian male completely. As Lyman notes about himself, "I had always been more or less a macho kind of guy, and vegetarian just wasn't how I saw myself" (1998:81). Lyman, president of the International Vegetarian Union (IVU), was a co-defendant in a case pressed by the Texas Beef Cattleman's Association, after having appeared on the Oprah Winfrey Show in April 1996, where he announced that "Mad Cow Disease could make AIDS look like the common cold!" (Texas Department of Agriculture 1996). A former fourth generation cattleman, Lyman (1998) became a vegetarian after developing severe health problems. For the past several years, Lyman has been delivering hundreds of lectures per year about animal agriculture, Mad Cow Disease, and vegetarianism.

Although Lyman reports having lost 130 pounds on a vegan diet (1998), he appears somewhat overweight. Yet, some vegetarians feel that this makes him a good exemplar. For example, in her review of Lyman's book, a local group leader writes:

> [P]hysically he is a great spokesperson as well: His persona of the all-American college football type and cattle rancher as well as being a vegetarian but still carrying some weight around the middle is a wonderful contrast to some of the more brainy medical types who look like they could use a little fat on them. (Simon 1998)

Similarly, a discussant on an e-mail list about scientific aspects of vegetarian diets writes about her reaction to Howard Lyman being elected president of the IVU:

My immediate reaction, which I never said out loud, was that one of the things holding back people from the vegetarian diet was the image of us as scrawny along with the idea that there just wasn't enough to eat on such a diet, and accordingly, it would be good to have people show that one can, in fact, get overweight on a vegan diet, because that would show there was plenty of good food.

Ironically then, Lyman, with some excess baggage around the middle, may be seen as a positive exemplar of vegetarianism. Visual images often "speak louder" than words; exemplars who demonstrate that not all vegetarians are skinny and emaciated may help to neutralize stereotypes generated in the cultural environment about vegetarians and body weight.

NEUTRALIZING THE "SKINNY VEGETARIAN" IMAGE

Movement leaders and organizations attempt to neutralize negative impressions of vegetarianism in the cultural environment by de-emphasizing the weight loss aspects of vegetarian diets; focusing on the lightness and health-giving properties of vegetarian foods; and using current vegetarian constituents as healthful, moral exemplars. Neutralizing negative stereotypes is an important, yet previously underemphasized aspect of creating successful social movement performances. Negative connotations about a social movement in the cultural environment—whether spread by "experts," the media, bystanders, or countermovements—may have deleterious consequences for attracting new adherents. Therefore, an important aspect of any social movement's public performance is likely to be the neutralization of these negative connotations.

Certainly, vegetarian diets have found increasing public acceptance since the 1960s, when they were associated with hippie counterculture (Apte and Katona-Apte 1986; Belasco 1993). But to what degree can the increasing acceptance of vegetarian diets be attributed to social movement efforts? My data do not specifically permit such an evaluation, but I would suggest that—in addition to the movement's neutralization efforts—three important factors in the cultural environment have contributed to a gradual acceptance of vegetarian diets: increasingly negative attitudes about red meat, increasing expert acceptance of vegetarian diets, and the commercialization of vegetarian food products.

First, increasingly negative attitudes about red meat (with negative media publicity about *e. coli*, bovine spongiform encephalopathy, and cholesterol), make the move toward a vegetarian diet seem more positive. For example, in a recent study conducted by the National Live Stock and Meat

Board, one-third of the consumers surveyed said "their diets would be healthier if they did not eat red meat" (cited in Putnam and Duewer 1995:4). Most people who gradually become vegetarians eliminate red meat first (Jabs, Devine, and Sobal 1998b; Maurer 1989); negative publicity about red meat is a positive force toward vegetarianism in the cultural environment.

Second, positive public proclamations by scientific experts and government agencies about vegetarian diets contribute to the cultural environment in which the promotion of vegetarian diets takes place. As discussed earlier, the American Dietetic Association has issued periodic position papers on vegetarian diets, which have included increasingly positive evaluations. In addition, in 1995, the U.S. Department of Agriculture and the U.S. Department of Health and Human Services issued their revised *Federal Dietary Guidelines for Americans*, which, for the first time, announced, "Vegetarian diets are consistent with the *Dietary Guidelines for Americans* and can meet Recommended Dietary Allowances for nutrients" (Putnam and Duewer 1995:7). Granted, such official proclamations often stir up additional controversy, but, in general, they lend more professional legitimacy to promoting vegetarian diets.

Finally, the food industry's promotion of vegetarian foods, especially meat analogs (e.g., soy "burgers," tofu "hot dogs," and tempeh "bacon"), has contributed positively to the promotion of vegetarian diets. Sales of these meat analog products totalled $56 million in 1994 (Golbitz 1996). These products enable people to explore a vegetarian diet while maintaining the conventions of the typical U.S. meal (Maurer 1996). Advertising promotions by large food companies—such as an ad featured on the weekly Sunday television talk-shows promoting a veggie burger by Green Giant—contribute positively to the vegetarian environment by normalizing vegetarian foods. As the food industry continues to profit from the sales of meat analogs and other specialty vegetarian products, we are likely to see a continued "mainstreaming" of vegetarian diets (Beardsworth and Keil 1993, 1997:238–41).

These features of the vegetarian movement's cultural environment exemplify the complexity of circumstances that may affect a social movement's impression management techniques. Successful techniques of neutralizing negative images in the cultural sphere will likely take advantage of such positive conditions as those discussed above. Managing a social movement's collective self depends on reflective leaders and advocates who are aware of positive and negative cultural circumstances, and who negotiate strategies that will capitalize on the existing environment. How these leaders accomplish these important tasks in an interactional setting is an area worthy of further exploration.

ACKNOWLEDGMENTS

Thanks to Joel Best, Thomas Burger, Jeffery Sobal, and Rhys H. Williams, whose ideas all contributed to the development of this chapter. I also would like to thank Susan Quarti for her research assistance.

REFERENCES

Amato, P., and S. Partridge. 1989. *The New Vegetarians: Promoting Health and Protecting Life.* New York: Plenum.

American Academy of Pediatrics. 1977. "Nutritional Aspects of Vegetarianism, Health Foods, and Fad Diets." *Pediatrics* 59(3):460–64.

American Dietetic Association. 1975. "Position Paper on Food and Nutrition Misinformation on Selected Topics." *Journal of the American Dietetic Association* 66:277–80.

———. 1980. "Position Paper on the Vegetarian Approach to Eating." *Journal of the American Dietetic Association* 77:61–68.

———. 1988. "Position of the American Dietetic Association: Vegetarian Diets." *Journal of the American Dietetic Association* 88(3):351–55.

———. 1993. "Position of the American Dietetic Association: Vegetarian Diets." *Journal of the American Dietetic Association* 93(11):1317–19.

———. 1997. "Position of the American Dietetic Association: Vegetarian Diets." *Journal of the American Dietetic Association* 97(11):1317–21.

Appleby, P. N., M. Thorogood, J. I. Mann, and T. J. Key. 1998. "Low Body Mass Index in Non-Meat Eaters: The Possible Roles of Animal Fat, Dietary Fibre, and Alcohol." *International Journal of Obesity* 22:454–60.

Apte, M. L., and J. Katona-Apte. 1986. "Diet and Social Movements in American Society: The Last Two Decades." Pp. 26–33 in *Food in Change: Eating Habits from the Middle Ages to the Present Day,* edited by A. Fenton and E. Kisban. Scotland: John Donald.

Attwood, C. R. 1996. "When Vegetarian Families Encounter the Law . . . " *New Century Nutrition* (July):6–7.

Bakan, R., C. L. Birmingham, L. Aeberhardt, and E. M. Goldner. 1993. "Dietary Zinc Intake of Vegetarian and Nonvegetarian Patients with Anorexia Nervosa." *International Journal of Eating Disorders* 13(2):229–33.

Bargen, R. 1979. *The Vegetarian's Self-Defense Manual.* Wheaton, IL: Theosophical.

Barnard, N. 1992. *A Physician's Slimming Guide for Permanent Weight Control.* Summertown, TN: The Book.

Beardsworth, A., and T. Keil. 1992. "The Vegetarian Option: Varieties, Conversions, Motives, and Careers." *Sociological Review* 40:253–93.

———. 1993. "Contemporary Vegetarianism in the U.K.: Challenge and Incorporation?" *Appetite* 20:229–34.

———. 1997. *Sociology on the Menu.* London: Routledge.

Belasco, W. J. 1993. *Appetite for Change.* Ithaca, NY: Cornell University Press.

Benford, R. D., and S. Hunt. 1992. "Dramaturgy and Social Movements: The Social Construction and Communication of Power." *Sociological Inquiry* 62(1):36–55.

Best, J. 1994. "Troubling Children: Children and Social Problems." Pp. 3–19 in *Troubling Children: Studies of Children and Social Problems*, edited by J. Best. Hawthorne, NY: Aldine de Gruyter.

Brody, J. 1998. "Many Experts Question Spock's Diet for Children." *New York Times*, 20 June, p. A1.

Brown, J. 1995. "Summerfest Points to Ponder." *Grapevine* (Newsletter of the Triangle Vegetarian Society) 9(4):11.

Brulle, R. J. 1996. "Environmental Discourse and Social Movement Organizations: A Historical and Rhetorical Perspective on the Development of U.S. Environmental Organizations." *Sociological Inquiry* 66(1):58–83.

Burke, E. C., and D. M. Huse. 1979. "Multiple Nutritional Deficiencies in Children on Vegetarian Diets." *Mayo Clinic Proceedings* 54(8):549–50.

Charles, N., and M. Kerr. 1988. *Women, Food, and Families*. Manchester: Manchester University Press.

Cooper, C. K., T. N. Wise, and L. S. Mann. 1985. "Psychological and Cognitive Characteristics of Vegetarians." *Psychosomatics* 26(6):521–27.

Dietz, T., A. S. Frisch, L. Lalof, P. C. Stern, and G. A. Guagnano. 1995. "Values and Vegetarianism: An Exploratory Analysis." *Rural Sociology* 60(3):533–42.

Dwyer, J. T., R. F. Kandel, L. D. Mayer, and J. Mayer. 1974. "The 'New' Vegetarians." *Journal of the American Dietetic Association* 64:376–82.

Eisman, G., with M. Ball and A. Green. 1994. *The Most Noble Diet: Food Selection and Ethics*. Burdett, NY: Diet Ethics.

Erhard, D. 1973. "The New Vegetarians: Part One—Vegetarianism and Its Medical Consequences." *Nutrition Today* 8(6):4–12.

———. 1974. "The New Vegetarians: Part Two—The Zen Macrobiotic Movement and Other Cults Based on Vegetarianism." *Nutrition Today* 9(1):20–27.

Friedson, E. 1970. *Professional Dominance*. Chicago: Atherton.

Gamson, W. A. 1988. "Political Discourse and Collective Action." *International Social Movement Research* 1:219–44.

Garner, D. M. 1997. "The 1997 Body Image Survey Results." *Psychology Today* 30(January/February):30–44, 75–84.

Goffman, E. 1959. *The Presentation of Self in Everyday Life*. Garden City, NY: Doubleday.

Golbitz, P. 1996. "Meat Alternative Sales Sizzling." *Natural Foods Merchandiser*, January. On-line: http://www.newhope.com/public/nfm/.

Gregory, D. 1973. *Dick Gregory's Natural Diet for Folks Who Eat: Cookin' with Mother Nature*. New York: Harper & Row.

Hesse-Biber, S. 1996. *Am I Thin Enough Yet?* London: Oxford University Press.

Hill, G. 1984a. "Special Diet Set for Sisters Who Refused to Eat." *Washington Post*, 15 June, p. C1.

———. 1984b. "Women Defend Faith, Seek Return of Children." *Washington Post*, 24 June, p. C1.

———. 1984c. "Underweight Girl Leaves Hospital." *Washington Post*, 6 July, p. B3.

Hurlburt, V. J., and M. Nouri. 1998. "On Becoming and Being a Vegetarian: Decisions and Commitments." Paper presented at the Eastern Sociological Society meetings, Philadelphia, PA.

Jabs, J., C. M. Devine, and J. Sobal. 1998a. "Personal Factors, Social Networks, and Environmental Resources in Maintaining Vegetarian Diets." *Canadian Journal of Dietetic Practice and Research* 59(4):183–189.

———. 1998b. "A Model of the Process of Adopting Vegetarian Diets: Health Vegetarians and Ethical Vegetarians." *Journal of Nutrition Education* 30:196–202

Janelle, K. C., and S. Barr. 1995. "Nutrient Intakes and Eating Behavior Scores of Vegetarian and Nonvegetarian Women." *Journal of the American Dietetic Association* 95(2):180–86.

Kadambari, R., S. Gowers, and A. Crisp. 1986. "Some Correlates of Vegetarianism in Anorexia Nervosa." *International Journal of Eating Disorders* 5(3):539–44.

Kalucy, R. S. 1987. "The 'New' Nutrition." *Medical Journal of Australia* 147:529–30.

Key, T., and G. Davey. 1996. "Prevalence of Obesity Is Low in People Who Do Not Eat Meat." *British Medical Journal* 313:816–17.

Knutsen, S. F. 1994. "Lifestyle and the Use of Health Services." *American Journal of Clinical Nutrition* 59 (suppl.):1171S–75S.

Krizmanic, J. 1992. "Here's Who We Are." *Vegetarian Times* (October):72–80.

Kubal, T. J. 1998. "The Presentation of Political Self: Cultural Resonance and the Construction of Collective Action Frames." *Sociological Quarterly* 39(4):539–54.

Lipsky, M. 1968. "Protest as a Political Resource." *American Political Science Review* 62:1144–58.

Lyman, H. No date. "Voice for a Viable Future." Audiotape from EarthSave Foundation, Santa Cruz, CA.

———. 1998. *Mad Cowboy: Plain Truth from the Cattle Rancher Who Won't Eat Meat.* New York: Scribner's.

Maurer, D. 1989. *Becoming a Vegetarian: Learning a Food Practice and Philosophy.* Unpublished master's thesis, East Tennessee State University, Johnson City.

———. 1995. "Meat as a Social Problem: Rhetorical Strategies in the Vegetarian Literature." Pp. 143–63 in *Eating Agendas: Food and Nutrition as Social Problems,* edited by D. Maurer and J. Sobal. Hawthorne, NY: Aldine de Gruyter.

———. 1996. "Tofu and Taste: Explicating the Relationships between Embodiment, Language, and Food Choice." *Humanity and Society* 20(3):61–76.

———. 1997. *The Vegetarian Movement in North America: An Examination of Collective Strategy and Movement Culture.* Unpublished doctoral dissertation, Department of Sociology, Southern Illinois University-Carbondale.

McAdam, D., J. D. McCarthy, and M. N. Zald. 1988. "Social Movements." Pp. 695–737 in *Handbook of Sociology,* edited by N. J. Smelser. Newbury Park, CA: Sage.

Messina, M., and V. Messina. 1996. *The Dietician's Guide to Vegetarian Diets.* Gaithersburg, MD: Aspen.

North American Vegetarian Society. No date. "Vegetarianism: Answers to the Most Commonly Asked Questions." Brochure. Dolgeville, NY: Author.

O'Connor, M. A., S. W. Touyz, S. M. Dunn, and P. J. V. Beumont. 1987. "Vegetarianism in Anorexia Nervosa? A Review of 116 Consecutive Cases." *Medical Journal of Australia* 147:540–42.

Ornish, D. 1993. *Eat More, Weigh Less*. New York: HarperCollins.

Ossipow, L. 1995. "Vegetarianism and Fatness: An Undervalued Perception of the Body." Pp. 127–43 in *Social Aspects of Obesity*, edited by I. de Garine and N. J. Pollack. Luxembourg: Gordon and Breach.

Parham, B. 1979. *What's Wrong with Eating Meat?* Boulder, CO: Ananda Marga.

Powell, K. 1992. *Lifestyle as a Dimension of Social Movement Study: A Case Study of the Vegetarian Movement in the United States*. Unpublished Ph.D. dissertation, Department of Speech Communications, University of Georgia, Athens.

Putnam, J. J., and L. A. Duewer. 1995. "U.S. Per Capita Food Consumption: Record-High Meat and Sugars in 1994." *Food Review* 18(2):2–11.

Roberts, I. F., R. J. West, D. Ogilvie, and M. J. Dillon. 1979. "Malnutrition in Infants Receiving Cult Diets: A Form of Child Abuse." *British Medical Journal* 1:296–98.

Robeznieks, A. 1986. "How Many Are There?" *Vegetarian Times* (October):16–17.

Roe, D. A. 1986. "History of Promotion of Vegetable Cereal Diets." *Journal of Nutrition* 116:1355–63.

Sadalla, E., and J. Burroughs. 1981. "Profiles in Eating: Sexy Vegetarians and Other Diet-Based Stereotypes." *Psychology Today* (October):51–57.

Sapon, S. M., F. Berg, and L. Campanile. 1993. "Vegetarianism . . . A Diet for Life." Brochure. Dolgeville, NY: North American Vegetarian Society.

Simon, M. 1998. "Book Review of Mad Cowboy: Plain Truth from the Cattle Rancher Who Won't Eat Meat by Howard Lyman with Glen Merzer" *Vegan On-line Magazine*, June. www.geocities.com/RainForest/Vines/9234.

Snow, D. A., L. A. Zurcher, Jr., and S. Ekland-Olson. 1980. "Social Networks and Social Movements: A Microstructural Approach to Differential Recruitment." *American Sociological Review* 45:787–801.

Spencer, C. 1995. *The Heretic's Feast: A History of Vegetarianism*. Hanover, NH: University Press of New England.

Spock, B., and S. J. Parker. 1998. *Dr. Spock's Baby and Child Care*, 7th edition. New York: Pocket Books.

Stahler, C. 1994. "How Many Vegetarians Are There?" *Vegetarian Journal* 12(4):6–9.

Sykes, G. M., and D. Matza. 1957. "Techniques of Neutralization: A Theory of Delinquency." *American Sociological Review* 22:667–70.

Texas Department of Agriculture. 1996. "Perry Asks Attorney General to Seek Legal Action Against Talk Show Guest Over Mad Cow Comments." Press release on-line: http://www.agr.state.tx.us.

Todhunter, E. N. 1973. "Food Habits, Faddism, and Nutrition." *World Review of Nutrition and Dietetics* 16:286–317.

Toronto Vegetarian Association. 1995. "Vegetarianism—On the Rise." TVA Fact Sheet. Toronto: Author.

Twigg, J. 1979. "Food for Thought: Purity and Vegetarianism." *Religion* 9:13–35.

———. 1983. "Vegetarianism and the Meanings of Meat." Pp. 18–30 in *The Sociology of Food and Eating*, edited by A. Murcott. Aldershot: Gower.

Varner, G. E. 1994. "In Defense of the Vegan Ideal: Rhetoric and Bias in the Nutrition Literature." *Journal of Agricultural and Environmental Ethics* 7(1):29–40.

Wasserman, D., and C. Stahler. 1996. *Meatless Meals for Working People*. Baltimore: Vegetarian Resource Group.

Weber, M. 1922, 1963. *The Sociology of Religion.* Translated by E. Fischoff. Boston: Beacon.

West, E. D. 1972. "The Psychological Health of Vegans Compared with Two Other Groups." *Plant Foods and Human Nutrition* 2:147.

Whorton, J. 1977. "'Tempest in a Flesh-Pot': The Formulation of a Physiological Rationale for Vegetarianism." *Journal of the History of Medicine and Allied Sciences* 32:115–39.

Williams, R. H. 1995. "Constructing the Public Good: Social Movements and Cultural Resources." *Social Problems* 42:124–44.

Woolsey, M. M. 1997. "The Eating Disordered Vegetarian." *Healthy Weight Journal* 11(2):32–34.

Worsley, A., and G. Skrzypiec. 1997. "Teenage Vegetarianism: Beauty or the Beast?" *Nutrition Research* 17(3):391–404.

Zdrodowski, D. 1996. "Eating Out: The Experience of Eating in Public for the 'Overweight' Woman." *Women's Studies International Forum* 19(6):655–64.

Zey, M. and W. A. McIntosh. 1992. "Predicting Intent to Consume Beef: Normative Versus Attitudinal Influences." *Rural Sociology* 57(2):250–65.

Zmora, E., R. Gorodischer, and J. Bar-Ziv. 1979. "Multiple Nutritional Deficiencies in Infants from a Strict Vegetarian Community." *American Journal of Diseases of Children* 133(February):141–44.

12

The Size Acceptance Movement and the Social Construction of Body Weight

JEFFERY SOBAL

INTRODUCTION

Social problems are often tightly intertwined with organized social movements that work to define, draw attention to, and change the conditions associated with those particular problems (Blumer 1971; Bash 1995; Mauss 1975; Troyer 1989). This chapter will examine how a social movement that opposes the stigmatization of obese individuals that has come to be called the size acceptance movement has played a role in the way body weight is constructed as a social problem in the United States and other postindustrial societies. The size acceptance movement has been the subject of historical chronologies by leaders in the movement (e.g., Fabrey 1995; Stimson 1995), reflective discussion by movement participants (e.g., Cooper 1998), journalistic reports (e.g., Fraser 1997), and acknowledgment by the mainstream weight loss community (e.g., Brownell 1993). While social scientists have examined participants in the size acceptance movement (e.g., Allison, Basile, and Yuker 1991; Hughes and Degher 1993), little social science analysis has examined size acceptance as a movement (Sobal 1995).

A variety of perspectives offer viewpoints for examining social movements (Lofland 1996; Morris and Mueller 1992; Oberschall 1973). A social constructionist orientation assumes that a process operates where social movement organizations and their participants actively interpret, define, negotiate, and manage themselves to advance their interests as they engage with contextual challenges and opportunities. The variety of individuals and organizations that are included in a social movement operate in a coordinated way to make claims to advance their interests in relationship to similar and opposing claims made by others (Lofland 1996). Con-

231

structionist perspectives tend to focus on cultural, symbolic, and ideological aspects of social movements, as seen in new social movement theory
(Larana, Johnston, and Gusfield 1994), and are often contrasted with the
more objectivist focus of resource mobilization theories (Cohen 1985),
which focus on instrumental and rational use of resources to achieve
movement goals (McCarthy and Zald 1977).

Information for this analysis came from a variety of sources. Content
analysis (Weber 1985) was used to analyze published and computerized
information generated by the size acceptance movement, the mass media,
and medical sources. Literature from the size acceptance movement is frequently cited here as evidence because it is visible, concrete, has a dated
origin, and can be widely disseminated for individual consumption. However, much of the important discourse and many events of the movement
operate beyond the scope of publications, and are less accessible and permanent as a social and historical record. In addition to publications,
participant observation (Spradley 1980) was performed at national and
local events of size acceptance organizations. Ethnographic interviews
(Spradley 1979) were conducted with leaders and participants in the size
acceptance movement, medical organizations, and the public.

BODY WEIGHT AS A SOCIAL PROBLEM

In contemporary postindustrial societies the interpretation, evaluation,
and management of body weight has become a highly contested social
arena. The weight arena can be seen as a social space where competing
interest groups attempt to define, typify, draw attention to, and promote
various aspects of weight as social problems (Hilgartner and Bosk 1988).
There is limited carrying capacity in an arena such as body weight, and
competing groups draw upon different themes in attempts to receive
attention. Discourses about weight employ many deeper social and cultural concerns about health, gender, beauty, class, race, and other contentious social concerns.

Over the course of the twentieth century an increasing emphasis on slimness has emerged and developed (Brumberg 1988; Schwartz 1986; Seid
1989; Stearns 1997). The emphasis on thinness has broadened and intensified since the 1960s (Garner, Garfinkel, Schwartz, and Thompson 1980;
Morris, Cooper, and Cooper 1989; Wiseman, Gray, Mosimann, and Ahrens
1992), with weight concerns salient and even obsessive among women
(Germov and Williams 1996; Rodin, Silberstein, and Striegel-Moore 1984;
Schoenfielder and Wieser 1983; Tiggemann and Rothblum 1988). The rising
attention and concern about weight has led to a focus on women's bodies
as a lifelong project to be managed and achieved (Brumberg 1997).

The rise in emphasis on thinness was accompanied by a parallel rejection of fatness. Obesity became a stigmatized condition, a discredited characteristic that was perceived as a moral failure of fat people (Allon 1981; Sobal 1991a, 1995, 1999). Prejudice against fatness led to a labeling of large individuals as deviant (Goode 1996; Hughes and Degher 1993). Discrimination against large people permeated many arenas of life, including work, family, health, and everyday interactions (Sobal 1999).

The cultural focus on slimness in recent decades led to the development of a system of weight industries that developed vested social, economic, and political interests in portraying high levels of body weight as a social problem (Sobal 1995). These included the weight loss, medical, pharmaceutical, fitness, food, dieting, apparel, fashion, and insurance industries, all of which operated in the role of moral entrepreneurs who have vested interests in promoting slimness and rejecting fatness (Becker 1963; Conrad 1975; Reissman 1983).

EMERGENCE OF THE SIZE ACCEPTANCE MOVEMENT

The size acceptance movement focuses on advocating for fat people who are stigmatized and discriminated against. Many movement participants use the term *fat* to describe themselves, and attempt to neutralize its connotation as seen in Schroeder's (1992) book title *Fat Is Not a Four Letter Word*. Body size dimensions other than weight could be, but have not been dealt with by a size acceptance movement. Thin people are typically admired, and have not developed a social movement to advance their acceptance. Tall people are also socially valued, although short people are negatively evaluated (Roberts and Herman 1986), but they have not been part of the size acceptance movement.

Size acceptance did not begin to emerge as a social movement until the late 1960s and early 1970s (Sobal 1995). Before then, a few individual pioneers spoke out for size acceptance in various arenas and some isolated groups were active for specific size cases, but a broader consciousness about the problem and organization around the issue did not exist. Understanding the development and growth of the size acceptance movement requires consideration of its social location with respect to other precursor and parallel social movements and particular social conditions related to the movement.

Precursor Movements. Postwar society in the United States bred skepticism and opposition to many established social patterns and institutions. During the 1960s social structures and values became unsettled, volatile, and turbulent. A variety of social movements developed, many challenging inequalities in the way particular segments of society were treated. Civil rights, women's rights, age rights, gay rights, and other movements emerged, mobilized resources, and changed social identities (Freeman 1983). These social movements developed and shared reform paradigms as well as strategies and techniques that were used as tools for social change. Social movements of the 1960s and 1970s captured the attention and imagination of the public (Freeman 1983), and led to a climate of protest that generated a variety of oppositional movements that dealt with other causes, such as the antiwar, antinuclear, and antipollution movements (Minkoff 1997).

The size acceptance movement was a product of race, gender, age, sexuality, and other precursor movements that blazed the trail, established methods for creating social change, and served as a training ground for some size activists. Size acceptance concerns arose from consciousness raising about inequality, stigmatization, and discrimination developed and modeled by other movements. Tactics and procedures pioneered by other movements laid the foundation for methods employed to advance size acceptance.

Precedent social movements continue to parallel the size acceptance movement, forming a networked set of movements that sometimes share ideology, enthusiasm, and strategies. For example, the many components of the women's movement (Buechler 1990) have provided institutional structures such as women's centers that have housed some size acceptance activities. However, few fat feminists (Stimson 1995) have come from or been tied to the mainstream women's movement and often feel alienated by the lack of recognition and attention to size acceptance issues.

Nondieting as an Allied Movement.   In addition to larger precursor movements, an alliance with another movement catalyzed attention and resources for body weight. Joining the streams of development of two movements at a particular juncture can produce a special window of opportunity for social reform (Kingdon 1984). What was widely called the nondiet movement (Berg 1992) became a close ally of size acceptance, even though the two movements draw from different populations of leaders and participants. The interaction of the two movements promoted developments beyond what might have otherwise occurred. The nondiet movement was a backlash against dieting and a reaction to public concerns about thinness and eating disorders, which fit well with size acceptance ideas, although people associated with nondieting may not actually endorse acceptance of very large people.

Widespread dissatisfaction with the emphasis on thinness and promotion of dieting for women emerged in response to body weight concerns becoming what Rodin et al. (1984) termed "normative discontent." By

1980 there were increasing attacks on the emphasis on thinness and dieting. The orientations of these challenges ranged from feminist (Orbach 1978, 1982) to sociological (Allon 1981; Millman 1980). Dieting to lose weight had become almost obligatory among many women beyond puberty, but was plagued by a terrible lack of reported success in achieving and maintaining weight loss (Cogan and Rothblum 1992; Holmes, Zysow, and Delbanco 1989; Stuart, Mitchell, and Jensen 1981; Wing and Jeffery 1979). Backlash against stringent thinness standards, compulsive aspects of dieting, low weight loss success rates, and fraudulent and even harmful side effects of some diets fueled the nondiet movement. The nondiet movement is partially a reaction to overmedicalization of eating and weight, where health professionals, often dietitians and nutritionists, became "food cops" (Bergman 1992) and "health Nazis" (Edgley and Brissett 1990) in their zeal to promote thinness, despite conclusions as early as Stunkard and McLaren-Hume (1959) concluding that dieting is rarely successful.

The weight loss industry has been criticized and attacked from several directions. For several decades journalists have produced exposés of dieting practices and services (e.g., Wyden 1965; Fraser 1997). The medical and nutritional community regularly criticized most diets as "fads" and critiqued commercial weight loss organizations (e.g., Dwyer 1980; Dwyer and Lu 1993). Government agencies investigated false claims and fraudulent practices in dieting organizations (e.g., U.S. Congress 1990a, 1990b). All of these challenges to the weight loss industry damaged its attractiveness and credibility and typified its public image as untrustworthy and ineffective.

A crucial element in the emergence of the nondiet movement was the fear of eating disorders and broad efforts to protect women from what was widely construed as a scourge of anorexia nervosa and bulimia nervosa. Attention to and concern about pathological eating and eating disorders grew in the 1970s, escalated in the 1980s, and matured during the 1990s (Brumberg 1988; Hof and Nicolson 1996). Claims about an epidemic of anorexia nervosa and bulimia grew, but then declined under closer scientific scrutiny (Hof and Nicolson 1996). Eating disorders moved from being curiosities and even glamorous conditions to being stigmatized forms of deviance (Sobal and Bursztyn 1998; Way 1995). The reaction against eating disorders provided a basis for opposition to notions that thinness is always desirable, and generated strong negative reactions to dieting and weight loss in general. Broad publicity about eating disorders engendered widespread concern about epidemics of adolescent girls starving themselves to death.

A therapeutic community for treating eating disorders developed, gained power, and established vested interests in continuing its efforts to emphasize the harms of pursuing thinness. The nondieting orientation was often grounded in psychological and psychiatric ideas, offering individual therapy rather than focusing on political changes. Another strand of nondiet thinking drawn from health and fitness professionals who converted from or were outside mainstream activities in their professions that emphasized thinness and weight loss. Dissatisfaction with the existing weight loss culture and concern about eating disorders fed the development of the nondiet movement. Nondieting therapies and programs emerged to help women deal with weight as a personal problem (Ciliska 1990; Kano 1989; Polivy and Herman 1992). It is notable that some weight loss plans recognized the dissatisfaction with dieting and also claimed that they were nondiet programs, joining the bandwagon of the rejection of dieting when they were actually recycled diets that took on new names.

A concept underlying the shift toward nondieting was that restrained eating violates natural hungers, leading to bingeing and consequent weight gain (Polivy and Herman 1983). A variety of other nondiet concepts emerged as variations on the theme of escape from the rigid and diet-based compulsive eating (Hirschmann and Munter 1988), including intuitive eating (Tribole and Resch 1995), purposeful eating (Siegel 1997), and enjoyable eating (Omichinski 1993). Nondiet efforts to prevent and curb eating disorders were compatible, for the most part, with size acceptance movement ideology, and the two movements often reinforced each other and aligned efforts.

Social Conditions.   Demographic changes that resulted from the aging of the baby boom cohort contributed to conditions that facilitated the earlier culture of thinness and later reactions of size acceptance. During the 1960s an accelerating emphasis on thinness was based in the growing focus on the youth culture of the baby boom, with thin adolescents adopted as ideals for body shape. Mass media and mass marketing in the fashion industry blossomed to emphasize thinness during this period. Pressures to be thin continued to diffuse and penetrate throughout society, and body dissatisfaction and dieting continued to be almost normative among women. The general aging of the population as the baby boom matured and the rise in fatness in the United States in the 1980s (Kuczmarski, Flegal, Campbell, and Johnson 1994) moved many away from the earlier youth culture and its focus on appearance.

Simultaneously, the medical community accelerated the medicalization of obesity and increased its attention and efforts to encouraging weight loss to enhance health and prevent illness (Sobal 1995). However, medical authority and medical dominance among the health professions began eroding during the 1980s (Starr 1982). Other professions such as psychology began to intrude into medical turf, bringing different concerns and therapeutic perspectives about eating disorders and body image that conflicted with the physiological focus of the biomedical model.

THE SIZE ACCEPTANCE MOVEMENT: STRUCTURE AND PROCESSES

Size acceptance ideas developed in the United States in the late 1960s as reactions to pervasive stigmatization and discrimination against fat people. The movement grew and developed a structure that included a loose collective of organizations, groups, and individuals connected through interpersonal relationships and more formal communication channels such as publications, and more recently the Internet. The underlying ideology of the size acceptance movement focused on exposing, combating, and preventing fatism, weightism, and sizism; promoting size diversity and tolerance; and developing a size-accepting, size-neutral, and size-friendly society. Size acceptance became a new conceptual model that was used in the broader social construction of body weight, opposing the moral and medical models that dominated discourse about fatness and thinness (Sobal 1995). The major strategies of the size acceptance movement were to use political changes to collectively challenge mainstream beliefs and practices and, at the same time, create cultural change in ideas about weight in their emphasis on fat pride, fat liberation, and fat power.

Like most social movements, several organizations have played a crucial role in advancing the size acceptance movement. The National Organization to Advance Fat Acceptance (NAAFA) is the oldest membership organization for people of size, founded in 1969. Association for the Health Enrichment of Large Persons (AHELP) held its first conference in 1991 as an organization for health professionals, including psychologists, dietitians/nutritionists, nurses, exercise professionals, social workers, educators, and researchers (but few physicians) tied more to the nondieting movement than the size acceptance movement. Many other allied groups have existed in the size acceptance network, including diverse small activist groups (Fat Underground, Fat Liberation Front, Council on Size and Weight Discrimination) and other types of groups (Abundia, Ample Opportunity, Body Image Task Force, Largesse). The structure of the size acceptance movement has been and continues to be highly diffuse. NAAFA, the largest organization, has forty local chapters, which all have considerable autonomy.

The number of people involved in the size acceptance movement is relatively small. NAAFA is the largest and only national organization, claiming approximately five thousand members. This is only a tiny fraction of the estimated third of the U.S. adult population defined by health researchers as overweight (Kuczmarski et al. 1994) or the large number of people who are trying to lose weight (Serdula, Williamson, Anda, Levy, Heaton, and Byers 1994). Size activists who form the size acceptance movement's leadership, act as crusaders, and serve as experts probably number only in the hundreds.

The size acceptance movement includes two major components (1) political activism that attempts to reform the values and practices of society about body weight, and (2) social support that provides a refuge for large people from the intolerance of a thin society through assistance and companionship. This duality of function is characteristic of many social movement organizations, with different organizations offering varying balances between sociality and activism. The concept of dual group function has long been discussed by social scientists, with small groups being seen as having both task and social functions. Consideration of the presence and change of such duality may offer insights into current debates about structure versus identity in social movements (Cohen 1985). Shifts in social and political balance in size acceptance are evidenced in the change of name (but not the acronym) of NAAFA from the National Association to Aid Fat Americans to the National Association to Advance Fat Acceptance.

Political Activism. The size acceptance movement organizes and engages in a variety of political activities to promote its causes. Several types of protest events (Minkoff 1997) are employed, including rallies (the Million Pound March was held in 1998), boycotts (e.g., of Coca-Cola, Southwest Airlines, and other companies), and other forms of civil disobedience like protests and picketing. Other strategic tactics include activism to gain attention to size issues by designating events (International No-Diet Day, Size Acceptance Month), workshops (Treating the Dieting Casualty), support groups, letter writing, educational services, and programs.

An important component of the size acceptance movement is producing materials to communicate its concerns and ideas. Popular books describing the problems of being large and promoting size acceptance began with Louderback (1970). By the 1990s such books were streaming out of publishing houses (e.g., Cooper 1998; Erdman 1995; Garrison 1993; Goodman 1995; Thone 1997). Self-help books offering practical and instrumental support for large people emerged and proliferated, offering help in exercise and fitness (Kingsbury 1988; Lyons and Burgard 1990; Smith 1984), beauty and fashion (Aronson 1997; Nanfeldt 1996), health care (Sullivan 1997), and other areas. Glossy magazines for large people are distributed to general audiences (*Radiance, Extra!*), women of color (*Belle*), women with fashion interests (*Mode, Big Beautiful Woman*), and men who are fat admirers (*Dimensions*) and seek erotica (*Plumpers and Big Women,*

Buf). Nonglossy "zines" exist for general audiences (*Fat!So?*, *Rump Parlia-ment*), lesbians (*FaT GiRL*), and gay men (*Bulk Male*). Formal size accept-ance organizations and informal groups also distribute newsletters. Numerous computerized web sites, listservers, and other electronic ser-vices function to promote the movement and facilitate communication among those who are involved but scattered across various locations.

Size acceptance and nondieting agendas have been promoted by gain-ing access to practitioners in the health professions, where the relativistic concept of paradigm developed by Kuhn (1970) was employed to claim that a "new weight paradigm" had emerged (e.g., Parham 1996; Robinson, Hoerr, Petersmark, and Anderson 1995). Strategies for gaining attention, disseminating their message, and developing converts included establish-ing an alternative image, making professional presentations, and dissem-inating publications. During the mid-1990s, size activists and nondiet practitioners worked to get on the agenda of many conferences of health professionals, including nutrition educators, dietitians, psychologists, public health workers, and exercise scientists. Size acceptance has received some legitimation by the presence of activists within established institu-tions, such as large HMOs (Kaiser Permanente) and government nutrition programs (USDA Cooperative Extension). Size activists established offi-cially recognized membership groups in some professional nutrition organizations, such as the Society for Nutrition Education's 1995 charter-ing of a Division of Nutrition and Weight Realities. *Obesity and Health* was a journal established in 1987 primarily for weight loss professionals, and its name was changed to *Healthy Weight Journal* in 1994 to expand its cov-erage to all aspects of weight within its scope, with a new emphasis on nondieting and size acceptance.

Crusaders are individuals who take leadership in advancing particular causes (Sobal 1995). There are a number of people who play that role in the size acceptance movement, often portraying themselves as size activists. The role of a crusader is to gain positive public attention, make strong pub-lic claims, counter opposing claims, and produce ideas and resources for the movement. Crusaders are perceived as leaders within and outside the movement, and serve as role models for recruiting new participants and inspiring current participants to additional activism. Some size acceptance crusaders use their positions in academia or the health care system to pro-mote the cause of the movement, others spend their nonworking hours in movement activities, while yet others leave their jobs and earn a living through their movement work. Without the efforts of crusaders, social movements have difficulty maintaining or expanding their influence among competing interests.

Experts are authorities who are called upon to make and refute specific claims (Conrad 1992; Sobal 1995). Experts are invoked for support by claimants about contested issues, with rival groups of experts competing to develop more adherents to their portrayal of reality (Berger and Luckmann 1966). The size acceptance movement searches for experts in the scientific community who can be invoked to support the goals of the movement, and opposing camps do the same. Different types of expertise exist, including technical and experiential. Most, but not all technical experts about body weight in the medical community do not support acceptance of fatness, instead applying a biomedical model to obesity that assumes thinner is healthier (Sobal 1995). However, fat people are experiential experts about the psychological, social, and cultural aspects of weight, and they often serve as important experts in making claims under a political model of body weight that focuses on human rights aspects of weight such as discrimination and stigmatization.

Social Support. As an organized social movement, size acceptance offers several forms of social support to its participants. Emotional social support is an important resource supplied by the size acceptance movement. In the broader society thinness is the reigning value, but the size acceptance movement offers its large sized participants who may weigh 300, 400, 500, or more pounds a refuge from a world organized for thinner people. By offering large people acceptance and positive evaluation, the movement can become a functional "family" for individuals oppressed because of their size.

Fat Admirers ("FAs" as they call themselves) are sexually attracted to large and often extremely fat people. The most visible FAs are men attracted to large women (Goode 1983; Klein 1996; NAAFA 1995), although there are gay male FAs who have their own organizations (e.g., Girth and Mirth). Women FAs attracted to large men, and large women, also exist but are less widely known outside their circles. FAs play a role in developing and maintaining the size acceptance movement by providing romantic opportunities that make the movement more socially attractive to people of size. FAs also make some contributions to activist activities of the movement, with some playing important roles in founding and leading size acceptance organizations as well as contributing some important financial support. However, for most FAs involvement in the movement is more social than political. Overall, FAs help legitimate the social functions of the movement, drawing large people into becoming involved and attending organized movement activities.

Another function of the size acceptance movement is to provide instrumental social support for its members. The women's fashion industry has largely emphasized extreme slimness and is seen by many in the movement as a barrier or even an opponent to size acceptance. Obtaining clothing, particularly for women, is a problematic experience for large people.

However, a segment of the fashion world is recently beginning to cater to larger women (and the market for products that they offer) and members of the size acceptance movement offer important marketing opportunities for such "plus size fashions" (women's dress size 12 and above). However, women who are labeled "supersize" (women's dress size 28 or greater) have extreme difficulty buying clothes, except at size movement functions and through mail order channels promoted through the size acceptance movement. Large women models spread messages about self-acceptance and beauty, like Stella Jolles Reichman (1977), who served as spokeswoman for the Lane Bryant clothing stores for larger women, and more recently Emme Aronson (1997), who is a leading model for plus sizes. In 1996, *Mode* appeared as the first fashion magazine for full-figured women, beginning to legitimize the size acceptance niche in the broader fashion world and to make more clothing styles available to large women.

Size Acceptance and the Social Construction of Body Weight

The size acceptance movement has struggled to gain acknowledgment in the body weight arena, and appears to have gained a place on the agenda. In the weight arena, size activists and size acceptance organizations have broken into the circle of sources that the news media seek out, becoming a part of what has been conceptualized as the news web (Tuchman 1978). This may not have led to large changes in the way most of the general population deals with weight, but has influenced some individuals and groups. Most significantly, size acceptance has gained sufficient attention to offer a political counterpoint to the largely medical and moral discussion of body weight, altering the shape of current social discourse on weight issues.

The impacts of size acceptance on the public construction of body weight reflect the size and structure of the movement, with the relatively small and diffuse organizations, groups, and individuals influencing a variety of specific and local decisions, but not leading to sweeping social changes. The power of the movement tends to be cultural, rather than economic and political, with few financial or governmental resources to draw upon. While there are powerful moral entrepreneurs that profit from encouraging thinness, such as pharmaceutical companies, there is less overt profit to be made in promoting size acceptance. That has led to difficulty in producing allies with financial and political power.

Tannen (1998) suggests that the contemporary United States is an "argument culture" that uses a model of opposition for structuring social interaction. This requires oppositional discourse, where there is an expectation that people will take different sides about issues and offer competing opinions. Often this is justified on the basis of fairness, where multiple viewpoints are given attention even though the issue is left unresolved. The use of oppositional discourse has created an important niche for the size acceptance movement in public discussion about body weight, which is a topic of great interest in the United States. Forums that discuss weight are increasingly offering spokespeople for the size acceptance agendas seats at the discussion table. Crusaders and experts in the size acceptance movement often accept such opportunities to offer counterclaims against advocates of thinness. This occurs across a range of settings, from medical forums where body weight issues are discussed to television talk shows that seek out of the ordinary and contrasting perspectives to draw audiences.

Advocates of thinness, whether for health or esthetic reasons, also benefit from the existence of the size acceptance voice in public discourse about weight. Attention to weight by the mass media focuses discussion on the topic, setting the public agenda and influencing people "not so much by telling them what to think, but by telling them what to think about" (Milio 1990:41). When proponents of size acceptance draw attention to weight as an issue, they also provide opportunities for those promulgating thinness to contribute an opposing view. Publicity for either side is advantageous to both because it draws attention to weight as a problem in society, setting a weight agenda that can be shaped in either direction. The presence of size acceptance advocates also helps supporters of weight control locate themselves by contrast in the landscape of weight discourse.

CONCLUSION

Currently the size acceptance movement includes a complex, constantly changing diversity of components, alliances, and oppositions that share some common as well as differing agendas. Size acceptance interests raise issues about obesity, but they are framed as political problems rather than the moral or medical problems used in past discourse about weight (Sobal 1995). The size acceptance movement has offered an alternative paradigm for discussing body weight as a social problem, providing an oppositional voice to medical and corporate interests that focus on thinness. Alliances with interests and use of tactics from the women's, civil rights, age rights, and other movements have been developed. These current characteristics of the size acceptance movement are shaped by several attributes that will influence future developments.

The size acceptance movement is highly gendered, with a majority female membership. The gendered nature of the movement strongly shapes its activities, both facilitating and hindering ties to the broader women's movements. After an intensive lobbying effort, the National

Organization for Women (NOW) passed an antisize discrimination resolution in 1990 (Smith 1995). However, most mainstream feminists are unre-
ceptive to size acceptance ideas, retaining normative esthetic values in
favor of thinness (Rothblum 1994). Radical fat feminism is a long-standing
part of the size acceptance movement, but draws less from the core of the
women's movement and more from radical left and progressive lesbian
quarters. The gendered nature of the size acceptance movement offers
both opportunities and constraints for its future development.

The size acceptance movement deals with issues that are culture bound,
with both obesity and eating disorders occurring primarily in Western,
postindustrial societies (Ritenbaugh 1982; Swartz 1985). The concept and
activities of size acceptance developed largely in the United States, but dif-
fusion to other countries has occurred. The U.S.-based NAAFA has members in other nations, and other organized groups are emerging, such as
the Canadian Association for Size Acceptance (CASA), Size (United Kingdom), and Size Acceptance Network (Australia). Size groups in other
nations may differ in their goals from those of the United States, such as
the Swedish group, which is more of an interest group for obese patients
seeking weight loss services than an activist group seeking fat acceptance.
Virtually all size acceptance activity has occurred in Western societies, and
it is not clear how other parts of the world such as Asia or Africa will react
to the concept of size acceptance.

The size acceptance movement includes relatively few minorities. In the
United States, many members of minority groups more positively value
larger bodies, while white Americans more often value thinness
(Kumanyika, Morssink, and Agurs 1992; Kumanyika, Wilson, and Guilford-Davenport 1993; Nichter and Nichter 1991; Parker, Nichter, Nichter,
Vuckovic, Sims, and Ritenbaugh 1995). It is not clear how the rising ethnic
diversity of the population (O'Hare 1992) will influence recruitment,
receptiveness, and resources for the size acceptance movement.

The size acceptance movement is linked to class, with few very low or
very high socioeconomic status participants. Obesity is associated with
low socioeconomic status (Sobal and Stunkard 1989; Sobal 1991b) in contrast to eating disorders, which are associated with high socioeconomic
status (Brumberg 1988). This contributes complex class associations and
problems for the movement. Alliances between size acceptance and nondieting movements may broaden the class base for both.

The recent alliances between the size acceptance movement and the
nondieting movement take advantage of commonalities between the two,
advancing both in a joint quest linking rejection of sizism and avoidance
of body discontent to gain broader public recognition of the body as a
social problem locus. The size acceptance movement has benefited greatly
by drawing upon professionals from the nondieting movement as experts

and crusaders. It is possible that these interests of the two movements may diverge in the future as conditions change, but currently the interaction of the two movements, primarily at the leadership level, has produced a synergy that has advanced alternative weight paradigms in many arenas.

Size acceptance has established a niche in the current arena of interests that deal with body weight, and its claims have shaped the discourse about weight in contemporary society. The location of the movement with respect to gender, ethnicity, culture, and class may shape future developments. The future trajectory of the size acceptance movement is not clear, and further social science analysis will be useful in interpreting whether it declines, is small and marginal, or grows in influence.

REFERENCES

Allison, D. B., V. C. Basile, and H. E. Yuker. 1991. "The Measurement of Attitudes towards and Beliefs about Obese Persons." *International Journal of Eating Disorders* 10(5):599–607.

Allon, N. 1981. "The Stigma of Overweight in Everyday Life." Pp. 130–74 in *Psychological Aspects of Obesity: A Handbook,* edited by B. J. Wolman. New York: Van Nostrand Reinhold.

Aronson, Emme (with Daniel Paisner). 1997. *True Beauty: Positive Attitudes and Practical Tips from the World's Leading Plus-size Model.* New York: Putnam.

Bash, H. H. 1995. *Social Problems and Social Movements: An Exploration into the Sociological Construction of Alternative Realities.* Highlands, NJ: Humanities.

Becker, H. S. 1963. *Outsiders.* New York: Free Press.

Berg, F. M. 1992. "Nondiet Movement Gains Strength." *Obesity and Health* 6(5): 85–90.

Berger, P., and T. Luckmann. 1966. *The Social Construction of Reality: A Treatise in the Sociology of Knowledge.* New York: Doubleday.

Bergman, Y. 1992. *Food Cop: Yolanda, Tell Us What to Eat.* New York: Bantam.

Blumer, H. 1971. "Social Problems as Collective Behavior." *Social Problems* 18: 298–306.

Brownell, K. D. 1993. "Whether Obesity Should Be Treated." *Health Psychology* 12(5): 339–41.

Brumberg, J. J. 1988. *Fasting Girls: The History of Anorexia Nervosa.* Cambridge, MA: Harvard University Press.

———. 1997. *The Body Project: An Intimate History of American Girls.* New York: Random House.

Buechler, S. M. 1990. *Women's Movements in the United States: Women's Suffrage, Equal Rights, and Beyond.* New Brunswick, NJ: Rutgers University Press.

Ciliska, D. 1990. *Beyond Dieting: Psychoeducational Interventions for Chronically Obese Women: A Non-dieting Approach.* New York: Brunner/Mazel.

Cogan, J., and E. Rothblum. 1992. "Outcomes of Weight Loss Programs." *Genetic, Social and General Psychology Monographs* 118:387–415.

Cohen, J. L. 1985. "Strategy or Identity: New Theoretical Paradigms and Contemporary Social Movements." *Social Research* 52(4):663–716.

Conrad, P. 1975. "The Discovery of Hyperkinesis: Notes on the Medicalization of Deviant Behavior." *Social Problems* 23:12–21.

———. 1992. "Medicalization and Social Control." *Annual Review of Sociology* 18:209–32.

Cooper, C. 1998. *Fat and Proud: The Politics of Size.* London: Women's Press.

Dwyer, J. T. 1980. "Sixteen Popular Diets: Brief Nutritional Analyses." Pp. 276–91 in *Obesity,* edited by A. J. Stunkard. Philadelphia: W. B. Saunders.

Dwyer, J. T., and D. Lu. 1993. "Popular Diets for Weight Loss: From Nutritionally Hazardous to Healthful." Pp. 231–52 in *Obesity: Theory and Therapy,* 2nd edition, edited by A. J. Stunkard and T. A. Wadden. New York: Raven.

Edgley, C., and D. Brissett 1990. "Health Nazis and the Cult of the Perfect Body: Some Polemical Observations." *Symbolic Interaction* 13(2):257–79.

Erdman, C. K. 1995. *Nothing to Lose: A Guide to Sane Living in a Larger Body.* San Francisco, CA: Harper Collins.

Fabrey, W. J. 1995. "A Mini-History of the Size Acceptance Movement: The First 25 Years." P. 7 in *Size Acceptance and Self Acceptance,* 2nd edition, edited by NAAFA, Inc. Sacramento, CA: NAAFA.

Fraser, L. 1997. *Losing It: America's Obsession with Weight and the Industry That Feeds on It.* New York: Dutton.

Freeman, J. 1983. *Social Movements of the Sixties and Seventies.* New York: Longman.

Garner, D. M., P. E. Garfinkel, D. Schwartz, and M. Thompson. 1980. "Cultural Expectations of Thinness in Women." *Psychological Reports* 47:483–91.

Garrison, T. (with D. Levitsky). 1993. *Fed Up! A Woman's Guide to Freedom from the Diet/Weight Prison.* New York: Carroll and Graf.

Germov, J., and L. Williams. 1996. "The Sexual Division of Dieting: Women's Voices." *Sociological Review* 44:630–47.

Goode, E. 1983. "The Fat Admirer." *Deviant Behavior* 4(2):175–202.

———. 1996. "The Stigma of Obesity." Pp. 332–40 in *Social Deviance,* edited by E. Goode. Boston: Allyn and Bacon.

Goodman, W. C. 1995. *The Invisible Woman: Confronting Weight Prejudice in America.* Carlsbad, CA: Gurze.

Hilgartner, S., and C. Bosk. 1988. "The Rise and Fall of Social Problems: A Public Arenas Model." *American Journal of Sociology* 94:53–78.

Hirschmann, J. R., and C. H. Munter. 1988. *Overcoming Overeating.* New York: Addison-Wesley.

Hof, S., and M. Nicolson. 1996. "The Rise and Fall of a Fact: The Increase in Anorexia Nervosa." *Sociology of Health and Illness* 18(5):581–608.

Holmes, M. D., B. Zysow, and T. L. Delbanco. 1989. "An Analytic Review of Current Therapies for Obesity." *Journal of Family Practice* 28:610–16.

Hughes, G., and D. Degher. 1993. "Coping with Deviant Identity." *Deviant Behavior* 14:297–315.

Kano, S. 1989. *Making Peace with Food: Freeing Yourself from the Diet/Weight Obsession.* New York: Harper and Row.

Kingdon, J. 1984. *Agendas, Alternatives, and Public Policy.* Boston: Little, Brown.

Kingsbury, B. D. 1988. *Full Figure Fitness.* Champaign, IL: Life Enhancement.

Klein, R. 1996. *Eat Fat*. New York: Pantheon.

Kuczmarski, R. J., K. M. Flegal, S. M. Campbell, and C. L. Johnson. 1994. "Increasing Prevalence of Overweight among U.S. Adults: The National Health and Nutrition Examination Surveys 1960–1991." *Journal of the American Medical Association* 272:205–11.

Kuhn, T. 1970. *The Structure of Scientific Revolutions*, 2nd edition. Chicago: University of Chicago Press.

Kumanyika, S., C. Morssink, and T. Agurs. 1992. "Models for Dietary and Weight Change in African-American Women: Identifying Cultural Components." *Ethnicity and Disease* 2:166–75.

Kumanyika, S., J. F. Wilson, and M. Guilford-Davenport. 1993. "Weight-Related Attitudes and Behaviors of Black Women." *Journal of the American Dietetic Association* 93:416–22.

Larana, E., H. Johnston, and J. R. Gusfield. 1994. *New Social Movements: From Ideology to Identity*. Philadelphia, PA: Temple University Press.

Lofland, J. 1996. *Social Movement Organizations: A Guide to Research on Insurgent Realities*. Hawthorne, NY: Aldine de Gruyter.

Louderback, L. 1970. *Fat Power: Whatever You Weigh Is Right*. New York: Hawthorne.

Lyons, P., and D. Burgard. 1990. *Great Shape: The First Fitness Guide for Large Women*. Palo Alto, CA: Bull.

Mauss, A. 1975. *Social Problems and Social Movements*. New York: J. B. Lippincott.

McCarthy, J. D., and M. Zald. 1977. "Resource Mobilization and Social Movements." *American Journal of Sociology* 82:1212–41.

Milio, N. 1990. *Nutrition Policy for Food-Rich Countries: A Strategic Analysis*. Baltimore, MD: Johns Hopkins University Press.

Millman, M. 1980. *Such a Pretty Face: Being Fat in America*. New York: W. W. Norton.

Minkoff, D. C. "The Sequencing of Social Movements." *American Sociological Review* 62:779–99.

Morris, A., T. Cooper, and P. J. Cooper. 1989. "The Changing Shape of Female Fashion Models." *International Journal of Eating Disorders* 8:593–96.

Morris, A. D., and C. M. Mueller (eds.). 1992. *Frontiers in Social Movement Theory*. New Haven, CT: Yale University Press.

National Association to Advance Fat Acceptance (ed.). 1995. *Size Acceptance and Self Acceptance*, 2nd edition. Sacramento, CA: Author.

Nanfeldt, S. 1996. *Plus Style: The Plus Size Guide to Looking Great*. New York: Penguin.

Nichter, M., and M. Nichter. 1991. "Hype and Weight." *Medical Anthropology* 13:249–84.

O'Hare, W. P. 1992. "America's Minorities: The Demographics of Diversity." *Population Bulletin* 47:1–46.

Oberschall, A. 1973. *Social Conflicts and Social Movements*. Englewood Cliffs, NJ: Prentice Hall.

Omichinski, L. 1993. *You Count, Calories Don't*. Winnipeg, Manitoba: TAMOS.

Orbach, S. 1978. *Fat Is a Feminist Issue*. New York: Berkeley.

———. 1982. *Fat Is a Feminist Issue II*. New York: Berkeley.

Parham, E. S. 1996. "Is There a New Weight Paradigm?" *Nutrition Today* 31(4):155–61.

Parker, S., M. Nichter, M. Nichter, N. Vuckovic, C. Sims, and C. Ritenbaugh. 1995. "Body Image and Weight Concerns among African American and White Adolescent Females: Differences That Make a Difference." *Human Organization* 54(2):103–14.

Polivy, J., and P. Herman. 1983. *Breaking the Diet Habit*. New York: Basic Books.

———. 1992. "Undieting: A Program to Help People Stop Dieting." *International Journal of Eating Disorders* 11:261–68.

Reichman, S. J. 1977. *Great Big Beautiful Doll: Everything for the Body and Soul of the Larger Woman*. New York: E. P. Dutton.

Reissman, C. K. 1983. "Women and Medicalization: A New Perspective." *Social Policy* 14:3–18.

Ritenbaugh, C. 1982. "Obesity as a Culture-Bound Syndrome." *Culture, Medicine, and Psychiatry* 6:347–61.

Roberts, J. V., and C. P. Herman. 1986. "The Psychology of Height: An Empirical Review." Pp. 113–40 in *Physical Appearance Stigma and Social Behavior*, edited by C. P. Herman, M. P. Zanna, and E. T. Higgins. Hillsdale, NJ: Lawrence Erlbaum Associates.

Robinson, J. I., S. L. Hoerr, K. A. Petersmark, and J. W. Anderson. 1995. "Redefining Success in Obesity Intervention: A New Paradigm." *Journal of the American Dietetic Association* 95(4):422–23.

Rodin, J., L. Silberstein, and R. Striegel-Moore. 1984. "Women and Weight: A Normative Discontent." Pp. 267–303 in *Nebraska Symposium on Motivation*. Lincoln: University of Nebraska Press.

Rothblum, E. D. 1994. "I'll Die for the Revolution but Don't Ask Me Not to Diet: Feminism and the Continuing Stigmatization of Obesity." Pp. 53–76 in *Feminist Perspectives on Eating Disorders*, edited by P. Fallon, M. A. Katzman, and S. C. Wooley. New York: Guilford.

Schoenfielder, L., and B. Wieser (eds.). 1983. *Shadow on a Tightrope: Writings by Women on Fat Oppression*. Iowa City, IA: Aunt Lute.

Schroeder, C. R. 1992. *Fat Is Not a Four Letter Word*. Minneapolis, MN: Chronimed.

Schwartz, H. 1986. *Never Satisfied: A Cultural History of Diets, Fantasies, and Fat*. New York: Free Press.

Seid, R. P. 1989. *Never Too Thin: Why Women Are at War with Their Bodies*. New York: Prentice Hall.

Serdula, M. K., D. F. Williamson, R. F. Anda, A. Levy, A. Heaton, and T. Byers. 1994. "Weight Control Practices in Adults: Results of a Multistate Telephone Survey." *American Journal of Public Health* 84:1821–24.

Siegel, K. 1997. "Purposeful Eating in the Nondiet Approach." *Healthy Weight Journal* 11:52.

Smith, A. 1984. *The Gifted Figure: Proportioning Exercises for Large Women*. Santa Barbara, CA: Capra.

Smith, S. 1995. "Building Bridges in the Movement between Past and Future." *Healthy Weight Journal* 9(3):53–54.

Sobal, J. 1991a. "Obesity and Nutritional Sociology: A Model for Coping with the Stigma of Obesity." *Clinical Sociology Review* 9:125–41.

———. 1991b. "Obesity and Socioeconomic Status: A Framework for Examining

Relationships between Physical and Social Variables." *Medical Anthropology* 13(3):231–47.

———. 1995. "The Medicalization and Demedicalization of Obesity." Pp. 67–90 in *Eating Agendas: Food and Nutrition as Social Problems*, edited by D. Maurer and J. Sobal. Hawthorne, NY: Aldine de Gruyter.

———. 1999. "Sociological Analysis of the Stigmatization of Obesity." Pp. 187–204 in *A Sociology of Food and Nutrition: The Social Appetite*, edited by J. Germov and L. Williams. New York: Oxford University Press.

Sobal, J., and M. Bursztyn. 1998. "Dating People with Anorexia Nervosa and Bulimia Nervosa: Attitudes and Beliefs of University Students." *Women and Health* 27(3):71–87.

Sobal, J., and A. J. Stunkard. 1989. "Socioeconomic Status and Obesity: A Review of the Literature." *Psychological Bulletin* 105(2):260–75.

Spradley, J. P. 1979. *The Ethnographic Interview*. New York: Holt.

———. 1980. *Participant Observation*. New York: Holt.

Starr, P. 1982. *The Social Transformation of American Medicine*. New York: Basic Books.

Stearns, P. 1997. *Fat History: Bodies and Beauty in the Modern West*. New York: New York University Press.

Stimson, K. W. 1995. "A Fat Feminist Herstory." Pp. 8–10 in *Size Acceptance and Self Acceptance*, 2nd edition, edited by NAAFA, Inc. Sacramento, CA: NAAFA.

Stuart, R. B., C. Mitchell, and J. A. Jensen. 1981. "Therapeutic Options in the Management of Obesity." Pp 321–53 in *Medical Psychology: Contributions to Behavioral Medicine*, edited by C. K. Prokop, and L. A. Bradley. New York: Academic.

Stunkard, A., and M. McLaren-Hume. 1959. "The Results of Treatment of Obesity." *Archives of Internal Medicine* 103:79–85.

Sullivan, J. 1997. *Size Wise: A Catalog of More Than 1000 Resources for Living with Confidence and Comfort at Any Size*. New York: Avon.

Swartz, L. 1985. "Anorexia Nervosa as a Culture-bound Syndrome." *Social Science and Medicine* 20:725–30.

Tannen, D. 1998. *The Argument Culture: Moving from Debate to Dialogue*. New York: Random House.

Thone, R. R. 1997. *Fat—A Fate Worse Than Death? Women, Weight, and Appearance*. New York: Haworth.

Tiggemann, M., and E. D. Rothblum. 1988. "Gender Differences in Social Consequences of Perceived Overweight in the United States and Australia." *Sex Roles* 18:75–86.

Tribole, E., and E. Resch. 1995. *Intuitive Eating*. New York: St. Martin's.

Troyer, R. 1989. "Are Social Problems and Social Movements the Same Thing?" Pp. 41–58 in *Perspectives on Social Problems*, Vol. 1, edited by J. Holstein, and G. Miller. Greenwich, CT: JAI.

Tuchman, G. 1978. *Making News*. New York: Free Press.

U.S. Congress. 1990a. *Juvenile Dieting, Unsafe Over-the-Counter Diet Products, and Recent Enforcement Efforts by the Federal Trade Commission*. Hearing before the Subcommittee on Regulation, Business Opportunities, and Energy of the Committee on Small Business, House of Representatives. Washington: U.S. Government Printing Office.

————. 1990b. *Deception and Fraud in the Diet Industry*. Hearing before the Subcommittee on Regulation, Business Opportunities, and Energy of the Committee on Small Business, House of Representatives. Washington: U.S. Government Printing Office.

Way, K. 1995. "Never Too Rich . . . or Too Thin: The Role of Stigma in the Social Construction of Anorexia Nervosa." Pp. 91–113 in *Eating Agendas: Food and Nutrition as Social Problems,* edited by D. Maurer and J. Sobal. Hawthorne, NY: Aldine de Gruyter.

Weber, R. P. 1985. *Basic Content Analysis*. Newbury Park, CA: Sage.

Wing, R., and R. W. Jeffery. 1979. "Outpatient Treatments of Obesity: A Comparison of Methodology and Clinical Results." *International Journal of Obesity* 3:261–79.

Wiseman, C., J. J. Gray, J. E. Mosimann, and A. H. Ahrens. 1992. "Cultural Expectations of Thinness in Women: An Update." *International Journal of Eating Disorders* 11:85–89.

Wyden, P. 1965. *The Overweight Society*. New York: William Morrow.

Biographical Sketches of the Contributors

S. Bryn Austin is a Doctoral Candidate in the Department of Health and Social Behavior at the Harvard School of Public Health in Cambridge, Massachusetts. Her primary areas of interest are the prevention of eating disorders and the uses of the media in public health. Her work has appeared in *Culture, Medicine and Psychiatry, Cultural Critique, Journal of Studies on Alcohol,* and in several book chapters.

John Germov is a Lecturer in Sociology in the Department of Sociology and Anthropology at the University of Newcastle, Australia. He is author or coauthor of several books, including *Second Opinion: An Introduction to Health Sociology* (1998) and *Social Appetite: An Introduction to the Sociology of Food and Nutrition* (1999), and articles on health policy, legal aid, education, and medical fraud. His research interests include health policy, post-Fordist/postbureaucratic workplace change, public sector restructuring, gender, dieting, and body image.

Mark T. Hamin received his doctorate in 1998 from the Department of History and Sociology of Science at the University of Pennsylvania. His dissertation was titled *Tables Turned, Palates Curbed: Elements of Energy, Economy, and Equilibrium in American Food Science, 1880–1930.* His research interests focus on the history of nutrition and food research, and he has contributed papers on the topic to books such as *Landscapes of Technology* (1998). He currently resides in Ames, Iowa.

Sally Horrocks is a Lecturer in the Department of Economic and Social History at the University of Leicester, United Kingdom. Her work includes analysis of research and development in the food manufacturing industry, examining the response of the industry to developments in the nutritional sciences during the interwar period. Currently she is studying research and development in British manufacturing industries since 1945, as well as the history of medicine and nutritional sciences.

Donna Maurer is a John S. Knight Postdoctoral Fellow in the Writing Program at Cornell University. In 1997, she received her doctorate in Sociology from Southern Illinois University-Carbondale, where she won the Outstanding Dissertation Award. She coedited, with Jeffery Sobal, *Eating Agendas: Food and Nutrition as Social Problems* (1995). She is currently completing a book on the North American vegetarian movement.

Martha McCaughey is an Assistant Professor of Women's Studies in the Center for Interdisciplinary Studies at Virginia Tech and teaches courses in Women's Studies, Sociology, and Science and Technology Studies. She received her doctorate in Sociology from the University of California at Santa Barbara. Her work examines the embodied discourses of gender, sexuality, and aggression, with a focus on scientific narratives and popular culture. She is the author of *Real Knockouts: The Physical Feminism of Women's Self-Defense* (1997), and is coediting a book on violent women in popular culture.

Nita Mary McKinley is an Assistant Professor of Psychology at Allegheny College in Pennsylvania, where she teaches Developmental Psychology, Psychology of Women, Psychology of the Adolescent Girl, and Body Image and the Psychology of Physical Appearance. Her research interests include objectified body consciousness, body satisfaction, and eating problems across the lifespan and their relationship to factors such as political activism. She is also particularly interested in fat stigmatization and resistance to cultural appearance norms.

Ellen S. Parham combines teaching, research, and practice related to nutrition and weight issues as a Professor and Coordinator of Dietetics at Northern Illinois University, including a graduate course on Obesity and Eating Disorders. Her research deals with control of food intake, social support and weight, size acceptance, and weight-related attitudes. She is a registered dietitian and licensed professional counselor and has developed and led weight management and size acceptance programs for individuals and groups. She is one of the founders of the Division of Nutrition and Weight Realities in the Society for Nutrition Education.

Paula Saukko is a Lecturer in the Centre for Mass Communication Research at the University of Leicester in the United Kingdom. She is currently completing her dissertation on the discourse of eating disorders at the Institute of Communications Research, University of Illinois, Urbana-Champaign. Her research interests encompass cultural studies, qualitative research, media, gender, and social theory. She has recently published articles in the *Cultural Studies Research Annual* and *European Journal of Cultural Studies*.

David Smith is Wellcome Lecturer in the History of Medicine in the Department of History at Aberdeen University, where he teaches in the Faculties of Arts and Divinity and Medicine. His research interests focus on the interactions between science, medicine and government in connection with food and nutrition. He is editor of *Nutrition in Britain: Science, Scientists and Politics in the Twentieth Century* (1997).

Jeffery Sobal is a Sociologist who is an Associate Professor in the Division of Nutritional Sciences at Cornell University. His research interests focus on social patterns of obesity, especially body weight and marriage, and the role of weight in society, particularly stigmatization of obese individuals and medicalization of obesity as a social problem, as well as additional work on the food choice process and the food and nutrition system. He coedited, with Donna Maurer, *Eating Agendas: Food and Nutrition as Social Problems* (1995).

Peter N. Stearns is the Heinz Professor of History and Dean of the College of Humanities and Social Sciences at Carnegie Mellon University. He is a social historian devoted to the exploration of research topics not previously open to historical analysis. He founded and is editor-in-chief of the *Journal of Social History* and editor of the *Encyclopedia of Social History*. He has published more than fifty books and seventy articles, including *Fat History: Bodies and Beauty in the Modern West* (1997), and completed two television programs for the Arts and Entertainment Network's History Channel.

Lauren Williams is a Lecturer in Nutrition and Dietetics at the University of Newcastle in Australia with tertiary qualifications in Science, Dietetics and Social Science. She previously worked in the Australian health system in community and public health nutrition, and has been involved in the Dietitians Association of Australia (DAA). Her interests in the social side of nutrition resulted in collaboration with sociologists, most recently in the area of dieting among women. Recent publications include a coedited book with John Germov, *The Social Appetite: An Introduction to the Sociology of Food and Nutrition* (1999).

Index